Morality and Social Justice

Studies in Social and Political Philosophy

General Editor: James P. Sterba, University of Notre Dame

Morality and Social Justice
Point/Counterpoint

**James P. Sterba, Tibor R. Machan,
Alison M. Jaggar, William A. Galston,
Carol C. Gould, Milton Fisk, and
Robert C. Solomon**

Rowman & Littlefield Publishers, Inc.

ROWMAN & LITTLEFIELD PUBLISHERS, INC.

Published in the United States of America
by Rowman & Littlefield Publishers, Inc.
4720 Boston Way, Lanham, Maryland 20706

3 Henrietta Street
London WC2E 8LU, England

Copyright © 1995 by Rowman & Littlefield Publishers, Inc.

Portions of Chapter 4 originally appeared in *Liberal Purposes: Goods, Virtues, and Diversity in the Liberal State* (Cambridge: Cambridge University Press, 1991). Reprinted with permission.
Portions of Chapter 7 originally appeared in *A Passion for Justice* (Reading, Mass.: Addison Wesley, 1990). Reprinted with permission.

British Cataloging in Publication Information Available

Library of Congress Cataloging-in-Publication Data

Morality and social justice: point/counterpoint / James Sterba . . . [et al.].
p. cm. — (Studies in social and political philosophy)
Includes bibliographical references and index.
1. Justice. 2. Social justice. 3. Social ethics. I Sterba, James P. II. Series: Studies in social and political philosophy.
JC578.M67   1994   303.3'72—dc20   94-3534   CIP

ISBN 0-8476-7977-2 (cloth : alk. paper)
ISBN 0-8476-7978-0 (pbk. : alk. paper)

Printed in the United States of America

♾™ The paper used in this publication meets the minimum requirements of American National Standard for Information Sciences—Permanence of Paper for Printed Library Materials, ANSI Z39.48-1964.

Contents

Preface

The idea of bringing together a diverse group of well known contemporary political philosophers to discuss their views occurred to me soon after completing my book *How To Make People Just* in which I argue that five contemporary conceptions of justice, when properly interpreted, all support the same practical requirements. I realized that the best way to test out the book's thesis was to get contemporary political philosophers to talk about the differences and similarities of their views. My earlier efforts centered on my book and its reconciliationist argument. In 1991, there appeared a special issue of the *Journal of Social Philosophy* devoted to the book, and in 1992, there was a special symposium devoted to my reconciliationist argument at the American Philosophical Association Central Division Meeting. The present book brings together seven well known contemporary political philosophers, Milton Fisk, William A. Galston, Carol C. Gould, Alison M. Jaggar, Tibor R. Machan, Robert C. Solomon and myself to explore the possibility of achieving agreement in political theory. For the most part, the essays in this book focus on the topic of social justice. Each author defends his or her own view in a principal essay and also comments on two or more of the other essays. The reader will probably be struck more by the points of disagreement rather than the points of agreement among the essays and comments, but several of the authors in their comments do stress points of agreement and suggested ways by which that agreement could be extended in the future. In any case, I know of no better way of doing political philosophy than by bringing people together with divergent views and getting them to talk to each other.

I want to take this opportunity to thank my co-authors for all they did to make this volume possible. With seven authors who travel extensively and are always busy, it was not easy the maintain the coordination and collaboration necessary to produce a work of this sort. In this regard, the staff at Rowman & Littlefield were always helpful, in particular, Jennifer Ruark, Julie E. Kirsch, and Lynn Gemmell. Finally, I would like to especially thank Jonathan Sisk, Editor-in-Chief at Rowman & Littlefield, who encouraged this project from the start.

James P. Sterba
Notre Dame, Indiana

1

Reconciling Conceptions of Justice

James P. Sterba

It is widely believed that alternative conceptions of justice are incommensurable such that no nonarbitrary reason can be given for accepting one conception of justice over another. So we find libertarians with their ultimate political ideal of liberty endorsing the practical requirements of a minimal state, welfare liberals with their ultimate political ideal of fairness endorsing the practical requirements of a welfare state, and socialists with their ultimate political ideal of equality endorsing the practical requirements of a socialist state, and so on. Each political ideal is said to lead to different practical requirements, yet there is no nonarbitrary way to determine which ideal to accept. Alasdair MacIntyre seemed to champion this view in *After Virtue*, but even an opponent of MacIntyre like John Rawls in his recent work seems to grant that the conception of justice he favors is rooted in a prior acceptance of modern social democratic traditions, from which many have concluded that without a prior and seemingly arbitrary acceptance of those traditions, one would not be led to endorse Rawls's conception of justice.

For a number of years now I have argued that this incommensurability thesis is mistaken and that alternative conceptions of justice in their most defensible contemporary formulations are not, in fact, incommensurable but can be shown to lead to the same practical requirements.[1] Thus I claim that a libertarian conception of justice with its ideal of liberty, a welfare liberal conception of justice with its ideal of fairness, a socialist conception of justice with its ideal of

1

equality, a communitarian conception of justice with its ideal of the common good, and a feminist conception of justice with its ideal of androgyny can all be seen to support the same practical requirements, specifically, the practical requirements that are usually associated with a welfare liberal conception of justice, namely, a right to welfare and a right to equal opportunity. Since most people endorse one or another of these conceptions of justice, to reach agreement in practice it should suffice to show them that all these conceptions support the same practical requirements of a right to welfare and a right to equal opportunity.[2] Nevertheless, to make my practical reconciliation argument even more compelling, I further argue that the conception of rationality required by rational egoism leads at least to the libertarian conception of justice, which, in turn, has been shown to lead to the same practical requirements as the other four conceptions. So I argue that there is no escaping my practical reconciliation of alternative conceptions of justice by rejecting morality altogether and endorsing rational egoism.

Now obviously I cannot in this paper lay out my entire practical reconciliation argument. What I propose to do then is to focus on two related parts of my argument where I attempt to show that libertarians and feminists should endorse the same practical requirements of a right to welfare and a right to equal opportunity. In setting out these two parts of the argument, I will try to make the argument more perspicuous than I have in the past and relate the argument to recent work done by libertarians and feminists, especially work done by my two distinguished commentators. I cannot think of any better way on this occasion to put my practical reconciliation argument to the test.

The Libertarian Conception of Justice

Libertarians have interpreted their ideal of liberty in basically two different ways. Some libertarians, following Herbert Spencer, have (1) taken a right to liberty as basic and (2) derived all other rights from this right to liberty. Other libertarians, following John Locke, have (1) taken a set of rights, including typically a right to life and a right to property, as basic and (2) defined liberty as the absence constraints in the exercise of these rights. Both groups of libertarians regard liberty as the ultimate political ideal, but they do so for different reasons. For Spencerian libertarians, liberty is the ultimate political ideal because all other rights are derived from a right to liberty. For Lockean libertarians, liberty is the ultimate political ideal because liberty is just the absence of constraints in the exercise of people's fundamental rights.

Spencerian Libertarians

Let us begin by considering the view of Spencerian libertarians, who take a right to liberty to be basic and define all other rights in terms of this right to liberty. According to this view, liberty is usually interpreted as being unconstrained by other people from doing what one wants or is able to do. Interpreting liberty this way, libertarians like to limit constraints to positive acts (that is, acts of commission) that prevent people from doing what they otherwise want or are able to do. By contrast, welfare liberals and socialists interpret constraints to include, in addition, negative acts (acts of omission) that prevent people from doing what they otherwise want or are able to do. In fact, this is one way to understand the debate between defenders of "negative liberty" and defenders of "positive liberty." This is because defenders of negative liberty interpret constraints to include only positive acts of others that prevent people from doing what they otherwise want or are able to do, while defenders of positive liberty interpret constraints to include both positive and negative acts of others that prevent people from doing what they otherwise want or are able to do.

In order not to beg the question against libertarians, suppose we interpret constraints in the manner favored by libertarians to include only positive acts by others that prevent people from doing what they otherwise want or are able to do. Libertarians go on to characterize their political ideal as requiring that each person should have the greatest amount of liberty commensurate with the same liberty for all. From this ideal, libertarians claim that a number of more specific requirements can be derived, in particular a right to life, a right to freedom of speech, press, and assembly, and a right to property.

Here it is important to observe that the libertarian's right to life is not a right to receive from others the goods and resources necessary for preserving one's life; it is not a right to welfare: it is simply a right not to be killed unjustly. Correspondingly, the libertarian's right to property is not a right to receive from others the goods and resources necessary to meet one's basic needs, but rather a right to acquire goods and resources either by initial acquisitions or by voluntary agreements.

Of course, libertarians would allow that it would be nice of the rich to share their surplus resources with the poor. Nevertheless, libertarians deny that government has a duty to provide for such needs. Some good things, such as the provision of welfare to the needy, are requirements of charity rather than justice, libertarians claim. Accordingly, failure to make such provisions is neither blameworthy nor punishable. As a consequence, libertarians contend that such acts of charity should not be coercively required. For this reason, libertarians are opposed to any coercively supported welfare program.

For a similar reason, libertarians are opposed to coercively supported opportunity programs. This is because the basic opportunities one has under a libertarian conception of justice are primarily a function of the property one controls, and since unequal property distributions are taken to be justified under a libertarian conception of justice, unequal basic opportunities are also regarded as justified.

Lockean Libertarians

The same opposition to coercively supported welfare and equal opportunity programs characterizes Lockean libertarians who take a set of rights, typically including a right to life and a right to property, as basic and then interpret liberty as being unconstrained by other people from doing what one has a right to do. For according to this view, a right to life is simply a right not to be killed unjustly; it is not a right to receive welfare. Correspondingly, a right to property is a right to acquire property either by initial acquisitions or by voluntary transactions; it is not a right to receive from others whatever goods and resources one needs to maintain oneself. Understanding a right to life and a right to property in this way, libertarians reject both coercively supported welfare programs and equal opportunity programs as a violation of liberty.

Spencerian Libertarians and the Problem of Conflict

To evaluate the libertarian view, let us begin with the ideal of liberty as defended by Spencerian libertarians and consider a typical conflict situation between the rich and the poor. In this situation, the rich have more than enough resources to satisfy their basic needs. By contrast, the poor lack the resources to meet their most basic needs even though they have tried all the means available to them that Spencerian libertarians regard as legitimate for acquiring such resources. Under circumstances like these, libertarians usually maintain that the rich should have the liberty to use their resources to satisfy their luxury needs if they so wish. Spencerian libertarians recognize that this liberty might well be enjoyed at the expense of the satisfaction of the most basic needs of the poor; they just think that liberty always has priority over other political ideals, and since they assume that the liberty of the poor is not at stake in such conflict situations, it is easy for them to conclude that the rich should not be required to sacrifice their liberty so that the basic needs of the poor may be met.

Of course, Spencerian libertarians allow that it would be nice of the rich to share their surplus resources with the poor. Nevertheless, according to Spencerian libertarians, such acts of charity cannot be required because the liberty of the poor is not thought to be at stake in such conflict situations. In fact, however, the liberty of the poor is at stake in such conflict situations. What is at stake is the liberty of the poor to take from the surplus possessions of the rich what is necessary to satisfy their basic needs.[3]

Needless to say, Spencerian libertarians would want to deny that the poor have this liberty. But how could they justify such a denial? As this liberty of the poor has been specified, it is not a positive right to receive something, but a negative right of noninterference. Nor will it do for Spencerian libertarians to appeal to a right to life or a right to property to rule out such a liberty because, on the Spencerian view, liberty is basic and all other rights are derived from a right to liberty. Clearly, what Spencerian libertarians must do is recognize the existence of such a liberty, and then claim that it conflicts with other liberties of the rich. But when Spencerian libertarians see that this is the case, they are often genuinely surprised, one might even say rudely awakened, for they had not previously seen the conflict between the rich and the poor as a conflict of liberties.

Now when the conflict between the rich and the poor is viewed as a conflict of liberties, we can say that the rich should have the liberty to use their surplus resources for luxury purposes, or we can also say that the poor should have the liberty to take from the rich what they require to meet their basic needs. If we choose one liberty, we must reject the other. What needs to be determined, therefore, is which liberty is morally preferable: the liberty of the rich or the liberty of the poor.

Two Principles

In order to see that the liberty of the poor to take from the surplus resources of the rich what is required to meet their basic needs is morally preferable to the liberty of the rich to use their surplus resources for luxury purposes, we need appeal to one of the most fundamental principles of morality, one that is common to all political perspectives. This is the "ought" implies "can" principle: People are not morally required to do what they lack power to do or what would involve so great a sacrifice that it would be unreasonable to ask them to perform such an action, and/or in the case of severe conflicts of interest, unreasonable to require them to perform such an action.[4]

For example, suppose I promised to attend a departmental meeting on Friday, but on Thursday I am involved in a serious car accident which puts me into a coma. Surely it is no longer the case that I ought to attend the meeting now that I lack the power to do so. Or suppose instead that on Thursday I develop a severe case of pneumonia for which I am hospitalized. Surely I could legitimately claim that I cannot attend the meeting on the grounds that the risk to my health involved in attending is a sacrifice that it would be unreasonable to ask me to bear. Or suppose the risk to my health from having pneumonia is not so serious that it would be unreasonable to ask me to attend the meeting (a supererogatory request). It might still be serious enough to be unreasonable to require my attendance at the meeting (a demand that is backed up by blame or coercion).

What is distinctive about this formulation of the "ought" implies "can" principle is that it claims that the requirements of morality cannot, all things considered, be unreasonable to ask, and/or in cases of severe conflict of interest, unreasonable to require people to abide by. The principle claims that reason and morality must be linked in an appropriate way, especially if we are going to be able to justifiably use blame or coercion to get people to abide by the requirements of morality. It should be noted, however, that while major figures in the history of philosophy, and most philosophers today, including virtually all libertarian philosophers, accept this linkage between reason and morality, this linkage is not usually conceived to be part of the "ought" implies "can" principle. Nevertheless, I claim that there are good reasons for associating this linkage between reason and morality with the "ought" implies "can" principle, namely, our use of the word "can" as in the example just given, and the natural progression from logical, physical, and psychological possibility found in the traditional "ought" implies "can" principle to the notion of moral possibility found in this formulation of the "ought" implies "can" principle. In any case, the acceptability of this formulation of the "ought" implies "can" principle is determined by the virtual universal acceptance of its components and not by the manner in which I have proposed to join those components together.[5]

When we apply the "ought" implies "can" principle to the case at hand, it seems clear that the poor have it within their power willingly to relinquish such an important liberty as the liberty to take from the rich what they require to meet their basic needs. Nevertheless, it would be unreasonable to ask or require them to make so great a sacrifice. In the extreme case, it would involve asking or requiring the poor to sit back and starve to death. Of course, the poor may have no real alternative to relinquishing this liberty. To do anything else may involve worse consequences for themselves and their loved ones and may invite a painful death. Accordingly, we may expect that the poor would acquiesce, albeit unwillingly, to a political system that denied them the right to welfare supported by such a liberty, at the same time that we recognize that such a system imposed an unreasonable sacrifice upon the poor—a sacrifice that we could not morally blame the poor for trying to evade.[6] Analogously, we might expect that a woman whose life was threatened would submit to a rapist's demands, at the same time that we recognize the utter unreasonableness of those demands.

By contrast, it would not be unreasonable to ask and require the rich to sacrifice the liberty to meet some of their luxury needs so that the poor can have the liberty to meet their basic needs.[7] Naturally, we might expect that the rich, for reasons of self-interest and past contribution, might be disinclined to make such a sacrifice. We might even suppose that the past contribution of the rich provides a good reason for not sacrificing their liberty to use their current surplus for luxury purposes. Yet, unlike the poor, the rich could not claim that relinquishing such a liberty involved so great a sacrifice that it would be unreasonable to ask and require them to make it; unlike the poor, the rich could be morally blameworthy for failing to make such a sacrifice.

Notice that in virtue of the "ought" implies "can" principle this argument establishes that

(1a) Since it would be unreasonable to ask or require the poor to sacrifice the liberty not to be interfered with when taking from the surplus resources of the rich what is necessary to meet their basic needs, (1b) it is not the case that the poor are morally required to make such a sacrifice.

(2a) Since it would not be unreasonable to ask and require the rich to sacrifice the liberty not to be interfered when using their surplus resources for luxury purposes, (2b) it may be the case that the rich are morally required to make such a sacrifice.

What the argument does not establish is that it is the case that the rich are *morally required* to sacrifice (some of) their surplus so that the basic needs of the poor can be met. To clearly establish that conclusion, we need to appeal to a principle, which is, in fact, simply the contrapositive of the "ought" implies "can" principle. It is the conflict resolution principle: What people are morally required to do is what is either reasonable to ask everyone affected to accept, or in the case of severe conflicts of interest, reasonable to require everyone affected to accept.

While the "ought" implies "can" principle claims that if any action is *not reasonable to ask or require* a person to do, all things considered, that action is *not morally required* for that person, all things considered [-R(A v Re) -> -MRe], the conflict resolution principle claims that if any action is *morally required* for a person to do, all things considered, that action is *reasonable to ask or require* that person to do, all things considered [MRe -> R(A v Re)].

This conflict resolution principle accords with the generally accepted view of morality as a system of reasons for resolving interpersonal conflicts of interest. Of course, morality is not limited to such a system of reasons. Most surely it also includes reasons of self-development. All that is being claimed by the principle is that moral resolutions of interpersonal conflicts of interest cannot be contrary to reason to ask everyone affected to accept, or in the case of severe interpersonal conflicts of interest, unreasonable to require everyone affected to accept. The reason for the distinction between the two kinds of cases is that when interpersonal conflicts of interest are not severe, moral resolutions must still be reasonable to ask everyone affected to accept but they need not be reasonable to *require* everyone affected to accept. This is because not all moral resolutions can be justifiably enforced; only moral resolutions of severe interpersonal conflicts of interest can and *should* be justifiably enforced. Furthermore, the reason why moral resolutions of severe interpersonal conflicts of interest should be enforced is that if the parties are simply asked but not required to abide by a moral resolution in such cases of conflict, then it will be morally permissible, and even likely, that the stronger party will violate the resolution and that would be unreasonable to ask or require the weaker party to accept.

When we apply the conflict resolution principle to our example of severe conflict between the rich and the poor, there are three possible moral resolutions:

I. A moral resolution that would require the rich to sacrifice the liberty not to be interfered with when using their surplus resources for luxury purposes so that the poor can have the liberty not to be interfered with when taking from the surplus resources of the rich what is necessary to meet their basic needs.

II. A moral resolution that would require the poor to sacrifice the liberty not to be interfered with when taking from the surplus resources of the rich what is necessary to meet their basic needs so that the rich can have the liberty not to be interfered with when using their surplus resources for luxury purposes.

III. A moral resolution that would require the rich and the poor to accept the results of a power struggle in which both the rich and the poor are at liberty to appropriate and use the surplus resources of the rich.

Applying our previous discussion of the "ought" implies "can" principle to these three possible moral resolutions, it is clear that 1a (it would be unreasonable to ask or require the poor . . .) rules out II, but 2a (it would not be unreasonable to ask and require the rich . . .) does not rule out I. But what about III? Some libertarians have contended that III is the proper resolution of severe conflicts of interest between the rich and the poor.[8] But a resolution, like III, that sanctions the results of a power struggle between the rich and the poor is a resolution that, by and large, favors the rich over the poor. So all things considered, it would be no more reasonable to require the poor to accept III than it would be to require them to accept II. This means that only I satisfies the conflict resolution principle by being a resolution that is reasonable to require everyone affected to accept. Consequently, if we assume that however else we specify the requirements of morality, they cannot violate the "ought" implies "can" principle or the conflict resolution principle, it follows that, despite what Spencerian libertarians claim, the basic right to liberty endorsed by them, as determined by a weighing of the relevant competing liberties according to these two principles, actually favors the liberty of the poor over the liberty of the rich.

Yet couldn't Spencerian libertarians object to this conclusion, claiming that it would be unreasonable to require the rich to sacrifice the liberty to meet some of their luxury needs so that the poor could have the liberty to meet their basic needs? As has been pointed out, libertarians don't usually see the situation as a conflict of liberties, but suppose they did. How plausible would such an objection be? Not very plausible at all.

Consider what Spencerian libertarians are going to say about the poor. Isn't it clearly unreasonable to require the poor to sacrifice the liberty to meet their basic needs so that the rich can have the liberty to meet their luxury needs? Isn't it clearly unreasonable to require the poor to sit back and starve to death? If it is, then, there is no resolution of this conflict that would be reasonable to require both the rich and the poor to accept. But that would mean that libertarians could not be putting forth a moral resolution because according to the conflict resolution principle, in cases of severe conflict of interest, a moral resolution resolves conflicts of interest in ways that it would be reasonable to require everyone affected to accept. Therefore, as long as libertarians think of themselves as putting forth a moral resolution for cases of severe conflict of interest, they cannot allow that it would be unreasonable *both* to require the rich to sacrifice the liberty to meet some of their luxury needs in order to benefit the poor and to require the poor to sacrifice the liberty to meet their basic needs in order to benefit the rich. But I submit that if one of these requirements is to be judged reasonable, then, by any neutral assessment, it must be the requirement that the rich sacrifice the liberty to meet some of their luxury needs so that the poor can have the liberty to meet their basic needs; there is no other plausible resolution, if libertarians intend to be putting forth a moral resolution.

Lockean Libertarians and the Problem of Conflict

The same conclusions can be established against Lockean libertarians who take a set of rights, typically including a right to life and a right to property, as basic and then interpret liberty as being unconstrained by other people from doing what one has a right to do. In this context, the "ought" implies "can" principle and the conflict resolution principle can be shown, as I have argued elsewhere, to favor a conditional right to property over an unconditional right to property.[9] Consequently, if we assume that however else we specify the requirements of morality, they cannot violate the "ought" implies "can" principle and the conflict resolution principle, it follows that, despite what Lockean libertarians claim, the right to life and the right to property endorsed by them actually support a right to welfare.

Now it might be objected that the rights that this argument establishes from libertarian premises are not the same as the rights to welfare endorsed by welfare liberals and socialists. This is correct. We could mark this difference by referring to the rights that this argument establishes as "negative welfare rights" and by referring to the rights endorsed by welfare liberals and socialists as "positive welfare rights." The significance of this difference is that a person's negative welfare rights can be violated only when other people through acts of commission interfere with their exercise, whereas a person's positive welfare rights can be violated not only by such acts of commission but by acts of omission as well. Nonetheless, this difference will have little practical import. For once libertarians come to recognize the legitimacy of negative welfare rights, then in order not to be subject to the discretion of rightholders in choosing when and how to exercise these rights, libertarians will tend to favor the only morally legitimate way of preventing the exercise of such rights: they will institute adequate positive welfare rights that will then take precedence over the exercise of negative welfare rights. Accordingly, if libertarians adopt this morally legitimate way of preventing the exercise of such rights, they will end up endorsing the same sorts of welfare institutions favored by welfare liberals and socialists.

A Right to Equal Opportunity

It is possible that libertarians convinced to some extent by the above arguments might want to accept a right to welfare but then deny that there is a right to equal opportunity. Such a stance, however, is plausible only if we restrict the class of morally legitimate claimants to those within a given (affluent) society, for only then would a right to equal opportunity require something different from a right to welfare which entails a right to the basic opportunities necessary for the satisfaction of one's basic needs.[10]

Consider that at the present time there is probably a sufficient worldwide supply of goods and resources to meet the normal costs of satisfying the basic nutritional needs of all existing people. According to former U.S. Secretary of Agriculture Bob Bergland, "For the past 20 years, if the available world food supply had been evenly divided and distributed, each person would have received more than the minimum number of calories."[11] Other authorities have made similar assessments of the available world food supply.

Needless to say, the adoption of a policy of supporting a right to welfare for all existing people would necessitate significant changes, especially in developed countries. For example, the large percentage of the U.S. population whose food consumption clearly exceeds even an adequately adjusted poverty index would have to substantially alter their eating habits. In particular, they would have to reduce their consumption of beef and pork so as to make more grain available for direct human consumption. (Presently the amount of grain fed to

American livestock is as much as all the people of China and India eat in a year.) Thus, at least the satisfaction of some of the nonbasic needs of the more advantaged in developed countries would have to be forgone if the basic nutritional needs of all existing people in developing and underdeveloped countries are to be met. Furthermore, to raise the standard of living in developing and underdeveloped countries will require substantial increases in the consumption of energy and other resources. But such an increase would have to be matched by a substantial decrease in the consumption of these goods in developing countries, otherwise global ecological disaster would result from increased global warming, ozone depletion, and acid rain, lowering virtually everyone's standard of living.[12]

In addition, once the basic nutritional needs of future generations are also taken into account, the satisfaction of the nonbasic needs of the more advantaged in developed countries would have to be further restricted in order to preserve the fertility of cropland and other food-related natural resources for the use of future generations. Obviously, the only assured way to guarantee the energy and resources necessary for the the satisfaction of the basic needs of future generations is by setting aside resources that would otherwise be used to satisfy the nonbasic needs of existing generations. And once basic needs other than nutritional needs are taken into account as well, still further restrictions would be required. For example, it has been estimated that presently a North American uses fifty times more resources than an Indian. This means that in terms of resource consumption the North American continent's population is the equivalent of 12.5 billion Indians. Obviously, this would have to be radically altered if the basic needs of distant peoples and future generations are to be met. Accordingly, recognizing a right to welfare applicable both to distant peoples and to future generations would significantly affect the right to equal opportunity that people can be guaranteed.

Now the form of equal opportunity that Rawls defends in *A Theory of Justice* requires that people who have the same natural assets and the same willingness to use them have an equal chance to occupy roles and positions in society commensurate with their natural assets.[13] So construed, equal opportunity provides two sorts of benefits. It benefits society as a whole by helping to ensure that the most talented people will fill the most responsible roles and positions in society. It benefits individuals by ensuring that they will not be discriminated against with respect to filling the roles and positions in society for which they are qualified, thereby giving them a fair chance of securing whatever benefits attach to those roles and positions in society.

I have argued, however, that once it is recognized that the class of morally legitimate claimants includes distant peoples and future generations, then guaranteeing a right to welfare to all morally legitimate claimants would lead to a state of affairs in which few resources are available for directly meeting nonbasic needs, although such needs may still be met indirectly though the satisfaction of basic needs. As a consequence, there won't be greater benefits attaching to certain roles and positions in society, since people can expect only to have their basic needs directly met in whatever roles and positions they happen to occupy. Of course, we will still want the most talented people occupying the most responsible roles and positions in society, it's just that occupying those roles and positions will not secure greater benefits to those who occupy them. Therefore, to ensure that the most talented people occupy roles and positions that are commensurate with their abilities, we will need to do something like the following. First, borrowing an idea from socialist justice, we will need to make the roles and positions people occupy as intrinsically rewarding as possible. Second, we will need to convince the more talented that they have a moral responsibility to the less talented and to society as a whole to use their talents to the fullest. Consequently, the equal opportunity that will be guaranteed to everyone in society will only be a fair means of ensuring that everyone's basic needs are met, not a means of providing differential rewards or of directly serving to meet nonbasic needs.

Accordingly, my practical reconciliation argument fails to guarantee a right to equal opportunity that provides greater benefits to the talented, enabling them to directly meet nonbasic as well as basic needs. But the failure to guarantee this sort of equal opportunity is no objection to my argument, given that having this sort of equal opportunity is incompatible with the more fundamental requirement of meeting everyone's basic needs. On this account, both libertarians and welfare liberals would come to endorse the same right to equal opportunity—an equal right not to be discriminated against in filling the roles and positions in a society that satisfies its obligations to meet everyone's basic needs.

What these arguments show, therefore, is that a libertarian conception of justice supports the same practical requirements as a welfare liberal conception of justice. Both favor a right to welfare and a right to equal opportunity. This is not to deny, of course, that there won't be disagreements concerning how to interpret a right to welfare understood as a right to the resources necessary for meeting one's basic needs and a right to equal opportunity understood as an equal right not to be discriminated against in filling the roles and positions in a society that satisfies its obligations to meet everyone's basic needs, but there is no reason to think that libertarians will disagree with welfare liberals any more than welfare liberals will disagree with themselves over the interpretation of these rights, especially over what is required for meeting people's basic needs.[14] Recall that it is generally thought that what divides welfare liberals from libertarians is that the former are committed to rights to welfare and equal opportunity whereas the latter rejected both of these rights. It is quite evident that libertarians want to reject rights to welfare and equal opportunity because they think (wrongly) that to endorse these rights is to abandon their ideal of liberty. No libertarian has argued that it will do just as well to grant such rights and then disagree as to how these rights are to be interpreted. Thus, given my argument that both libertarians and welfare liberals are required to endorse a right to welfare understood as a right to the resources necessary for meeting one's basic needs and a right to equal opportunity understood as an equal right not to be discriminated against in filling the roles and positions in a society that satisfies its obligations to meet everyone's basic needs, it is implausible for us to think that comparable differences will now emerge between libertarians and welfare liberals over the interpretation of these rights. Differences between welfare liberals and libertarians over what constitutes a basic needs minimum are likely to be no greater than differences among welfare liberals themselves over what constitutes such a minimum. Moreover, once libertarians and welfare liberals have taken the first practical steps to implement a right to welfare and a right to equal opportunity for distant peoples and future generations, they will both be in an even better position to know what is required for meeting people's basic needs. This is because sincerely attempting to live out one's practical moral commitments helps one to interpret them better, just as failing to live out one's practical moral commitments makes interpreting them all that more difficult.

In brief, what I have argued is that a libertarian conception of justice supports the same rights to welfare and equal opportunity as endorsed by a welfare liberal conception of justice.

Libertarian Objections

In his book *Individuals and Their Rights*, Tibor Machan criticizes the above argument that a libertarian ideal of liberty leads to a right to welfare, accepting its theoretical thrust but denying its practical significance.[15] He appreciates the force of the argument enough to grant that if the type of conflict cases that we have described between the rich and the poor actually obtained, the poor would have a right to welfare. But he denies that such cases—in which the poor have done all that they legitimately can to satisfy their basic needs in a libertarian society—actually obtain. "Normally," he writes, "persons do not lack the opportunities and resources to satisfy their basic needs."[16]

But this response virtually concedes everything that the above argument intended to establish. For the poor's right to welfare is not claimed to be unconditional. Rather it is said to be conditional principally upon the poor doing all that they legitimately can to meet their own basic needs. So it follows that only when the poor lack sufficient opportunity to satisfy their own basic needs would their right to welfare have any practical moral force. Accordingly, on libertarian grounds, Machan has conceded the legitimacy of just the kind of right to welfare that the above argument hoped to establish.

The only difference that remains is a practical one. Machan thinks that virtually all of the poor have sufficient opportunities and resources to satisfy their basic needs and that, therefore, a right to welfare has no practical moral force. In contrast, I would think that many of the poor do not have sufficient opportunities and resources to satisfy their basic needs and that, therefore, a right to welfare has considerable practical moral force.

But isn't this practical disagreement resolvable? For who could deny that most of the 1.2 billion people who are currently living in conditions of absolute poverty "lack the opportunities and resources to satisfy their basic needs"?[17] And even within our own country, it is estimated that some 32 million Americans live below the official poverty index, and that one-fifth of American children are growing up in poverty.[18] Surely, it is impossible to deny that many of these Americans also "lack the opportunities and resources to satisfy their basic needs." Given the impossibility of reasonably denying these factual claims, Machan would have to concede that the right to welfare, which he grants can be theoretically established on libertarian premises, also has practical moral force.[19]

If we turn to Jan Narveson's recent work on libertarianism, we find significant points of agreement and disagreement with my preceding analysis and argument. The basic point of agreement is that Narveson implicitly grants the relevance of the "ought" implies "can" principle and the conflict resolution principle in evaluating the acceptability of libertarianism. He says, for example, "To have the *right* to something you are using is for there to be good and sufficient reasons why everyone ought to let you do so."[20] In another place, he says that the "criterion of betterness is that better principles are more acceptable to people."[21] And in still another place, he suggests that "we should expect support for our theory from the people to whom it is addressed: namely, everybody."[22] In the light of these statements, I think Narveson and I agree that the proper distribution of basic liberties cannot be unreasonable to require the rich and the poor to accept (as the "ought" implies "can" principle demands). Or put positively, I think we agree that the distribution of basic liberties must be reasonable to require both the rich and the poor to accept (as the conflict resolution principle demands).

However, what Narveson and I disagree over is what sort of a distribution of basic liberties satisfies these two principles. In a very interesting recent paper, Narveson contends that the rule of first use should govern the distribution of basic liberties.[23] As Narveson interprets it, this rule permits first appropriators to take whatever they want of previously unowned goods and resources from the State of Nature provided that they do not interfere with the rights of others, which he thinks is easy to do with respect to unowned goods and resources. He allows that such appropriations deprive others of the opportunity to appropriate the same goods and resources. But he takes this fact to be morally irrelevant because he claims that people do not have a right to any such opportunity with respect to unowned goods and resources in the State of Nature.

Obviously, Narveson thinks that his first-use rule supports strong property rights and precludes anything like my negative rights to welfare. Nevertheless, I propose to show that he reaches this conclusion by focusing on certain cases of first appropriation while neglecting others. Specifically, he wants to focus on cases involving person A and person B, where both have the opportunity to appropriate some unowned goods and resources, but A acts first to appropriate those goods and resources. In one variant of this case, B would just never have gotten around to appropriating the goods and resources herself. In another variant, B would have, in time, gotten around to appropriating those goods and resources, but she lost out in this case, let us suppose, through her own fault by being lazy. Now when reflecting on this case in light of our two principles, it is difficult to see how we could reasonably object to A's appropriation. Given that A looks like the proverbial ant and B like the proverbial grasshopper, it is difficult to raise any serious objection. Yet we need to consider other cases.

Consider a case only briefly mentioned by Narveson and then set aside. Suppose A and B both have the opportunity to appropriate some unowned goods and resources, and both attempt simultaneously to do so. Narveson allows that in such a case A and B could have equal claims to those goods and resources.[24] So here we have a case that leads to equality rather than inequality.

Consider now another case which turns out to be crucial. Here A, B, and C have the opportunity to appropriate all the valuable unowned goods and resources at time *t* while D does not. Through no fault of her own, D arrives on the scene too late; A, B, and C have already appropriated all the valuable goods and resources. If D had only been there at *t,* she too would have appropriated a share of those resources, but now it's too late. She offers to work for A, B, or C, but they refuse; they are doing quite well by themselves. D would go elsewhere but she lacks the resources to do so. She asks A, B, and C for help, but they refuse. They would rather use their surplus goods and resources to meet their luxury needs.

Applying the "ought" implies "can" principle and the conflict resolution principle, I consider this to be a case where D would have a negative right to welfare, that is, a right not to be interfered with when taking from the surplus goods and resources of A, B, or C what she requires to meet her basic needs. Does Narveson agree?

In one interesting passage, Narveson remarks,

> One leaves "enough and as good" for others in the sense that one leaves them with *whatever they have.* . . . If all fails, they either are thrown upon the mercy of others or, if one accepts the other Lockean (and popular) idea of a right to a "sufficiency" then the better-off may have to help them out. But they are *not* owed anything, any "compensation" for *the sheer fact that they didn't get x first.*[25]

It is not entirely clear from the passage whether Narveson accepts what he refers to as the Lockean (and popular) idea of a right to a "sufficiency" in the case we are considering. What he explicitly rules out is regarding a right to a "sufficiency" as a compensation, and with this I agree. But wouldn't a right to a "sufficiency" in this case be supported by the "ought" implies "can" principle and the conflict resolution principle? Isn't it clear, even using Narveson's own formulation, that there are good and sufficient reasons why everyone ought to let D exercise such a right?

Narveson sometimes argues for his first-use rule by claiming that "stopping people from doing what they are doing is a paradigm case of interference."[26] Here Narveson has in mind interference with actions like A, B, and C's appropriation of unowned goods and resources. But D is also acting. She is doing what she can to stay alive and meet her basic needs. This continuing action of D and the actions of

A, B, and C are, of course, on a collision course. Who then is interfering with whom?

Narveson says "there is no possible better example of an interference with someone's liberty than a case in which someone interferes to prevent the continuation of an action already begun."[27] But D's continuing action of doing what she can to stay alive and meet her basic needs may have begun before A, B, and C's actions of appropriation. Does that show on Narveson's account that A, B, and C are interfering with D?[28]

What seems clear from our discussion of this example is that who acted first is not morally decisive nor even always morally relevant. Rather what is crucial is how the "ought" implies "can" principle and the conflict resolution principle assess the options people have or could have available to them. For this example, these principles favor the liberty of D over the liberty of A, B, and C to the extent necessary to allow D to secure the goods and resources necessary for meeting her basic needs.

Assuming that Narveson accepts the relevance of the "ought" implies "can" principle and the conflict resolution principle to the evaluation of libertarianism, and the quotes I've cited seem to indicate that he does, I have argued that a more expansive discussion of the relevant cases where these principles apply would lead by an argument virtually identical with the one that I've already presented in this paper to a practical reconciliation of a libertarian conception of justice and a welfare liberal conception of justice. I turn now to a consideration of feminist justice.

Feminist Justice

Contemporary feminists almost by definition seek to put an end to male domination and to secure women's liberation. To achieve these goals, many feminists support the political ideal of a gender-free or androgynous society.[29] According to these feminists, all assignments of rights and duties are ultimately to accord with the ideal of a gender-free or androgynous society. Since a conception of justice is usually thought to provide the ultimate grounds for the assignment of rights and duties, I shall refer to this ideal of a gender-free or androgynous society as "feminist justice."

The Ideal of Androgyny

But how is this ideal to be interpreted? A gender-free or genderless society is a society where basic rights and duties are not assigned on the basis of a person's biological sex. Being male or female is not the grounds for determining what basic rights and duties a person has in a gender-free society. But this is to characterize the feminist ideal only negatively. It tells us what we need to get rid of, not what we need to put in its place. A more positive characterization is provided by the ideal of androgyny. Putting the ideal of feminist justice more positively in terms of the ideal of androgyny also helps to bring out why men should be attracted to feminist justice.

In a well-known article, Joyce Trebilcot distinguishes two forms of androgyny.[30] The first form postulates the same ideal for everyone. According to this form of androgyny, the ideal person "combines characteristics usually attributed to men with characteristics usually attributed to women." Thus, we should expect both nurturance and mastery, openness and objectivity, compassion and competitiveness from each and every person who has the capacities for these traits.

By contrast, the second form of androgyny does not advocate the same ideal for everyone but rather a variety of options from "pure" femininity to "pure" masculinity. As Trebilcot points out, this form of androgyny shares with the first the view that biological sex should not be the basis for determining the appropriateness of gender characterization. It differs in that it holds that "all alternatives with respect to gender should be equally available to and equally approved for everyone, regardless of sex."

It would be a mistake, however, to sharply distinguish between these two forms of androgyny. Properly understood, they are simply two different facets of a single ideal. For, as Mary Anne Warren has argued, the second form of androgyny is appropriate *only* "with respect to feminine and masculine traits which are largely matters of personal style and preference and which have little direct moral significance."[31] However, when we consider so-called feminine and masculine *virtues*, it is the first form of androgyny that is required because then, other things being equal, the same virtues are appropriate for everyone.

We can even formulate the ideal of androgyny more abstractly so that it is no longer specified in terms of so-called feminine and masculine traits. We can specify the ideal as requiring no more than that the traits that are truly desirable in society be equally available to both women and men, or in the case of virtues, equally expected of both women and men.

There is a problem, of course, in determining which traits of character are virtues and which traits are largely matters of personal style and preference. To make this determination, Trebilcot has suggested that we seek to bring about the second form of androgyny, where people have the option of acquiring the full range of so-called feminine and masculine traits.[32] But surely when we already have good grounds for thinking that certain traits are virtues, such as courage and compassion, fairness and openness, there is no reason to adopt such a laissez-faire approach to moral education. Although, as Trebilcot rightly points out, proscribing certain options will involve a loss of freedom, nevertheless, we should be able to determine at least with respect to some character traits when a gain in virtue is worth the loss of freedom. It may even be the case that the loss of freedom suffered by an individual now will be compensated for by a gain of freedom to that same individual in the future once the relevant virtue or virtues have been acquired.

So understood, the class of virtues will turn out to be those desirable traits that can be reasonably expected of both women and men. Admittedly, this is a restrictive use of the term "virtue." In normal usage, the term "virtue" is almost synonymous with the term "desirable trait."[33] But there is good reason to focus on those desirable traits that can be reasonably expected of both women and men, and, for present purposes, I will refer to this class of desirable traits as virtues.

Unfortunately, many of the challenges to the ideal of androgyny fail to appreciate how the ideal can be interpreted to combine an expected set of virtues with equal choice from among other desirable traits. For example, some challenges interpret the ideal as attempting to achieve "a proper balance of moderation" among opposing feminine and masculine traits and then question whether traits like feminine gullibility or masculine brutality could ever be combined with opposing gender traits to achieve such a balance.[34] Other challenges interpret the ideal as permitting unrestricted choice of personal traits and then regard the possibility of Total Women and Hells Angels androgynes as a *reductio ad absurdum* of the ideal.[35] But once it is recognized that the ideal of androgyny can be interpreted not only to expect of everyone a set of virtues (which need not be a mean between opposing extreme traits), but also to limit everyone's choice to desirable traits, then such challenges to the ideal clearly lose their force.

Actually, the main challenge raised by feminists to the ideal of androgyny is that the ideal is self-defeating in that it seeks to eliminate sexual stereotyping of human beings at the same time that it is formulated in terms of the very same stereotypical concepts it seeks to eliminate.[36] Or as Warren has put it, "Is it not at least mildly paradoxical to urge people to cultivate both 'feminine' and 'masculine' virtues, while at the same time holding that virtues ought not to be sexually stereotyped?"

But in response to this challenge, it can be argued that to build a better society we must begin where we are now, and where we are now people still speak of feminine and masculine character traits. Consequently, if we want to easily refer to such traits and to formulate an ideal with respect to how they should be distributed in society, it is plausible to refer to them in the way that people presently refer to them, that is, as feminine or masculine traits.

Alternatively, to avoid misunderstanding altogether, the ideal could be formulated in the more abstract way I suggested earlier so that it no longer specifically refers to so-called feminine or masculine traits. So formulated, the ideal requires that the traits that are truly desirable in society be equally available to both women and men, or in the case of virtues, equally expected of both women and men. So formulated the ideal would, in effect, expect that men and women have in the fullest sense an equal right of self-development. The ideal requires this because an equal right to self-development can only be effectively guaranteed by expecting the same virtues of both women and men and by making other desirable traits equally available to both women and men.

So characterized the ideal of androgyny represents neither a revolt against so-called feminine virtues and traits nor their exaltation over so-called masculine virtues and traits.[37] Accordingly, the ideal of androgyny does not view women's liberation as *simply* the freeing of women from the confines of traditional roles, thus making it possible for them to develop in ways heretofore reserved for men. Nor does the ideal view women's liberation as *simply* the revaluation and glorification of so-called feminine activities like housekeeping or mothering or so-called feminine modes of thinking as reflected in an ethic of caring. The first perspective ignores or devalues genuine virtues and desirable traits traditionally associated with women, while the second ignores or devalues genuine virtues and desirable traits traditionally associated with men. By contrast, the ideal of androgyny seeks a broader based ideal for both women and men that combines virtues and desirable traits traditionally associated with women with virtues and desirable traits traditionally associated with men. Nevertheless, the ideal of androgyny will clearly reject any so-called virtues or desirable traits traditionally associated with women or men that have been supportive of discrimination or oppression against women or men. In general, the ideal of androgyny substitutes a socialization based on natural ability, reasonable expectation, and choice for a socialization based on sexual difference.

Of course, in proposing to characterize feminist justice in terms of the ideal of a gender-free or androgynous society, I recognize that not all feminists start off endorsing this ideal. Christina Sommers, for example, has attracted attention recently by distinguishing liberal feminism, which she endorses, from androgynous feminism, which she opposes.[38] But as one gets clearer and clearer about the liberal feminism which Sommers endorses, it begins to look more and more the androgynous feminism which she says she opposes. There is nothing surprising about this, however. We cannot have the genuine equal opportunity for men and women that Sommers wants without reforming the present distribution of gender traits. Women cannot be passive, submissive, dependent, indecisive, and weak and still enjoy the same opportunities enjoyed by men who are aggressive, dominant, independent, decisive, and strong. So I contend that liberal feminism and androgynous feminism go together because genuine equal opportunity requires the feminist ideal of a gender-free or androgynous society.

It also seems that those who claim we cannot escape a gendered society are simply confused about what a gender-free society would be like.[39] For they seem to agree with those who favor a gender-free or androgynous society that the assignments of roles in society should be based on (natural) ability, rational expectation, and choice. But what they also hold is that some of these assignments will be based on sex as well because some of the natural abilities that people have will be determined by their sex. But even assuming this is the case, it wouldn't show that society was gendered in the sense that its roles in society are based on sex *rather than* being based on (natural) ability, rational expectation, and choice. And this is the only sense of gendered society to which defenders of feminist justice would be objecting.[40] So once the notion of a gender-free society is clarified, there should be widespread agreement that the assignments of roles in society should be based on (natural) ability, rational expectation, and choice. The ideal of androgyny simply specifies this notion of a gender-free society a bit further by requiring that the traits that are truly desirable in society be equally open to (equally qualified) women and men, or in the case of virtues, equally expected of (equally capable) women and men.

Of course, insofar as natural abilities are a function of sexual difference, there will be differences in the desirable traits and virtues that women and men acquire even in a gender-free or androgynous society. And some contend that these differences will be substantial.[41] But given that we have been slow to implement the degree of equal opportunity required by the ideal of a gender-free or androgynous society, it is difficult to know what differences will emerge that are both sex-based and natural ability-based. What we can be sure of is that given the variety and types of discrimination employed against women in existing societies, a gender-free or androgynous society will look quite different from the societies that we know.

Defenses of Androgyny

Now there are various contemporary defenses of the ideal of androgyny. Some feminists have attempted to derive the ideal from a welfare liberal conception of justice. Others have attempted to derive the ideal from a socialist conception of justice. Here I will consider only the attempt to derive the ideal of androgyny from a welfare liberal conception of justice.[42]

In attempting to derive the ideal of androgyny from a welfare liberal conception of justice, feminists have tended to focus on the right to equal opportunity, which is a central requirement of such a conception of justice. Of course, equal opportunity could be interpreted minimally as providing people only with the same legal rights of access to all advantaged positions in society for which they are qualified. But this is not the interpretation given the right by welfare liberals. In a welfare liberal conception of justice, equal opportunity is interpreted to require in addition the same prospects for success for all those who are relevantly similar, where relevant similarity involves more than simply present qualifications. For example, Rawls claims that people in his original position would favor a right to "fair equality of opportunity," which means that people who have the same natural assets and the same willingness to use them would have the necessary resources to achieve similar life prospects.[43]

Yet any attempt to derive the feminist ideal of androgyny from the right to equal opportunity endorsed by welfare liberals can only be partially successful because the ideal still transcends this right by requiring not only that desirable traits be equally available to both women and men but also that the same virtues be equally inculcated in both women and men. Of course, part of the rationale for inculcating the same virtues in both women and men is to support a right to equal opportunity. And if support for such a right is to be fairly allocated, the virtues needed to support this right must be equally inculcated in both women and men. Nevertheless, to hold that the virtues

required to support a right to equal opportunity must be equally inculcated in both women and men is different from claiming, as the
ideal of androgyny does, that human virtues, sans phrase, should be
equally inculcated in both women and men. Thus, the ideal of androgyny clearly requires an inculcation of virtues beyond what is
necessary to support a right to equal opportunity. What additional
virtues are required by the ideal obviously depends upon what other
rights should be recognized. In this regard, the ideal of androgyny is
somewhat open-ended. Feminists who endorse the ideal would simply
have to go along with the best arguments for additional rights and
corresponding virtues.

In particular, I would claim that they would have to support a right
to welfare that is necessary for meeting the basic needs of all legitimate claimants given the strong case that can be made for such a
right from welfare liberal, socialist, and libertarian perspectives.

Obviously, in order to provide all legitimate claimants with the
resources necessary for meeting their basic needs, there has to be a
limit on the resources that will be available for each individual, and
this limit will definitely have an effect on the implementation of the
ideal of androgyny. Of course, some feminists would want to pursue
various possible technological transformations of human biology in
order to implement their ideal. For example, they would like to make
it possible for women to inseminate other women and for men to lac-
tate and even to bring fertilized ova to term. But bringing about such
possibilities would be very costly indeed.[44] Consequently, since the
means selected for meeting basic needs must be provided to all legitimate claimants, including distant peoples and future generations, it
is unlikely that such costly means could ever be morally justified.
Rather it seems preferable to radically equalize the opportunities that
are conventionally provided to women and men and wait for such
changes to ultimately have their effect on human biology as well. Of
course, if any "technological fixes" for achieving androgyny should
prove to be cost efficient as a means for meeting people's basic needs,
then obviously there would be every reason to utilize them.

Androgyny and the Family

The primary locus for the radical restructuring required by the ideal
of androgyny is the family. Here two fundamental changes are needed. First, all children irrespective of their sex must be given the same
type of upbringing consistent with their native capabilities. Second,

mothers and fathers must also have the same opportunities for education and employment consistent with their native capabilities.

Yet at least in the United States this need to radically modify traditional family structures to guarantee equal opportunity confronts a serious problem. Given that a significant proportion of the available jobs are at least 9 to 5, families with pre-school children require day care facilities if their adult members are to pursue their careers. Unfortunately, for many families such facilities are simply unavailable. In New York City, for example, more than 144,000 children under the age of six are competing for 46,000 full-time slots in day care centers. In Seattle, there is licensed day care space for 8,800 of the 23,000 children who need it. In Miami, two children, three and four years old, were left unattended at home while their mother worked. They climbed into a clothes dryer while the timer was on, closed the door, and burned to death.[45]

Moreover, even the available day care facilities are frequently inadequate either because their staffs are poorly trained or because the child/adult ratio in such facilities is too high. At best, such facilities provide little more than custodial care; at worst, they actually retard the development of those under their care. What this suggests is that at least under present conditions if pre-school children are to be adequately cared for, frequently, one of the adult members of the family will have to remain at home to provide that care. But since most jobs are at least 9 to 5, this will require that the adult members who stay at home temporarily give up pursuing a career.

However, such sacrifice appears to conflict with the equal opportunity requirement of feminist justice. Families might try to meet this equal opportunity requirement by having one parent give up pursuing a career for a certain period of time and the other give up pursuing a career for a subsequent (equal) period of time. But there are problems here too. Some careers are difficult to interrupt for any significant period of time, while others never adequately reward latecomers. In addition, given the high rate of divorce and the inadequacies of most legally mandated child support, those who first sacrifice their careers may find themselves later faced with the impossible task of beginning or reviving their careers while continuing to be the primary caretaker of their children.[46] Furthermore, there is considerable evidence that children will benefit more from equal rearing from both parents.[47] So the option of having just one parent doing the child-rearing for any length of time is, other things being equal, not optimal.

It would seem, therefore, that to truly share child-rearing within the family what is needed are flexible (typically part-time) work schedules that also allow both parents to be with their children for a significant period every day. Now some flexible job schedules have already been tried by various corporations. But if equal opportunity is to be a reality in our society, the option of flexible job schedules must be guaranteed to all those with pre-school children. Of course, to require employers to guarantee flexible job schedules to all those with pre-school children would place a significant restriction upon the rights of employers, and it may appear to move the practical requirements of feminist justice closer to those of socialist justice. But if the case for flexible job schedules is grounded on a right to equal opportunity, then at least defenders of welfare liberal justice will have no reason to object. This is clearly one place where feminist justice with its focus on equal opportunity within the family tends to drive welfare liberal justice and socialist justice closer together in their practical requirements.

Feminist Objections

In her recent book, *Justice, Gender and the Family*, Susan Okin also examines the capacity of a welfare liberal ideal to support the ideal of a gender-free society, which I take to be the same as an androgynous society.[48] Noting Rawls's failure to apply his original position-type thinking to family structures, Okin is skeptical about the possibility of using a welfare liberal ideal of fairness to support feminist justice. She contends that in a gender-structured society like our own, male philosophers cannot achieve the sympathetic imagination required to see things from the standpoint of women. In a gender-structured society, Okin claims, male philosophers cannot do the original position-type thinking required by the welfare liberal ideal of fairness because they lack the ability to put themselves in the position of women. As Okin puts it,

> For if principles of justice are to be adopted unanimously by representative human beings ignorant of their particular characteristics and positions in society, they must be persons whose psychological and moral development is in all essentials identical. This means that the social factors influencing the differences presently found between the sexes— from female parenting to all the manifestations of female subordination and dependence—would have to be replaced by genderless institutions and customs.[49]

So, according to Okin, original position-type thinking can only really be achieved in a gender-free society.

Yet at the same time that Okin despairs of doing original position-type thinking in a gender-structured society, like our own, she herself purportedly does a considerable amount of just that type of thinking. For example, she claims that Rawls's principles of justice "would seem to require a radical rethinking not only of the division of labor within families but also of all the nonfamily institutions that assume it."[50] She also claims that "the abolition of gender seems essential for the fulfillment of Rawls's criterion of political justice."[51] More specifically, she contends that

> if those in the original position did not know whether they were to be men or women, they would surely be concerned to establish a thorough-going social and economic equality between the sexes that would protect either sex from the need to pander to or servilely provide for the pleasures of the other. They would emphasize the importance of girls' and boys' growing up with an equal sense of respect for themselves and equal expectations of self-definition and development. They would be highly motivated, too, to find a means of regulating pornography that did not seriously compromise freedom of speech. In general, they would be unlikely to tolerate basic social institutions that asymmetrically either forced or gave strong incentives to members of one sex to serve as sex objects for the other.[52]

But which is it? Can we or can we not do the original position-type thinking required by a welfare liberal ideal of fairness? I think that Okin's own work, as well as my own, demonstrates that we can do such thinking and that her reasons for thinking that we cannot are not persuasive. For to do original position-type thinking, it is not necessary that everyone be able to put themselves imaginatively in the position of everyone else. All that is necessary is that some people be able to do so. For some people may not be able to do original position-type thinking because they have been deprived of a proper moral education. Others may be able to do original position-type thinking only after they have been forced to mend their ways and live morally for a period of time.

Moreover, in putting oneself imaginatively in the place of others, one need not completely replicate the experience of others, for example, one need not actually feel what it is like to be a murderer to adequately take into account the murderer's perspective. Original position-type thinking with respect to a particular issue requires only a general appreciation of the benefits and burdens accruing to people affected by that issue. So with respect to feminist justice, we need to be able to generally appreciate what women and men stand to gain and lose when moving from a nonandrogynous or gendered society to an androgynous or gender-free society.

Of course, even among men and women in our gendered society who are broadly capable of a sense of justice, some may not presently be able to do such original position-type thinking with respect to the proper relationships between men and women; these men and women may only be able to do so after the laws and social practices in our society have significantly shifted toward a more gender-free society. But this inability of some to do original position-type thinking does not render it impossible for others, who have effectively used the opportunities for moral development available to them to achieve the sympathetic imagination necessary for original position-type thinking with respect to the proper relationships between men and women. Accordingly, Okin has not provided any compelling reason to reject my previous argument that a welfare liberal ideal of fairness supports the ideal of androgyny.[53]

In examining the series of articles that Alison Jaggar has written on the topic of feminist justice, one notices what appears to be a significant change in Jaggar's view. In her earlier work, she seems to be defending a strong form of sexual equality, but in her more recent work her commitment to sexual equality appears to be importantly qualified. Accordingly, one might think that my own conception of feminist justice is more compatible with Jaggar's earlier view than with her more recent view. I will argue, however, that this is not the case.

In her widely anthologized article "On Sexual Equality" written more than fifteen years ago, Jaggar attempts to defend "the traditional conception of sexual equality as the de-institutionalization of sexual difference."[54] Here she refuses to define woman "as having a particular kind of body, having a recent history of being brought up in a patriarchal society, having an inherited history of female archetypes, having present experiences which occur because one is female, and having a future which calls for a revolution from being oppressed."[55] Rather she favors a starker account. She writes, "For me, to be a woman is no more and no less than to be a female human being."[56] She goes on to reject special rights for women. She argues that "so long as we view the difference between the sexes as a simple physiological difference—and we have no conclusive grounds for doing more—then there is no reason to draw up a special bill of rights for women in order to ensure our equality."[57] Near the end of this article, it becomes quite clear that Jaggar is endorsing the same ideal of feminist justice that I am endorsing. She writes, "we must . . . create a new androgynous culture which incorporates the best elements of both the present male and the present female cultures . . ."[58]

When we turn to one of Jaggar's most recent articles, however, her commitment to sexual equality and androgyny seems to be qualified by a recognition of sexual difference.[59] At first, Jaggar simply points out that there are enumerable cases where because of differences in the social situation of men and women "identical treatment of the sexes appears to promote women's inequality rather than their equality, at least in the short term."[60] She gives as examples no-fault divorce settlements, joint custody statutes, and an ordinance forbidding firefighters to breast-feed between calls.[61] The strategy here, of course, is to recognize certain differences in order to eliminate them. Later in this article, however, Jaggar contends that we need to recognize that there are ways in which women are different that should not be eliminated but valorized. Here she cites approvingly Sara Ruddick's work postulating a connection between mothering and opposition to militarism and Carol Gilligan's work which purports to discover a different voice among many women—a voice characterized by a caring ethic. She also notes the need to recognize the differences between women, differences of race, class, sexual preference, religion, age, ethnicity, marital status, physical ability, and so on.[62] Jaggar concludes that feminists "seem caught in the dilemma of simultaneously demanding and scorning equality with men," and recommends that feminists abandon neither their short-term goal of achieving equality nor their long-term goal of a world where "equality [is] overshadowed by the goods of mutual care."[63]

Yet despite the fact that Jaggar's more recent work on feminist justice may appear to be a departure from her earlier work with which my own conception of feminist justice is more clearly compatible, I think it is possible to see Jaggar's more recent work as simply a development and extension of her earlier work, and in no way incompatible with it. This becomes clear once we see that in her earlier work Jaggar was primarily trying to determine, as I am, what would be required by feminist justice in an ideal society. This is not a society, like our own, plagued by a variety of different sexist practices that have left women disadvantaged in various ways. Nor is it a society, like our own, characterized by racism, classism, homophobia, ageism, and various other institutional prejudices. Rather, it is a society where past injustices have been corrected and men and women have for some time been treated equally. So for such a society, it makes sense for feminist justice to require that women and men continue to be treated equally. Or to put the claim in terms of my formulation of feminist justice, it makes perfectly good sense in such a society to require that the traits that are truly desirable in society be equally available to both women and men, or in the case of virtues, equally inculcated in both women and men.

However, in a sexist society, like our own, where women have been disadvantaged through unequal treatment, simply treating women and men equally, that is, in exactly the same way, would not be just, for it would serve to perpetuate the previous injustices. For such a society, the only acceptable route to sexual equality is through a transitional stage where sexual inequalities of the past are corrected by compensating for them with unequal treatment. To achieve a fair outcome in a race in which some runners have been disadvantaged by being forced for some time to run with weights tied to their legs, we may need to transfer the weights to other runners who were advantaged by this unfair practice at least for a corresponding period of time.

That is why in my book *How to Make People Just*, I defended not only a right to equal opportunity, but in addition a right to affirmative action in cases where there was a denial of equal opportunity in the past. So in an unjust society, there is a need to recognize differences created by past injustices and to correct for them with unequal treatment. Moreover, this unequal treatment is required by the ideal of equality itself.

Nevertheless, differences between women and men that are due to past injustices are not the only differences that Jaggar wants to recognize. As she puts it, there are other differences that should not be eliminated but valorized and here, as we already noted, Jaggar has in mind women's commitment to mothering and the caring ethic as extolled by Sara Ruddick and Carol Gilligan respectively. While I agree that these traits should be valorized, I think, for that very reason, steps should be taken to eliminate them as differences. For as Ruddick rightly points out, men can be mothers too, and I think it follows from my ideal of feminist justice that if men are to be parents, then they should share equally the roles of mother and father properly understood. And the same holds true with respect to Gilligan's caring ethic. To the degree to which commitment to a caring ethic is desirable, then such a commitment should be encouraged and even inculcated in both women and men. And if this is effectively done, then, over time, these difference between women and men will, in fact, disappear. So I would argue that a correct interpretation of Jaggar's recent stress on the importance of sexual difference is perfectly compatible with her earlier commitment to sexual equality and the ideal of androgyny. So, in this respect, our views do not differ at all.

Nevertheless, there are at least two important respects in which Jaggar and I do disagree. The first concerns the ability of a welfare liberal conception of justice to support an adequate ideal of sexual equality or androgyny. Here Jaggar thinks that liberalism fails to adequately support a feminist conception of justice because it is committed to an ahistorical, abstract conception of human nature.[64] But while this criticism may have some validity when addressed to classical liberalism, as I have argued elsewhere,[65] it doesn't apply to contemporary versions of the theory. Of course, it might be objected that people in the original position look a lot like the abstract individuals to which Jaggar claims liberals are committed. But appearances can be deceiving, and to see why they are in this case, we need only recall why the theoretical construction of the original position was introduced in the first place. It was introduced to draw out the implications of widely shared moral judgments about fairness such as the judgment that no one deserves his or her native abilities or starting place in society. It was in no way intended to suggest that people are actually behind a veil of ignorance in real life. Moreover, the only information that is abstracted from in the original position is the prejudicial information concerning what positions particular people actually occupy in society, and so there is no reason to think that that knowledge is required for working out a morally adequate conception of justice.

A second respect in which Jaggar and I disagree concerns the usefulness of interpreting the welfare liberal ideal of fairness as hypothetical consent. In a recent interesting paper, Jaggar grants that "the theoretical device of hypothetical consent initially may be attractive to feminists working in practical ethics."[66] But she then goes on to argue that "hypothetical consent is [in fact] an inappropriate conceptual tool for this sort of feminist ethical work."[67] Her main objection to arguing from hypothetical consent comes "from the fact that this reasoning is about ideal rather than actual societies."[68] On this account, Jaggar recommends that feminists who work in practical ethics "refrain from speculations about hypothetical consent and devote their energy instead to reflecting on and indeed actively pursuing real life moral consensus."[69]

Unfortunately, the idea that reasoning from hypothetical consent is about ideal rather than nonideal or actual societies derives from Rawls's self-imposed limit on the type of hypothetical consent theory he chose to develop. Since Rawls only sought to construct principles of justice for ideal conditions for which it was assumed that everyone would strictly comply with the chosen principles of justice, many have thought that the device of hypothetical consent can only be usefully applied in ideal conditions. Yet there is no reason why a hypothetical consent account of fairness cannot be extended to nonideal conditions as well. In fact, I have done just that in some of my earlier work where I have developed a hypothetical consent theory of punishment, by assuming behind a veil of ignorance that one might be a criminal, a victim of crime, or a member of the general public and then deriving principles of punishment.[70] So, in general, there seems to be no problem with the application of a hypothetical consent theory of fairness to nonideal conditions.

Yet perhaps what is really troubling Jaggar is not the possibility of developing a hypothetical consent theory that applies to nonideal conditions, but rather the realization that under nonideal conditions we must deal with people constituted through institutions of domination such as gender, race and class. Such people, and they include ourselves, are not only unequal in knowledge and power but often also prejudiced, confused—even brutal or sadistic.[71] Here the problem is that such individuals may not be able to achieve the sympathetical imagination required by a hypothetical consent theory of fairness. Of particular relevance to feminist justice is that such individuals may not be able to imaginatively put themselves in the place of women. But this is the same problem raised by Okin that we discussed earlier, and the solution remains the same: We must recognize that in an unjust society only some people will be capable of doing original position type thinking. Others, either through improper moral education or their own fault, may simply not have this ability. Notice also that under nonideal conditions, the possibility of achieving an actual consensus that is morally acceptable and the ability of individuals to do original position-type thinking go hand in hand; for only when a considerable number or people in a society have achieved the sympathetic imagination necessary to put themselves in the position of others will the actual consensus that emerges under real life conditions be morally acceptable. So feminists really can't follow Jaggar's advice and "refrain from speculations about hypothetical consent and devote their energy instead to reflecting on and indeed actively pursuing real life moral consensus" because speculations about hypothetical consent and real life moral consensus are actually intimately connected.

In sum, what I have argued in this paper is that a libertarian conception of justice and a feminist conception of justice support the practical requirements that are usually associated with a welfare liberal conception of justice, namely, a right to welfare and a right to equal opportunity. I have also attempted to show that recent work done by libertarians and feminists neither undercuts nor is incompatible with this argument for reconciling conceptions of justice.

Notes

An earlier version of this paper was presented as a symposium paper at the 1992 Central Division American Philosophical Meeting held in Louisville, Kentucky. Alison Jaggar and Jan Narveson were the commentators.

1. See James P. Sterba, "Neolibertarianism," *American Philosophical Quarterly* (1978); *The Demands of Justice* (Notre Dame: University of Notre Dame Press, 1980); "The Welfare Rights of Distant Peoples and Future Generations: Moral Side-Constraints on Social Policy," *Social Theory and Practice* (1981); "Recent Work on Alternative Conceptions of Justice," *American Philosophical Quarterly* (1986); "Justifying Morality: The Right and the Wrong Ways," *Synthese* (1987); *How to Make People Just* (Totowa, N.J.: Rowman & Littlefield, 1988); "Feminist Justice and the Family," reprinted in my anthology, *Justice: Alternative Political Perspectives*, 2nd ed. (Belmont, Calif.: Wadsworth, 1991).

2. It is interesting to note that in his recent work Alasdair MacIntyre has significantly qualified his commitment to the incommensurability thesis with which he is so widely associated. He now allows that while alternative political ideals are incommensurable, it is still possible for a sensitive interpreter to come to adequately understand competing ideals so as to raise problems for those ideals that should lead either to their abandonment or to their modification. He credits Aquinas with being a sensitive interpreter of Aristotelianism and Augustinianism who showed the need to modify each perspective to produce a more adequate synthesis. In his most recent work, MacIntyre sees himself as being the sensitive interpreter of two views he calls the encyclopedist (which he apparently thinks contains the core view of liberalism) and the genealogist (which represents an ugly form of relativism). He then attempts to show that both of these views are plagued with internal contradictions which he takes to provide support for the Augustinian-Aristotelian synthesis that he derives from Aquinas. Obviously, I welcome MacIntyre's newly stated recognition that it is possible to argue nonarbitrarily with respect to alternative political ideals. Nevertheless, I think that while MacIntyre in his most recent work may have correctly refuted the genealogist, the liberalism he criticizes is only a caricature of contemporary liberalism. Ironically, it turns out that contemporary liberalism, correctly

understood, is in fact one variant of the general Augustinian-Aristotelian synthesis that MacIntyre derives from Aquinas! See Alasdair MacIntyre, *Three Rival Versions of Moral Enquiry* (Notre Dame: University of Notre Dame Press, 1990).

3. It is not being assumed here that the surplus possessions of the rich are either justifiably or unjustifiably possessed by the rich. Moreover, according to Spencerian libertarians, it is an assessment of the liberties involved that determines whether the possession is justifiably or not.

4. I first appealed to this interpretation of the "ought" implies "can" principle to bring libertarians around to the practical requirements of welfare liberalism in an expanded version of an article entitled "Neo-Libertarianism," which appeared in the fall of 1979. In 1982, T. M. Scanlon, in "Contractualism and Utilitarianism," appealed to much the same standard to arbitrate the debate between contractarians and utilitarians. In my judgment, however, this standard embedded in the "ought" implies "can" principle can be more effectively used in the debate with libertarians than in the debate with utilitarians, because sacrifices libertarians standardly seek to impose on the less advantaged are more outrageous and, hence, more easily shown to be contrary to reason.

5. I am indebted to Alasdair MacIntyre for helping me make this point clearer.

6. See James P. Sterba, "Is There a Rationale for Punishment?" *American Journal of Jurisprudence* (1984).

7. By the liberty of the rich to meet their luxury needs I continue to mean the liberty of the rich not to be interfered with when using their surplus possessions for luxury purposes. Similarly, by the liberty of the poor to meet their basic needs I continue to mean the liberty of the poor not to be interfered with when taking what they require to meet their basic needs from the surplus possessions of the rich.

8. See, for example, Eric Mack, "Individualism, Rights and the Open Society," in *The Libertarian Alternative*, ed., Tibor Machan, (Chicago, 1974) Nelson Hall and "Libertarianism Untamed," *Journal of Social Philosophy*, Special Issue (1991).

9. For a sketch of this argument, see *How to Make People Just*, pp. 92–97.

10. Moreover, libertarians have not restricted the class of morally legitimate claimants in this fashion. After all, the fundamental rights recognized by libertarians are universal rights, that is, rights possessed by all people, not just those who live in certain places or at certain times. Of course, to claim that these rights are universal rights does not mean that they are universally recognized. Obviously, the fundamental rights that flow from the libertarian ideal have not been universally recognized. Rather, to claim that they are universal rights, despite their spotty recognition, implies only that they ought to be recognized at all times and places by people who have or could have had good reasons to recognize these rights, whether or not they actually did or do so.

Nor need these universal rights be unconditional. This is particularly true in the case of the right to welfare, which, I have argued, is conditional on people doing all that they legitimately can to provide for themselves. In addition, this right is conditional on there being sufficient resources available so that everyone's welfare needs can be met. So where people do not do all that they can to provide for themselves or where there are not sufficient resources available, people simply do not have a right to welfare.

Yet even though libertarians have claimed that the rights they defend are universal rights in the manner I have just explained, it may be that they are simply mistaken in this regard. Even when universal rights are stripped of any claim to being universally recognized or unconditional, still it might be argued that there are no such rights, that is, that there are no rights that all people ought to recognize.

But how would one argue for such a view? One couldn't argue from the failure of people to recognize such rights because we have already said that such recognition is not necessary. Nor could one argue that not everyone ought to recognize such rights because some lack the capacity to do so. This is because "ought" does imply "can" here, so that the obligation to recognize certain rights applies only to those who actually have or have had at some point the capacity to do so. Thus, the existence of universal rights is not ruled out by the existence of individuals who have never had the capacity to recognize such rights. It would only be ruled out by the existence of individuals who could recognize these rights but for whom it would be correct to say that they ought, all things considered, not to do so. But we have just seen that even a minimal libertarian moral ideal supports a universal right to welfare. And I have also argued elsewhere that when "ought" is understood prudentially rather than morally a non-question-begging conception to rationality favors morality over prudence. (See *How to Make People Just*, Chapter 11.) So for those capable of recognizing universal rights, it simply is not possible to argue that they, all things considered, ought not to do so.

11. Bob Bergland, "Attacking the Problem of World Hunger," *National Forum* (1979) Vol. 69, No. 2, p. 4.

12. For a discussion of these causal connections, see Cheryl Silver, *One Earth One Future* (Washington, D.C.: National Academy Press, 1990); Bill McKibben, *The End of Nature* (New York: Anchor Books, 1989); Jeremy Leggett, ed., *Global Warming* (New York: Oxford University Press, 1990); Lester Brown, ed., *The World Watch Reader* (New York: Nelson, 1991).

13. John Rawls, *A Theory of Justice* (Cambridge: Harvard University Press, 1971).

14. For further discussion of a basic needs minimum, see *How to Make People Just,* pp. 45–48.

15. Tibor R. Machan, *Individuals and Their Rights* (La Salle: Open Court, 1989), pp. 100-111.

16. Ibid., p. 107.

17. Alan Durning, "Life on the Brink," *World Watch* (1990) Vol. 3, No. 2, p. 24.

18. Ibid., p. 29.

19. In *Individuals and Their Rights* and in correspondence, Machan has distinguished between poverty and hunger that results from natural causes and poverty and hunger that results from "political tyrannies" or from other human causes. Machan suggests that only the first sort of poverty and hunger need concern libertarians. But unless the victims are morally responsible for their fate, then, it seems to me, others will have at least a prima facie obligation not to interfere with relief efforts, even when those relief efforts happen to be utilizing their own surplus possessions.

20. Jan Narveson, "Property Rights: Original Acquisition and Lockean Provisos" (unpublished manuscript), p. 11. I want to thank Narveson for sending me a copy of this paper. It was very helpful to have it when I was preparing this symposium paper, as was a series of letters he and I exchanged just a year ago.

21. Ibid., p. 15.

22. Ibid., p. 7

23. Ibid., p. 6; see also his *The Libertarian Idea* (Philadelphia: Temple University Press, 1990), Chapters 6 to 8.

24. Narveson, "Property Rights," p. 9.

25. Ibid., p. 10.

26. Ibid., p. 6.

27. Ibid., p. 6.

28. If one tries to apply my distinction between Spencerian libertarians and Lockean libertarians to Narveson's analysis, we find that he seems to endorse the Spencerian view on some occasions (ibid., p. 6) and the Lockean view on others (ibid., pp. 10–11). This, of course, is inconsistent, but at least Narveson is in good company in this regard. See Robert Nozick, *State, Anarchy, and Utopia* (New York: Basic Books, 1974), pp. 67n, 161–64, 179n.

29. See, for example, Ann Ferguson, "Androgyny as an Ideal for Human Development," in *Feminism and Philosophy,* Mary Vetterling-Braggin et al., eds. (Totowa, N.J.: Rowman & Littlefield, 1977) pp. 45–69; Mary Anne Warren, "Is Androgyny the Answer to Sexual Stereotyping?" in *"Femininity," "Masculinity," and "Androgyny,"* Mary Vetterling-Braggin, ed. (Totowa, N.J.: Rowman & Littlefield, 1982) pp. 170–86; A. G. Kaplan and J. Bean eds. *Beyond Sex-Role Stereotypes: Reading Toward a Psychology of Androgyny* (Totowa, N.J.: Rowman & Littlefield, 1976); Andrea Dworkin, *Women Hating* (New York: Dulton, 1974), Part IV; Carol Gould, "Privacy Rights and Public Virtues: Women, the Family and Democracy," in *Beyond Domination,* Carol Gould, ed. (Totowa, N.J.: Rowman & Littlefield, 1983), pp. 3–18; Carol Gould, "Women and Freedom," *Journal of Social Philosophy* (1984) pp. 20–34; Linda Lindsey, *Gender Roles* (Englewood Cliffs, N.J.: Prentice-Hall, 1990); Marilyn Friedman, "Does Sommers like Women?" *Journal of Social Philosophy* (1991), pp. 75–90.

30. Joyce Trebilcot, "Two Forms of Androgynism," in *Feminism and Philosophy,* pp. 70–78.

31. Warren, "Is Androgyny the Answer," pp. 178–79.

32. Trebilcot, "Two Forms of Androgynism," pp. 74–77.

33. On this point, see Edmund Pincoffs, *Quandaries and Virtue* (Lawrence: University of Kansas Press, 1986), Chapter 5.

34. See, for example, Kathryn Paula Morgan, "Androgyny: A Conceptual Critique," *Social Theory and Practice* (1982), pp. 256–57.

35. See, for example, Mary Daly, *Gyn-Ecology: The Meta-ethics of Radical Feminism* (Boston: Beacon, 1978), p. xi.

36. Margrit Erchler, *The Double Standard* (New York: St. Martin's Press, 1980), pp. 69–71; Elizabeth Lane Beardsley, "On Curing Conceptual Confusion" in *"Femininity," "Masculinity," and "Androgyny,"* pp. 197–202; Mary Daly, "The Qualitative Leap Beyond Patriarchal Religion," *Quest* (1975) Vol. 1, pp. 20–40; Janice Raymond, "The Illusion of Androgyny," *Quest* (1975), Vol. 2, pp. 57–66.

37. For a valuable discussion and critique of these two viewpoints, see Iris Young, "Humanism, Gynocentrism and Feminist Politics," *Women's Studies International Forum* (1985), Vol. 8, No. 3, pp. 173–83.

38. See Christina Sommers, "Philosophers Against the Family," in *Person to Person,* George Graham and Hugh LaFollette, eds. (Philadelphia: Temple University Press, 1989), pp. 82–105; "Do These Feminists like Women?" *Journal of Social Philosophy* (1990), pp. 66–74; "Argumentum Ad Feminam," *Journal of Social Philosophy* (1991), pp. 5–19.

39. Elizabeth Wolgast, *Equality and the Rights of Women* (Ithaca: Cornell University Press, 1980).

40. Moreover, given that the basic rights that we have in society, e.g., a right to equal opportunity, are equal for all citizens and are not based on our differing natural abilities, these rights are not even in this derivative sense based on one's sex.

41. Anne Moir and David Jessel, *Brain Sex* (Secaucus: Carol Publishing, 1991).

42. For an attempt to derive the ideal of androgyny from a socialist conception of justice, see "Feminist Justice and the Family," pp. 319–20.

43. Rawls, *A Theory of Justice*, p. 73.

44. See Barbara Katz Rothman, " How Science Is Redefining Parenthood," *Ms* (August 1982), pp. 154–58.

45. *New York Times*, November 25, 1987.

46. See Lenore Weitzman, *The Divorce Revolution: The Unexpected Social and Economic Consequences for Women and Children in America* (New York: Free Press, 1985).

47. Dorothy Dinnerstein, *The Mermaid and the Minotaur* (New York: Harper & Row, 1977); Nancy Chodorow, *Mothering: Psychoanalysis and the Sociology of Gender* (Berkeley: University of California Press, 1978).

48. Susan Okin, *Justice, Gender and the Family* (New York: Basic Books, 1989), Chapter 5.

49. Ibid., p. 107.

50. Ibid., p. 104.

51. Ibid., p. 104.

52. Ibid., pp. 104–5.

53. It is worth pointing out that my previous argument for androgyny actually benefited from criticisms raised by Okin in private correspondence in 1987.

54. Alison Jaggar, "On Sexual Equality," in *Sexual Equality*, Jane English, ed. (1977), p. 97.

55. Ibid., p. 99.

56. Ibid., p. 99.

57. Ibid., p. 102.

58. Ibid., p. 105.

59. Alison Jaggar, "Sexual Difference and Sexual Equality," in *Theoretical Perspectives on Sexual Difference*, Deborah Rhode, ed. (New Haven: Yale University Press, 1990), pp. 239–54.

60. Ibid., p. 242.

61. Ibid., p. 241.

62. Ibid., p. 246.

63. Ibid., pp. 253–54.

64. Alison Jaggar, *Feminist Politics and Human Nature* (Totowa, N.J.: Rowman & Littlefield, 1983), pp. 42–43.

65. Ibid., pp. 69–71.

66. Alison Jaggar, "Taking Consent Seriously: Feminist Practical Ethics and Actual Moral Dialogue," in *Applied Ethics: A Reader*, Earl Winkler and Jerold Coombs, eds. (Oxford: Basic Blackwell, 1993), pp. 69–70.

67. Ibid., pp. 69–70.

68. Ibid., p. 79.

69. Ibid., pp. 81–82.

70. James P. Sterba, "Retributive Justice," *Political Theory* (1977); "Contractual Retributivism Defended," *Political Theory* (1979); "Is There a Rationale for Punishment?" *American Journal of Jurisprudence* (1984); "A Rational Choice Theory of Punishment," *Philosophical Topics* (1990).

71. Jaggar, "Taking Consent Seriously," *Op. Cit.*, p. 79.

Comments by Tibor R. Machan

In his paper for this book Sterba takes classical liberalism—or libertarianism, as it has come to be known and been developed into a more coherent political outlook in our time—seriously, only to transform its defense so that it supports, paradoxically it might seem at first blush, the quite antiliberal system of the welfare state. (I use "liberal" here, as elsewhere, not in its corrupted socialist but original individualist sense.) Sterba thinks that classical liberalism or libertarianism—including its Lockean version—must, based on its own conception of justice, give philosophical backing to the redistributivist welfare state.

In response I will argue, in essence, that Sterba (a) overstates the place of poverty and misfortune in free, capitalist societies (by reading history as if it gave us a great many examples of such a system and failing to note that the fractions of existing systems that are capitalist tend to contribute to the elimination of poverty and misfortune), and (b) wishes to remedy the remaining fraction of poverty and misfortune in free, capitalist systems by throwing out the baby with the bath water, that is, by undermining the integrity of the right to individual liberty, thereby inviting the high probability of the abolition of such a right through and through.

Even though Sterba has gone some rounds with various philosophers who take it that libertarian politics serves the cause of justice better than others, it may be useful here to continue the discussion. Sterba addresses my own argument for libertarianism and concludes that it, too, involves the problem of failing to appreciate the impact of the fundamental metaethical idea that "ought" implies "can." Here is how he puts the point against my position: "[Machan] appreciates the force of the argument enough to grant that if the type of conflict cases that we have described between the rich and the poor actually obtained, the poor would have a right to welfare."[1]

Actually, what I say is this: "If Sterba were correct about Lockean libertarianism typically contradicting '"ought" implies "can"',' his argument would be decisive."[2] I do not deny that such conflict cases could obtain in a libertarian system, but do deny that they would be typical. To this Sterba responds as follows:

> For who could deny that most of the 1.2 billion people who are currently living in conditions of absolute poverty "lack the opportunities and necessities to satisfy their basic needs"? And even within our own country [U.S.A.], it is estimated that some 32 million Americans live below

the official poverty index [$14,000 per annum for a family, $7,000 per annum for an individual], and that one-fifth of American children are growing up in poverty. Surely, it is impossible to deny that many of these Americans also "lack the opportunities and resources to satisfy their basic needs."[3]

This response is a non sequitur because it speaks not of what may be expected in a country that functions within the framework of laws guided by Lockean libertarian principles—individual human negative rights, including the rights to life, liberty, and property—but of what is true of (a) the world at large and (b) the United States in the 1990s. The world is clearly very far from adhering to Lockean libertarian principles of justice and the United States has only the mildest resemblance to such a system, having for nearly all of its history had its proclaimed Lockean libertarian principles contradicted (e.g., slavery, conscription, blue laws, eminent domain laws, police power provisions) and powerfully watered down (e.g., federal regulations, federal, state, county, and municipal income, property, and sales taxes). It is, furthermore, admitted by nearly all economists that the expansion of free trade throughout the globe, via provisions such as privatization and removing trade barriers—approaching Lockean libertarian conditions of justice at least in the realm of commerce—would improve the terrible conditions Sterba so unfairly links to libertarianism. And without our embarking on a detailed analysis of conditions in the United States, it may just help here to consider that for over one hundred years the country's federal government has been moving in the direction of a democratic welfare state, away from any semblance of laissez-faire. Yet each year the number of the poor is reported to be increasing, there is more and more evidence of homelessness, and the relative standard of living of the citizenry is reported to be worsening. If there is a way to help the situation of the poor, it does not appear to be by moving toward the welfare state.

Let me, then, summarize my complaint about Sterba's argument for welfare statism, as it emerges from his analysis of libertarian politics.

First of all, Sterba believes that there is much evidence of poverty and misfortune amid the free, capitalist society with its commitment to the (realistically) full protection of private property rights. This is a mistake. What there is evidence of is much poverty and misfortune going unattended in all kinds of societies that fall very, very short of being free, capitalist systems which protect private property rights. One cannot point even to the United States, with its massive welfare state and it history of extreme violation of private property rights, as in the case of the failure to have protected these rights for the bulk of black Americans and compromised their full protection for others, as well.[4]

Second, Sterba is correct to note that under the free, capitalist system of economics that would prevail in a classical liberal, libertarian polity—based on its constitution of natural, individual rights—no legal guarantee would exist against being poor and misfortunate, no one could be coerced to supply one with provisions to alleviate these conditions. Would this constitute grounds for compromising that system? Or, to put it more theoretically, would this possibility warrant choosing a system in which full protection of private property rights would not be attempted via the law?

The answer is that this would not warrant abandoning the libertarian alternative in favor of some other, say the welfare state. The reason is as follows.

A political system, such as socialism, the welfare state, libertarianism, or fascism, is one reasonably coherent answer to a problem that human beings, who are social animals (among other things), face in their community living. No actual community ever fully exhibits such a system in its pure form, mainly because even if members of a community tried with all their good will and intelligence, they would probably fail to implement the system fully and completely. But people have tried, throughout history, to implement various systems—or, to put it differently, to use the standards of justice identified via the conceptualization of such systems, as their guide to establishing and maintaining political societies. But to do this they needed to use a system of such standards that is consistent, that has no built-in conflict. If, say, a libertarian system were indeed the best of all the alternatives, and it would imply that private property rights ought to be fully protected, this would require that no official compromise be made on that protection. Failing that, the legal system would include elements leading to its own disintegration. Legal precedents of compromises on private property rights would quickly devour the system's integrity—one case of a supposedly just violation of private property would serve as the justification for subsequent cases.

Now there are, no doubt, instances in human life where supposedly firmly established principles of conduct or political organization ought to be abandoned, disregarded.[5] In personal ethics, for example, honesty, generosity, courage, prudence, and such ought, in very special circumstances, to be abandoned so as to address some exceptional problems, ones that are inherently abnormal, as when one lives in a concentration camp or deals extensively with Nazis, gangsters, or terrorists. An individual, by employing *phronesis* or practical reason, will have the opportunity to rebound from these exceptions and resume a life of virtue appropriate to human living in general. A legal system, on the other hand, operates differently. It represents official policy and any abridgment of its principles can come to haunt it later as a means for its disintegration. I believe we have ample evidence for this in how the welfare state has spawned a tremendously intrusive state, huge bureaucracies, corruption galore, yet has not eliminated what nearly everyone who advocates it promises it will eliminate, namely, poverty and misfortune.

So, even if we agree with Sterba, as we surely must, that not everyone is equally well positioned in their lives—or as he might put it, is not equally free to achieve the same goals as everyone else, this does not justify altering the legal system that rests on a sound understanding of human nature and its requirements in a community. It is not that there may not *occasionally* be people who are drastically limited by natural happenstance in their abilities to cope and reach for success. But if a community is to be rendered suitable to human life, *as such*, the principles by which it should be governed need to be derived not from exceptional or emergency situations but from human nature and a life normally to be expected for human beings. As the saying goes, hard cases make bad law.

I argue elsewhere[6] that the occasional (as distinct from typical) presence of the crucially incapacitated (e.g., totally neglected orphan or abandoned cripple) does not warrant amending the legal system to accommodate their "nature." Sterba takes it that in this argument I differ from him only practically—that is, I grant that such poor possess "action rights."[7]

What I do grant is that innocent people whose sole alternative to perishing is to steal ought, indeed, to steal. This does not include the 1.2 billion people Sterba cites who are living in poverty around the globe, since their lot rests in large measure on lacking a legal system of natural rights in their political organization. (Thus, lacking a system of private property rights in farming, Ethiopians and Somalians face famines in light of the absence of efficient food production that is best supported by such a system.) The same applies to the 32 million Americans who supposedly live below the poverty line, as understood in one of the richest nations in world history, one that has been famous for its championing of private property rights, if not their full protection. Were property rights fully protected rather than officially violated nearly everywhere—including for purposes of expropriating people's wealth for innumerable governmental projects that thwart productivity in various ways—the bulk of poverty would most likely be alleviated. (Considering the record of societies with largely protected private property rights and those without, this is not a speculative claim. There's little doubt the Soviet Union failed largely because of collectivization and the "tragedy of the commons.")

When we focus on those individuals who have failed to flourish within a system in which property rights are protected, then we may claim that if they have been innocent of rights violation and have made every effort to succeed but failed through misfortune, then they ought to take the drastic measure of *disregarding* the rights of others. In their scale of moral principles the goal of flourishing, which is primary, would not be achievable without such stealing. But this does not mean they have any (political) right to steal—that is, that a human community ought to have as one of its principles of organization to accommodate such exceptional cases.

Rights, as I have argued, are political principles, not personal moral edicts. Thus, the existence of a few such people from truly libertarian societies on whom Sterba focuses does not serve as grounds for assigning the positive political rights of some people to other people's services and belongings. Freak cases do not warrant modifying the principles of morality and politics. They do not generate basic possible human rights.

Exceptional cases such as those focused upon by Sterba do raise serious moral issues for people in a free society. Such people will have to be generous enough to (voluntarily) take care of such innocent people in dire straits. This applies to those, especially, who are close to them and thus understand their specialness. It may be tempting to amend the legal system in their behalf, motivated by compassion and generosity, but since this will undermine the integrity of the just polity, it would be the wrong thing to do.

Notes

1. See Sterba's "Reconciling Conceptions of Justice" in this book.
2. Tibor R. Machan, *Individuals and Their Rights* (LaSalle, Ill.: Open Court, 1989), p. 103.
3. See Sterba's paper in this book.
4. For a good account of this see Jonathan R. T. Hughes, *The Governmental Habit*, 2nd ed. (New York: Basic Books, 1986).
5. I discuss this in Tibor R. Machan, "Prima Facie v. Natural (Human)

Rights," *Journal of Value Inquiry* (Summer 1976), Vol. 10, pp. 119–31; see also Eric Mack, "Egoism and Rights," *The Personalist* (Winter 1973) Vol. 54, pp. 5–33, and "Libertarianism Untamed," *Journal of Social Philosophy* (1992), Vol. 22.

    6. In Machan, *Individuals and Their Rights,* pp. 100–111.

    7. See the "Introduction" in James P. Sterba, *Alternative Political Perspectives* (Belmont, Calif.: Wadsworth, 1991), p. 6.

Comments by Alison M. Jaggar

Sterba's essay springs from his book *How to Make People Just* and is an updated version of his paper "Reconciling Conceptions of Justice" delivered at the 1992 Central Division meeting of the American Philosophical Association. As in his earlier works, Sterba's project is to convince the adherents of seemingly different conceptions of justice that they should all accept two rights. In this essay, these are identified as a right to welfare and a right to equal opportunity, though earlier Sterba has asserted a right to affirmative action rather than to equal opportunity. I was one of two commentators on Sterba's symposium paper and I have published a discussion of his book in the *Journal of Social Philosophy* (Winter 1991), Vol. 2, No. 3. This is therefore my third opportunity to comment on Sterba's practical reconciliation project and, as on previous occasions, his work leaves me feeling ambivalent.

I certainly admire Sterba's attempt to draw on academic philosophical theory in order to illuminate significant issues of current public policy; I also think his strategy of approaching people on their own ground, beginning with premises they accept already, is an excellent way to begin. As someone committed to the importance of dialogue, I appreciate his persistent efforts to persuade philosophers from a variety of different traditions to communicate with each other, as he has done in this book, which was his idea and which he coordinated. Finally, since I personally agree that some version of welfare and equal opportunity should be promoted in contemporary democratic societies, I should be delighted if Sterba could persuade everyone else of this.

I continue to be unhappy, however, with his characterizations of the various views he seeks to reconcile. His invariable method is to distill rich and complex intellectual traditions down to tidy conceptions of justice, each defined in terms of one "ultimate political ideal" whose identity is flagged with a capital letter. One of my objections to his procedure is that his definition of each political tradition in terms of a different basic value exaggerates the contrasts between the traditions and obscures their convergences. This problem is clearly illustrated by Sterba's classification of individual philosophers; for instance, he places Susan Okin and me in the same category because we are both feminists, even though Okin is a liberal and I am a socialist, and puts himself, as a liberal, into a different category, even though he too is a feminist. This grouping is unfortuate because his views in fact are closer to Okin's than are mine. A more flexible approach would have allowed Sterba to categorize both Okin and himself as liberal feminists and to identify me as a socialist feminist. I recognize that the creation of taxonomies always requires a certain amount of pushing and pulling—indeed, the restrictiveness of my own categories of feminism has been criticized—but I find Sterba's specific taxonomy of theories of justice to be quite distorting. In my *JSP* paper, I argued that his reductionist method not only seriously mischaracterized the politics of the socialist, feminist, and communitarian traditions but, by presenting them all as conceptions of justice in the liberal sense, he reduced each to a common denominator that diverted attention from the deeper philosophical issues it raised.

One issue over which Sterba and I have disagreed continually is his insistence on defining feminism as a commitment to androgyny, regardless of the fact that many feminists have explicitly and repeatedly distanced themselves from this ideal. Sterba is aware of their rejection but he argues that androgyny is a logical consequence of views characteristically held by feminists. In my comments on Sterba's APA presentation, I offered several reasons for disagreeing with his proposal to define feminism in terms of androgyny and I shall take this opportunity to recapitulate and elaborate some of them here.

Sterba's argument for his claim that feminism should be defined as a commitment to androgyny begins from the assumption that all feminists are committed to equality of opportunity, continues with the assertion that genuine equality of opportunity requires the abolition of gender and concludes with the claim that the ideal of androgyny is logically equivalent to the ideal of a gender-free society. In response, I would argue that:

(1)   None of the three concepts or ideals that Sterba associates with feminism is capable of defining it. Some feminists are critical of the ideal of equal opportunity, while others explicitly reject genderlessness and still others reject androgyny.

(2)   Even if one of these three concepts did comprehend the spirit of feminism, this would not license defining feminism in terms of any of the others since they are not logically equivalent to each other. In particular, androgyny is an ideal different in kind from equality of opportunity and genderlessness.

First let us consider equal opportunity. This ideal is certainly endorsed by most Western feminists but it is definitive only of liberal feminism. Nonliberal feminists endorse equal opportunity only with reservations or they regard it as only a minor feature of their larger feminist vision. For instance, socialist feminists find the ideal of equal opportunity problematic insofar as it presupposes a competitive and meritocratic society that fails to support such socialist values as shared responsibility and community. "Difference" feminists criticize equal opportunity as an ideal springing from a liberal tradition that they regard as characteristically masculine; in their view, feminism's distinctive contribution lies in its revalorization of such culturally feminine characteristics as nurturing and caring. Finally, rather than endorsing traditional ideals, radical feminists call for a transvaluation or rethinking of all values. Equality of opportunity may be part of nonliberal feminisms but it cannot be said to define them.

Even those feminists who wholeheartedly endorse the ideal of equal opportunity do not necessarily commit themselves to abolishing gender. Sterba names Christina Sommers as one self-identified feminist who makes an emphatic distinction between a commitment to equal opportunity and a commitment to abolishing gender. Sommers insists that those she labels "gender feminists" are extreme radicals whose views are quite incompatible with those of liberal feminists such as herself. Sterba responds by arguing that a thoroughgoing commitment to equality of opportunity requires the abolition of gender, regardless of whether or not this is acknowledged by Sommers and some other liberals. I think Sterba is correct on this point; I also believe a thoroughgoing commitment to equality of opportunity requires abolishing economic class. But even though I regard the abolition of economic class as a requirement for achieving the egalitarian ideals of both liberalism and liberal feminism, I do not think this belief justifies defining either liberalism or feminism as a commitment to the abolition of class. For one thing, other aspects of liberalism and at least liberal versions of feminism are often thought incompatible with abolishing class. Moreover, because so many liberals and feminists would disagree with such a definition, it would be confusing at best and presumptuous or provocative at worst. In the present U.S. political climate, such a definition would also be likely to discredit both liberalism and feminism because it would confirm widespread conservative beliefs that feminism and liberalism were merely covers for a dangerously radical and discredited socialism. It is surely useful on occasion to show how class differences may undermine equality of opportunity, but it would be counterproductive as well as misleading to insist that liberalism and all feminisms could be defined in terms of a commitment to a classless society.

My argument so far has been that feminism should not be defined in terms of a commitment to either equal opportunity or the abolition of gender because these fail to encapsulate the feminist vision of substantial numbers of feminists. Many feminists have also distanced themselves from androgyny, but Sterba believes that he has succeeded in redefining this ideal in such a way as to take account of their objections. Sterba's definition of androgyny requires that the traits that are truly desirable in society be equally available to both women and men, or in the case of virtues, equally expected of both women and men. He regards his redefinition as virtually equivalent to a very strong sense of equal opportunity and no more than a "positive" formulation of the "negative" ideal of genderlessness. In Sterba's view, androgyny, so defined, is sufficiently broad and uncontroversial that it is capable of encompassing all the diverse feminist views.

I dispute Sterba's assertions that androgyny is equivalent either to equality of opportunity or to genderlessness. Creating equality of opportunity is a matter primarily of changing social structures; so is a commitment to abolishing gender, since gender is essentially a system of social norms prescribing different behavior for individuals of different sexes. By contrast, androgyny is an ideal of individual development, and a commitment to achieving androgyny is a commitment to changing people.

As an ideal of individual development, androgyny is different from the ideals attributed by Sterba to the nonfeminist political traditions, because liberty, equality, and community are all ideals of social relations. I would oppose taking an ideal of individual development as the primary focus of efforts for social change because to do so would create a direct threat to people's autonomy. For instance, a commitment to androgyny might well be taken to license extensive social intervention in the formation of individuals' characters; Sterba's own earlier talk about "inculcating virtues," for instance, suggests an intrusive form not just of social but of human engineering. By contrast, focusing on abolishing gender rather than creating androgyny would eliminate any direct threat to autonomy and put feminism on all fours with Sterba's other political traditions.

Political movements that focus primarily on individual rather than social reform are likely to be ineffectual as well as intrusive. Addictive drug use is more likely to be reduced by changing the social conditions that make using and selling drugs an almost irresistible temptation than by urging people to "Just say No!" As a feminist, I certainly try to avoid raising my daughters as stereotypically feminine and my son as stereotypically masculine, not to mention working to overcome aspects of my own feminine socialization, but my very limited success in changing myself or in raising children markedly different from their peers has brought home to me very clearly the limits of individual effort in the absence of supporting social structures. Insofar as my daughters are more assertive and athletic than I am, for instance, I think this is less the result of my refraining from saying to them the sorts of things that were said to me, such as "Don't be a tomboy" and "Children should be seen and not heard" and even "Be good, sweet maid, and let who will be clever," and more the result of changes in the social norms of gender, themselves linked closely with gendered changes in the composition of the paid labor force. Of course, these changes in the paid labour force are in part the results of feminist efforts—but efforts directed primarily toward reforming social structures rather than reforming individuals. I entirely agree with Sterba that a new society will certainly encourage the emergence of new people but I think political movements should focus on reforming social relations and let people work out their own responses to social changes.

It is interesting to note that many women's present reluctance to label themselves feminists may spring precisely from a fear that feminism entails androgyny. An article in *Atlantic Monthly* puts the point explicitly:

> To the extent that it challenges discrimination and the political exclusion of women, feminism is relatively easy for many women to embrace. It appeals to fundamental notions of fairness; it suggests that social structures must change but that individuals, particularly women, may remain the same. . . . But to the extent that feminism questions (women's familial) roles and the underlying assumptions about sexuality, it requires profound individual change as well, posing an unsettling challenge that well-adjusted people instinctively avoid. Why question norms of sex and character to which you've more or less successfully adapted? (October 1993)

The author then goes on to reassure such women that "the popular image of feminism as a more or less unified quest for androgynous equality, promoted by the feminists' nemesis Camille Paglia, is at least ten years out of date."

Equating equality of opportunity with androgyny is not only misleading but likely to discredit feminism among women who value their femininity. Sterba would certainly respond that the ideal of androgyny does not deny to anyone character traits that are culturally feminine; it merely makes them available for men as well. This is a respectable argument that deserves serious consideration, but Sterba should be clear that it reflects the views of only some feminists, not all. Insisting on defining feminism in terms of ideals and values that many feminists explicitly reject is confusing, even if the feminists' rejection stems from failure to understand Sterba's sense of "androgyny" or to acknowledge the full implications of their own views.

Imposing definitions on people who prefer a different terminology is also likely to provoke resistance, a fact to which Sterba seems oblivious. He seems similarly unaware of the possibility that the resistance provoked by his controversial definition of feminism may be intensified by his chacterization of himself as a welfare liberal. Self-identified feminists may well resent an attempt to redefine their tradition by someone they perceive as an outsider, whose primary loyalties are not to feminism. Even when his feminist credentials are acknowledged, as they certainly should be, this recognizes Sterba only as a contributor to feminism; it does not authorize him to define it. Anyone is free to stipulate the meaning of feminism for herself, as well as to offer her understanding of what others mean by it, but no one has the authority to stipulate what feminism should mean for all feminists.

There is something hubristic or presumptuous about any attempt to redefine a tradition in terms explicitly rejected by many of its adherents. As I noted in my *Journal of Social Philosophy* article, previous claims to identify "true" or "essential" or "authentic" liberalism or socialism or feminism typically have been used for sectarian and authoritarian purposes; current postmodernist jargon sometimes calls them "terroristic" because often they have been used to excommunicate dissenting voices. All such claims obviously depend on assuming that there is a single proper or correct way of understanding intellectual and political ideals and traditions, an assumption I think is mistaken. I do not deny either that some interpretations of political traditions may be incorrect, in the sense of misrepresenting or distorting the understandings of historical agents, nor that we may often find good reasons for construing a political ideal one way rather than another. But I regard it as important for the health of any political tradition that controversial suggestions for interpreting it in particular ways be offered as proposals to be evaluated on their merits rather than presented as definitions. Definitions make a claim to authority and, if their authority is accepted, they operate to legitimate one view as orthodoxy while discrediting others as heresy. Dissidents then become heretics silenced by being denied the *imprimatur* of true liberalism or socialism or feminism. In order not to foreclose important political debates, it is advisable to define movements such as feminism in terms that are as minimal and widely accepted as possible. Beginning from a relatively uncontroversial definition of feminism, such as a commitment to ending the subordination of women, would also better promote Sterba's reconciliationist goals.

Sterba concludes his paper with a brief discussion of the procedure of justifying moral claims by presenting them as postulated agreements among hypothetical people who are rational, equal, and uncoerced. He wishes to defend this approach to moral justification against what he takes to be my objections. I presume that the reason he raises this methodological issue here is that he regards his own conclusions as established by this method. Certainly his discussion of libertarianism appeals to what he thinks it would be reasonable for everyone to accept, although this type of reasoning is not explicit in his discussion of feminism. Regardless of Sterba's motive for introducing the topic, I welcome the opportunity to clarify my views.

Sterba attributes to me three objections to hypothetical consensus reasoning. The first is that the parties in a Rawlsian original position are abstract individuals and Sterba notes that I have published some criticisms of abstract individualism. In fact, however, this objection to hypothetical consensus reasoning is better attributed to Michael Sandel than to me. My own criticisms of abstract individualism were developed several years before my objections to hypothetical consensus reasoning and for purposes that were quite different.

Rawls explicitly restricts the use of hypothetical consensus reasoning to deriving principles of justice in ideal circumstances, including full compliance with whatever is agreed. At first sight, therefore, hypothetical consensus reasoning seems an inappropriate method for addressing those moral problems that arise in less than ideal circumstances, which include most of those with which feminists are concerned. Sterba disputes Rawls's restriction of the method of hypothetical consensus to constructing normative principles for ideal societies, citing as an example of the possibility of using the method in nonideal circumstances his own appeal to hypothetical consensus in developing a theory of punishment. However, my own objections to using hypothetical consensus reasoning in nonideal situations do not rest on an appeal to the authority of Rawls—though in fact I believe he was wise to restrict the use of postulated hypothetical consensus to the circumstances of perfect justice, since attempts to use the method in situations of imperfect justice clearly bring out its weaknesses. In particular, the divergence in the practical conclusions reached by various philosophers claiming to use this method raise serious doubts about its reliability.

Both Rawls and Sterba admit that the method of hypothetical consensus cannot be used by everyone. Rawls sees it as too demanding intellectually, noting that it may require the ability to do advanced mathematics. Sterba sees it as too demanding imaginatively, noting that "in an unjust society only some people will be capable of doing original position-type thinking . . . either through improper moral education or their own fault." I cannot accept the explicit elitism and covert authoritarianism of a method of moral justification whose proponents acknowledge that it is available only to a relatively privileged few.

My main objection to the method of hypothetical consensus, however, rests on what I regard as the impossibility of anyone's speaking authoritatively for everyone, especially when the situations of many other people are very different from that of the speaker. Drawing on the history of contemporary Western feminism, I have offered several examples of the mistakes and resentments arising out of some women's presuming to speak for others. I believe that no individual can properly represent the views of everyone else, regardless of her intellectual or imaginative capacity or her mathematical or her moral training. Hypothetical agreements have no more moral weight than thought experiments have scientific weight. They may sometimes be useful in moral discovery but add nothing to moral justification.

Hypothetical consensus reasoning utilizes a monological reasoning process that I regard as both presumptuous and unreliable. Fair and open empirical discourse is indispensable, despite the undoubted difficulty of instantiating it, and it is for this reason, among others, that I prefer to approach moral justification through the method of Feminist Practical Dialogue.

Comments by Carol C. Gould

The thrust of Sterba's closely reasoned paper is to develop an argument for the moral requirement to meet people's basic needs. The form of the argument is to show that alternative conceptions of justice, often viewed as incommensurable, can in fact be reconciled in terms of their practical conclusions concerning welfare rights. He also advances a useful argument for a more androgynous account of desirable character traits and moral virtues. I find myself in strong agreement with the direction of Sterba's moral and political concerns. However, I would like to note a number of questions about his arguments, first with respect to how to persuade libertarians concerning welfare rights, and second, concerning some possible refinements of the account of androgyny.

Before turning to Sterba's discussion of the libertarian view of justice, I have a preliminary remark to make about his characterization of all five alternative conceptions of justice that he is concerned with in his larger project. It seems misleading to demarcate these conceptions, even in a summary way, in terms of what appear to be exclusive ideals of each of them, that is, liberty as the ideal for libertarianism, fairness for welfare liberalism, equality for socialism, the common good for communitarianism, and androgyny for feminism. This suggests a reductive simplification of each view, which is incorrect for many of their formulations. Thus, for example, several important types of socialist theory base themselves on a conception of liberty or freedom, which to be sure differs from the acceptation of that term in libertarian views. Or again, feminist conceptions of justice and indeed of androgyny itself cannot be understood without an appeal to the ideal of equality, etc.

More relevant to this particular paper is what I would characterize as Sterba's rather undialectical approach to the reconciliation of the libertarian and welfare liberal views. Sterba's assumption is that the concept of liberty goes through unchanged in his argument that libertarians are required by their own concept of liberty, together with a commitment to moral reasonableness, to arrive at a practical conclusion in accord with the welfare liberal's concept of welfare rights. But I would argue that it is only by a reinterpretation of the concept of liberty that it can be seen to have the implication of welfare rights. In short, it does not seem to me that within the framework of libertarianism, retaining the self-identical concept of liberty, that Sterba's argument can go through. For a libertarian would cite a difference between the liberty of the rich to keep the excess wealth that they possess and the liberty of the poor to take it from the rich for their own use. If liberty means freedom from external interference or harm by others or the state with what one chooses to do (compatible with a like liberty for others), then the libertarian could argue that the rich person's retention of their wealth is not an external constraint of this sort upon the poor, whereas the liberty of the poor to take this wealth would involve an interference or harm, since it would presumably proceed by some kind of force or ingression, at least with respect to what the rich possess. Therefore, the libertarian concept of liberty cannot be extended to equate the liberty of the poor to take with the liberty of the rich to keep, contrary to Sterba's argument that liberty, being universal on the libertarian view, makes these two liberties equivalent.

Instead, I think it is necessary to reinterpret the concept of liberty in terms of a conception of positive liberty and it is such a conception that entails welfare rights. Since this notion of positive liberty is based on the primary value of the individual and of individual rights, it is compatible with the libertarian's concern with this and has nothing in common with the statist caricature that Isaiah Berlin gives of it.[1] Nonetheless, it is of course not identical with the libertarian's original view and instead requires a dialectical transformation of it. Such a view of positive liberty presupposes the importance of free choice and the absence of external constraint, that is, negative liberty, but also the exercise of this choice in the realization of long-term projects and the development of capacities over time. But this can be seen to require access to the conditions for such self-development, including among them the satisfaction of basic needs.[2]

There is another aspect of Sterba's reconciliation argument that I would like to comment on here and that concerns his notion of reasonableness in moral contexts. Sterba is rightly concerned with conflict resolution in moral arguments and he uses the notion of moral reasonableness in a helpful way. However, here too, I think he makes things too easy. Appealing to what we would in applied contexts generally accept as reasonable and unreasonable, Sterba is able to override what seem to be conflicting conclusions from alternative conceptions of justice by the expedient of appealing to our ordinary intuitions. His everyday example about the required attendance at department meetings works very well to get our assent to what it is or what it is not reasonable to ask or require in that case. But the translation of this into a general conflict resolution principle and its application to the libertarian/welfare liberal difference seems to me something of a slippery slope. It is one thing for us to exercise our moral intuitions and agree that it is not unreasonable to ask the rich to give something of their excess to the poor who are desperately in need of it, and it is equally acceptable to argue that the libertarian would want to have a moral resolution of a serious conflict between rich and poor, rather than a simple victory of the stronger. But to conclude from this that the libertarian would therefore agree that the rich would be morally required to sacrifice and that a policy of positive welfare rights would be rationally supported on prudential grounds seems beyond plausibility. For in this case, the argument from reasonableness would have to override any conceptual differences about justice and reduce all of the philosophical issues to prudential accommodation, which is hardly the kind of thing a libertarian would go along with.

Throughout his essay, Sterba adopts a radical position concerning the requirement to meet basic needs universally—on a worldwide basis and for future generations. This implies a normative requirement for a radical redistribution of available goods and resources such that, in his view, all but only basic needs could be met. Presumably, have and have-not nations would be leveled to a common and equal distribution and this, on Sterba's account, would leave nothing over for non-basic needs. He accordingly holds that the question of equal opportunity for meeting nonbasic needs would simply be eliminated.

While I do not deny the importance of meeting the needs for basic means of subsistence universally, one problem that emerges is Sterba's apparent disregard for the role of states in the provision and redistribution of available resources, for as things stand, states are the political and economic frameworks for the organization of their society's redistributive activities. Furthermore, to assume a universal pool of goods and resources available for worldwide redistribution disregards completely the production processes and the complex network of entitlements of those who have done the work to produce the goods (most often socially) and which may be necessary to keep the production and distribution processes going. Sterba needs to give more of an argument about how he proposes to take such considerations into account in his suggested worldwide redistribution.

Furthermore, we may question his implicit empirical assumption that there will be only enough goods and resources to meet basic needs and that equal opportunity beyond this would be irrelevant. That is, he presupposes a subsistence economy if not worse—a Malthusian economy of scarcity as a permanent condition into the future. However, there is no way to predict that our technologies and social organization will prove inadequate to the provision of a significant range of nonbasic needs on a worldwide scale in the future. Straight-line projections from presently available resources are highly unreliable.

Turning now to Sterba's discussion of feminist conceptions of justice, which he sees as based on an ideal of androgyny, I would like to raise three points of refinement or difference. The first problem concerns his interpretation of androgyny as involving both a choice among desirable traits or characteristics and a list of virtues that men and women would equally be expected to develop. What makes me uncomfortable is Sterba's suggestion that there is a canonical set of androgynous virtues which may involve a loss of freedom, in contrast with the optional character of the desirable traits that are not virtues. This is not to deny that there are virtues and that in fact they may turn out to be universal and gender-free. But to tie the conception of androgyny to them seems to miss the point. For, contrary to Sterba's view, androgyny in itself is not the ultimate ideal of a feminist conception of justice. As involving gender-free modes of personal and social development, androgyny is desirable because of the requirement to be free from oppressive gender definitions of one's person, in terms of fixed, imposed, or restrictive gender roles and characteristics. But the criticism of such oppressive or restrictive definitions in fact appeals to an ideal of equal freedom, that is, that people should be free to choose their modes of self-development. Sterba, by contrast, claims that "an equal right to self-development can only be effectively guaranteed by expecting the same virtues of both women and men. . . ." Such an expectation presumably has its grounds beyond the choices to be made and rather suggests the choices that ought to be made. But this is to give a perfectionist or natural law reading to the notion of self-development, which is at variance with its basis in freedom.

A second problem arises from Sterba's laudable attempt to be inclusive and to reconcile alternative views. This concerns his supposing that it would be consistent with an androgynous ideal to accept an assignment of roles in society based on natural abilities, even where these abilities are determined by sex. His argument is that the assignment still takes place on the basis of the natural ability (which would be justified on his account) rather than on the basis of its source in sexual difference.

In the first place, it seems to me better and more just to base an assignment of roles in society on demonstrated abilities where equal conditions are provided rather than on presumed natural abilities, for it is very difficult to determine what the "natural abilities" are apart from their manifestation, and then the question of what distinguishes socially acquired from innate abilities becomes even more unclear. In the second place, if the assignment of social roles is based on so-called natural abilities where these are taken to be sex-based, this would reproduce the old sexually oppressive division of labor and the mere claim that one is basing this assignment on natural abilities alone does not make the process gender-free. Finally, it is odd to include within the framework of androgyny characteristics that are claimed to be based on natural sex differences since it is just this that the concept of androgyny was introduced to reject.

A third problem concerns a refinement of Sterba's view about the changes needed to "radically modify traditional family structures" in line with the ideal of androgyny. Sterba helpfully points out two fundamental changes that are needed, namely, equal upbringing of children irrespective of their sex and equal opportunities for education and employment for both mothers and fathers. I would argue that he needs to add to this list a third fundamental change which he mentions only casually later but does not include among the two fundamental changes that he does propose nor is it implicit in them. This is the need for mothers and fathers to assume equal obligations in child-raising. Without this, I would suggest that the equal upbringing of children and the equal opportunities for mothers and fathers cannot be realized.

Sterba's essay, for all the above reservations and questions, goes a long way in enlarging the scope of current discussion of concepts of justice and in turning our attention to the concrete contexts of their application.

Notes

1. Isaiah Berlin, "Two Concepts of Liberty," in *Four Essays on Liberty* (Oxford: Oxford University Press, 1970).

2. See Carol C. Gould, *Rethinking Democracy* (Cambridge: Cambridge University Press, 1988), chapter 1.

2

Justice, Self, and Natural Rights

Tibor R. Machan

The intellectual arena is alive with arguments and controversies concerning a perennial moral and political problem much more fundamental than whether one or another practice in our society is just or right. They concern whether certain basic standards exist for human personal and community life as such. Perhaps no such standards exist. In that case do various communities, cultures, regions of the globe, or other groupings of people decide on such matters, with no objective standard to rely upon in the last analysis?[1]

Developments in Eastern Europe, the former Soviet Union, South Africa, Nicaragua, Chile, China, and other parts of the geopolitical sphere have thrust this question into virtually any thinking person's life. Could we judge most white South Africans of the part by objective standards or only by ones which we happen to judge institutions in North America or in Western Europe? Can we say that the Chinese or the South African government ought, in fact, to submit to democratic processes, or is that just a wish we happen to have that others simply do not share and have no reason to take seriously unless they wish to? Can we say with conviction and confidence that, for example, a more individualist system of economic organization is more suitable to human community life than a collective command system? Or is it all really quite relative and indeterminate how a human community should be constituted?[2]

My plan here is to defend the position in political philosophy that the right to liberty or negative freedom is the proper standard of justice in human community life. It will also be argued that a good or just human community is such that in such a community moral virtue not only is accidentally possible but is necessarily enhanced. Furthermore, it will be shown that this conception of political justice rests on an objective, and at a basic level, universalizable foundation. That foundation is naturalism, including naturalistic ethics and rights theory.[3]

My task here will be somewhat laborious, since so much about the position I wish to lay out is in dispute in our time. The first task will be to examine some metaethical and metapolitical challenges a naturalist approach faces in our time. Next a case for a sound (objectively valid) idea of human nature will be advanced, one showing that human life is teleological and normative—it is goal-directed and involves moral responsibilities. From this it will be maintained that given the moral nature of human beings, political justice must be grounded in the effort to establish, maintain, and preserve what our moral nature requires in a social-political-legal context. In the end some critical objections to this position will be taken up.

Current Philosophy and Naturalism

Before I develop the case for the natural rights classical liberal position on justice, some metaethical and political problems that stand in the way of such a task are worth noting. During the past two and a half decades a lively discussion has ensued about natural law ethics. In the mid-twentieth century most prominent philosophy departments espoused some variety of noncognitivism. When one mentioned natural or human rights, one was quickly directed to read Margaret Macdonald's famous emotivist essay, "Natural Rights."[4] This was essentially an application of A. J. Ayer's logical positivism to political morality.

The philosophical climate has undergone some changes since. Now there does not exist a comparably firm orthodoxy in metaethics or metapolitics. Yet, even today the more prestigious philosophers and departments tend to look with disdain toward naturalist ethics and politics. What's more, the naturalist politics that we associate—albeit somewhat problematically—with John Locke has come under fire from several classical liberal and conservative political theorists from whom one might expect support.

Locke's natural rights theory has also been deprecated recently by some admirers of Plato's political thinking.[5] These thinkers essentially lump Locke's political views with those of Thomas Hobbes, at least at the basic philosophical level.[6] A more recent line of criticism of the natural rights classical liberal stance is deeply skeptical and broader based.[7] It would avoid Platonism even more than natural law classical liberals or libertarians for the very reason that it finds fault with naturalism as such.[8]

The criticism of naturalism advanced from some of these position-thinkers will be taken up later. Let us see, for now, the position they believe justifies their disdain for naturalism.

Judging by some of its champions, the criticism finds the idea of human nature without foundation.[9] Some of these points are owed to the philosophical orientation of Karl Popper.[10] Just as do positivist critics, such as Macdonald, as well as most existentialist critics of the Platonic-Aristotelian tradition, these critics reject the concept of "the nature of X" if it is supposed to involve anything that is not purely conventional. Accordingly, human nature is not objective but nominal and even historically or culturally relative and conditioned.

There is another recently revived doctrine antithetical to naturalism. This is political intuitionism, combined with the claim that one is able to reach substantive moral and political conclusions without any reliance on work in other branches of philosophy. This thesis, of "the independence of moral theory,"[11] has had considerable influence. One need but read the major journals of ethics and political theory, where papers often begin with a claim about our "considered moral judgments" and proceed from such intuitive beginnings to reach various moral and public policy conclusions.

In advancing a naturalist foundation for political justice, it would be imprudent to avoid confronting the metapolitical positions sketched above. A kind of Kuhnean result is in evidence from the widespread promulgation of these views. Most prominent ethicists and political theorists share the attitude captured. This is made evident, in a slightly different but not entirely unrelated context, by Russell Hardin, when he notes that "Anyone who tries to defend an unvarnished right of contract for any two parties to do whatever they want to do under any circumstances will be met with vacant stares from most moral and political theorists today."[12]

Naturalists in the classical liberal school aim at uncovering some objective ground that would enable us to "defend an unvarnished right" to life, liberty, and property—including, derivatively, freedom of contract (though not of the type caricatured by Hardin). Thus, not facing up to the challenges placed before naturalism by these various prominent theorists will render it impossible to make convincing advances.

The paradigm of noncognitivist, antinaturalist metaethics and meta-politics needs to be shown to be inadequate before the naturalist position can even gain a hearing. That will be my first task in this essay.

Naturalism

Why is there so much skepticism about the idea of "the nature of X"? The doubtfulness is similar to that which motivates deconstructionists in contemporary literary criticism. We can go all the way back to Heraclitus and, especially, his pupil Cratylus to locate the lineage of this school of thought.[13]

The skeptic's persuasiveness can be understood, given one version of naturalism that has *bona fide* historical roots. This is a troublesome doctrine. It could justifiably lead classical liberals and British conservatives—that is, those who are weary of leviathan for various reason (especially in the United States and in the United Kingdom)—to fear dogmatism and authoritarianism.

The naturalism in question, linked to the Platonic natural law tradition, posits the existence of transcendent, permanent or timeless, and perfect natures for every being.[14] Yet, with this Platonic idea of what the nature of something must be, we are stymied from the start. If to know "the nature of X is a, b, and c" would also require knowing that the proposition is a timeless truth, a temporal human being could not affirm this. Forever there would *have to be* doubt about any proposition affirming that kind of truth.

Therein lies one of the major objections to naturalism. I argue, later, that the Platonist conception of what "the nature of X" must mean is not the best way to understand what "the nature of X" must mean. There is a neo-Aristotelian approach—which may be called, following Ayn Rand, contextualism[15]—that has a far better prospect.

Human Nature

If there is an objective moral foundation of the classical liberal system of polity, its earliest (albeit still halting and by no means fully consistent) expression is to be found in the natural rights theory of Locke. Contrary opinion exists, of course—some claim that Hobbes is the actual grandfather of this polity.[16] But it is widely admitted, at least, that if this polity rests on a normative political framework, it is that which we inherited from the political works of Locke. Such other thinkers as Hobbes or Adam Smith either did not advance a sufficiently normative theory or did not exert sufficient (early) influence. Locke, as other thinkers, borrowed from others (e.g., the Levellers). But he put together the most coherent position in his day favoring the idea that each human individual is politically sovereign, in possession of basic rights that it is the proper task of government to secure.

I stress the normativity of the Lockean legacy because it is in Locke that we find such ideas defended as that every person *ought to* respect every other person's equality, freedom, and independence and that each individual human being should have a sphere of personal authority accorded to him. The rights Locke claims everyone possesses are political *norms*, not, as in the case of Hobbes, innately prompted strategies for survival. Locke not only held—though he did not prove—that such social/political norms were binding on all persons in a human community, he also believed that these norms were themselves based on more basic edicts of personal conduct, namely, "the law of Nature." Individuals are free, in the sense that they, in adulthood, are able to bring it about on their own to follow these laws. They *ought to* do the former: "The state of Nature has a law of Nature to govern it, which obliges everyone, and reason, which is that law, teaches all mankind who will but consult it, that being all equal and independent, no one ought to harm another in his life, health, liberty or possessions" (Chapter II, Section 6, *Second Treatise on Civil Government*).

Now the Lockean view has come under attack from both the right and the left.[17] The right sees basic rights as mere individualist artifacts, invented in defiance of the much more reliable streams of tradition and custom that grow, through trial and error, over the centuries, to become the most dependable devices for social living. The left takes these rights to be (to use Marx's phrase) "insipid illusions," beliefs produced so as to legitimize certain historically inevitable impulses of human beings at a given time period. They are mere rationalizations, not genuine philosophical/moral foundations.

The most severe damage to the doctrine of natural rights has arisen from the philosophical system that has given rise to the scientism found mostly in the social sciences. This view denies that a normative outlook on human community life even makes sense. It is empiricist and skeptical. It mostly yields conservative conclusions about politics since, in the absence of convincing guidelines for public policy, the best guide is the past—including class structures, coercive laws, and other edicts based on tradition and custom.

I will try to cast the Lockean perspective in a contemporary light, without losing any of its crucial features and power. I will spell out, in several paragraphs, what the natural rights perspective is. This will make it possible to judge whether it is warranted to dismiss it as many philosophers and social scientists do. Finally I will focus on some objections, ones advanced recently by utilitarians, skeptics, and historicists.[18]

Natural Rights in Outline

What is a natural rights theory? It is an answer to a question that arises in connection with human community life; namely, "How, in the most general terms, should we (human beings) live with each other?" In particular, this answer rests on an investigation of human nature. The community in question embraces people who are unrelated—that is, they may not stand to each other as kith and kin, friends, colleagues, etc. Among family members, friends, colleagues, and so forth, special, narrower ethical principles could probably handle the problems a theory of natural rights aims to handle among human beings unknown to each other. But the situation of large human communities, with strangers as members, is familiar enough, so it isn't difficult to imagine why our question would arise. How should we interact with human beings as such, never mind other ties?

Now this question has been answered in very different ways, for very different reasons. I won't canvass all. It is probable that most people have some familiarity with them.

For example, one answer has been to model human community life on some such life in heaven—the city of God. Another has been to advise the community to ensure the equality of all of its members (at least in terms of crucial goods and services), or to purify the race, or to service God, or to help the forces of history. These have all been defended, in elaborate treatises, as answers to the question addressed by natural rights theory, namely, "How should we live as a community?"

Numerous questions that arise in the various areas of human inquiry have a bearing on the study of politics. This shouldn't really be surprising. Politics concerns the basic principles of human community life. The issue is certainly complicated by all sorts of factors about human beings, their relationships, environment, health, sustenance, goals and purposes, etc. Political theory subsumes virtually all other fields of inquiry.

Here is the natural rights approach to answering our question: First we need to grasp some points about reality and our knowledge of it. Then we need to learn how we would best understand what is meant by such judgments as "We should act so and so" or "He should not act so and so" or "This is good" or "This is evil." The reason is that in politics we are, after all, concerned with how we *should* or *should not* act, what institutions we should support, and so forth. So we need to consider how to answer such questions. Next we need to explore the application of the ideas of *should* and *should not* to human conduct and human institutions. This will involve considering what it is to be a human being, what is human nature. We need to investigate personal and social moral life—the realm of ethics or natural law, and whether it is even possible to speak of what individuals morally should do in their own lives and toward their fellows. We need, next, to consider public or political conduct, mainly the conduct that would be appropriate, first of all, toward other people *as such*, as a bare minimum, within a social political context.

By following this naturalist approach, we will come to the topic of basic human rights theory, our main concern.

Some Basic Philosophical Issues

First, existence *cannot be* inherently confusing—we may be confused about it but it *must* make sense once closely studied. If this is denied, then all bets are off, not just in human affairs and the studies of them but in all realms of inquiry, *including the denial itself.* The words we speak, even as we affirm or deny anything, will lack clear and unambiguous identity and the meanings of our concepts will be indeterminate. This will include whatever we ourselves might wish those meanings to be as a matter of our intentions. For example, as we state that by "rights" we mean only social devices invented by us, we will have to admit that these devices may or may not be what we want them to be. If reality is itself something in a total flux, all the way to its most basic structure, our statement that this is so cannot be depended upon. It will mean nothing firm or stable. And, not insignificantly, in the realm of ethics and politics, that will tend to imply that the powerful—by virtue of their power and not the clarity and truth of some ideas that justify some conduct—must rule and no check on them, based on what is really right and wrong, is possible. So, insofar as we admit that we can make sense of even the minimum of our lives, we affirm that reality hangs together in a reasonably orderly fashion, at least at the most basic level.[19]

Moreover, we can know the facts above well enough, also. We can also know a lot more than that, if only we work hard to find things out. Knowing reality *as it is* is not impossible, as some people have claimed, provided we do not have an impossible ideal as a conception of what is meant by doing so. From what we have already learned, we can infer that we can learn about reality. The task is one of finding out about it, through extensive and hard work.[20]

Among other areas of reality of the greatest interest to us is human nature itself, that is, what we are as human beings, quite apart from our individual identity, our special origins, sex, race, professional competence, etc. These all can be crucial in some contexts, but for now what concerns us is human nature. We are concerned because we are interested in how human beings should conduct themselves toward each other qua human beings, and that cannot be answered without knowledge of what human beings are simply as human beings. Once we have got a glimpse at human nature, as it were, we can then ask how considerations of "should" apply in the case of human beings as such. And that provides us with the basic material needed to determine the basic norms of interpersonal conduct, that is, the norms of political life.

The point about the general integrity of reality is complicated but perhaps a clue or so would suffice so that it can be understood without much difficulty. Everything that exists abides by some very minimal principles, namely, those that pertain to existence itself. That is, just for being something, anything at all, whatever exists abides by certain principles, namely, the principles of existence—the necessary conditions for something being at all, whatever it is then identified to be. Those principles are, as might be suspected, very general in character, since they apply to everything, past, present, future, and even the possible. (The very possibility of the existence of something involves these basic principles.) And because of this generality, these principles have to be extremely broad in scope but limited in content, in what they imply. This is because granted that all existence, necessarily, exists, there is a great deal of variety in all of what does exist.

The most basic principle of existence is that what exists must be something specific, something definite. A chair must be a chair, a table a table, a dog a dog, a person a person, an act of justice an act of justice. This sounds terribly broad, even "empty," but that is because the point bears on everything whatever, so it cannot include very much in the way of variations. Things are what they are, and this is true about everything. Contrary to what may appear to be true, however, there is quite a lot embedded in this point. The main thing embedded in it is that no contradictory situations can exist in reality—that is, it cannot be the case that something both is a table and is not a table. Perhaps a quick example will show how deeply we all require this point in our understanding of reality. Thus, when in a court of law some testimony is subjected to cross-examination, if the testimony is shown to contain contradictions—for example, someone is found saying both that he was in New York on June 4, 1988, and that he was not in New York on June 4, 1988—then we have found something terribly wrong with the testimony. The same would be the case if he said that he had a hat on yesterday afternoon and that he did not have a hat on at that time. Or that he is married to Susie as well as that he is not married to Susie. This is all wrong because such things simply cannot be.

Now this and some related considerations about reality inform us of the absolute requirement of keeping our understanding of reality consistent. There is a lot else we need, but this minimum requirement is entirely indispensable. Everything else about our way of dealing with reality requires that this central point be adhered to.[21] That is why, for instance, if a theory, say of natural rights, contains a contradiction, it cannot be considered even possibly right, let alone true. The same is clear of any scientific theory, a legal contract, or a plan of action. Reality does not tolerate—embody—contradictions, that is, facts that are of one kind and not that kind all at once in the same fashion.[22]

From the above remarks very little follows except for a few points already hinted at. Knowledge may not involve contradictions or inconsistencies. This general point about knowledge follows the general point about existence, because knowledge is our correct awareness or identification of existence, whatever else it is. The way we obtain knowledge differs from one sort of cases to others. For example, in history the records left to us, involving trusting others a great deal, give us knowledge; in biology experimentation with members of the same species of living beings, and our awareness of differences and similarities in the behavior of these members and their various parts, will provide us with knowledge. In sociology the careful observation of how groups of people behave and the interpretation of this observation by reference to our broader knowledge can be found in each case of knowledge. This is important because sometimes it is thought that unless the knowledge in one field of inquiry abides by the standards of knowledge in all others, it is impossible that we have knowledge in the former.[23]

That is why some people think that we can have knowledge only in the physical sciences, because they believe that knowledge must always and exclusively rest on our awareness of physical properties and attributes. Here is why empiricism is so popular—because knowledge that is guided by the dictates of the empirical sciences is taken to be the only kind of knowledge.

But then we would rule out at the start any knowledge of whatever lacks strictly physical properties. And that would be a prejudice. Such prejudice is encouraged by theories of knowledge that require that all cases of knowledge be exactly like all others. There is no justification for this, even though it is a widespread view. (The same prejudice creates our problem with beauty or moral goodness—a theory demands that all things beautiful or morally good be identical, and we cannot confirm this, so it is concluded that beauty or moral goodness is purely relative, even subjective.) Yet just as there can be trees, equally healthy, that are very different yet still trees, so there can be knowledge, equally sound, yet different and still knowledge.

A few other, more special, points need to be made about knowledge. First, to know something is to have correctly concluded on the basis of the relevant evidence that something is the case (even if this means only that something is probably so and so, or that some thing is possibly so and so). Second, the evidence involved is something we may obtain by various means at our disposal—by simply looking; looking and touching; looking, touching, and hearing; looking, touching, hearing, and comparing to something else, and so forth. The minds we have, and the sensory organs we have, working together by our direction, is how we obtain knowledge. And even if we don't get knowledge immediately but get only well-supported beliefs, even good or educated guesses, it is by way of the mind in its highly complicated ways of operation with the senses that we get this much.

Basically, when we attempt to obtain knowledge, we aim for knowing what is what and how something becomes (or became, or will become) another thing; why this has occurred and not that; and where things have occurred, etc. In all our efforts we need to recall that contradictions are prohibited and that different kinds of evidence may have to be used to discover different facts about the world.

The above discourse is brief but necessary. From there we can take a very long jump to advance to something much closer to what interests us here, namely, politics. What we need to turn to is a consideration of the place of norms in existence. We are familiar enough with knowledge about facts concerning inanimate and animate existence— rocks are hard, dogs often bark, penicillin can cure disease, governments often wage war. These kinds of facts can be known without much debate about them, although very soon after we have come to admit that we know something along these lines, we find that other matters we might think we know are extremely controversial. But that is not what is at issue—controversy is a social problem that anyone who wishes to tell others what he knows (claims to know) will encounter; first we need to find out whether there is anything we know about controversial topics. Such a topic is the topic of norms, principles of human conduct. That Napoleon should have prepared his men better for the battle at Waterloo, or that Teddy Roosevelt should not have led the United States into war, or that President George Bush should have fought against inflation by refusing to print more money, or that one should respect the wishes of one's spouse in consideration of where to live—all these are facts or alleged facts about which much controversy arises. Yet that is not the issue, but how we might come to know about these matters. The natural rights theory (which I find sound) answers this question by noting, first, that considerations of what one should or should not do pertain to considerations of what is good and evil. That which is good (and possible) for one to pursue is something one should pursue, and that which is evil (and possible) for one to pursue one should not pursue, to put the matter plainly. But this just shifts our problem.

How do we come to know what is good? Here we need to consider what "good" means. It means the fullest realization of some particular thing as an instance of its kind—a good peach is a fully realized peach, or a peach that has most fully completed the nature of being a peach. A good tennis game is a fully realized tennis game, or a tennis game that has fully reached the crux of a tennis game. The idea is not a very simple one, but whenever we appraise tomatoes, peaches, apples, chickens, parking lots, or whatever, we can learn whether we should praise it or criticize it by reference to the fact that the thing (or activity or whatnot) in question has more or less fully reached its distinctive nature in the given case at hand. This tennis game is a good one if the players play by satisfying the central ingredients of tennis and whatever those ingredients imply for the particular game at hand. (The particular game at hand may require realizing the game somewhat differently from another particular game.) A good skiing slope or a good knife or a good source of light—all these pertain to how fully some particular case realizes the essence of what it is in its own instance. We don't always talk of a good this or a good that, or a bad this or a bad that, but such expressions as "great" or "neat" or "swell" or "far out" or "fantastic," and numerous others (I no longer remember), make the same point for us, as do "lousy," "rotten," "poor," etc. When we consider what good is most generally, it has to do with whether something has realized its nature in the case at hand. The nature of something, what it is that makes it the kind of thing it is—a tennis game, a golf ball, or a Christmas tree—is the place or category it occupies in the most rational way of classifying attributes, properties, and whatever else we perceive about existence. This process yields our knowledge of trees, chairs, furniture, balloons, time, days, weeks, months, space, field, meadow, galaxy, mind, memory, imagination, idea.[24] There is nothing mysterious about the point that everything has a nature, since everything that exists is most successfully classified as one kind of thing or another, and it must be so classifiable for it to exist and for us to understand it and for it to be anything at all. (This follows from the previous discussion.) In the case of human beings, this all leads to the issue of the relationship between their actions and being good. Being a good human being, like being a good anything, requires the fullest possible realization of human nature in the particular case of a given person. Thus we—that is, at least some widely read or heard human beings—need to know what human nature is so we can tell what it is to be good at being a human being. In other words, some clear enough idea of human nature is required for anyone to be able to judge, with reasonable success, what it is to be a good human being.

What then is a human being as such, that is, what is human nature? This is where the naturalism of natural rights theory comes into full focus. Natural rights theory can produce an understanding of the rights human beings have by reference to an understanding of human nature. That is why they are called *natural* rights—rights someone has (or we are justified to ascribe to someone) by virtue of his or her human nature within communities of others.

Human nature is the set of facts that are true of human beings just insofar as they are human beings, nothing else (e.g., not as students, mothers, Germans, and those 25 years old, or as animals, objects, geometrical figures, etc.). What is that set of facts?

Without repeating my earlier points, this set includes that human beings are animals (with a biological nature and all of what that involves) and capable of rational thought (having the capacity to think in terms of principles, to think at the level of general ideas or concepts and what these imply). The ancient idea that man is a rational animal is still sound, although some of it, and what exactly it implies, has had to be modified in the light of our greater understanding of some of the issues involved. Still, the crucial point is that human beings are by nature animals and capable of rationality. A good human being would, then, be one who, speaking very generally (with all the very important details left out deliberately, so this can apply to everyone), is biologically healthy and fully alert (except of course, when continued alertness requires rest). As to what this implies about how we should conduct ourselves personally and in public, we come to this next.[25]

The first normative area we are concerned with is personal ethics—the code or laws of nature that pertain to how we should conduct ourselves. By nature we live a most fully human life by being rational. We thus achieve well-being on all possible levels (which excludes any interference that we cannot control). But here is the rub. To the best of our knowledge the bulk of the animate world behaves as guided automatically—by instincts, drives, reflexes, and so forth (given the environment surrounding it). Human beings, however, are not compelled by their inner drives, instincts, etc., to behave as they do. To put the matter plainly, they are able to choose between genuine alternatives. Maybe some animals can, too. Those cases are rare enough not to pose a problem here. Human beings may also have some instincts, but this too is negligible. The point is that people in maturity are able to choose what they will do. (In short, we are not discussing childhood, even adolescence, although a fuller discussion would have to consider those stages, as many other things.)

Now it is central that human beings enjoy the freedom that other animals lack at first in the area of thinking. Human beings, unlike other animals, cope with reality mainly through the medium of ideas, theories, principles, concepts, etc. To live, even to the minimum degree of viability, a solitary adult needs to figure things out, and then he can take the actions his life requires for sustenance. An adult, of course, can choose to whither away, to die, not to live, in which case thinking is not required for him. But we are not concerned about those human beings who do not choose to live and thus have no interest in the principles of human conduct, of human action, of human living! The norms we are interested in have application for us because we haven't got innate drives, etc., to guide us in living but if we will not live, then the norms are beside the point.[26]

The first point, then, about basic moral norms is that they are required only for the living. But this is inseparable—in the case of an investigation of the human good—from the fact that our capacity for thought needs to be initiated or put into effect by us. If we don't put thinking into effect, we merely coast or float about—usually on the opinions of others—voluntarily at the disposal of others. In the morality underlying natural rights theory, living requires thought, rational observation, reflection, consideration, recollection, assessment, evaluation, comparison, etc. Without choosing this kind of activity we in fact also reject the requirements of human life, and to the extent that we fail to engage in rational thought, etc., we are failing in the commitment we make when we choose to live, namely, to live as fully as is possible to us.[27]

For a rational animal to choose life is to choose a rational life, and one that isn't rational just now and then. This is a choice one can renege on, but to that extent one will be less than a good human being. Not living in accordance with one's nature is to fail to be good. The requirements for being good, then, include, first and foremost, the exercise of one's rational faculty, something that human beings must do by choice. It is now clear that goodness is being in full accord with one's nature. That is the function or point of the concept, as it were. Thus, given our human nature, namely, being a rational animal, it is possible to understand what being a good human being is.[28] It is to be in full accord with the requirement of rationality. It is clear from an understanding of human nature that one's capacity for rationality, one's distinctive humanity as it were, is kept in force by choice.

So the first moral responsibility of any human being who has chosen to live is to be mentally alert, to think rationally, and to act accordingly.[29] This is a responsibility of each individual person. It is a matter of personal choice that one does what one should do, otherwise it makes no sense that one should do it. What one cannot help but do cannot be something one should do. Choice, the capacity to initiate action, is of the essence of moral responsibility.

But this is not all there is to it. To live our lives according to our nature is the human good. Only individual human beings can proceed to act so as to achieve or neglect human moral good. Others cannot do it for them. All that can be done even for children is to provide them with good examples and shield them from gross errors.

Alongside the universal moral responsibility to live a human life rationally, there are endless diverse details. They are less crucial for now because they can vary; they don't form a system of laws for all. What will be rational for one person at one time need not be for another. Still, numerous general principles are pertinent outside the norm that we should think and act rationally. For example, it is generally rational to be honest, productive, generous, prudent, well integrated, and courageous. These are the virtues one will find articulated by most moralists, more or less intact. What they differ on is what comes first and why. Suffice it to summarize that human life requires that a person live rationally because that is what living the life of a human being amounts to and that is to what a person commits himself when he chooses to live.

The natural rights theory outlined here is based on an ethical view in terms of which the morally good human life consists of a person living rationally. Success, excellence, or happiness (in the sense of full flourishing), as a human being, is best pursued by living in accordance with the requirements of one's nature as a rational animal.

What, if anything, does this tell us about human community life? That only a human community the fundamental organizing principles of which incorporate the basic facts of human morality can be said to accord with human nature, be conducive to human moral goodness, and thus be characterized as just. Just communities are not those populated only by good human beings.[30] The latter could come about by way of accident: people might gather together and all at once be at their best, regardless of the organizational characteristics—constitution—of their community. A good human community is such that it makes moral goodness more than accidentally possible; indeed, it enhances human goodness. This is where natural rights surface.

The just political community is what it is because it accurately reflects the requirements of human nature within the context of community life—that is, it meets the requirements of morally sovereign individuals by means of respecting and protecting individual human rights to life, liberty, and property. These rights are the standards of justice for the organization of a human community—the criteria for how to establish, maintain, and promote justice in community life.

That these negative rights can be the foundation of justice is disputed often on the grounds that justice requires greater activism, not merely protection from untoward acts. A just state or government would, accordingly, engage in certain promotional activities—legislate appropriate conduct, further the good behavior of its citizens, repair past social wrongs, etc. How, then, could the administration of a system of basically negative rights—protecting against murder, assault, robbery, fraud, embezzlement, kidnapping, and the adjudication of charges of the commission of such deeds—count as the maintenance of justice?

If one appreciates, however, that adult human beings possess a moral nature, whereby it is crucial that they make decisions within their sphere of authority, circumscribed by their negative rights, then one can see why a just political and legal system would provide primarily protective rather than active or legislative policies. Given the naturalist basis of this idea of justice and given the idea of human nature that makes the best sense, it would appear evident that a just system must be engaged in securing peace and the respect of negative rights rather than promoting certain ends or objectives for people, something only individual initiative may facilitate.[31]

Consider in contrast John Rawls's conception of "justice as fairness." The central difference between the Lockean individual rights perspective and that offered by John Rawls is that for Rawls human beings are cast into situations from which they cannot extricate themselves of their own free will—even their moral character is determined by chance. Accordingly, it is not possible to envision human beings as autonomous, sovereign, and morally responsible[32] and, therefore, in need of what Robert Nozick has called "moral space."[33] Rather all persons are in the same boat of having been cast into a situation quite apart from their choices or best alternatives. So as to remedy the unfairness that is experienced by them, justice is needed *via* the establishment of equality of circumstances.[34] This involves the active promotion of certain states of affairs, ends, or objectives, as the substance of justice.

The Rawlsian conception of human nature is unjustified—it would be unable to explain the enormous advances human beings constantly make on their own lives, their successful creative accomplishments, even the philosophic and scientific innovations that characterize so much of human living. The kind of passivity ascribed by Rawls and his followers to all of us does not even square with how Rawlsians behave, namely, as creative political partisans of the downtrodden, the poor, and the needy.

Instead of this passive conception, the institutions of a political community should be rested on the more accurate view that human beings are by nature creative, free agents, capable of self-direction in nearly any circumstance, except where political justice is not possible, for example, in the midst of an earthquake or when they are crucially incapacitated. The range of their creativity may not be identical, but in normal circumstances each person has ample opportunity to initiate the effort to advance his or her own life, to become more able to cope, and to succeed at the innumerable tasks that may provide fulfillment to human individuals.[35]

Within the present framework, however, basic negative rights are the standards or principles of just human interaction that arise from nature.[36] Of course, conduct in line with these standards can give rise to rights that arise from contract, promises, and familial relations. A child has rights which parents or equivalent agents must respect, and parents, too, have rights children must respect.[37]

Rights then are those principles which govern some of the basic relations between human beings, but their source may be varied. The most basic source of rights, however, is human nature, which implies moral requirements for community life such that every person may be forced to abide by certain principles: It is everyone's natural right to be respected for what one is, namely, a human being, capable of choosing to live, to think, and to act rationally, and to interact by respecting the rationality of all others, as well as to protect against their violation.

The rights to life, liberty, and property state these points somewhat cryptically, meaning:

(1) Since it is one's basic nature to be able to choose to live, one's life (as the outcome of one's essential human choice) is something no one other than the agent is permitted to terminate or take (except once the person is refusing to respect the life of another and elicits self-defensive action that may kill).

(2) Since the choice to live entails the commitment to think and act rationally, it is unjustifiable that others who have explicitly or implicitly[38] joined a community would be authorized to subvert one's liberty to make this choice (it would be the negation of another's humanity to subvert his choice between rational thought and action or irrational mental life and behavior).[39]

(3) Since rational choice should lead one to interact with others, who also will find it rational to associate with others, the association of individuals and the results of such association (e.g., cooperation, competition, trade, bequeathal, and so forth) may not be violated.

All told, then, the rights to life, liberty, and property—not to be murdered, not to be assaulted or coerced, and not to be robbed or have one's property expropriated—are natural rights. They emerge because we are human beings, we have the power of choice, as such, to live and to flourish, and we should do so in societies.

The crucial point is that natural rights theory rests on the moral nature of human life, on the requirement of each person to choose life and flourishing for oneself. The main complaint against this idea is that if another lives badly, neglects one's life, or suffers misfortune, help may be forced upon or demanded of the person. But this destroys the human dignity of the person, however needy or earnest he or she might be. Nor may others force someone to engage in the sort of conduct often deemed to be honorable, namely, charitable conduct, since coerced charity is not charity but robbery. Those who urge such measures fail to observe the requirements of human nature. That failure only appears to be useful, helpful, necessary, moral, nice, unavoidable, etc.

Once these matters are carefully considered, the resulting alleged welfare state is not really one that promotes welfare at all. It is impossible to be of value to human beings—promote their overall welfare—if one acts out of accord with human nature (except, perhaps, entirely accidentally).[40]

Let me summarize my points. First, natural rights theory aims to address the central question of political life, namely, what norms should guide us in our basic relationship to other human beings? Natural rights theory aims to answer this basic question by consulting nature, specifically human nature. It adheres to certain fundamental points about reality and our knowledge of reality, and it has a certain view about what goodness is, namely, the flourishing of something in accordance with its nature. With respect to ethics or how we should morally conduct our lives, the question is what human nature amounts to and how it may be fully actualized in an individual human being (which is to say, by an individual human being who possesses the capacity to realize this human nature consistently in his or her case). By choosing life-and-rationality, one conducts himself in a morally proper manner. A community is good—a just human community—if its principles are in accord with the moral requirements of human (personal and social) life. The libertarian political stance stresses the primary significance of human freedom or liberty ("negative freedom"), that is, the foremost significance of each person's right to liberty of conduct in the context of social or interpersonal affairs. Respecting the right—and taking measures to resist its violation—is warranted on the basis of the natural rights theory outlined in this discussion.

Some Points of Criticism

At least an outline of the case for the natural rights classical liberal position has been spelled out. The case for the objectivity of the moral foundations of a natural rights theory with libertarian content has also been sketched in sufficient detail so that the position can be plainly considered. It is now possible to take a critical look at some of the objections raised against the naturalist—natural law, natural rights—stance of which the present position is a variant.

Let me turn first to a criticism that combines two vital elements of contemporary conservatism, namely, a belief in the significance of tradition with a commitment to a utilitarian value theory. The former belief keeps such a critic close to some of the individualist features of the American polity since, after all, that polity has for more than two centuries embodied such features—that is, it has become traditional to embrace individualism in America. The latter is the view implicit in David Hume's antirationalist conservatism, whereby the values to be pursued by us find their overarching justification in their public utility. The only element of contemporary conservatism not directly present in this approach is religion. However, religion is presupposed within the traditionalist element, since by reference to tradition religion emerges as a vital feature of culture.

A conservative utilitarian criticism of the natural rights position involves the following points: It may be true that there are various necessary conditions that are required for human existence and flourishing or excellence. Yet it does not follow at all that from these (or from knowing these) it is possible to infer norms or virtues or principles of human conduct. (This is plainly a restatement of the is/ought gap thesis of Hume and the subsequent empiricist/positivist movement in epistemology and metaethics.)[41]

From this position it would seem both hopeless and undesirable to forge and sustain a free society or legal system by relying on natural laws or rights (whether in the Aristotelian/Thomistic or Kantian/Gewirth tradition). If we assume that negative freedom is in most cases a good thing (i.e., it is good when human beings do not intrude on each other's lives and properties),[42] there is reason to believe that within the framework of natural law or naturalist ethical and political thinking this good thing would be jeopardized. We are reminded of the historical fact that most ethical theorists, those who have supposed that we can derive "oughts" from the "is" of what human nature comes to, have promulgated ethical and political views that have given meager respect to negative liberty. Plato, Hegel, and Marx, to name but three outstanding figures, have all advocated holistic or totalist moral-political systems.[43] While that does not prove natural law or essentialist/naturalist views wrong, the critics would wish us to consider the matter as perhaps suggestive and warn those fond of negative freedom against the temptation to rely on anything like the naturalist tradition.

To put it more succinctly, conservative utilitarian critics of the natural law/natural rights position firmly cling to the Humean is/ought argument against the possibility of naturalist ethics and politics. So they claim that our better theoretical alternative is utilitarianism, which does not insist on the full, uncompromising protection of negative rights and allows plenty of room for various paternalistic and welfare policies by governments of human communities.

Now every theory that is flawed needs in the end to be provided with a substitute that holds up. For merely lacking full adequacy—completeness and consistency—will not be fatal to a theory while no better one is available. Some critics of natural rights liberalism also defend—as well as consider problems with—the sort of ethical/political doctrine we may expect from a utilitarian or consequentialist approach. Here, following a prudent strategy of not denying the troublesome aspects of the view being favored, utilitarians preempt the sort of criticism of the positivist/utilitarian ethical/political stance which has led Rawls and Nozick, among others, toward its rejection. This is that the position does not guarantee public policies that are in perfect accord with our moral intuitions. For example, one major criticism of utilitarianism is that the pursuit of the greatest happiness of the greatest number (or the general welfare or Pareto optimality) may lead to policies in law and politics which are on their face morally intolerable[44]—solving the population problem by means of random killing, giving important and widely admired people (VIPs) organs from the bodies of those no one cares about, etc.[45] Utilitarianism, thus, seems to make possible the justification of what would normally be considered moral callousness. And it is extremely doubtful that any theory can hope to justify such callousness.

But it can be replied that these impressions are essentially unjustified because the position won't generate any more callousness when carefully understood than would other ethical positions. In short, a utilitarian critic of the natural rights stance can hold that the theory provides us with better results in our efforts to understand our moral problems in life than does the natural rights theory. The reason is mainly that the latter view is philosophically flawed while the former is no worse than the latter when it comes to handling difficult moral problems.

Another criticism important to address comes from out-and-out skeptics. The objection to the present thesis advanced by some such critics has three main parts. First, it claims that naturalism has been invalidated by contemporary empirical science.[46] This is especially true as far as the naturalist depends on some type of teleological thesis. Second, it finds fault with the attempt to develop a case for liberalism based on an ethics of individual flourishing, drawn from Aristotle. One such critic tells us, for example, that "Writing in an age of mass democracy and wage-labour, Aristotle's latter-day liberal followers prescribe a life of bourgeois virtue—of thrift, industry, prudence, and creative work. However one assesses these ideals, the salient point is that in each of them the content given to human flourishing is taken wholly from the conventional norms of the theorist's local culture. It is far from clear what is the claim on reason attributed to these ideals."[47] He also maintains that "the attribution to Aristotle of a belief in the moral centrality of choice-making (made by Machan and others) is all the more incongruous in that the belief plainly presupposes an affirmation of the freedom of the will which Aristotle does not make."[48]

Third and last, the skeptical critic is doubtful about applying the ideals of classical liberalism to different cultures, thus denying their universalizability, certainly implicit in natural (human) rights theories. The critic can claim, for example, that the individualism involved in the West's political legacy will probably not—and certainly need not—apply to a tribal culture. Therein, the critic can point out, individuals—or, at least, their freely chosen goals, projects, tastes, desires, preferences, etc.—are not regarded to be important. Individuals are important only as members of the group.[49]

This is a point very similar to that made by certain historicist critics of the natural rights position. Their criticism of Western political thought centers on the alleged fallacy of seeking some stable, transhistorical foundation for political justice. They argue, implicitly at least, that standards of justice, of goodness, etc., are going to have to be relative to given stages of human historical development.

The historicist objections of the natural rights tradition rest on the premise that the individualism implicit in the Lockean doctrine is false to the facts and is merely an invention of a certain historical period.[50] This criticism, reminiscent of Marxist objections to bourgeois politics and law, contends that the self or ego is an invention, something intellectuals created so as to rationalize certain public institutions and policies. Based on what we have learned from the history of ideas, political history, and cultural anthropology, we can see, the argument goes, that the idea of the individual self, the autonomous or sovereign person, is a modern contrivance, instead of a successful identification or true discovery of some fact about the human species.[51]

Of course when fully elaborated, this criticism goes on to maintain that in fact human beings are by nature collective. It is maintained that the human individual is a part of a larger whole and thus the good life for the human being is never anything that is derivable from his or her nature as an independent, sovereign, morally equal being. Let me now take a look at these objections to natural rights.

Against Utilitarian Criticism

There are two lines of argument that I will suggest against the utilitarian position. First, I will refute the objections to naturalism. Second, I will argue that the position itself requires something of a naturalist foundation to be coherent and complete. Since what I have presented earlier—in my outline of the natural rights position—should provide the grounding of the refutation of these two criticisms, I will be somewhat brief.

The is/ought gap troubles moral philosophy only if we accept a questionable, albeit prominent, theory of what it is both to be something and to know something, as well as the belief that a rational argument must have a deductive form. Thus, first, the empiricism underlying this skepticism begs the question of what there can be—to wit, it holds that only beings which are capable of being sensed can be ascertained to exist.[52] This rules out any type of existence that could involve characteristics we associate with values and morality. Since the empiricist view is open to serious doubt and there is reason to believe that a more pluralistic ontology would be more sound—based on common sense and its integration into a logically coherent order of existence—the is/ought gap suggested by empiricism need not be accepted as binding on a serious effort to inquire into the issue of values.[53] Second, the deductivism assumes that the formation of valid concepts could only proceed by way of deducing ideas from other ideas that fully contain them already, which basically denies any kind of growth of knowledge. So accepting the sting of the is/ought argument cuts much too deep—it undermines not just morality but all substantive (nontautological) claims to knowledge.[54]

There is, of course, an additional problem with the subjective utility or positivist approach to understanding justice: it leaves it entirely undecidable whether to embrace that theory. For, after all, whether a theory should be embraced is itself something of a normative question. The positivist—in economics or in law, not to mention in ethics—is, after all, advocating something. The positivist is addressing us with the proposal that what we ought to do is embrace a theory about values and virtues that has it that values and virtues are all subjective, a matter of personal taste or preference. But then why would not the positivist's own theory come to anything more than something we ought to embrace if we like it but not if we do not?[55]

As to the suggestion some make that the natural law (i.e., objective morality) position poses a threat to human ("negative") liberty, that is a justified concern only with an intrincisist conception of values and moral goodness. This view has it that in and of themselves, by virtue of certain innate traits or characteristics or properties, some items in nature are good, and they command support from those capable of seeing their goodness. The stress is on an enforceable, obligatory command which may be acted on by anyone, including someone who understands the command as it bears on another person and can coerce this other's adherence.

The crucial difference between this intrincisist conception of goodness and the present naturalist view is that the former omits from consideration the relational element of choice involved between a human individual and the values appropriate for him or her to pursue.[56] In other words, regardless of whether one chooses to act in certain ways, the mere behavior or movement furthering some goal can count as morally adequate in this intrincisist framework, since that alone will satisfy the implication that the good should be pursued. Yet, of course, if "ought implies can," as it must, this intrincisist view stumbles very badly. Having made someone behave so that this behavior promotes some goal has not succeeded in producing moral value, since the latter is dependent on choosing the appropriate behavior, that is, on acting rightly. It is clear, of course, that here there appears only a somewhat cumbersome technical difference between some authoritarian conceptions of moral and political virtue and the libertarian position presented above. But sometimes a lot hinges on small differences.

At this point I must discuss ethical and political anomalies since some utilitarians believe that their defense of the antinaturalist/positivist stance is helped a great deal by recalling them. They seem to think that these sorts of cases cannot be handled by the natural law/ rights position, which would be a failing since they evidently occur and need to be handled by us. If a moral/political/legal framework cannot guide us in this task, that framework is seriously flawed.

There are peculiarities about anomalous cases. These may cast them in a different light from that which favors the utilitarian position. To begin with, each anomalous case involves an emergency. That is to say, it places people in unique circumstances that no ethical theory is able to render manageable. Typical are desert island or lifeboat examples so often raised in judging ethical theories. Ethical theories are general guidelines to human conduct. So if they cannot handle the desert island or lifeboat examples, they must fail as ethical theories. So, even though it is argued, for example along Kantian lines, that honesty is a duty, if there is an imaginable case where it is not, the theory that so maintains must fail. Prudence is a virtue but sometimes one ought, first, to practice the virtue of courage. Moderation is good policy but clearly not always. It is not possible to find any kind of specific behavior or conduct, outside of following the very general policy of being rational, that will always be the right one for the situation, especially when the situation is extraordinary.[57]

One point to recall about natural rights is that they are supposed to guide the formation of law and government, not personal conduct. Natural rights are the application of ethics to public policy, so necessarily they apply only in circumstances where public life is possible. Some examples of the alleged inadequacy of natural rights theory as applied in practice presuppose that such rights are to guide conduct at the individual, personal level. So these simply fail to appreciate the purpose of natural rights theory.

Libertarian natural rights theorists have taken their clue from Locke who distinguished between situations "where peace is possible"[58] as distinct from those where it is not. Ayn Rand, too, has addressed the issue of the relationship between circumstances in one's life that are exceptional and the moral position that is most suitable to human life in general. Are the principles or virtues that are to guide ordinary human conduct and relationships identical to those that might help with the bizarre? The same type of question may be asked of a scientific theory.[59] In all of its realms, especially in that which is open to choice (as that involving human beings), nature can confront us with odd cases in which principles designed to treat normal circumstances do not smoothly apply.

But there is also the consideration that some anomalies illustrate that moral wrongs of the past produced the character of the case such that we seem to be faced with a dilemma. Thus one might be persuaded that someone's rights should be violated so as to correct a previous wrong—as in affirmative action policies—and thus accept the view that rights are not compossible.[60] And even though libertarian natural rights theorists have actually addressed the class of such cases, many utilitarians, following Russell Hardin's lead, have not found their work compelling enough to indicate how they have gone wrong.[61]

The general thrust of the natural law/rights approach in handling anomalies may be summarized as follows: The purpose of ethics or moral systems is to provide for the guidance of human living, with political theory and law to provide for the guidance of human life in the company of other human beings. To the extent that an ethical and/ or political system helps achieve the purpose it naturally has—that is, the purpose assumed in asking the question that gives rise to it as one of the many competing answers—it is a sound system. But even a sound system of ethics and/or politics can face difficulties, so the question is whether one or another faces them more successfully—more comprehensively, with greater integrity, etc.

What of the relationship between the ethical system and the political one (the principles of which would form a constitution or set of common laws on which positive law would most appropriately be made to rest in human community aimed at justice)? Ethics is prior to politics—how *I* should live is logically prior to how *we* should act together. So the relationship between ethics and politics is best seen in light of the fact that each person, as an adult, faces questions of living concerning oneself logically prior to facing questions of living with others who are strangers to oneself. (Of course, there are ethical questions pertaining to living with members of one's family, neighborhood, etc.; these are not political but social in the sense of pertaining to rather intimate or specialized yet close human interaction, not to the organizational principles of a large human community.) This is a matter of the ontology of the situation. That is, because one is the initiator of one's own behavior, in need of guiding one's conduct, one needs to have the answer to what one should do or how one should carry on per se before advancing to the problem of what one should do or how one should carry on vis-à-vis others. The ethical dimension of one's life has priority and the political is subsidiary to it, so when a conflict arises the ethical is decisive. (The political realm is nearly always subject to ethical or moral scrutiny, whereas political principles are not usually invoked in evaluating ethical principles.) For official representatives of the political dimension this may not be advisable to stress publicly, of course, and as far as their own conduct is concerned, given their personal loyalties, the priority issue may not arise at all. (The point is well played out in Melville's *Billy Budd*.) The natural law is prior. The natural rights each person has vis-à-vis others (who are strangers to one but are members of one's human community) may on occasion have to be disregarded in the face of the responsibilities of natural law. Anomalous cases seem to me all best explainable in terms of the naturalist stance just sketched.

Of course, this sketch immediately calls to mind some elements of utilitarianism's consequentialist character. There is one major difference, however, between utilitarianism's and natural rights theory's teleological position. Utilitarianism is usually uncommitted to some definitive conception of the human purpose and, therefore, of the summum bonum. With the human good left essentially subjective, the question of moral right and political rights is also undecidable. The escape clause, namely, that what right and justice and the like come to is "stipulated along the lines of Ulpian's maxims, or along Roman or Common law lines"[62] just cannot make clear sense, in utilitarianism's own theoretical terms, of the assertion, for example, that there is "a right or even the moral duty to be unjust to individuals in certain circumstances."[63]

The point here is not to deny that difficulties can arise in reconciling principles of morality and principles of politics and law. There is some reason to doubt that such difficulties must turn into moral dilemmas for all normative frameworks.[64] I myself have made the case that there is no good reason to even reidentify basic human rights as prima facie rights just so as to accommodate the alleged conflicts that can exist between different basic human rights.[65] But wherever it is suspected that such difficulties face us, the proper course that would seem to me warranted would be to attend very carefully to the intricacies of the circumstances. (The positive law is itself indicative of this point, when we consider how it handles alleged wrongdoings in exceptional circumstances, such as those involving shipwrecks, famine, earthquakes, etc.) Such cases tend to beg for the fullest possible knowledge of all the factors, since only then can we learn if the people involved made full use of their faculties so as to arrive at the most rational—that is, morally most suitable, given the nature of man as a rational being—decision under the unusual circumstances. Sketching such cases won't suffice.

Some utilitarians give us the clue to the last criticism I wish to level at the positivist elements of the utilitarian stance. They inform us that "the legal never exhausts the moral." What we could learn from this is that the law is a narrower scope and might very well be aimed at guiding us through normal elements of our lives, with its very general and very few edicts, compared to morality, which bears on every aspect of life under our volitional control.

Against Political Skepticism

Both of the central points advanced by the skeptic can be answered. First, Aristotle, as the representative of the objectivist and universalist stance in ethics and politics, is the first to admit that not everything that is morally right and wrong is universalizable, even though fundamental virtues may be. And in my own position, as well as in the positions of those who share it, *rationality* is the central virtue— just as in Aristotle, *right reason* fills that role. Other virtues are more contextual, which is entirely consistent with Aristotle and with an Aristotelian approach to moral theory. Moreover, all the virtues spelled out by "latter-day liberal followers" can be conceptually related to the original virtues spelled out by Aristotle. (Whatever is added can be defended, as well, and this may simply show some learning in the field, not relativism at all.)

Second, Aristotle does address the issue of choice-making in his distinction between the intellectual and the moral virtues. The latter require choice, which makes sense, since morality involves self-responsible conduct or neglect, something that could not be without the capacity for choice.[66] Aristotle did have a doctrine of free will—only it was not a major aspect of his moral theory. He located freedom of the will in the process of deliberation. As Weaner Jeager notes, "Aristotle's notion of free will is the exact complement of the notion of most perfect deliberation in the *Epinomis*."[67] And David Ross notes that "On the whole we must say that [Aristotle] shared the plain man's belief in free will but that he did not examine the problem very thoroughly, and did not express himself with perfect consistency."[68]

In the main, most skeptics do not bother to investigate these issues at any greater length[69] and thus it is not possible to argue with them. Suffice it to say that many of the skeptical claims advanced directly against natural rights theory are unsupported and some are evidently false.

We should add that, no doubt, a normative naturalist would have to invoke a teleological conception of human behavior—where else would the standards of right and wrong, good or evil come from? If by nature human beings are not destined—that is, it would not be more healthy or suitable or fitting for them—to be doing one thing rather than another, why insist that doing it is a good or right thing? The only alternative would be a theistic doctrine, which of course also embraces some variety of teleology and would, thus, come under similar fire from some allegedly devastating empiricist thesis.

Only there is no such devastating empiricism around, no decisive blow against teleology. Given all the new philosophizing about metaphysics, epistemology, philosophy of mind, etc., one would have to be rather steeped in a discredited logical positivism to think that teleology can be dismissed so cavalierly and thus normative naturalism (i.e., natural law and rights ethics and politics) swept away with ease. Furthermore, antinaturalists are also very suspicious of free will, once again because of their scientism—thinking that somehow the belief in free will is antiscience, antiempirical, anticool! Poppycock! No more so than many other doctrines and, by my lights, far less so than any other. Science is fully compatible with the free will idea.[70] Empiricism in epistemology need not be taken as decisive about anything.

Finally, there is that old saw about how natural law and rights theory is a danger to political liberty. It is odd enough that people so wedded to scientism and determinism would worry about political liberty—why not just say, *qué será, será*? But then to claim that having any idea of human nature *must* endanger human liberty is really difficult to fathom.

Presumably, as Karl Popper argued in *The Open Society and Its Enemies*[71]—and as argue virtually all of his followers—a stable idea of human nature authorizes us to force people to conform to the standards we may derive from this idea.

First of all, it is a curious position to take in philosophy or any other discipline that aims to learn the truth about the world that we shall avoid some theory if it has certain consequences we do not favor. That is precisely the ideological thinking so many believe liberals are guilty of. If learning about human nature does happen to justify coercion, so much the worse for liberty. That this seems unwarranted to me is not here the issue. What matters is that philosophers have to follow the argument, not evade those results they fear.

As another prospect, however, what if, as in the case of Locke and most natural law classical liberals, precisely the opposite is warranted by reference to what we learn is human nature? What if it turns out that human beings ought to live the sort of life that places them in the position of moral responsibility, thus precluding the forcible imposition of any but the most minimal standards (i.e., protection of their basic rights so that justice may prevail and self-governing virtue can flourish)?

Even if there were any problem with naturalism along these lines, certainly noncognitivism or skepticism cannot help—if there is no reason for imposing standard A (which limits liberty because human nature so requires), surely there is no reason impose standard B (which protects liberty because human nature so requires). Without standards nothing can be concluded, *either for or against intrusive action,* but the right standards may give aid and comfort to the champion of liberty—which is just what I think is the case. (Some skeptics, e.g., John Gray, seem to exemplify this point.)

Maybe what is wrong is that naturalism is a morally demanding position, after all, and many classical liberals just don't want to hear about that. Let us all be free, they want to cry out, but they don't much want to know about what to do with their liberty. Never mind that no one has the authority to *make* them do anything within the Lockean naturalist tradition. They don't even want to know about what they might be morally obligated to do as free agents. (The problem is that often those who claim to know what someone ought to do jump quite illogically to the conclusion that they are justified in forcing another to do the right thing. But this is just wrong. What is also wrong, however, is the belief that being a free agent, sovereign or autonomous, means that the standards of right conduct are invented by one rather than derivable from an understanding of one's nature and who one is.).

The trouble with the skeptical defense of liberty is that it can boomerang right back at those with a preference for liberty—if it is no more than a preference. (This point is made very well by Renford Bambrough.[72])

So, all in all, natural law theorists need not be taken aback all that much by the dismissal they experience from Popperians and other skeptics. (Some of these, by the way, have stopped being great friends of political liberty.[73]) Once they have made the points I have hinted at here—and added some of the nuances one needs with each new incarnation of the basic skeptical thesis—it is time to move on to more constructive work. As we have seen, when skeptics claim that teleology is obsolete and that empiricism is the right theory of knowledge, they are off base. Such a position is untenable, not to mention odd for a skeptic to embrace.

It is worth adding that for a long time mechanistic materialism had been the reigning metaphysics. It was believed, at least by secular philosophers, that here lies the foundation for the solution to many human problems. Hobbes placed all his hopes on this view, as did many others. Even Kant accepted that at least the phenomenal world—what science is concerned with—yields fully to the laws of mechanics. Only the mysterious noumenal world escapes it, though we are left in the dark as to just how this is possible.

But mechanistic materialism is not even the favored ontology in physics. Any of the varieties of reductionism is certainly not self-evidently true. Arguably, also, a much more pluralistic metaphysics—akin to what I outlined earlier—makes much better sense of what we find around us as well as within us in reality.[74]

This leads us to the following conclusions. If there are different kinds and types of beings—substances—that have a fundamentally irreducible nature, the explanation of how they behave could also be very different. Efficient causality—the mode of the action of one thing upon another that is favored by reductive materialism and physicalism—need by no means be the only form of causality. Teleological causation—such as we invoke when we explain much of human (but a good deal of plant and animal) behavior—cannot be ruled out.

It is a matter of discovery, not a fundamental metaphysical assumption, as skeptical critics of the natural rights position assume, whether we affirm the reality of one or another kind of causal interaction. And there is evidence enough pointing to self-determined behavior when human action is at issue not to dismiss this on the ground of some a priorist reductionism.[75]

Similar points can be raised against the assumption that empiricism is the hands-down winner in the competition between theories of knowledge. Clearly, the empiricist theory itself is not capable of being shown true by reference to the standards of truth and knowledge its adherents propound. Instead, a view of knowledge I sketched above makes better sense, namely, whereby what is known has a decisive impact on the standards of truth and knowledge about that kind or type of being. It is our task to see to it that we keep tracking what is known as we make our claims to knowing this or that, as well as try to find out more about it. This again yields a pluralism, this time in the theory of knowledge—there are some general criteria that all successful knowledge claims need to satisfy. But there are also criteria that are relative to the context of the different kind and type of thing known. Thus what will be known about musical harmony will be a case of knowledge for different reasons from what will be known about the War of 1812 or the number of consecutive 7s that may occur in the calculation of *pi*.

This pluralism and contextualism handles very well, I propose, the problems derived from the fact of cultural diversity, without requiring us to accept cultural relativism. It makes the justifiable versus the unjustifiable diversions possible to identify, based on certain stable enough, transhistorical standards of good, right, and just.[76] The present natural rights approach would appear to manage that very well; it may explain why the "human rights" approach has been so widely invoked in international criticisms of political and legal practices through the past several decades.[77]

Arguing with Historicism

The objections historicists make against natural rights have greater punch than those made by skeptics, who are usually hoisted on their own petard.[78] One of them states that "there is no expression in any ancient or medieval language correctly translated by our expression 'a right' until near the close of the middle ages: the concept lacks any means of expression in Hebrew, Greek, Latin or Arabic, classical or medieval, before about 1400, let alone in Old English, or in Japanese even as late as the mid-nineteenth century."[79] This critic also construes individualism as basically wrong, referring to "that newly invented social institution, the individual."[80]

Plainly put, the historicists contend that stable, transhistorical principles of political life cannot be identified. Both human nature and our understanding of the world change constantly; what we know is known from a given historical perspective. Human nature itself changes because we look at the world differently at different historical periods; our minds are influenced by when we use them and the resulting "knowledge" is, thus, conditioned, which does not yield stable principles of ethics, politics, economics, or any other sphere of human concern.

Yet much of this is wrong on its face. The rest of it is subject to dispute on conceptual grounds.

There is evidence that the dominant language of human life in certain earlier periods of human history paid scant attention to the human self, to individuality, to the moral autonomy and political sovereignty of human beings. No doubt, Plato and even Aristotle considered human beings in their relation to other social wholes—the family, tribe, city, class, race, etc. But what of this? Why should any such historical evidence be decisive in questions of ontology and, eventually, ethics and politics?

Conceptual development can be both gradual as well as uneven, radical, or dormant. If human beings possess the capacity to make choices, they may exercise it differently as they will, constrained by some factors but with plenty of elbowroom to work in. Also, in the domain of human knowledge many false starts, misunderstandings, prejudices, etc., are possible. To look to what in fact people believed throughout history is only one avenue of discovery as to what actually exists.

The claim that because the dominant modes of belief had been different from some belief system being considered, the latter is flawed, simply won't settle the issue. In many sciences we find advances toward a more and more fully developed conception of some thing—the solar system, the atom, the liver, the human mind, etc. To claim that because in the past there was little talk about a potentially infinite universe, that idea cannot be sound, would be quite out of order in astronomy or cosmology.

Similarly, it may be granted that in the past—say prior to the eleventh century—extensive or even sufficient moral concern for individual human beings as such had been negligible (though by no means absent). Most philosophers focused on the place human beings occupy on the social landscape and what this implies as to their proper behavior vis-à-vis some supposedly greater body. (But let us not forget that this same talk is prevalent today—e.g., in Marx's phrase "the organic whole [or body]" of humanity.[81])

Furthermore, a dialectical point needs also to be made against the historicist thesis. Such a thesis will backfire because it purports to be correct even while many disbelieve it. Most people who have written on these matters have thought that what they say is true, whether they have been right or wrong. They have not believed that what they believe is true only for some period of time, only in some phase of human history, etc. And the historicist must implicitly propose that the thesis about the temporality of the idea of the human individual is universally valid—that is, for example, in 10,000 years it should still be accepted as true that the idea of the human individual was only a temporary myth, not something true.[82] But if this fails to be the dominant view, should it be dismissed for that reason alone? I doubt that historicists would be so giving.

The dominance of some position may be due to many factors, including the obvious one that those who advanced it may have found it convincing, may have benefited from advancing it, maybe focused their gaze too narrowly, etc. The real issue is whether the view can hold its own against alternative positions. The task is for historicists and all others to get into the fray and argue it all out, not to keep invoking the authority of history or numbers in defense of some position.

Finally, the historicist position is false to the fact of its own promulgation. It is, after all, individual human beings who propound ideas, who criticize them, who stand apart from the rest with their doctrines and skepticism. This testifies to the individuality of the advocate, at least—a human being who can act independently, who can think for himself or herself, and whose kind of individualistic life may therefore require certain socioeconomic and political conditions for it to flourish.[83] The natural rights position pays very close attention to just this scenario about human life.

Naturalism: Some Final Reflections

Perhaps the central thesis of this essay should once again be stated, this time as simply as possible. It is that, because of the kind of beings they are and numerous other facts about their lives, it is more just for human beings to live in freedom than even in the slightest condition of slavery. Or, even more bluntly, free men and women live more justly as human beings than do slaves of any degree. It is this thesis that I have been defending.

Despite the simple truth of the above claim, it is also true that the naturalist normative framework may be difficult to identify and work out. No doubt many have tried to erect it and have failed, though the mere lack of widespread acceptance of natural law/rights views is no proof of this. The main reason for much of the actual failure is not so much a matter of moral and political inadequacy but the flawed metaphysical and epistemological doctrines that have guided the enterprise of developing the naturalist position.[84] If we had heeded Gilbert Harman's idea, that "we must take care not to adopt a very skeptical attitude nor become too lenient about what is to count as knowledge,"[85] especially in how we conceive of moral and political knowledge and what tests we expect claims to such knowledge and the underlying arguments to meet, the task of developing the naturalist position would probably have fared better.

A theory in any field of investigation is an answer to a question that human beings raise. Which theory is the best one may be determined by which of the ones proposed answers the question best, which is itself determined by what we want from an answer. In political theory we want an answer that helps us guide our organized community affairs with the least degree of inherent conflict, the most comprehensive applicability to such community life, the facilitation of human living while in the company of others human beings to whom one is not intimately related. Whether the present theory meets these criteria cannot be known without a comparative analysis. What may be valuable in the present undertaking is entering a contending answer with a clearly important perspective, one that places the individual in the center of political affairs. If we do not allow a fruitless idealism to stand in the way of identifying the best theory in this sphere of inquiry, we will recognizing that nature is the best guide to how we need to cope with our human personal and community lives, a matter to which each of us pays heed quite naturally, after all.

Notes

I wish to thank Mark Turiano for his advice on the preparation of this work, as well as James Sterba for his criticisms. I believe the paper has benefited considerably from discussing various features of it with James Chesher, Douglas J. Den Uyl, Gregory Johnson, and Douglas B. Rasmussen.

1. It is arguable that exactly this problem was tackled by Socrates in his various discussions, namely, whether a firm standard of right judgment in matters of justice could be identified. See Leo Strauss, *Natural Right and History* (Chicago: University of Chicago Press, 1953). See also Tibor R. Machan, *Human Rights and Human Liberties: A Radical Reconsideration of the American Political Tradition* (Chicago: Nelson-Hall, 1975).

2. The way the alternative is stated or expressed is often one of the points in hot dispute. Interestingly, many of those who would deny that there are objective standards in any of these areas are, nevertheless, insistent on describing the dispute in ways they alone deem appropriate!

3. Although I will be dealing with the naturalist metaethics and meta-politics that I argue support the classical liberal or libertarian polity of individual (negative) rights, it should be noted right off that there are philosophers who argue that naturalism does not support such a position. The concept "objective" should here be understood to mean "capable of being demonstrated on the basis of evidence of existing (natural) beings, attributes, etc." It is a concept that need not be interpreted differently from how it is used in, say, instructions to a jury to be objective in their assessment of a case presented to them, that is, to consider only what is evident to them—facts, valid inferences from them, etc.—and not permit their wishes, desires, or biases to undermine their judgment. Of course, what is at issue in the debate is whether such objectivity is possible to human beings. For more, see notes 19 and 20 below.

4. In A. I. Melden, ed., *Human Rights* (Belmont, Calif.: Wadsworth, 1970). I discuss Macdonald at some length in my doctoral dissertation, Human Rights: A Metaethical Inquiry (University of Michigan Microfilms, 1972), as well as in *Human Rights and Human Liberties*.

5. Strauss, *Natural Right and History*.

6. The one major exception is Harry V. Jaffa, who finds much in Locke that is philosophically valuable. See his *How to Think About the American Revolution* (Durham: Carolina Academic Press, 1978).

I should make it clear that while I treat Locke's political thinking as the precursor to the kind of classical liberal or libertarian position I defend, I do not mean to imply that Locke himself was a full-blown, uncompromised libertarian. Clearly Locke was willing to take political steps against atheists and others, for reasons we do not now need to consider. When I invoke Locke, Aristotle, or anyone else in clarifying the position I want to develop here, it is mostly so as to indicate some basic similarities of approach, thus making it simpler to understand the present position. One cannot always say everything pertinent, so these indices are very useful.

7. Perhaps the most general attack on natural rights theory comes from Richard Rorty, e.g., in his *Objectivity, Relativism, and Truth* (Cambridge: Cambridge University Press, 1991), p. 31. Rorty is a pragmatist/historicist who denies any transhistorical knowledge, even in the natural sciences. That his historicist claims are themselves purported transhistorical claims about how human beings cope with their environment does not seem to faze him

much, yet they would appear to involve him in a flat-out contradiction. I present a case for what might be termed a minimalist foundationalism in Tibor R. Machan, "Evidence of Necessary Existence," *Objectivity* Vol. 3, (Fall 1992), pp. 31–62.

8. See, however, note 16, for a strange affinity between Strausseans and Rorty et al.

9. See, e.g., John Gray, *Liberalism* (Minneapolis: University of Minnesota Press, 1986) and *Liberalisms* (London: Routledge, 1989). See also Larry Briskman, "Skinnerism and Pseudo-Science," *Philosophy of the Social Sciences* (Summer 1981), Vol. 3 and Norman Barry, *On Classical Liberalism and Libertarianism* (New York: St. Martin's Press, 1989).

10. John Gray has gone through several changes in his political orientation, yet he has throughout remained a Pyrrhonist in his epistemology. His most recent hero in political theory is Michael Oakeshott.

Some have observed that Gray has changed his mind on several occasions concerning the merits of liberalism and related doctrines. Yet what has remained entirely unchanged in his views is his Phyrronism or skepticism concerning not only morality but any kind of knowledge claim. Ever since I have known Gray, we have argued about the same issue, namely, whether human knowledge is possible at all. And, of course, when one denies that it is, one is rather unconstrained about choosing political positions, since they can now be entirely a matter of one's alternating preferences.

Incidentally, the source of skepticism in Gray is not much different from what it is in other skeptics, namely, the misguided conception of what knowledge must be, namely, timeless certainty. What many take to be the limits of knowledge really amount to no more than the fact that knowledge isn't something else, namely, becoming what one knows. To complain that we know reality only as it appears to us or in its knowable aspect is to (a) attribute to reality features that have nothing to do with reality as such, namely, that it is known or knowable by us, and (b) confuse knowing reality with somehow acquiring it in toto into consciousness. For more on this, see Tibor R. Machan, *Individuals and Their Rights* (LaSalle, Ill.: Open Court, 1989).

11. John Rawls, "The Independence of Moral Theory," *Proceedings and Addresses of the American Philosophical Association* (1975), Vol. XLVII, pp. 5–22.

12. Russell Hardin, "The Utilitarian Logic of Liberalism," *Ethics* (1986), Vol. 97, pp. 73–74.

13. For a very informative discussion, see Stephen Cox, "Devices of Deconstruction," *Critical Review* (Winter, 1989), Vol. 3, pp. 56–76. For the more constructive case supporting the foundationalist approach to moral and political theory, see some of the contributions to the special issue on this topic, "Rethinking Foundationalism," in *Reason Papers* (Fall 1991), No. 16. It bears noting that all the talk about postmodernism, as if these doctrines hadn't been thought of prior to our times, is more of a press agent publicity stunt than fidelity to fact. So-called postmodern thinking is much better described as pre-ancient (pre-Socratic, pre-Aristotelian) thinking. Or rather,

more or less developed versions of these ideas surrounding these issues have been around in *every* age, with more or less popularity.

14. Some Strausseans seem to acknowledge the difficulty of establishing such foundations, yet insist on the need to look for them (at least implicitly—e.g., Allan Bloom, *The Closing of the American Mind* [New York: Simon and Schuster, 1987], who eschews a thorough discussion of absolute or fundamental realities, even as he severely lambastes those who have given up on it and embrace some variety of relativism).

There has always been some question about just how genuine this Straussean endorsement is, since Leo Strauss has claimed that for bona fide philosophers it is okay to deceive the ordinary folk and, also, that few so-called philosophers are *bona fide*. See, for an interesting discussion, Carl Page, "The Truth About Lies in Plato's Republic," *Ancient Philosophy* (1991), Vol. 11, pp. 1–33. Perhaps it is the search alone, and the fate of those who are committed to it, never mind what one finds, that Strausseans see as significant, but it would be too dangerous to admit this to all and sundry. Some of those who have studied with Strauss have openly endorsed nihilism—e.g., Harry Newman. See, for a good summary, Paul A. Basinski and Harry Newman, "Nihilism Challenged . . . and Defended," *Claremont Review of Books* (Fall 1985), pp. 26–28. Newman probably articulates openly the essential features of Rorty's thinking, as well, as he does those of all epistemological skeptics.

15. See Ayn Rand, *Introduction to Objectivist Epistemology,* 2nd ed. (New York: New American Library, 1990).

16. See, e.g., Frank M. Coleman, *Hobbes and America* (Toronto: University of Toronto Press, 1977). See also Edward Andrew, *Shylock's Rights* (Toronto: University of Toronto Press, 1988), for an elaborate and especially virulent denigration of the Lockean idea of individual rights. Leo Strauss and many of his students maintain that while Locke is to be credited with laying the foundations for the American polity, there is not any substantial philosophical difference between Locke and Hobbes. See, e.g., Walter Berns, *The First Amendment and the Future of American Democracy* (New York: Basic Books, 1976). The basic argument of the Strausseans is that since Locke's basic philosophy (metaphysics, epistemology) fails to cohere with his allegedly natural law ethics and politics, the latter is largely a rhetorical device for justifying certain special political objectives. This, incidentally, resembles closely the Marxist view, whereby not a concern for truth but one of vested interest accounts for the "convictions" underlying the American polity. See C. B. Macpherson, *Possessive Individualism* (London: Oxford University Press, 1962). Cf. also Andrew C. MacLaughlin, *The Foundations of American Constitutionalism* (Greenwich, Conn.: Fawcet, 1961) and op. cit., Jaffa, *How to Think About the American Revolution.*

Whatever motivations we may attribute to Locke, the crucial question is whether his basic argument holds up. And if it is possible to find a philosophical groundwork that gives the Lockean portion credibility, the Lockean theory may be in good shape. After all, every level of an edifice need not be designed and built by the same engineers.

17. I use these labels while aware of the controversies and fine distinctions stressed by those to whom they apply. Essentially, though, the right supports spiritual welfarism or paternalism, urging government to act as soul crafters (see George Will, *Statecraft as Soulcraft* [New York: Simon and Schuster, 1983]), while the left supports economic or material welfarism or paternalism, urging the state to guard us against our mismanaging of our households. The dispute is probably at the metaphysical level, namely, about which is more important, our souls or our bodies. The present position sees the person as an integrated, multifaceted entity with a most fundamental need for self-directedness. I deal with this in Tibor R. Machan, *Business Bashing, Why Commerce Is Maligned* (forthcoming).

18. Although I discuss the views in terms of their philosophical characterization, I will cite particular theorists so that we can get a clear statement of the criticism rather than having to produce a statement that members of these schools could contend is a caricature. Those I will consider have addressed the natural rights position quite directly.

19. I note this because it is contested in contemporary metaphysics (most prominently by Willard Van Orman Quine, who advocates ontological relativism, or Richard Rorty, who simply denies that we can have bona fide knowledge of the nature of what exists—i.e., of the foundation of knowledge). To claim, as some of these thinkers do, that all this proves is that for us reality must be consistent is to attempt something that by their own thinking one cannot do, namely, gain an independent perspective of the relationship between reality and the human understanding. In other words, the very enterprise in which such thinkers are involved belies their own doctrine's soundness.

20. Here, again, the view I am sketching is implicitly or explicitly contested by such philosophers as Richard Rorty and Paul Feyerabend. And their skepticism has direct bearing on whether the thesis I sketch below can be defended. Both seem to me, however, to be captivated by the mistaken notion that when we know X, we must be influencing X and this brings into question whether what we know is in fact X or X + our-impact-on-X. But knowing X is not influencing but grasping it, not attacking but embracing it, as it were. Part of the confusion arises from thinking that when we know X *as it is*, we somehow must have implanted into our knowing faculty the X itself, which of course does not happen—what is there is not *X as it is* but *our knowledge of X as it is. Knowing X* is not the same as *being X*!

This should also allay worries about knowledge having always to be final, complete, closed. In this connection it is still very instructive to read J. L. Austin, "Other Minds," in his *Philosophical Papers* (Oxford: Clarendon Books, 1961), and Barry Straud, "Wittgenstein and Logical Necessity," in George Pitcher, ed., *Wittgenstein* (Garden City, N.Y.: Anchor, 1969).

21. Tibor R. Machan, "C. S. Peirce and Absolute Truth," *Transactions of the C. S. Peirce Society* (Spring 1980), Vol. 16, pp. 153–61.

22. This metaphysical position is not without its challengers and there is ample literature on the subject. Yet all I want to point out is that a challenge is itself something and if one denies that the above holds universally, it is an open issue what the challenge itself must mean. Aristotle still had the best defense of the law of noncontradiction as a basic fact of reality, not just of our mode of apprehending it.

23. Tibor R. Machan, "Epistemology and Moral Knowledge," *Review of Metaphysics* (September 1982), Vol. 36. I discuss in this paper the nature of natures—i.e., what it is to be the nature of something. I carry further this discussion in *Individuals and Their Rights*.

24. Here the naturalism of the present position emerges most distinctively. For more, see Machan, *Human Rights and Human Liberties*, and Douglas B. Rasmussen, "Essentialism, Values and Rights," in *The Libertarian Reader*, T. R. Machan, ed. (Totowa, N.J.: Rowman & Littlefield, 1982), pp. 37–52. See also Machan, *Individuals and Their Rights*.

25. I develop at some length the case for this definition as I try to answer a challenge by M. P. Golding, advanced in his "Toward a Theory of Human Rights," *The Monist* (October 1968), Vol. 52, p. 495, in, e.g., *Individuals and Their Rights*.

26. The argument for this conception of free will is advanced by Roger W. Sperry in his more technical paper, "Changing Concepts of Consciousness and Free Will," *Perspectives in Biology and Medicine* (Autumn 1976), Vol. 9, pp. 9–19. See also Tibor R. Machan, "Applied Ethics and Free Will, Some Consequences of Independence," *Journal of Applied Philosophy* (1993), Vol. 10, pp. 59–72.

27. The choosing in question may perhaps be characterized better by the term "initiating (of thought)." It is done, as it were, by willing—the person's most basic act of paying heed or becoming alert or focused in life, something the person needs to sustain and maintain as an individual commitment. When this choice or initiation of the process of awareness is abnegated, even partially or temporarily—except, of course, during required rest—the commitment to living a good human life is faltering.

28. Machan, "Epistemology and Moral Knowledge."

29. I am here drawing on the work of Ayn Rand, "The Objectivist Ethics," in *The Virtue of Selfishness: A New Concept of Egoism* (New York: Signet, 1964). See, for more, Tibor R. Machan, "Reason, Individualism, and Capitalism: The Moral Vision of Ayn Rand," in *The Philosophic Thought of Ayn Rand,* D. Den Uyl and D. Rasmussen, eds. (Urbana: University of Illinois Press, 1983).

30. Plato's conception of justice is broader than the justice that can characterize a political community. The just state for Plato is really the perfectly good human community, one in which everything goes right. For the difference between Plato's conception of justice and that which is considered here,

see Hannah F. Pitkin, *Wittgenstein and Justice* (Berkeley: University of California Press, 1972), pp. 303ff. Consider, also, that in Plato's *Republic* what is at stake is not political justice as such but the nature of the just or morally, ethically good or excellent human being. Justice, in that context, is a more encompassing concept than in the context of political theory as an effort to conceptualize the best constituents of a large community or nation state.

31. I develop in detail the argument for the obligatory nature of these rights for human individuals in the context of their community lives, in *Individuals and Their Rights*. Since I argue from the basis of classical egoism or individualism, it may be significant to appreciate just how one may establish the obligation to respect others' basic rights from such a moral foundation. Chapter 7, "Individualism and the Problem of Political Authority," concerns just this issue. See also Tibor R. Machan, "Reply to Critics of Individuals and Their Rights," *Reason Papers* (Fall 1992), No. 17.

32. John Rawls, *A Theory of Justice* (Cambridge: Harvard University Press, 1971), p. 104. Rawls may, of course, reject this characterization of his position, but it is very difficult to see how he can make any room for moral responsibility given his view that character itself is a function of luck, etc. See, for more on this point vis-à-vis Rawls, Machan, *Human Rights and Human Liberties,* pp. 167–68. Consider the following: "The assertion that a man deserves the superior character that enables him to make the effort to cultivate his abilities is . . . problematic; for his character depends in large part upon fortunate family and social circumstances for which he can claim no credit." One may wonder whether Rawls is fully aware of the deterministic implications of this claim. He may as well embrace B. F. Skinner's doctrine in *Beyond Freedom and Dignity* (New York: Bantam, 1971), in which the ontological foundations of ethics are explicitly denied. Yet for Rawls it is problematic to sweep aside free will entirely, for then how could he argue, as he evidently does, that human beings ought to act in accordance with his conception of justice as fairness. If we *ought to* be fair, it must be true that we have the choice to be fair or not to be fair. If whether we possess the character to be fair depends upon fortunate family and social circumstances, then we either will be or will not be fair and there is nothing Rawls or anyone else can do about the matter, nor can anyone blame people for failing to be fair or for failing to support institutions of fairness throughout society. Does Rawls wish to embrace the view that whether one supports, say, affirmative action or opposes it is irrelevant to one's moral virtue? It would have to be, however, if our family and social circumstances made us supporters or opponents of such policies.

33. Robert Nozick, *Anarchy, State, and Utopia* (New York: Basic Books, 1974), p. 57. Nozick has since writing this book rejected his libertarian views—see his *The Examined Life* (New York: Simon and Schuster, 1989), pp. 286–96, mainly on grounds that even if individuals require such moral space, as spelled out by means of their Lockean negative rights, they may be made to conform to certain public purposes we all need to share. "The lib-

ertarian position I once propounded now seems to me seriously inadequate, in part because it did not fully knit the humane considerations and joint cooperative activities it left room for more closely into its fabric" (pp. 288–87). Nozick thinks that such considerations and activities need to be given symbolic expression via certain government projects that give it meaning as such. The libertarian who shares the concern with such common goals and meanings will stress, however, that when these are instilled in the membership of the community by force, they lose their significance and, indeed, via such coercion will undermine the chances of their realization. Forced belief and practice is alienating and saps the society of its moral life blood.

34. Rawls, *A Theory of Justice*, pp. 101–2.

35. Rawls subsequently published *Political Liberalism* (New York: Columbia University Press, 1993), in which, as Stephen Holmes points out in his review (*The New Republic*, October 11, 1993, p. 42), Rawls "unexpectedly combines this [*A Theory of Justice's*] argument [about social determinism] with its opposite. Alongside strong claims about unequal upbringing and the redistributions it implies, we now find the observation that people are 'responsible' for their character and desires, whatever disadvantages their social upbringing heaped upon them," and that "those who surf all day off Malibu must find a way to support themselves and would not be entitled to 'public funds'."

I should at this point call attention to Sterba's efforts to demonstrate that from a classical liberal or libertarian negative rights theory one can reach conclusions that would support the supportive welfare state. I address this position in my responses to Galston and Sterba at another place in this volume.

36. Some, such as Heather Gert, in "Rights and Rights Violators: A New Approach to the Nature of Rights," *Journal of Philosophy* (1990), Vol. 90, pp. 688–94, have argued that rights are superfluous since all human wrongs can be reduced to injuring or harming people. As she puts it, "To say that I ought not to punch you because it would hurt you is sufficient—there is no further need to invoke that alleged thing that is your right not to be punched or hurt. Clearly, much of what is to be taken into account is the harm caused by our actions and the significance we give to the harm" (p. 694).

Yet this is wrong—rights violations often involve depriving people of choices, and some of these choices, if they had not been made, would have resulted in greater injury to the person than what resulted from the rights violation itself. Concerning some other aspects of what amounts to violating rights, see J. Roger Lee, "Choice and Harms," in *Rights and Regulation* M. Bruce Johnson and T. R. Machan, eds. (Cambridge: Ballinger, 1983), pp. 157–73. Interestingly Gert does not consider *any* libertarian analysis of rights—e.g., those by Eric Mack, Jan Narveson, Lee, or Rasmussen and Den Uyl. This is not surprising since most of her analysis focuses on what are called positive rights, such as "persons in underdeveloped countries" having "the right to even a minimal amount of food" (p. 693). But then her essay ought to have been entitled "Positive Rights and Positive Rights Violators."

37. See, for more on this, Tibor R. Machan, "Between Parents and Children," *Journal of Social Philosophy* (1992), Vol. 23, pp. 16–22.

38. For why implicit consent is a binding commitment to a principle of social life, see my *Individuals and Their Rights*, Chapter 7.

39. This holds even for those few who may have no means available to them to further their lives via the protection of their right to negative liberty—e.g., the utterly incapacitated poor—since those who do have those capacities ought to strive to preserve the general, unexceptional conditions of human flourishing, meaning they ought to maintain those rights that will help them to do so as human beings. (Incidentally, those thoroughly incapacitated are not usually the ones who violate negative rights since they are by definition unable to do such strenuous things. It is, thus, moot to argue that they have the authority to engage in such conduct. It is more important to consider why others, not so incapacitated, might have that authority instead of the responsibility to provide the remedies needed.)

40. That the welfare state now and then does help some people is not a counterexample here. Some people fall out of airplanes and live to write best-selling books about it. Moreover, the good done *via* the welfare state is demonstrably costly to those who were taxed so as to produce it and that much of this cost ought not to be borne by them is not an implausible thesis. Yet, it is more likely that the welfare state supports those who manage it more successfully than those in whose behalf such "management" is supposed to occur. See John Gray, "Classical Liberalism, Positional Goods, and the Politicization of Poverty," in *Dilemmas of Liberal Democracies,* Adrian Ellis and Krishan Kumar, eds (London: Tavistock, 1983). Gray notes that studies have demonstrated that "The greatest net beneficiaries from the welfare state in Britain have been the professional middle classes, whose political pull and social skills have enabled them to create and then exploit a vast range of services largely sustained by tax subsidies derived from the poorer majority. The largest net losers from British welfarism, on the other hand, have been the working poor and the victims of the artificial poverty trap created by the extremely high marginal tax rates to which they are subject" (p. 180).

41. Ernest van den Haag, "Against Natural Rights," *Policy Review* (Winter 1983), No. 23, pp. 143–75. Appendix 1 of *Individuals and Their Rights* is a direct response to van den Haag's arguments.

42. This point, incidentally, is difficult to support philosophically without a natural law/natural rights underpinning. In other words, how do we tell, without reference to human nature, that freedom is a (nonarbitrary) good thing for a human being living in a community?

43. Renford Bambrough, in *Moral Skepticism and Moral Knowledge* (Atlantic Highlands, N.J.: Humanities Press, 1979), disposes of the alleged conceptual connection between essentialist or objectivist moral theories and authoritarianism.

It does not follow from the true premise "[I know that] A ought to do X" that "Therefore, [I know that] someone ought to force A to do X." The further premise "[I know that] (for any A and for any X) if A ought to do X, someone ought to force A to do X" would have to be true, as well. While there may be some cases such that if A ought to do X, when someone, say B, knows this, someone, say B, ought to force A to do X—e.g., if A ought to respect the rights of others, and B is the government established to protect rights—it is certainly false that for all cases of "A ought to do X" this is so.

44. Strictly, to determine whether they are intolerable would require establishing a superior competing theory; yet moral beliefs need not all rest on explicit moral theories. There is a moral reality just as a physical, chemical, biological, or legal reality known to most ordinary people and to violate those beliefs should not remain unexplained.

Ethical dilemmas may appear to occur once one takes a close look at a situation that pits two or more equally sensible moral beliefs against one another. One way this might be resolved is to establish an ethical theory that succeeds in rationally ranking moral principles. A way of evading the problem is to claim that the world is simply too topsy-turvy for us to find an adequate theory to make sense of it (e.g., in the realm of ethics). An explanation of all this may involve the fact that no theory pertaining to dynamic matters such as human conduct could be final in its scope, so there will always be some areas yet to be integrated within a theory. Theories will at times need modification so as to accommodate this fact.

45. There is a more serious problem with the utilitarian stance, identified by Kenneth Arrow in *Social Choice and Individual Values* (New Haven: Yale University Press, 1962). The very ideas of rational choice and democracy (or liberty) combine to generate contradictory public policy. Furthermore, the idea of the greatest happiness of the greatest number is confused, based on the incommensurability of the two features to be quantified, namely, the universe of those who can be happy and happiness itself, so it would help to know just what exactly the value standard is that van den Haag is proposing. See, however, Chapter 2 in Tibor R. Machan, *Private Rights, Public Illusions* (New Brunswick, N.J.: Transactions Books, 1994), where I argue that no such problem faces a natural rights approach to social or public choice theory because it leaves a rationally delimited public scope wherein democracy is to function.

46. Gray, *Liberalism*.

47. Gray, *Liberalisms*, p. 258.

48. Ibid., p. 265n26.

49. Does this mean the individuals do not exist as individuals or are neglected as such? Presumably, for Gray's objection to go through, he would have to claim that a tribe is an individual or an organic whole, just as Karl Marx had claimed that "the human essence is the true collectivity of man" (in "On the Jewish Question") most likely because he regarded humanity an "organic whole" (in *Grundrisse*).

50. Alasdair MacIntyre, *After Virtue* (Notre Dame: University of Notre Dame Press, 1981).

51. In *Individuals and Their Rights* I defend a conception of the human individual that withstands most of the more plausible critical charges made

against individuals—for example, that it relies on an antisocial, atomic conception of human life. See also Tibor R. Machan, *Capitalism and Individualism, Reframing the Argument for the Free Society* (New York: St. Martin's Press, 1990). For a more fundamentally focused discussion of individuality, as it arises in metaphysics (vis-à-vis whether the entities populating reality are or could be individuals), see Jorge J. E. Gracia, *Individuality* (Albany: SUNY Press, 1988). In relation to denying individualism in an Aristotelian tradition—including, especially, the politics that emerges from it—it is worthwhile to note that Aristotle's metaphysics may be more individualistic than is widely believed. See, in this connection, Henry Teloh, "What Aristotle Should Have Said in Metaphysics Z," *Southern Journal of Philosophy*, (Summer 1982), Vol. 20, pp. 241–55. See also Emerson Buchanan, *Aristotle's Theory of Being* (Cambridge: Greek, Roman, and Byzantine Monographs, 1962), p. 2.

52. Machan, "Epistemology and Moral Knowledge." If radical or strict empiricism is correct, then knowledge of what ought to be done is of course impossible, since "good" and "ought to" are not radically (even though they could be commonsensically) empirical concepts.

53. For a discussion of the problems with the open question argument G. E. Moore advances against the naturalist metaethics, see Machan, *Individuals and Their Rights*, p. 94.

54. This development has, of course, occurred with the emergence of such views as those of Feyerabend and Rorty. There have always been intimations of it in the thinking of various relativist and historicist philosophers. See Tibor R. Machan, "Some Reflection on Rorty's Philosophy" *Metaphilosophy*, Vol. 24 (January/April 1993), pp. 123–35. See, also, op. cit., Machan, "Evidence of Necessary Existence."

55. The significance of this point may escape some but it should not, at least, not if one is interested in consistency. At a recent conference an advocate of legal positivism was arguing how unwise it is for justices of the Supreme Court as well as legal scholars to read the U.S. Constitution as if that document depended in the slightest on some notion of natural law. Lino Graglia invoked Hume's is/ought gap thesis and defended the positivist notion that all that justices ought to do is read the Constitution literally, placing limits on majority rule only on very rare occasions—such as in the unlikely event that some legislature enacted a law barring women from voting. In such a case, of course, the Constitution is quite explicit: no legislature may do such a thing.

Now from a positivist position there is no justification for this heartfelt advice. Graglia may feel strongly about this matter but by the tenets of Humean moral skepticism the fact, say, that the Constitution grants women the vote does not prove that justices ought to invalidate any law that prohibits the vote. From the "is" of what the Constitution asserts no "ought" could follow, according to Hume, as to what anyone ought to do. (As to how best to understand Hume in this context, I would defer to those who claim that he was opposing only the extreme rationalistic efforts to deduce moral oughts, not the more common ones of drawing moral inferences from our understanding of human affairs.)

If the response were that, well, it is inconsistent to be a justice of the Supreme Court and also refuse to uphold the provisions of that Court, the answer is, so what? Why ought one to be consistent? It is just some people's preference, is it not? Furthermore, neither does it hold, as many positivists maintain, that what ought to be honored in the law is what the people—i.e., the majority of those of them who vote and their elected representatives—want. So what if the people want A (the "is") and the justice honors not-A (the "ought")? No objection can be made against this by legal positivists.

On the score of consistency, incidentally, if the positivist admits that at least justices ought to be consistent in their decisions with the document they took an oath to uphold, it is then not much of a leap of logic for one to argue that they ought to be consistent with the implications of that document. For example, if the positivist accepts that the Constitution endorses nearly universal democracy, and if democracy presupposes certain societal provisions—e.g., the right to privacy, private property, political participation, freedom of speech, freedom of association, equal treatment under the law, etc.—the legal positivist would have to accept, also, that justices ought to reject all those laws that render democracy inoperable. Are the provisions listed above good candidates for what democracy—and thus the Constitution—requires? Well, democracy involves the uncoerced decision of a member of a community to select one of several alternatives to promote as a principle of community life. Without those provisions there is no such absence of coercion. If one has no right to privacy, private property, equal treatment under the law, etc., then democracy is impossible;—the voter lacks independence and will very possibly be threatened by any decision he or she reaches that does not favor the majority. The voter will be unable to retreat to his or her dominion to escape repercussions for voting against the majority. The voter may be treated differently from other voters if he or she is not part of the majority.

Thus, it appears that even the most minimal normative content legal positivism accords to the process of lawmaking and jurisprudence commits the positivist to nearly everything that natural rights theorists advocate. Most significantly, of course, the positivist has made it impossible for him or her to advocate any normative claim, including the claim that democratic decisions ought to be honored by justices. There is simply, for the positivist, nothing to be said in favor of what justices ought to do that one could not, with equal validity from the positivist framework, deny that the justices ought to do. And such a theory must simply be declared hopelessly fruitless, unworkable, void, and null.

56. Rasmussen, "Essentialism, Values and Rights"; Douglas Den Uyl and Douglas Rasmussen, "Nozick on the Randian Argument," in *Reading Nozick,* Jeffrey Paul, ed. (Totowa, N.J.: Rowman & Littlefield, 1981), pp. 232–69. In *Human Rights and Human Liberties,* I put the matter as follows: "There are no intrinsically beautiful or good or right things, only things that are good,

right, or beautiful in relation to living entities for which things can be good, right, and beautiful in terms of purposes and goals" (p. 66).

57. This is what's so unreal about the kinds of cases that analytic philosophers use to test ethical principles—ones so ingeniously devised by, for example, Judith Jarvis Thomson. No theory of ethics—indeed, no theory of any kind outside perhaps metaphysics—should be held responsible for managing all imaginable cases.

Despite overdoing the testing of ethics by reference to such cases, some of those that are realistic should, in fact, be considered in the examination of an ethical system. When I suggest, for example, that courage might now and then conflict with prudence, I have in mind a case such as when a soldier must defend against an attack from the enemy but could easily imagine hiding, instead. The act of defense would involve courage, the act of hiding would involve prudence. One needs to consider the proper hierarchy of ethical principles in order to handle such a case. That is just what would be done in the study of military ethics.

58. Quoted in H. L. A. Hart, "Are There Any Natural Rights?" in *Human Rights*, Melden, ed., p. 61n. This appears to be a paraphrase of Locke's point, advanced in his *Second Treatise of Government*, Book 2, Chapter 19, 211–48.

59. This is part of the value of all the hoopla that has emerged from T. Kuhn's work in the philosophy of science. But see Tibor R. Machan, "Kuhn's Impossibility Proof and the Moral Element in Scientific Explanations," *Theory and Decision* (December 1974), Vol. 5, pp. 355-74.

60. For a detailed discussion of compossibility, see David L. Norton, *Personal Destinies, A Philosophy of Ethical Individualism* (Princeton: Princeton University Press, 1976).

61. For example, Eric Mack, "Egoism and Rights," and "Egoism and Rights Revisited," *The Personalist* (Autumn 1977), Vol. 57, pp. 282–87. See also Machan, "Prima Facie versus Natural (Human) Rights," *Journal of Value Inquiry*, Vol. 10 (1976), pp. 119–131.

62. Van den Haag, p. 49.

63. Ibid., p. 48.

64. Earl Conee, "Against Moral Dilemmas," *Philosophical Review* (January 1982), Vol. XCI, pp. 87–97.

65. See, again, my "Prima Facie versus Natural (Human) Rights."

66. Here is a passage that illustrates Aristotle's view: "Virtue is concerned with feeling and actions; praise and blame are bestowed on voluntary ones, pardon (sometimes also pity) on involuntary ones. To define and distinguish the voluntary and the involuntary is, therefore, essential if one is enquiring into virtue—and useful for legislators too, in connection with the assigning of honours and punishment" (*Nicomachean Ethics* III, 1, 1109b30).

67. Werner Jeager, *Aristotle* (London: Oxford University Press, 1934), p. 152.

68. David Ross, *Aristotle* (London: Methuen, 1964), p. 201.

69. I have read a draft of a forthcoming paper by Gray in which some of these issues are explored in greater detail. We will have wait until it appears

before we can tell whether its case is telling, although it is difficult to see
how Gray could avoid his problems without recanting at least those of his
remarks that rest on his flawed textual analysis of Aristotle.

It is worth noting that Gray makes much of two points against classical
liberalism, namely, its subjective individualism and its aspiration to universalism. On the first point, Gray characterizes individualism in a strictly sub-
jectivist way and this is clearly not necessary for classical liberalism. See,
e.g., my *Capitalism and Individualism*, as well as my *Individuals and Their
Rights*, in which I develop what I have called classical individualism as a
contrasting individualist position. See also Norton, *Personal Destinies*.

Concerning the nonuniversalizability of liberalism's principles, it is
worth noting that while no doubt some implications of these principles may
not be universally applicable—ought, after all, implies can, and some societal circumstances make no room for certain possibilities—the real issue is
whether the basics are objective, not universal. Cultural diversity can be
divided into the sensible, contextually warranted and the morally and politically intolerable varieties. Without some sense of what is basically right,
that distinction is impossible to make and we are left with having to accept
the killing of wives in India for the sake of collecting a new dowry as simply a different cultural practice. Indeed, Gray's own effort to criticize cannot
escape a certain measure of universalization. After all, should someone in a
given culture advance the thesis of universalizability, Gray would argue against
such an individual. So his own criticism of the alleged cultural imperialism
of classical liberalism cannot help but amount to a kind of cultural imperialism. So we are left with the question, which of these transcultural systems
of standards or criteria is the sound one? We lack the option of engaging in
the discussion without any concern for that issue, as Gray seems to think we
may proceed.

70. Tibor R. Machan, *The Pseudo-Science of B. F. Skinner* (New Roch-
elle, NY: Arlington House, 1974). See also Roger W. Sperry, *Science and
Moral Priority* (New York: Columbia University Press, 1983).

71. Karl Popper, *The Open Society and Its Enemies* (Princeton: Princeton
University Press, 1953).

72. Bambrough, *Moral Skepticism and Moral Knowledge*.

73. Gray has recently identified himself with a rather forceful conserva-
tism. See, e.g., his review of Adam Seligman, *The Idea of Civil Society* (New
York: Free Press, 1992), in "Authority's Ghost," *The New York Times Book
Review* (September 13, 1992), p. 26.

74. I explore this in greater detail in *Individuals and Their Rights*. The
main point is that our encounter with the universe clearly suggests a great
variety of types and kinds of beings and while in some cases we may be
mistaken in the belief that there exists a difference of type or kind while it
merely appears to be so, in other cases it is not reasonable to expect the
success of a reduction, say, from musical harmony to physical matter or
process, from self-awareness to brain process, from literary excellence to
chemical events.

75. I have in mind, in particular, Sperry's work, as outlined in *Science and Moral Priority.*

76. "Transhistorical" is not the same as "transcendent." What transhistorical involves is the stability of certain standards of right and wrong throughout the history of a distinctive species of agents who must, given the kinds of beings they are, choose their conduct. Some fundamental choices are going to be sound for them any time, any place, although many of the derivative decisions may be different because of historical variables. Thus, while it may turn out that certain virtues, such as thoughtfulness or right reason, will never be dispensable for a good human life, other moral alternatives, vis-à-vis parenting, citizenship, or familial loyalty, will vary from culture to culture or even more particularly.

77. It may be instructive, and should be taken into consideration in the assessment of the respective views, that the natural rights theory of Locke gave impetus to the eventual emergence of such documents as the United Nations Universal Declaration of Human Rights, certainly a transcultural instrument of moral and political influence. While this may not be a document that fulfills its task flawlessly, it goes a good way toward stressing the propriety of such an approach. It is difficult, indeed, to see how Gray's multiculturalism—buttressed, at one point, with a reference to Feyerabend's epistemological anarchism—can make any sense of any kind of criticism, even that which he engages in, not to mention those involved in chiding a Soviet Union, South Africa, Chile, Iraq, or other cultures for inhumanities.

78. In the last analysis skepticism is so nihilistic that it robs the proponent of the position of any justification for saying anything at all, even critical. Why should we, from a skeptical perspective, accept any meaning of the words being spoken?

79. MacIntyre, *After Virtue*, p. 69. For whether the historicist position, e.g., of MacIntyre, is historically accurate about rights in particular, see Brian Tierney, "Origins of Natural Rights Language: Text and Contexts, 1150–1250," *History of Political Thought* (Winter 1989), Vol. 10, pp. 615–46, and "Conciliarism, Corporatism, and Individualism: The Doctrine of Individual Rights in Gerson," *Christianesimo hella Storia* (1988), Vol. 9, pp. 81–111.

80. Ibid., 228.

81. Karl Marx, *Grundrisse* (New York: Harper and Row, 1972, abridged), p. 33. For how well developed this idea has become, often not even clearly linked with Marx, see Catharine A. Mackinnon, *Feminism Unmodified* (Cambridge: Harvard University Press, 1987). See also Alan Freeman and Elizabeth Mensch, "The Public-Private Distinction in American Law and Life," *Buffalo Law Review* (1987), Vol. 36, pp. 237–57. It is instructive to note that if we are to understand philosophical arguments for natural rights along Marxist lines, such that they are designed, even if inadvertently, to serve some special or vested interests, this can cut deep enough to indict Marxism as well as other views that employ it. For example, arguably one likely consequence of implementing the anti-individualist, anti-individual rights position is to strengthen the power of the state or government over against the

claims of citizens. In short, this position fosters state power. One might then hold, consistent with the Marxist analysis, that these arguments against individuals have as their ulterior motive nothing other than statism, the gaining of full or totalitarian legal power over human individuals. Yet the real question is not what motivates these views but whether they are right.

82. Here the point earlier made vis-à-vis skepticism about universal principles holds against historicists, also. These self-reflexive arguments are not without their serious punch, using, as they do, the common logical rule of substitution to test various claims. For more on these kinds of issues, see *Reason Papers* (Fall 1991), No. 17, "Rethinking Foundationalism." See also Machan, "Evidence of Necessary Existence."

83. For an interesting history of ideas on the concept of the individual, see J. D. P. Boldton, *Glory, Jest and Riddle, A Study of the Growth of Individualism from Homer to Christianity* (New York: Barnes and Noble, 1973). But see also John O. Lyons, *The Invention of the Self* (Carbondale: Southern Illinois University Press, 1978).

84. See Tibor R. Machan, "Law, Justice and Natural Rights," *Western Ontario Law Review* (Fall 1975), Vol. 14, pp. 119–30.

85. Gilbert Harman, *Thought* (Princeton: Princeton University Press, 1973), p. 145.

Comments by Robert C. Solomon

I found much that was of interest in Tibor R. Machan's essay on justice, the self and natural rights, and there are any number of fairly predictable queries, elaborations and countermoves to be made following and against his familiar line of reasoning. But what I would like to note, unjustly at Professor Machan's expense, is a more general observation about the kind of essay it is, the type of argument it pursues, the questions it raises—and ignores.

On the one hand, I quite agree with his insistence on "naturalism," which he rightly contrasts with the "purely conventional." But I also share the "skeptics" fear that such thinking too readily lends itself to "dogmatism and authoritarianism." I do not think that Lockean naturalism presents such a clear and present danger in this regard, and despite the danger of political incorrectness I myself still find much to admire in Locke's own rather modest and much qualified conception of certain natural rights, although I would want to contextualize and historicize his discussion (and those rights) in a quasi-Hegelian framework that would no doubt be much to Machan's displeasure and much more cumbersome than this comment (or its readers) could bear.

Quite apart from the arguments over natural rights and the debates about which natural rights deserve our primary attention, there is the structure of the argument itself, which I will simply refer to, following Robert Nozick (but without attributing its originality to him), as a "top-down" account of justice. It is an account that formally begins with metaphysics and ontology and then derives certain controversial ethical conclusions. Some readers, no doubt, will be troubled by the "is-ought" inference that is embedded in such an argument. I have no problem with that, and, indeed, I agree with Machan that an adequate study of justice requires an investigation of human nature, but I would also argue, against his crude distinction between "instinct" and rationality (pp. 71–72), that this should include a careful study of "instinct" as well as (again going beyond his overly sharp distinction between nature and convention) the concrete cultivation and many variations of that nature in particular societies.

David Miller, in a too-neglected book called *Social Justice* some years ago, used a series of anthropological and historical studies to understand the very different conceptions of "nature" and "justice" that he found manifested in different human societies. Only one of these, not surprisingly, a predominately "market" society, included a primary conception of rights. Machan tells us that "human beings may also have some instincts, but this . . . is negligible," and "people in maturity are able to choose what they will do." As a card-carrying existentialist, I could hardly disagree with that, but what is missing here is the menu—including the psychological menu—from which mature people make their choices.

Maturity, I take it, has much to do with the cultivation and internalization of the mores, values and beliefs of a particular society. To become a mature English capitalist is not the same as becoming a mature Maori elder. I do not deny that there are choices, even radical choices, to be made against the grain of one's whole society and upbringing. An English capitalist could, with enormous effort, become part of and accepted into a nonindividualistic, nonpossessive tribal society, just as a Maori might migrate to Auckland in search of fun and fortune as an isolated, alienated individual. But culture provides the background, what Sartre calls "the situation," and justice is defined within culture—as is "nature." To be a naturalist in human affairs is to be, in part, an anthropologist. The mistake is thinking that "nature" implies universality, rather than the riches of variation and differences. I think that Machan gets it right, but without realizing just what he is admitting, when he writes that "the just political community is what it is because it accurately reflects the requirements of human nature within the context of community life." (p. 73)

What bothers me overall is the familiar fuss about "grounding" natural rights. Why does the universality of certain principles of justice—or at any rate of certain rational procedures—appear to be such a recurrent obsession with so many philosophers? Perhaps the unfortunate dichotomy between universal rationality and chaos is never far below the surface. But what would follow if there were (as there are) real differences in conceptions of justice (and occasionally *no* conception of justice) from culture to culture, from context to context? Why should we think all disagreements are "rationally" resolvable, and what if (as it happens) they are not? Apart from a rather obvious *political* agenda, why should we be concerned to show that some version of Lockean rights—"negative" rights—should apply equally well in cultures whose sense of self is irreducibly communal, whose sense of work, reward and responsibility is very different from ours. Machan's use of "nature" and "natural," despite their generous implications, thus serves an old and familiar purpose, to impose a very narrow political conception of human beings and their societies and render as a matter of logic the conclusion that everyone, "developing" or "developed," is ultimately just like us.

Behind every theory of justice lies a political agenda. This does not mean that theories of justice are merely devious, or that they are mere rationalizations, although, to be sure, some are. Some are self-congratulatory and self-serving. But some are guilt-ridden and self-condemning, some are merely self-righteous and some are intricate attempts to portray oneself as above the fray or, perhaps, to present oneself as a decent-minded and compassionate human being without, of course, allowing mere sentiment to sully one's philosophical credentials. Socrates had his own political agenda, and it was (as repeated by Plato) neither hidden nor, to our eyes, benign. We seem too conveniently to forget that his philosophical playfulness was ultimately a demolition of democracy, a demonstration of the ignorance of the many and a defense of the few (as it turned out, certainly the wrong few at that). Socrates seems to seek an answer to the question, "what is justice?" but I would suggest that this is precisely what Socrates so deftly shows cannot be done. Acts must always be viewed in context, and their justice (or injustice) depends upon the characters and circumstances involved. It is not just, for example, to return arms to a madman, nor is it just simply to reward one's friends (not to mention getting even with one's enemies). What the *Republic* gives us is *context*, not unlike the Athens of the Golden Age. But justice cannot be defined. It has to be lived, together.

Comments by James P. Sterba

There is much in Tibor Machan's "Justice, Self and Natural Rights" that I agree with. In this essay, Machan's main aim is to defend a natural rights view against opposing utilitarian, skeptical, historist and relativist perspectives.[1] With this general defense of natural rights, I am in full agreement. Machan's view and my own differ, however, with respect to certain particular details. But these details are very important. They concern the practical requirements of the libertarian ideal of liberty. I contend the libertarian's ideal of liberty, properly understood, requires a right to welfare and a right to equal opportunity. Machan maintains that these are not the practical requirements of the libertarian ideal for the societies in which we live.

In my own contribution to this volume, I discuss Machan's earlier response to my own argument concerning the practical requirements of the libertarian ideal of liberty. In this response, Machan criticizes my argument that a libertarian ideal of liberty leads to a right to welfare, accepting its theoretical thrust but denying its practical significance.[2] He appreciates the force of the argument enough to grant that if the type of conflict cases that we have described between the rich and the poor actually obtained, the poor would have a right to welfare. But he denies that such cases—in which the poor have done all that they legitimately can to satisfy their basic needs—actually obtain, or, as he puts it, "are typical."[3] "Normally," he writes, "persons do not lack the opportunities and resources to satisfy their basic needs."[4]

It would appear that the issue that Machan and I should settle is whether or not the poor today typically have opportunities and resources to satisfy their basic needs. This is the issue I was attempting to settle in my contribution to this volume. But there is another line of argument that Machan may want to pursue. It is touched on briefly in Machan's earlier critique, and it is taken up in greater detail in his comments on my paper in this volume.

In my paper, I responded only briefly to this line of argument because I really wasn't sure that Machan really wanted to pursue this line of argument given that it proceeds from premises that contradict his other response to my argument.[5] While Machan's first response turned on the claim that "normally, persons do not lack the opportunities and resources to satisfy their basic needs," Machan's second response concedes that many of the poor lack the opportunities and resources to satisfy their basic needs but then contends that this lack is the result of political oppression in the absence of libertarian institutions.

Now one might try to reconcile these two lines of argument by interpreting the first as claiming that normally *in libertarian societies* the poor do not lack the opportunities and resources to satisfy their basic needs, and the second as claiming that *in actual societies* many of the poor lack the opportunities and resources to satisfy their basic needs. But this won't do because when Machan makes his "normally claim" he goes on to refer to typical conditions in actual societies, whereas his second line of argument assumes that no actual society is sufficiently libertarian.[6]

But suppose Machan were to abandon his first line of argument for his second. Since Machan presents only his second line of argument in his comments on my paper in this volume, one might even speculate that the argument that I set out in my paper might have actually led Machan to take just this step, although in his comments Machan nowhere suggests that he is abandoning his first line of argument in favor of his second line of argument, which contradicts the first. In any case, how good is this second line of argument?

Machan's second line of argument seeks to place the main responsiblity for the fate of the poor on nonlibertarian political oppressors, but he also suggests that because of the existence of political oppression, there is something the poor can do to meet their basic needs which they are not doing: they can throw off their political oppressors and create libertarian societies. So, according to this line of argument, the poor's lack of resources to meet their basic needs is to some degree their own fault. They could throw off their political oppressors but they have not done so.

Clearly, this is to place responsibility for the fate of the poor where it does not belong. In actual societies, where the poor are oppressed they have little or no political power to change the political system under which they live. Under conditions of oppression, virtually all of the responsibility for the failure to meet the basic needs of the poor must be placed on the political oppressors themselves and on those who benefit from such a system but fail to oppose it.

Granting that this is the case, what is the remedy? We can all agree that oppressive societies must be transformed into nonoppressive ones, but Machan contends that this involves transforming them into libertarian societies as well. Actually, I have no objection to this, provided that it is recognized that within a libertarian society the liberty of the poor takes precedence over the liberty of the rich to the extent required to secure a right to welfare and a right to equal opportunity. Machan wants to resist this interpretation of libertarianism, but to do so he needs to show how the denial of these rights to the poor is not itself a form of oppression that conflicts with the "ought" implies "can" principle and the conflict resolution principle as I have interpreted them in my paper. I don't see how it can succeed in doing this.

There is the further question of how radical the transformations would have to be to change oppressive societies into libertarian societies. Machan suggests that the changes that are necessary are fairly minimal, but a closer analysis suggests that only a radical transformation would do the job. This is because in oppressive societies wealth and resources have usually been concentrated in the hands of a few. To transform an oppressive into a nonoppressive society, this inequality of wealth and resources would have to be eliminated. One way to do this would be to radically redistribute wealth and resources in favor of the poor. In fact, I have argued that such a radical redistribution of wealth and resources is required by the libertarian's own ideal of liberty. But Machan does not want to radically redistribute wealth and resources in this way. The kind of changes that Machan seems content with would not directly challenge the current unequal distribution of wealth and resources in existing oppressive societies, but only rule out certain oppressive or coercive ways of acquiring wealth and resources in the future. But this is like stopping a race in which some runners have been force to wear heavy weights while others were left unemcumbered, and then continuing the race after doing no more than letting the runners with weights remove them. Surely, this would not suffice to make the results of the race fair. There is a need for some kind of corrective to compensate for the advantage enjoyed by those runners who ran the whole race unemcumbered. Similarly, more needs to be done to transform oppressive societies into unoppressive ones than Machan seems willing to do. After blaming oppressive social structures for the plight of the poor, Machan seems reluctant to take the steps required to secure the basic needs of the poor. Why then does he balk at taking any further steps? Could it be that he does not see the oppression of the poor as truly oppressive after all? But that would be to return to his first line of argument (which contradicts his second) against which the argument of my paper would hold.

Notes

1. Not all utilitarian views need oppose a natural rights view. Some might

be quite compatible with such a view. Or at least this is what I contend in *How To Make People Just*, pp. 35–45.

2. *Individuals and their Rights* (La Salle, Ill.: Open Court, 1989), pp. 100–111.

3. *Ibid.*, pp. 106–110.

4. *Ibid.*, p. 107.

5. James P. Sterba, "Reconciling Conceptions of Justice."

6. *Ibid.*, p. 107.

3

Toward a Feminist Conception of Moral Reasoning

Alison M. Jaggar

This essay is part of a longer work in progress.[1] It is my first attempt to discuss in print some aspects of a model of moral reasoning practiced by several groups of North American feminist activists from the late 1960s until the present. I call the model "Feminist Practical Dialogue" or FPD. FPD continues the discursive tradition of moral reasoning developed by Western philosophers such as Plato, John Stuart Mill, John Rawls, and Jürgen Habermas but it suggests an alternative understanding of moral discourse, as well as alternative understandings of associated concepts such as moral subjectivity, moral community, and moral justification. These alternative understandings seem to me empirically, conceptually, morally, and pragmatically more satisfactory than those found in most nonfeminist conceptions of moral reasoning. In this essay, I begin to explore FPD's understandings of moral discourse as well as to raise some questions about its strengths and limits. First, however, I'd like to make some comments about the sense in which I take FPD to be feminist.

Certainly not all feminists subscribe to FPD; many have other views of how moral reasoning should be practiced.[2] In addition, FPD has drawn inspiration from various nonfeminist conceptions of moral reasoning and incorporates elements from these.[3] Nevertheless, FPD is feminist in a sense stronger than simply that of having been developed by self-identified feminists. Some have argued that consensual approaches to moral reasoning, of which FPD is one, come more easily to contemporary Western women than to their male counterparts since women are thought to be better listeners than men and more committed to the empowerment of others (Iannello 1992). Whether or not this is empirically true, FPD certainly incorporates features that, in Western culture, are symbolically feminine, including the values of caring for specific individuals, sharing intimate feelings, and emphasizing concrete experience over abstract ideals. But *feminine* thinking is not *feminist*, even though a reassessment of the traditionally feminine must be a part of the feminist project, and in any case FPD also embodies values, such as equality and fairness, that are associated with masculine moral thinking. Just as the incorporation of feminine values does not render FPD feminist, neither does FPD become feminist by adding masculine values to the feminine in a mix that might be called androgynous. Instead, I regard FPD as feminist primarily because it revises both feminine and masculine values in the light of a distinctively feminist commitment to ending women's subordination.

Feminist Practical Dialogue

Modern Western feminism has revolved around the complementary themes of women being silenced and women regaining their voices. It was the prohibition on women abolitionists speaking in public that sparked the emergence of nineteenth-century feminism in the United States, and the ensuing campaigns for women's suffrage may be seen as struggles to gain a voice for women in the conduct of public affairs. When North American feminism was revived in the late 1960s, it continued to be preoccupied with voice, a concern beautifully expressed by Adrienne Rich.

> One of the most powerful social and political catalysts of the past decade has been the speaking of women with other women, the telling of our secrets, the comparing of wounds and the sharing of words. This hearing and saying of women has been able to break many a silence and taboo; literally to transform forever the way we see . . . And so I begin tonight by urging each of you to take responsibility for the voicing of her experience, to take seriously the work of listening to each other and the work of speaking, whether in private dialogue or in larger groups. In order to change what is, we need to give speech to what *has been,* to imagine together what *might be* (Rich 1979).

Speaking was not invented by contemporary feminists, of course;

people have always talked with each other. Speech is a distinguishing characteristic of human beings and it is primarily through talking that we become members of a human community and acquire much of our most basic knowledge. In societies that have developed literacy, however, speech is usually thought to be less authoritative than the written word and the knowledge transmitted through oral discourse is typically regarded as suspect: as unreliable or, at best, as "folk wisdom." Nevertheless, even in advanced industrial societies speech remains an important source of insight or knowledge for some subcultural groups. Patricia Hill Collins asserts that, in the African American community, the use of dialogue continues to be vital in assessing knowledge claims. She writes: "the use of dialogue has deep roots in an African-based oral tradition and in African-American culture," and she cites the widespread use of the call-and-response discourse mode among African Americans as illustrating the continuing importance placed on dialogue (Collins 1990:212).

Recent feminist psychologists have claimed that North American women in general, including college-educated women of European ancestry, are more likely than their male counterparts to value discourse as a source of knowledge. They assert that women frequently "ground their epistemological premises in metaphors suggesting speaking and listening" rather than in "visual metaphors (such as equating knowledge with illumination, knowing with seeing, and truth with light)" (Belenky et al. 1986:18). Men talk to each other too, of course, but

> The differences between the women's conversation and the male bull session were strikingly reminiscent of the differences . . . noted between the play of fifth-grade girls and boys: intimate rather than impersonal, relatively informal and unstructured rather than bound by more or less explicit formal rules. Women have been practicing this kind of conversation since childhood (Belenky et al., 1986:114).

Given this cultural context, it is not surprising that contemporary Western feminists emphasize speaking between women as a primary means of determining feminist action and developing feminist understanding. In what follows, I offer several examples of how, over the past two decades, grass-roots activists have assigned a central role to spoken discourse. For description of the feminist discursive practices, I rely mostly, though not exclusively, on documents circulated among activists in typescript form or published by small "underground" or "alternative" presses.

Consciousness Raising

"Consciousness raising," often referred to affectionately as c.r., is one of the best-known inventions of contemporary Western feminism. Reaching the height of its popularity in the late 1960s and early 1970s, consciousness raising groups are small gatherings of women meeting in private to share experiences hitherto thought of as personal. The operating assumption of the consciousness raising process is that much so-called personal experience, rather than being idiosyncratic, in fact is characterized by a number of common features frequently manifesting male dominance—hence the slogan "The personal is political." During consciousness raising sessions, participants offer firsthand accounts of specific personal experiences, describing not only who said and did what to whom but also the speakers' own emotional responses to the events. Honesty and vulnerability are valued in c.r. groups, which emphasize that no aspect of experience is too trivial for respectful attention. Questions to clarify or stimulate reflection are encouraged, but hearers are expected to be "nonjudgmental," that is, to refrain from criticizing a speaker's conduct or disputing her account of her own experience. C.r. sessions are intended primarily to increase both the speakers' and the hearers' awareness of how women are subordinated in daily life, that is, to "raise their consciousness." The process is also designed, however, to provide emotional or moral support for individual women in order to strengthen them in resisting subordination.[4]

Feminist Health Care Activism

Our Bodies, Our Selves is now a best-selling feminist self-help manual, published in several editions by a major publishing house, but initially it was produced by a small "underground" press, the New England Free Press, and sold for 35 cents. It was written by the Boston Women's Health Course Collective as a text for a feminist course on "health, women, and our bodies," first offered at Boston's Emmanuel College in May 1969. The first edition of *Our Bodies, Our Selves* (originally titled *Women and Their Bodies* and published in December 1970) describes how a feminist conception of healthy embodiment was developed through collective discussion.

The course planners began by sharing their own experiences and their knowledge of sickness, health, and medical care, soon discovering that "there were no 'good' doctors and we had to learn for ourselves." For more information, they went to books and to medically trained people, deciding collectively on the topics for resarch and how those topics should be handled. They met weekly to discuss their research, "gave support and helpful criticisms to each other and rewrote the papers." They then shared their collective knowledge with other "sisters," who "added their questions, fears, feelings, excitement." They insisted that their published results were "not final," "not static," but rather "a tool which stimulates discussion and action, which allows for new ideas and for change" (Boston Women's Health Course Collective 1970:1).

> Often, our best presentations of the course were done by a group of women (we could see a collective at work—in harmony, sharing, arguing, disagreeing) with questions throughout. . . . It was more important that we talked about our experiences, were challenged by others' experiences (often we came from very different situations), raised our questions, expressed our feelings, were challenged to act, than that we learned any specific body of material.

> It was exciting to learn new facts about our bodies, but it was even more exciting to talk about how we felt about our bodies, how we felt about ourselves, how we could become more autonomous human beings, how we could act together on our collective knowledge to change the health care sytem for women and for all people." (Boston Women's Health Course Collective 1970:1–2).

In this account of its work process by the Boston Women's Health Course Collective, we find early statements of several themes that recur in later accounts of feminist process. The themes include a recognition that difference and even disagreement are not only inevitable but epistemically valuable, a willingness to acknowledge and explore people's emotional reactions, and an acceptance of technical expertise as necessary but not sufficient for an adequate understanding of women's health care needs. Above all, the themes include a conviction that, for students as well as instructors in the course, "the process that developed in the group became as important as the material we were learning." For these feminist activists, discussion was not just an efficient means to the end of acquiring new factual information about health care or even a means for developing critical evaluations of existing health care delivery systems. It was also a process that developed the moral capacities of each participant and the group as a whole.

Feminist Antimilitarist Activism

In another feminist enterprise, undertaken more than a decade later, antimilitarist activists developed an explicit formulation of the norms of feminist practical dialogue. This formulation can be found in the *Women's Encampment for a Future of Peace and Justice: Resource Handbook*. Inspired by the women besieging the U.S. military base at Greenham Common in England, a feminist "peace camp" was established in the summer of 1983 at Seneca Army Depot in upstate New York. The *Women's Encampment Handbook* is a 50-page pamphlet distributed free to camp participants. It includes information on Seneca Army Depot and the surrounding area, some history of feminist activism in the region and a great deal of feminist philosophy of nonviolence. It also sets out guidelines for collective decision-making by consensus.

The *Women's Encampment Handbook* echoes the aspirations of the Kantian (as opposed to the Hobbesian) contractarian tradition in stating clearly that consensus decision-making differs in principle not only from majority rule but also from bargaining. "Coercion and trade-offs are replaced with creative alternatives, and compromise with synthesis" (*Women's Encampment Handbook* 1983:42). It also offers a brief statement of the moral presuppositions of consensus decision-making. "The fundamental right of consensus is for all people to be able to express themselves in their own words and of their own free will. The fundamental responsibility of consensus is to assure others of their right to speak and be heard" (*Women's Encampment Handbook* 1983:42).

Most of the *Handbook*'s brief discussion is concerned less with elaborating philosophical assumptions than it is with the practical steps of moving towards consensus. In this connection, it identifies several roles that, if filled, may help consensus decision-making run smoothly. The roles include those of facilitator, recorder, and so-called "vibeswatcher," the last of whom "watches and comments on individual and group feelings and patterns of participation" (*Women's Encampment Handbook* 1983:42). The *Handbook* also lists various morally permissible alternatives if consensus cannot be reached. These are nonsupport, expressing reservations, standing aside, blocking, and withdrawing from the group.

An especially interesting feature of the *Handbook*'s account of consensus decision-making is its statement of what is required of individuals who engage in this process. The requirements are as follows:

Responsibility: Participants are responsible for voicing their opinions, participating in the discussion, and actively implementing the agreement.

Self-discipline: Blocking consensus should only be done for principled objections. Object clearly, to the point, and without putdowns or speeches. Participate in finding an alternative solution.

Respect: Respect others and trust them to make responsible input.

Cooperation: Look for areas of agreement and common ground and build on them. Avoid competitive, right/wrong, win/lose thinking.

Struggle: Use clear means of disagreement—no putdowns. Use disagreements and arguments to learn, grow and change. Work hard to build unity in the group, but not at the expense of the individuals who are its members (*Women's Encampment Handbook* 1983:42).

In striking contrast with Robert's Rules of Order, these requirements do not define specific procedures for the conduct of practical dialogue. Instead, they recommend the cultivation of certain moral attitudes or virtues and trust the reader to figure out how these attitudes or virtues should be manifested on specific occasions. They illustrate concretely what it means to pursue consensus rather than compromise, and show how, rather than fragmenting the community, the search for consensus may actually strengthen it and promote its moral development.[5]

Feminist Pegagogy

The preceding examples implicitly assume that participants in feminist dialogue enjoy something approaching a peer relationship. In fact, however, relations between women are frequently characterized by inequality rather than equality and some North American feminists have addressed this fact directly.[6] One good source for reflecting on inequality is feminist pedagogy, which addresses the dialogical constraints as well as opportunities inherent in the context of an academic institution, where credentialed instructors are paid to instruct, where students pay for instruction, and where credits and grades are conferred.

Classrooms do indeed offer a space for dialogue that is relatively free from some kinds of distractions and disruptions but in which the time available for speaking is rigidly limited and there are inevitable power differences between teachers and students. These inequalities are based not just on varying experience and expertise but also on the institutionally assigned power to grade—and to some extent on the student's power as a consumer of education. In addition, and except in the most homogeneous classrooms, there are power differences among students—and conflicts that often are related to these differences. Such inequalities, combined with the introduction of course material that may be highly emotive, are likely to stimulate extremely powerful feelings that must be somehow handled in the course of classroom discussion.

Instructors of courses in feminist studies see their job as being to facilitate open dialogue in the face of these difficulties and they have worked to develop specific ways of guaranteeing respect for all present, while acknowledging the variety and limitations of each person's experience, knowledge, ability, and social power. They have sought to acknowledge speakers' thoughts and feelings respectfully without accepting them uncritically. In short, they have tried to integrate "egalitarian content and process" into a situation where people in many respects are unequal (Schniedewind 1983:262).

Nancy Schniedewind begins her women's studies courses with interpersonal exercises for developing an "atmosphere of mutual respect, trust, and community in the classroom." She emphasizes that "Democratic processes among students are important for community and mutual respect," and notes that "the more aware each woman is of her use or abuse of time, attention, and power within the class, the more potentially democratic the group process" (1983:262). She also remarks that "festive procedures are community-builders. Refreshments during breaks, a potluck dinner, and the integration of poetry and songs into the course, all catalyze energy and build community" (1983:263). Like many other feminist teachers, Schniedewind uses various devices to foster cooperation among students and to integrate affective and practical learning with cognitive development. She suggests that pass/fail options or contract grading help both to reduce the instructor's power and to eliminate competitiveness between students (Schniedewind, 1983:268).

Schniedewind combines a strong commitment to feminist principles with a recognition of the difficulties in applying them. She endeavors to share leadership with her students but does not have "a totally egalitarian classroom." "I take more leadership and have more power than any of the students. I have found that students need an arena in which to *learn* to take responsibility for themselves and the group. For many, this is a new experience. I no longer expect that they automatically come to class with those experiences and skills." (Schniedewind 1983:265)

Rachel Martin, a white feminist working outside academia with black women who possessed few literacy skills, also found that a necessary prerequisite to dialogue was the establishment of a sense of community with her students. Like Schniedewind and her students, Martin and her students moved toward community through sharing personal experience and forms of mutual aid such as food, sympathy, massages, and haircuts (Martin 1989).

Feminist reflections on pedagogy provide one resource for considering how open and productive dialogue may occur even in a context that sets a variety of constraints. Especially noteworthy is feminist instructors' conscious concern with establishing a sense of community as a prerequisite to dialogue, despite the inevitable presence of inequalities. Working to establish such a sense of community requires feminists to recognize in practical ways that people are not simply "talking heads." Thus, feminists attend not only to the explicit content of assertions made but also to the speaker's emotional and physical needs, providing not only an attentive ear but food, drink, haircuts, and hugs. Finally, feminist instructors remain continually conscious that even adults are not finished or complete but are constantly changing and developing. This consciousness is especially clearly articulated in Schniedewind's assertion that democracy requires more than the institution of certain rules of procedure; the ability to utilize such rules appropriately requires that people possess certain moral capacities that can be developed only by practicing them.

African American Women's Dialogue

My final example of feminist reliance on spoken dialogue is drawn from the work of Patricia Hill Collins, who has asserted that the use of dialogue is especially characteristic of Afrocentric feminist epistemology insofar as it draws both on African American modes of gaining knowledge and on women's traditional "ways of knowing." Collins's account of black women's dialogue echoes many of the themes noted already. They include the importance of personal experience in assessing knowledge claims and the epistemic significance of emotion, characterized by Collins as part of an ethic of caring. For African American women, Collins writes, "personal expressiveness, emotions, and empathy are central to the knowledge validation process" (1990:215). She adds that, for African American women, "assessments of an individual's knowledge claims simultaneously evaluate an individual's character, values, and ethics." She reports that one of her classes of black women students "refused to evaluate the rationality of [a prominent Black male scholar's] written ideas without some indication of his personal credibility as an ethical human being" (1990:218). Thus, what Collins calls "an ethic of personal account-ability" is an additional dimension of an Afrocentric feminist episte-mology.

Collins insists that the dialogue in which black women engage is quite different from adversarial debate. Rather than being a weapon for verbal contest, dialogue is seen instead as fundamental to the cre-ation of community, the only context in which "people become more human and empowered" (1990:212).

FPD as an Idealization

Each of the practices described above offers a process for partic-ipants to recount their moral experience and then to reflect together critically on those accounts. While the practices differ somewhat from each other, I find them sufficiently similar to justify referring to them in the singular as FPD. In what follows, I discuss the conception of moral discourse implicit in FPD, drawing now on the work of other feminist philosophers as well as on the primary activist documents.

The conception of FPD that I discuss here is an idealization in the sense of being reconstructed from several different accounts. It is also an idealization in the sense that it focuses on the ideals that guide feminist discursive practices and the assumptions that underlie those ideals, ignoring questions about how far the ideals are ever instanti-ated. In fact, there is good reason to believe that in practice feminist dialogue often falls short of its own ideals. Many feminists, myself among them, can report efforts to engage in Feminist Practical Dia-logue that have been painful and unproductive and "free rider" prob-lems were reported at the Seneca Peace Encampment (Schwartz-Shea and Burrington 1990). This essay, however, is not an anthropological study of feminist culture nor an attempt either to romanticize or de-bunk it. Instead, it is a discussion of the philosophical assumptions and ideals implicit in one feminist model of moral reasoning.

Toward a Feminist Conception
of Moral Discourse

A discursive understanding of moral reasoning is not unique to contemporary feminism. Well over a century ago, John Stuart Mill extolled the benefits of free discussion in his classic essay *On Liber-ty*, and he has been followed in this century by neo-Kantian contractarian theorists such as John Rawls and communicative ethicists, such as Karl Otto Apel and Juergen Habermas. All have offered philosophical elaborations of the persistent conviction that the most reliable understandings are likely to emerge from unconstrained discussion between people who are clearheaded and well informed. But although FPD has arisen within the broad Western tradition of discursive approaches to justification/rationality, it offers distinctive perspectives on the crucial and contestible concepts of discursive openness, equality, freedom, and rationality.

Moral Deliberation in FPD

FPDs typically do not begin with the articulation of general moral rules or principles; instead, they begin with the creation of opportunities for participants to talk about their own lives. The importance placed on first-person narrative reflects the early radical feminists' conviction that the dominant understandings of reality, insofar as they had been male authored, had at best disregarded and at worst distorted or denied the truths of women's experience. The radical feminists of the late 1960s and early 1970s reacted to the neglect or misrepresentation of women's experience in moral and political analyses by asserting that the basis of moral and political understanding must be personal experience and the basis of feminist theory must be women's experience. In challenging accepted understandings of reality, therefore, feminists have been concerned that women begin by recounting their experience in their own terms. Rather than bracketing or disregarding their own experiences and concerns, participants in FPDs are encouraged to use them as the primary data of moral reflection. For FPDs, personal experience is a moral resource rather than a moral diversion.

First-person narratives may contribute to moral reflection in more than one way. Most obviously, they provide information about the lives of people whose situations may be very different from those of their hearers. It is a commonplace that our experience is broadened by learning about the experience of others. Of course, we may learn about other people's lives by reading or watching films or TV as well as by listening to them speak but personal interaction with a speaker makes a story especially vivid and immediate.

Listening to others recount their experience may increase our understanding of our own lives as well as those of others. It may help us to see hitherto unrecognized implications of our own actions; "helping" a disabled person without waiting for her request, for instance, may be to assume a position of power relative to her that reinforces a system of able-bodied privilege. Listening to others may also enable us to perceive commonalities in their experience and ours, a perception crucial to feminism. It has invariably been noticing similarities or patterns in the experience of different women that has precipitated the feminist recognition that many of women's supposedly "personal" problems result not from individual inadequacies but rather from social structures of male dominance (Frye 1990). With this recognition feminists become able to define as sexual harassment or date rape, for instance, moral and political problems that previously "had no name" (Friedan 1963).

Although FPD begins from the assumption that the experience of every woman is equally important, it does not assume that each person's account of her own experience is authoritative or incorrigible. For this reason, it would be misleading to describe feminist moral thinking as based in any simple sense on personal experience. While personal experiences are certainly the starting point of feminist moral thinking, they are not the building blocks of feminist moral theory. Instead, the experiences are reevaluated in a process of collective reflection that may transform the ways in which people think about their past situations and actions. To take a well-worn example, women may report enjoying male gallantry, interpreting this kind of attention as an expression of respect for women in general and themselves in particular. On further reflection, however, they may notice that this practice presupposes that women need male assistance and protection, thus covertly implying a lack of respect for their capabilities. Regardless of well-meaning intentions on both sides, men who behave gallantly toward women may then come to be seen as reinforcing male dominance and women who welcome this attention may be seen as colluding in reinforcing male dominant attitudes.

Although FPD begins with relatively naive descriptions of personal experience, it moves inevitably to revising these accounts by considering alternative modes of conceptualization. In the new conceptualizations, different elements are selected as morally significant; for instance, in discussing situations where women receive unwanted sexual attention or where they participate reluctantly in sexual interaction, feminists often emphasize elements of coercion that have been unremarked in previous accounts. A variety of discursive strategies may be employed in persuading others to perceive things differently. They include telling "counterstories" that highlight alternative features of situations, drawing attention to analogies with other situations, using language designed to arouse moral emotions such as disgust, pride, or shame, and encouraging imaginative identification with other people. Thus, feminist moral deliberation is typically herme-neutic, concerned to reinterpret experience and social reality.

Equality and Moral Deference

The broadening and deepening of moral experience envisioned by FPD is obviously much less likely to occur if we talk only with those whose experiences have been similar to our own. Enlarging our moral perspective requires that we speak with people whose lives have been very different from ours. FPD is concerned to include women of var-ious ages, physical abilities, class backgrounds, and racial or ethnic identifications, especially those women whose public silence has been the most profound. Since the few women permitted historically to participate in Western public discourse have been mostly women from the privileged classes, the most profoundly silenced women are pri-marily those from the working classes and other stigmatized groups, such as racial, ethnic, religious, or sexual minorities. Such women have found their voices not only muted but rendered virtually inaudi-ble, excluded almost completely from the public discourse.

FPD assumes that it is precisely those women who may be best able to provide moral insight and even moral inspiration, especially in certain areas. Socially located on the edges or the underside of the dominant culture, such women have firsthand experience of the far-reaching and subtle as well as immediate and blatant consequences of evils such as racism and class exploitation—and often they have de-veloped practical strategies for survival and resistance. Some femi-nists have asserted that the experience of less socially privileged women is not only different from that of women with more social advantages but also richer because it involves familiarity both with hegemonic and dissenting moral perspectives. Maria Lugones and Elizabeth V. Spelman write that "white/Anglo women are much less prepared for . . . dialogue with women of color than women of color are for dialogue with them in that women of color have had to learn white/Anglo ways, self-conceptions, and conceptions of them" (1983:577). To survive within a social system where they are at a systematic disadvantage, less privileged women must be acquainted with the dominant moral conceptualizations as well as with alterna-tive ways of thinking. Thus, they are sometimes said to have a kind of double vision or enlarged moral understanding or critical capacity.

Because the social location of less privileged women is thought to afford them a kind of moral epistemic privilege, FPD assumes that their speech is especially deserving of respectful attention, at least in certain areas. This assumption is reminiscent of the "moral deference" that Lawrence Thomas asserts we owe to what he calls "diminished social category" people, that is, to individuals who belong to social groups that are negatively and unjustly devalued. According to Thomas, moral deference involves a presumption in favor of the person's account of her experiences (1992–93). In the context of FPD, moral deference may also involve giving special weight to the meanings that the individual from the diminished social category assigns to the behavior of others as well as herself. If she is a woman of color, for instance, her allegations of racism on the part of others must be taken especially seriously.

Is the moral deference accorded to certain participants in FPD compatible with conceptions of moral reasoning that mandate the discursive equality of each participant? Certainly moral deference entails that the burden of justification is not distributed evenly among the participants: where relations between more and less privileged women are being evaluated, for instance, there is a presumption in favor of the account given by the less privileged speaker and in the next section we shall see that special pains are taken in FPD to ensure that women from disadvantaged groups may speak and be heard. These imbalances between participants in FPD clearly violate the principle of formal equality but they may be justified as strategies for assisting participants to attain a discursive equality that is substantive rather than formal. It is plausible to regard them as a kind of discursive affirmative action, necessary to counterbalance the socially imposed obstacles to some women's full participation in dialogue.

Even though FPD presumes that the contribution of hitherto silenced women is likely to be especially valuable, it does not assume that social deprivation results inevitably in superior moral understanding. On the one hand, as Thomas notes, it may fill its victims so full of bitterness and rancor that they perceive even innocent interactions as offensive. On the other hand, Uma Narayan has pointed out that women from subordinated cultures may be especially eager to conform with or assimilate into the dominant culture. Or they may be disempowered by feelings of schizophrenia or alienation or their critical capacities may be stunted or damaged rather than enlarged. Narayan writes:

> Certain kinds of oppressive contexts, such as the contexts in which women of my grandmother's background lived, rendered their subjects entirely devoid of skills required to function as independent entities in

the culture. Girls were married off barely past puberty, trained for nothing beyond household tasks and the rearing of children, and passed from economic dependency on their fathers to economic dependency on their husbands to economic dependency on their sons in old age. Their criticisms of their lot were articulated, if at all, in terms that precluded a desire for any radical change. They saw themselves as personally unfortunate, but they did not locate the causes of their misery in larger social arrangements (Narayan 1989:267–68).

She concludes,

[T]he alternative to buying into an oppressive social system need not be a celebration of exclusion and the mechanisms of marginalization. The thesis that oppression may bestow an epistemic advantage should not tempt us in the direction of idealizing or romanticizing oppression and blind us to its real material and psychic deprivations (Narayan, 1989:268).

While FPD requires that socially disempowered women be heard with special respect, it does not assume that any woman is a necessarily moral expert or authority. As Donna Haraway remarks, "*how to* see from below is a problem requiring . . . much skill with bodies and language" (1988:584). The same is presumably true for hearing from below or, to change the metaphor, from the margins. FPD is the practice that develops this skill.

Hearing Other Women

It is precisely because everyone's moral insight is limited that FPD emphasizes the need for interpersonal communication. But FPD is not easy; it is not simply a bunch of well-meaning people getting together and talking. Good will is necessary for the enterprise, but it is certainly not sufficient. Also required are effort, skill, and the practice of such virtues as responsibility, self-discipline, sensitivity, respect, and trust (*Women's Encampment Handbook* 1983:42). When the participants' past experiences have been very different from each other and when their present relations are quite unequal, practicing these skills and virtues may be especially necessary—and especially difficult.

From the earliest days of consciousness raising, FPD has emphasized the need to provide a nurturant and supportive environment so that participants will feel safe enough to speak openly of their experiences. Even when women voice their experience, however, we have seen that they cannot count on being heard. Lugones and Spelman have enumerated some of the difficulties that Hispana women face in communicating with white/Anglo women in the United States:

> We and you do not talk the same language. When we talk to you we use your language: the language of your experience and of your theories. We try to use it to communicate our world of our experience. But since your language and your theories are inadequate in expressing our experiences, we only succeed in communicating our experience of exclusion. We cannot talk to you in our language because you do not understand it. (Lugones and Spelman, 1983:575)

If white/Anglo women are to understand Hispana women, then, they must learn the Hispanas' "text." "But the text is an extraordinarily complex one: viz our many different cultures" (Lugones and Spelman 1983:580). Nevertheless,

> if white/Anglo women are to understand our voices, they must understand our communities and us in them. . . . This learning calls for circumspection, for questioning of yourselves and your roles in your own culture. . . . This learning is then extremely hard because it requires openness (including openness to severe criticism of the white/Anglo world), sensitivity, concentration, self-questioning, circumspection (Lugones and Spelman 1983:581).

Lugones and Spelman go on to ask why white/Anglo feminists should undertake the difficult project of learning to hear Hispana women. They suggest that possible motives include Anglo women's desires to make reparations for the past exclusion of women of color, to make alliances with them, or to facilitate the Anglo women's own self-growth or self-expansion. Lugones and Spelman, however, reject all such motives of duty, obligation or self-interest and conclude that "the motive of friendship remains as both the only appropriate and understandable motive" (1983:581).

In an article published four years later, Lugones elaborates her conception of intercultural discourse through the metaphor of "'world'-traveling," a metaphor that explains how some women may acquire a kind of double moral vision. Lugones writes that social outsiders, such as women of color in the United States, often are forced to practice world-traveling into the mainstream, whereas white/Anglo women often fail to see women of color, even *"while we are in their midst"* (author's italics). "(T)hey ignore us, ostracize us, render us invisible, stereotype us, leave us completely alone, interpret us as crazy" (Lugones 1987:7). Lugones remarks that these distorted perceptions are instances of what Marilyn Frye earlier had called "arrogant perception," and she herself characterizes them as failures of love.

Frye had written that those who see with arrogant eyes "organize everything seen with reference to themselves and their own interests" (Frye 1983:67). They misrepresent the moral situation "by mislabelling the unwholesome as healthy and what is wrong as right." One who sees with a loving eye, by contrast, is "separate from the other whom she sees" (1983:75). She "knows the independence of the other" and she "pays a certain sort of attention." She is attentive not only to the other, but also to herself, her own "interests, desires and loathings," her "projects, hungers, fears and wishes," and she is aware of how her own interests and emotions influence her perceptions of others (1983:75).

Patrocinio Schweickart develops this theme, noting that

> Being a good listener requires attentiveness to the needs and interests of two subjectivities. It means not only getting the speaker's arguments straight, but also trying to adopt his perspective, discern his assumptions and motives, identify with his feelings, feel his needs, understand what is at stake for him. In effect, the hearer must perform a service. She must put her subjectivity at the disposal of the speaker; she must cultivate and entertain, play host to, another subjectivity. At the same time, she must retain a lively sense of her own subjectivity; otherwise she risks losing the capacity for validating the speaker's claims, or of imposing her own subjective predispositions surreptitiously on the other (Schweickart, 1987:311).

For Frye, Lugones, and Schweickart, then, seeing and hearing are complex enterprises that may be done badly or well. They are active rather than passive processes which require, according to Frye, that listeners shift their loyalties away from men and men's projects and refocus their attention and their energy on women (Frye 1983:171–72). Such women include not only others but also oneself; self-knowledge is needed in order to hear others speak. In the context of a hierarchical, racist, and male-dominant society, seeing and hearing other women is said to require emotional and political reorientation, so that success in FPD becomes not simply a linguistic achievement but also a moral and political achievement.

This achievement is not made possible simply by the participants in the discourse committing themselves to certain abstract principles of discursive equality—or even to equal participation by representatives of certain groups.[7] Instead, FPD assumes that understanding between diverse people becomes possible only when those involved care for each other as specific individuals. It is significant that Lugones and Spelman propose the personal relation of friendship as the only appropriate motive for white/Anglo feminists to engage discursively with Hispanas and reject impersonal motivations such as duty. Only friendship, Lugones and Spelman write, will move white/Anglo women "to attain the appropriate reciprocity of care for your and our wellbeing as whole beings" (1983:581). Similarly, in the context of a paper describing the extreme difficulty of dialogue between English and Indian university women, Ann Seller asserts that some communication ultimately was made possible by "small acts of inclusion" such as sharing *puja* or invitations to watch television (1992:34). Ultimately, Seller writes, "I broke out of my isolation and they broke through the silence because of friendship, because of some shared political commitments and loyalties, and because sometimes we were in the same emotional world" (1992:29). Seller insists that dialogues occur only "intermittently on the basis of common concerns" and they take place between "people, not belief systems" (1992:33–34).

FPD insistence that communication occurs between particular people rather than abstract individuals or group representatives reflects its commitment to a kind of caring that requires knowing people in their concrete particularity rather than as representatives of certain disadvantaged groups. Such caring may be expressed in the process of dialogue by responses such as sympathy with another's anger, encouragement to overcome her timidity, or even concern for her physical needs. In insisting on the importance of caring for participants in discourse "as whole beings," as "concrete" rather than "generalized" others, feminists endorse one crucial aspect of the feminine value of care, namely, its focus on particular individuals, and refuse to reconceptualize it in abstract "masculine" terms.[8] However, because the caring practiced in FPD is critical as well as nurturant and because it consciously addresses social and political inequalities, it should be seen as a feminist rather than feminine form of care.

FPD as Nurturant rather than Adversarial

The most striking contrast between FPD and nonfeminist understandings of moral discourse is FPD's nurturant rather than adversarial nature. When described by nonfeminist moral theorists, the process of moral discussion sounds much like litigation or, at best, like collective bargaining—even when designed to produce an outcome that is morally justified and not simply pragmatically workable. For instance, Rawls refers to the participants in his hypothetical discourse in the legal terminology of "parties," Platonic dialogues resemble verbal battles in which Socrates invariably vanquishes his opponents and images of struggle are evoked when contemporary philosophers describe philosophical debates in terms of "protagonists" and the "force" of ideas. In the Western tradition, of course, an adversarial or agonistic understanding of argument is not peculiar to the moral philosophy. George Lakoff and Mark Johnson assert that it is common, in Western culture, to structure, perform, and talk about argument in terms derived from war (1980:5).

FPD, by contrast, distinguishes itself explicitly from adversarial debate (Collins 1990:212). In this context, feminists strive to develop modes of discursive interaction that are not structured by warlike metaphors. They do not seek to overwhelm each other by rational arguments. Instead, through a variety of specific practices, feminists try to support each other in reevaluating their initial conceptions of themselves and their experience, their history and culture, their relations to each other, and their perceptions of conflicting interests. In general, FPD is designed to promote an understanding and performance of moral discussion as a consciously cooperative and nurturant enterprise rather than a continuation of war by other means.

This is especially evident in the feminist insistence that moral discussion involves not only women's right to speak "in their own words and of their own free will" but also their responsibility "to assure others of their right to speak and be heard" (*Women's Encampment Handbook* 1983:42). FPD emphasizes good listening as much as, if not more than, good speaking and is distinguished by practices designed to encourage participants to feel that their contributions are welcome and will be heard sympathetically and respectfully while still critically. Such practices recognize "the obligation to be responsive to the voice of the other, to protect and nurture fragile speech, to assume responsibility for doing 'interactive labor,' to draw out, to facilitate, to engender and cultivate the speech of the other . . ." (Schweickart 1987:308). FPD cannot be understood, therefore, as an alternation of separate individual acts of speaking and listening—for it assumes that speaking and listening are not individual or separable acts. Often individuals would be unable to perform either of these acts unless they were encouraged and assisted to do so by the speaking and listening activities of others.

The nurturance displayed in FPD seems to be continuous with the discursive practices of Western women in general. Schweickart cites research findings that "men's discourse often takes on the quality of a verbal tournament," while women do more "interactive work" designed to keep conversations going (1987:304). Thus, "women see questions as part of conversational maintenance while men see them as requests for information; (and) women explicitly acknowledge previous utterances and try to connect with them while men have no such rule and often ignore preceding comments" (1987:304). Nurturant styles of discourse that are culturally feminine should not be interpreted as ways of compensating for supposed impairments in women's discursive competence, such as timidity or inarticulateness. Feminists reject suggestions that women's speech is "deviant in relation to a male norm . . . characterized as . . . direct, confident and straight-talking" (Mills 1992:5). Nor, in the context of moral discussion, should nurturance be seen simply as a culturally feminine-style "cooperative" alternative to a culturally masculine "competitive" style.[9] Instead, feminists regard nurturance as indispensable for collective moral reflection that is truly free and open.

It may not be immediately evident that nurturance promotes moral reflection more effectively than competition. Indeed, it may be thought that competition is more likely to promote the kind of critical questioning necessary to evaluate moral claims thoroughly—just as competition rather than cooperation has been alleged to promote progress in science (Hull 1988). But nurturing the speech of others does not preclude disagreeing with what they say. In the early days of consciousness raising, being supportive was thought to require that no one be "judgmental," but later it became evident that nurturance and support do not require the suppression of disagreement—that disagreement, indeed, is valuable insofar as it encourages speakers to reevaluate their accounts of their own experience. Thus, while FPD cannot countenance attempts to impose, rather than suggest, alternative ways of thinking about experience, it does recognize that sometimes it may be more nurturant and supportive to challenge than to accept a speaker's understanding even of her own life, for instance if she is blaming herself for being the victim of assault. Moreover, failure to express disagreement may even be a sign of disrespect.

Just as being nurturant does not preclude disagreement, neither does being nurturant mean that the tone of discussion must always be saccharine sweet. Cultures and subcultures vary in what they count as acceptable or offensive gestures and language; for instance, some Jewish American and African American women report finding the discursive style of some middle- and upper-class European Americans stilted and insincere, while some European American women from middle- and upper-class backgrounds report discomfort with what they perceive as the bluntness and loudness of Jewish American or African American speech. Deborah Tannen reports that Western men commonly pursue affiliative goals through an adversarial style that would intimidate many women but does not seem to trouble men (1990). The point of FPD is not to privilege any particular discursive style but rather to be sufficiently sensitive to varying cultural styles as to avoid intimidating, humiliating, or giving offense to other participants.

There are epistemological as well as moral reasons to avoid intimidating, humiliating, and offending others. Frightened, humiliated, or affronted people are ill-prepared for moral reflection; they are likely to be either defensively closed to alternative ways of thinking or so crushed that they cannot be critical. This is not to deny that participants in FPD sometimes experience uncomfortable or unpleasant emotions, such as uncertainty, embarrassment, anger, disappointment, or shame; as Lugones and Spelman remark, learning may be extremely hard. But inducing such emotions is not the primary goal of other participants; instead, they are inevitable concomitants of moral reevaluation.

Reflecting on FPD reveals that Western philosophical accounts of discourse often have been male-biased. When agonistic metaphors are taken as normative and discursive cooperation is regarded as no more than a culturally feminine deviation, the conceptual truth that cooperation is integral to *all* discourse becomes obscured.

The interdependence of speaking and listening is not merely a feminist pecularity; it is intrinsic to all productive discussion. Accounts of discourse that focus exclusively on speakers and their rights are incomplete and distorted. To describe discourse only in terms of speaking, while disregarding listening, is to rely on a mistaken view of meaning as representational and transparent, as a message packaged in language and needing only to be unwrapped by the hearer for the speaker's intention to become evident. In fact, meaning is something that listeners participate in constructing through their interpretations of utterances. Without interpretation by a listener, no communication occurs. Schweickart illustrates this point by reference to Sartre's play *No Exit,* writing: "Hell is being trapped forever in conversation not with people who disagree with you, but with people who cannot or will not be good listeners" (1987:309).

By recognizing the complementary roles of speakers and listeners, FPD works from a more complete and less distorted understanding of discursive interaction than philosophical accounts describing discourse only in terms of speech.

Process as Product

FPD simultaneously aims at consensus and recognizes that on any given occasion it may be unattainable (*Women's Encampment Handbook* 1983:42). Even in the absence of consensus, however, feminists regard the process of moral discussion as valuable for its own sake— unlike those philosophers who portray moral reasoning as a series of procedures or logical moves designed to generate justified conclusions but which themselves remain morally neutral. FPD's conception of moral reasoning, by contrast, embodies a number of dialogical or discursive virtues that go well beyond the Kantian values of mutual equality and respect.

Different theorists provide overlapping accounts of these virtues. The *Women's Encampment Handbook* lists responsibility, self-discipline, respect, cooperation, and struggle (1983:42). Lugones and Spelman mention courage and caring. Frye and Seller both emphasize political commitment and loyalty, while Frye adds self-knowledge and Seller adds empathy. Schweickart notes the need for imagination, sensitivity, and the ability to balance two subjectivities. Jane Braaten offers a list of what she calls intellectual virtues that include the ability to imagine another's response to a situation, given her subjective point of view, and to imagine a world based on alternative norms and values (1990:6–7).

Practicing these virtues is a valuable activity in itself. As Martha Nussbaum notes, "excursions of imagination and yearnings of sympathy do not serve as a means only, to an intellectual knowledge that is in principle (though perhaps not in fact) separable from them" (1990:92). She agrees with Aristotle that "the exercise of practical wisdom is itself a human excellence, an activity of intrinsic value apart from its tendency to produce virtuous actions." In the context of FPD, the practice of dialogical or discursive virtues also promotes the development of moral subjectivity and moral community, as well as moral justifiability. Consideration of these topics must await another occasion.

Some Strengths of Feminist
Practical Dialogue

FPD is both continuous with and divergent from mainstream philosophical conceptions of moral reasoning. Certainly it is not unique in its interest in discursive reasoning, in its determination that the values of freedom and equality should be expressed in the process of moral discourse, or in asserting the indispensability of empirical as opposed to imaginary dialogue. However, while many components of FPD may be found in other conceptions of moral reasoning, FPD combines them in a distinctive mixture that in my view offers several advantages.

FPD Is More Empirically and Conceptually Adequate

FPD emerges from an activist rather than an academic context and thus "constructs its alternative out of the concrete and shared experiences of women, rather than out of a romantic vision of precapitalist life or abstract ideal of human nature" (Ferguson, 1984:27). Because of this, FPD presupposes an understanding of moral discourse that is empirically and conceptually richer than that found in many philosophical theories, acknowledging the complexity and intrinsically cooperative nature of discourse and the opacity of meaning.

FPD Expresses Feminist Values

Second-wave feminists have always been clear that processes are inseparable from products; in consequence, they have insisted that feminist processes must embody feminist values. The following are among the values embodied in FPD.

1. *Respect for women's moral autonomy.* FPD expresses its respect for woman's autonomy by insisting that every woman be able to participate freely and equally in moral discourse. FPD, however, construes free and equal participation in a less abstract way than most philosophical accounts of discourse, a way that recognizes the complex realities of discursive interaction. Inherent in FPD, moreover, is a standard of discursive competence that seems attainable by any woman; specifically, and unlike most philosophical accounts of ideal discourse, FPD promotes a mode of discursive interaction that does not give systematic advantages to women with more formal education or other social privileges. FPD is therefore a deeply democratic model of moral reasoning that preserves the autonomy of all participants.

2. *Respect for women's experience and insights.* Feminists have asserted for over two decades that traditional moral theory ignores or devalues women's moral experience (Gilligan 1982). FPD regards attention to women's experience as indispensable to feminist ethics but,

at the same time, it does not treat as unchallengeable women's accounts and evaluations either of their own experience or the experience of others. Women, especially previously silenced women, must be treated with moral deference but not with moral obsequiousness.

3. *Care.* In addition to the symbolically masculine values of equality and reciprocity, FPD is informed by such symbolically feminine values as friendship, love, and care for concrete rather than generalized others. This certainly does not mean that manifesting anything other than positive or "vanilla" emotions violates of the ideals of FPD, FPD which recognizes that emotions such as suspicion, resentment, or hostility are inevitable and even appropriate in certain discursive contexts. However, it regards the occurrence of these emotions as compatible with care, friendship, and love which therefore, in the context of FPD, become critical rather than sentimental emotions.

The Pragmatic Optimism of FPD

FPD addresses not a philosophical ideal world but rather the world that we actually inhabit. By contrast, Rawlsian hypothetical dialogue is a philosophical thought experiment that addresses only the circumstances of what Rawls calls "perfect justice," while Habermas's conditions of ideal discourse are so stringent that they are quite inapplicable to daily life. Because FPD typically occurs in response to a perceived need to address specific moral problems, the recommendations it produces are likely to be more useful pragmatically than those produced by many philosophical theories. For instance, the conclusions of FPD are likely to be intuitively or motivationally acceptable to the participants, applicable in circumstances of less than perfect justice, and formulated at the level of determinacy or generality appropriate for the context.

FPD offers an alternative not only to philosophical conceptions of ideal discourse but also to a second kind of discourse mentioned in contemporary philosophical literature. This is "conversation," a way of talking that philosophers portray as free-ranging, unstructured, and involving no systematic attempt to compensate for discursive inequalities between the participants. Unlike ideal discourse, which is designed to represent the conditions of moral justification, philosophical conversations are not thought to bear any particular moral weight (Ackerman 1989; Walzer 1989–90).

Even though they are defined in opposition to each other, these two kinds of talk converge on the same unsatisfactory conclusion from the point of view of moral reasoning. Actual conversations can contribute to moral discovery but the agreements they may produce have no particular claim to moral legitimacy, while idealized discourse is never instantiated. Both kinds of talk thus lead quickly to skepticism in practical ethics.

It is certainly understandable why philosophers should be pessimistic about the ethical possibilities of empirical discourse. In the world we presently inhabit, even the aspiration to free and equal dialogue often seems next to hopeless, let alone capable of achieving moral consensus. People in the real world are unequal in resources, time, and power, and these inequalities cause severe imbalances in most empirical discourses. Few of our actual moral discussions resemble even the relatively fair circumstances of a philosophy seminar, and many of us can testify that socially constructed inequalities set powerful constraints on our discourse even here. Moreover, even if these obstacles to egalitarian discourse could somehow be overcome, the chance of consensus emerging seems remote indeed. People in the real world have sharply divergent values; the starting point of contemporary liberal theory, indeed, is the undisputed fact that modern societies are characterized by a plurality of conceptions of the good. Even more significantly, people also have interests that conflict in very real ways—which is not to say that they do not also share some significant interests.

It is easy to see why these unfortunately familiar facts of contemporary life should generate philosophical pessimism concerning the moral possibilities of empirical discourse. Such pessimism has led at least one influential contemporary philosopher, Bruce Ackerman, to deny explicitly that morality (unlike politics) requires dialogue. He says that "a little talk may go a long way; a lot may lead nowhere." Talking to others is not, in Ackerman's view, "of supreme importance in moral self-definition" because "The key decisions are made in silence: Whom to trust? What do I really think?" He concludes that "a morally reflective person *can* permissibly cut herself off from real-world dialogue" (1989:6).

FPD, by contrast, takes seriously the possibilities as well as the difficulties of empirical dialogue in the real world—and the moral potential as well as the moral limitations of real people. Although it is true that FPD is predicated on the assumption that everyone is fallible, it also assumes that we are all corrigible, capable of self-conscious reflection and deliberate action, of taking others' points of view and reevaluating our own positions from their perspectives. Because

FPD is designed specifically to tap the moral capacities of the participants, we can see that respect for the moral capacities of ordinary people, notably ordinary women, is inherent in this practice.

FPD thus constitutes an alternative to the two kinds of talk recognized by contemporary philosophers. In situations that are not and never will be ideal, it suggests a way in which women may talk with each other that is less than ideal but still superior to most ordinary conversations in hierarchical societies. In working to develop this alternative, the practitioners of FPD may be seen as accepting our real-life moral situation with good grace, rather than regretfully or grudgingly, and committing themselves to making the best of it. FPD offers a seemingly practicable method for promoting moral understandings that actually occur and may also claim to be morally justified.

Conclusion

Even in those relatively favorable situations where FPD can be practiced, it never guarantees moral consensus: some emotional responses may be too intransigent and some conflicts of interest too deeply entrenched. In such situations, FPD does not require us to talk forever. When talk becomes harassment, when understanding is not even on the horizon, when the need for action is urgent, FPD accepts that discussion may be abandoned—at least for the time being. However, it requires that dialogue be resumed as soon as possible. Given the inevitably limited nature of our experience and knowledge, including our limited knowledge even of our own capacities, needs, and motivations, FPD seems the best strategy currently available for improving the moral adequacy of our thinking and action.

One advantage of concentrating on the notion of empirical rather than hypothetical discourse and seeking actual rather than hypothetical consensus is that this encourages us to focus on the practical obstacles that make even domination-free communication, let alone moral consensus, so difficult to attain. Prominent among these obstacles, as we have seen, are socially constructed inequalities. We already have good reasons for working politically to reduce such inequalities, but if empirical discourse is recognized as crucial to feminist practical ethics, considerations of moral epistemology may now be added to these reasons. It becomes even clearer that moral progress is inseparable from political progress and feminist ethics from feminist politics.

FPD makes no pretence of being a tidy and unproblematic procedure, even in principle, for figuring out what we should to do. Utilizing FPD is no substitute for, and indeed requires, a kind of practical—especially political—wisdom: wisdom that enables us to weigh the claims of people who are never fully rational or uncoerced, but never completely puppets either, people who are, in addition, always in some power relation respective to us. Only such wisdom can tell us when, and especially with whom, it is morally incumbent to engage in dialogue—as well as when it is necessary to end the dialogue and commit ourselves to practical action.

Notes

1. I have received helpful comments on earlier drafts from many people, including Kathy Addelson, Hazel Barnes, Sandra Bartky, Lawrence Blum, Len Boonin, Luc Bovens, Dwight Boyd, Laura Brunell, Emily Calhoun, Frank Cunningham, Annette Dula, Marlene G. Fine, Lori Gruen, Sandra Harding, Virginia Held, Dale Jamieson, Jane Kneller, Gwyn Kirk, Marcia Lind, Bill McBride, Angela Miles, Jim Nickel, Linda Nicholson, Sally Ruddick, Richard Schmitt, Anne Seller, Gary Stahl, Karsten Struhl, and Iris Young. I have also benefited from comments made by audiences at the University of Toronto, the University of Frankfurt, the University of Quebec, the North American Society for Social Philosophy, and the Philosophy of Education Society as well as from SOFPHIA and from the political philosophy reading group and the women's studies work-in-progress at the University of Colorado at Boulder.

2. There is no orthodoxy in feminist ethics although it is a common mistake to identify feminist ethics with an ethics of care. In addition to several versions of an ethics of care, different feminists have proposed as models for feminist ethics the understandings of moral reasoning held by, among others, Aristotle, Hume, Kant, Hegel, Bentham, Mill, Sartre, Camus, Rawls, and Habermas.

3. For instance, the credits on the first page of the *Women's Encampment Handbook* (1983) thank "the tradition of handbooks from which some of this material has been obtained."

4. For descriptions of consciousness raising, see Arnold 1970; Gardner 1970; Hanisch 1970; Peslikis 1970; Sarachild 1970; Koedt et al. 1973; Payne 1973.

5. Space constraints do not permit me to discuss here a 1980 document circulated by the feminist battered women's movement, "A Feminist Perspective on the Ethics of Communication, Explored in the Context of an On-Going Group of Women with Decision-Making Responsibility" (Evans 1980). The author, Kit Evans, executive director of AWAKE, National Coalition

142 Alison M. Jaggar

Against Domestic Violence, offers "twelve basic principles for ethical communication at any level." These principles are grounded in a clear-eyed realization of the many ways in which free and open discourse may be subverted and provide practical suggestions for avoiding such subversion. Deborah Flick brought these principles to my attention and I obtained them from the Boulder Safehouse.

6. Some Italian feminists have also experimented with ways of utilizing inequality between women as a moral resource. See especially the Milan Women's Bookstore Collective (1990).

7. John Rawls specifies that the negotiating parties in his hypothetical discourse are "representative men" (1971).

8. The distinction between "generalized" and "concrete" others is made by Seyla Benhabib (1986). Lorraine Code insists that feminist caring is not impersonal but instead requires knowing the specific situations of the putative recipients of care, especially whether they need or want the type of care envisioned (1992).

9. Sara Mills, for instance, seems to suggest this (1992).

Bibliography

Ackerman, Bruce. "Why Dialogue?" *Journal of Philosophy* 86:1 (1989)

Arnold, June. "Consciousness-Raising." in *Women's Liberation: Blueprint for the Future*, Sookie Stambler, ed. New York: Ace, 1970, 155–61.

Baldwin, Margaret A. "Split at the Root: Prostitution and Feminist Discourses of Law Reform." *Yale Journal of Law and Feminism* 5:47 (1992) 47–120.

Belenky, Mary Field, Blythe McVicker Clinchy, Nancy Rule Goldberger, Jill Mattuck Tarule. *Women's Ways of Knowing: The Development of Self, Voice, and Mind.* New York: Basic Books, 1986.

Benhabib, Seyla. "The Generalized the Concrete Other: The Kohlberg-Gilligan Controversy and Feminist Theory." *Praxis International*, 5:4 (January 1986) 402–24.

Blum, Lawrence A. "Kant's and Hegel's Moral Rationalism: A Feminist Perspective." *Canadian Journal of Philosophy* 12:2 (June 1982) 287–302.

Boston Women's Health Course Collective. *Our Bodies, Our Selves.* Boston: New England Free Press, 1971.

Braaten, Jane. "Toward a Feminist Reassessment of Intellectual Virtue." *Hypatia* 5:3 (Fall 1990) 1–14.

Code, Lorraine. "Who Cares? The Poverty of Objectivism for a Moral Epistemology." *Annals of Scholarship* 19:1–2 (1992) 1–17.

Collins, Patricia Hill. *Black Feminist Thought: Knowledge, Consciousness, and the Politics of Empowerment*, Boston: Unwin Hyman, 1990.

Evans, Kit. "A Feminist Perspective on the Ethics of Communication, Explored in the Context of an On-Going Group of Women with Decision-Making Responsibility." National Coalition against Domestic Violence, August 1980. Unpublished manuscript.

Ferguson, Kathy E. *The Feminist Case Against Bureaucracy.* Philadelphia: Temple University Press, 1984.

Fisher, Roger, and William Ury with Bruce Patton. *Getting to Yes: Negotiating Agreement Without Giving In.* Boston: Houghton Mifflin, 1981.

Fraser, Nancy. "Toward a Discourse Ethic of Solidarity." *Praxis International* 5:4 (January 1986) 425–29.

Friedman, Marilyn. "The Impracticality of Impartiality." *Journal of Philosophy,* 86:11 (November 1989) 645–56

Frye, Marilyn. *The Politics of Reality: Essays in Feminist Theory.* Trumansburg, N.Y.: Crossing Press, 1983.

Frye, Marilyn. "The Possibility of Feminist Theory" in *Theoretical Perspectives on Sex Difference.* Debrel L. Rhode, ed. New Haven: Yale University Press, 1990.

Gardner, Jennifer. "False Consciousness." in *Notes from the Second Year.* Shulamith Firestone, ed. New York: 1970, 82–83.

Gibson, Mary. *To Breathe Freely: Risk, Consent and Air* Totowa, NJ: Rowman and Allanheld, 1985, 141–168.

Gilligan, Carol. *In a Different Voice: Psychological Theory and Women's Development.* Cambridge: Harvard University Press, 1982.

Hanisch, Carol. "The Personal Is Political." *Notes from the Second Year.* Shulamith Firestone, ed. New York: 1970, 76–78.

Haraway, Donna. "Situated Knowledges: The Science Question in Feminism and the Privilege of Partial Perspective." *Feminist Studies* 14:4 (Fall 1988) 575–99.

Hoagland, Sara Lucia. *Lesbian Ethics: Toward New Value.* Palo Alto: Institute of Lesbian Studies, 1988.

Hooks, Bell. *Talking Back: Thinking Feminist—Thinking Black.* Boston: South End Press, 1989.

Hull, David. *Science as a Process: An Evlutionary Account of the Social and Conceptual Development of Science.* Chicago: University of Chicago Press, 1988.

Iannello, Kathleen P. *Decisions without Hierarchy: Feminist Interventions in Organization Theory and Practice.* New York: Routledge, 1992.

Jaggar, Alison M. "Love and Knowledge: Emotion in Feminist Epistemology." *Inquiry* 32 (1989) 151–76.

Koedt, Anne, Ellen Levine, and Anita Rapone. "Consciousness Raising." in *Radical Feminism,* Anne Koedt, Ellen Levine, and Anita Rapone, eds. New York: Quadrangle, 1973, 280–81.

Lakoff, George, and Mark Johnson. *Metaphors We Live By.* Chicago: University of Chicago Press, 1980.

Lugones, Maria. "Playfulness, `World'-Travelling, and Loving Perception." *Hypatia* 2:2 (Summer 1987) 3–19.

Lugones, Maria C., and Elizabeth V. Spelman. "Have We Got a Theory for You! Feminist Theory, Cultural Imperialism and the Demand for 'the Woman's Voice'." *Hypatia* 1:1 (1983) 573–81.

Martin, Rachel. *Literacy from the Inside Out.* Boston: 1989.

Milan Women's Bookstore Collective. *Sexual Difference: A Theory of Social-Symbolic Practice.* Bloomington: University of Indiana Press, 1990

Mills, Sara. "Discourse Competence: Or How to Theorize Strong Women Speakers" *Hypatia* 7:2 (Spring 1992) 4–17.

Morgan, Kathryn Paula. "Women and Moral Madness." in *Science, Morality and Feminist Theory,* Marsha Hanen and Kai Nielsen, eds. Calgary: University of Calgary Press, 1987.

Narayan, Uma. "The Project of Feminist Epistemology: Perspectives from a Nonwestern Feminist." in *Gender/Body/Knowledge: Feminist Reconstructions of Being and Knowing,* Alison M. Jaggar and Susan R. Bordo, eds. New Brunswick: Rutgers University Press, 1989, 256–69.

Nussbaum, Martha. *Love's Knowledge.* Oxford: Oxford University Press, 1990.

Parker, Pat. "For the white person who wants to know how to be my friend." in *Making Face, Making Soul: Haciendo Caras: Creative and Critical Perspectives by Women of Color,* Gloria Anzaldua, ed. San Francisco: aunt lute foundation, 1990, 297.

Payne, Carol Williams. "Consciousness Raising: A Dead End?" in *Radical Feminism,* Anne Koedt, Ellen Levine and Anita Rapone, eds. New York: Quadrangle, 1973, 282–84.

Peslikis, Irene. "Resistances to Consciousness." in *Notes from the Second Year,* Shulamith Firestone, ed. New York: 1970, 81.

Piaget, Jean. *The Moral Judgement of the Child.* New York: Free Press, 1965.

Rawls, John. *A Theory of Justice.* Cambridge: Harvard University Press, 1971.

Rich, Adrienne. *On Lies, Secrets and Silences.* New York: Norton, 1979.

Sarachild, Kathie. "A Program for Feminist 'Consciousness Raising." in *Notes from the Second Year,* Shulamith Firestone, ed. New York: 1970, 78–80.

Schniedewind, Nancy. "Feminist Values: Guidelines for a Teaching Methodology in Women's Studies." in *Learning Our Way: Essays in Feminist Education,* Charlotte Bunch and Sandra Pollack, eds. Trumansburg, N.Y.: The Crossing Press, 1983, 261–71.

Schweickart, Patrocinio. "Engendering Critical Discourse." in *The Current in Criticism,* Clayton Koelb and Virgil Lokke, eds. West Lafayette: Purdue University Press, 1987, 295–317.

Schwartz-Shea, Peregrine, and Debra D. Burrington. "Free Riding, Alternative Organization and Cultural Feminism: The Case of Seneca Women's Peace Camp." *Women and Politics* 10:3 (1990) 1–37.

Seller, Anne. "Should the Feminist Philosopher Stay at Home?" unpublished manuscript, February 1992.

Spivak, Gayatri Chakravorty. "Can the Subaltern Speak?" in *Marxism and the Interpretation of Culture,* Cary Nelson and Lawrence Grossberg, eds. Urbana: University of Illinois Press, 1988, 271–313.

Sterba, James P. *How to Make People Just: A Practical Reconciliation of Alternative Conceptions of Justice.* Totowa, N.J.: Rowman and Allanheld, 1988.

Taylor, Charles. "The Dialogical Self." in *The Interpretive Turn,* David Hiley, James F. Bowman and Richard Shusterman, eds. Ithaca: Cornell University Press, 1991.

Thomas, Lawrence. "Moral Deference." *Philosophical Forum,* 14:1–3 (1992–93) 233–50.

Walzer, Michael. "A Critique of Philosophical Conversation." *Philosophical Forum,* 21:1–2 (Fall–Winter, 1989–90) 182–96.

Women's Encampment for a Future of Peace and Justice: Resource Handbook. New York: Romulus, 1983.

Comments by James P. Sterba

In my comments I would like to explore Jaggar's Feminist Practical Dialogue by examining a current instantiation of it by the two of us. Jaggar and I are both feminists, although unfortunately like most males my age I have not always been a self-identified feminist, and I am only very imperfectly one even now. Nevertheless, in my life and work I do strive to give expression to feminist values, and I certainly know that Jaggar does the same. So it is worth noting that for some time now Jaggar and I have been engaged in Feminist Practical Dialogue (FPD) while discussing the characterization of feminist justice that I defend in my paper.

This dialogue between Jaggar and me began when she was invited to contribute to a special issue of the *Journal of Social Philosophy* devoted to my book *How to Make People Just*. Jagger's paper was published in 1991 along with my response.[1] Our dialogue continued when Jaggar commented on my symposium paper at the American Philosophical Association's Central Division Meeting in 1992, where I also had the chance to respond. And it continues in this volume as well. As it turns out, in our practice of FPD, Jaggar and I are having a great deal of difficulty reaching consensus. Let me try to indicate what some of the stumbling blocks have been.

The first stumbling block to our reaching consensus seems to be the very project I set for myself in *How to Make People Just*. In that book, I set out five contemporary conceptions of justice: libertarian justice with its ideal of liberty, welfare liberal justice with its ideal of fairness, socialist justice with its ideal of equality, feminist justice with its ideal of androgyny, and communitarian justice with its ideal of the common good. I then claim that when these five conceptions of justice are correctly interpreted, they all lead to the same practical requirements, specifically the practical requirements of a right to welfare and a right to equal opportunity, and (where equal opportunity has been denied) a right to affirmative action. Now Jaggar objects to my approach to these five conceptions of justice because she doesn't think my approach allows people to identify with more than one of the conceptions. For example, Jaggar likes to think of herself not just as a feminist but as a socialist feminist as well, and she thinks that my approach to the above conceptions of justice makes this impossible. But nowhere in the book do I rule out people endorsing more than one of the conceptions of justice I discuss. Indeed, it would be quite odd for me to do so since the book aims to achieve a practical consensus among people who identify with the conceptions of justice that I discuss. So it seems the disagreement that Jaggar and I are having here suggests an additional norm for FPD. It is: Only disagree with the most favorable interpretation of another person's perspective.

A second stumbling block Jaggar and I have encountered in our practice of FPD concerns the way I characterize feminist justice.[2] Jaggar has less trouble with my *negative* characterization of feminist justice in terms of a gender-free or genderless society, but she is very critical of my *positive* characterization of feminist justice in terms of the ideal of androgyny. My discussion of this positive characterization notes that many feminists (whom I cite) have endorsed the ideal of androgyny and then goes on to argue that if the ideal is defined in the way I propose, the objections that other feminists have raised to the ideal cease to apply. Here Jaggar objects that because other feminists, herself included, don't accept my characterization of feminist justice, I should just give it up, and if I don't do that then I must be seeking to impose my own definition of feminist justice on others (and here I am doing some free interpretation), thereby revealing myself to be a male sexist pig in feminist clothing after all!

But I don't see why all feminists, myself included, don't have a right to defend their conceptions of feminist justice and give reasons why other feminists as well as nonfeminists should adopt those conceptions. Jaggar sees feminism as requiring an end to the subordination of women and then she wants to differentiate liberal, radical, Marxist, and socialist forms of feminism according to the means each would endorse to bring this about. I find this characterization useful. But I also think that the ideals of Marxist and socialist feminism have less appeal today than they once had, and that, consequently, we need to pursue new characterizations of feminist justice. This is my motivation for suggesting this new interpretation of the ideal of androgyny. So reflecting on the disagreement Jaggar and I are having here, I would propose another norm for FPD, one that might help build consensus among feminists. It is: Don't reject any feminist characterization until you have fairly evaluated the arguments for and against it.

A third stumbling block that has kept Jaggar and me from reaching consensus in our practice of FPD concerns the specific objections that Jaggar thinks are telling against my characteriziation of feminist justice in terms of the ideal of androgyny.[3] As I define it, the ideal of androgyny requires that the traits that are truly desirable in society be equally available to both women and men, or in the case of virtues, equally expected of both women and men.

Now Jaggar objects to this characterization on the grounds that feminist justice is an ideal for reforming social structures whereas androgyny is an ideal for reforming individuals.[4] Yet as I pointed out to Jaggar in private correspondence, the ideal of androgyny, as I define it, closely resembles the ideal of equal opportunity, and since the ideal of equal opportunity is thought to be an ideal for reforming social structures, the same should be true of the ideal of androgyny, as I define it.[5]

Nevertheless, Jaggar still wants to drive a wedge between androgyny, as I define it, and the ideal of equal opportunity, but to do this, she has to interpret the ideal of equal opportunity differently than I do so that it presupposes a competitive and meritocratic society. By contrast, the rights to welfare and equal opportunity as I defend them lead to an egalitarian society, which even socialists would find acceptable.[6]

Now it seems to me that some of these failures of interpretation suggest a desire to disagree and do verbal battle that wasn't supposed to characterize FPD.[7] This suggests that another specific norm for FPD might be needed. It is: Don't disagree when there is some way that you can constructively agree.

Indeed, as Jaggar and I continue to practice FPD, there seem to be even greater possibilities for constructive agreement. This is because despite her objections to my ideal of androgyny, in her own contribution to this volume, she endorses an ideal which looks very much like my ideal of androgyny. She says:

> Just as the incorporation of feminine values does not render FPD feminist, neither does FPD become feminist by adding masculine values to the feminine in a mix . . . Instead, I regard FPD as feminist primarily because it revises both feminine and masculine values in the light of a distinctively feminist commitment to ending women's subordination.[8]

Now compare this passage with the following passage which occurs in *How to Make People Just*, and which occurs as well in my symposium paper on which Jaggar commented and in my contribution to this volume on which Jaggar has also commented.

> So characterized the ideal of androgyny represents neither a revolt against so-called feminine virtues and traits nor their exaltation over so-called masculine virtues and traits. Accordingly, the ideal of androgyny does not view women's liberation as *simply* the freeing of women from the confines of traditional roles, thus making it possible for them to develop in ways heretofore reserved for men. Nor does the ideal view women's liberation as *simply* the revaluation and glorification of so-called feminine activities like housekeeping or mothering or so-called femi-

nine modes of thinking as reflected in an ethic of caring. The first perspective ignores or devalues genuine virtues and desirable traits traditionally associated with women, while the second ignores or devalues genuine virtues and desirable traits traditionally associated with men. By contrast, the ideal of androgyny seeks a broader based ideal for both women and men that combines virtues and desirable traits traditionally associated with women with virtues and desirable traits traditionally associated with men. Nevertheless, the ideal of androgyny will clearly reject any so-called virtues or desirable traits traditionally associated with women or men that have been supportive of discrimination or oppression against women or men.

As I read these two passages together, I feel confident that as Jaggar and I continue to practice FPD, despite our present disagreements, we shall some day soon actually reach that desired consensus at which FPD aims.

Notes

1. See Alison Jaggar, "A Critical Discussion of James P. Sterba's *How to Make People Just,*" *Journal of Social Philosophy* (1991), pp. 52–63, and my "Nine Commentators: A Brief Response," *Journal of Social Philosophy* (1991), pp. 100–118.

2. Alison Jaggar, "A Response to James P. Sterba's Reconciling Conceptions of Justice," presented at the APA Central Division Meeting in Louisville, Ky., in 1992. See also "A Critical Discussion of James P. Sterba's *How to Make People Just.*"

3. Ibid.

4. Jagger, "A Response to James P. Sterba's Reconciling Conceptions of Justice." In my response to Jaggar when she raised this same objection to my symposium paper at the APA Central Division Meeting, I responded that there was no tendency in my work to focus on changing people rather than changing social institutions, noting further Jaggar's approval of my discussion of how the ideal of androgyny would require significant changes in family structures.

5. Private correspondence, November 10, 1993.

6. For further argument on this point, see "From Liberty to Welfare," *Ethics* (1994).

7. Alison Jagger, "Toward a Feminist Conception of Moral Reasoning," p. 115.

8. Ibid. The omitted words are "that might be called androgynous." Does the omission of these words make a difference? Could it be that what Jaggar is really objecting to is just my use of the word "androgyny" and not the ideal I use the word to stand for?

Comments by Carol C. Gould

What contributions can feminism make to the understanding and practice of moral reasoning? This is the larger project that frames Jaggar's essay. She focuses more specifically on the delineation of a uniquely feminist mode of such reasoning and seeks to articulate its features by analyzing a number of examples. In these brief comments, I want to focus on three points: first, what exactly are the domain and purpose of the modes of discourse that Jaggar examines? Is it right to characterize all of them as "consensual approaches to moral reasoning," as she does, and further, is consensus an adequate characterization of participative discourse? Second, since Jaggar argues that such feminist discourse is by its nature critical, what grounds this critical stance; and how, in its emphasis on listening to the other, would her approach accommodate antifeminist views among women themselves? And third, is the proffered model of Feminist Practical Dialogue in fact distinctive as she claims it to be?

Jaggar's project is undoubtedly important and contributes to the ongoing discussion of feminist approaches to ethical discourse exemplified in such recent work as Virginia Held's *Feminist Morality*.[1] Jaggar makes interesting use of a number of concrete examples of feminist discussion. This very range, however, raises the first question I would like to pose, because the examples exhibit very different kinds of discourse, both in terms of their domain and their purpose. Thus, the first deals with the context of consciousness raising in which there is presumably no collective decision to be reached nor any specific action that is to be determined by the talking. The second is an account of the participative practices that went into the production of *Our Bodies, Our Selves* by the Boston Women's Health Collective. Here, the purpose was to pool collective knowledge and experiences of medical care and to jointly develop and publish a series of research papers on practical health care questions. The third was a specifically activist group, "The Women's Encampment," which set itself the task of collective decision-making by consensus for the sake of peace actions. The fourth has to do with contexts of feminist pedagogy and classroom practices, whereas the fifth deals with feminist reliance on spoken dialogue and women's traditional "ways of knowing," purportedly characteristic of African-American women. Later in her paper, she also draws on the example of relations of friendship as a model of nurturing speaking and listening.

These are clearly different contexts of discourse which can only be related to each other in the loosest sense as moral reasoning and

Jaggar has deliberately chosen such a wide range. However, in her general formulation of a feminist conception of moral discourse based on these examples, Jaggar seems to want to assimilate them all to a model of consensual decision-making, contrasting this practice with the alternatives of majority rule and bargaining. Yet, in many of these examples, there are no decisions to be made nor are there any requirements for or expectations of anything like consensus, which in fact would demand the full agreement of all parties involved in the discourse. Many of these examples would be better described in terms of *participative* discourse among free and equal individuals and Jaggar in fact does describe them that way as well. Through such participation, women come to self-understanding and develop moral capacities. However, such participative discourse is not always aimed at decision-making and may not require that the participants arrive at any agreements. For such contexts, the idea of consensus is clearly not appropriate. In this sense, too, it is misleading to analogize feminist practical dialogue to Habermassian discourse ethics, which explicitly sees the aim of moral reasoning as consensus or an agreement on a generalizable interest.

Moreover, in those examples where collective decision-making is involved, it is not clear that consensus is always the most democratic and participative means of reaching agreement, contrary to Jaggar's suggestion. Indeed, consensus, which requires unanimity, can put an extraordinary constraint on the freedom to maintain differences. No matter how respectful of alternative views such a process may be, it finally requires the concession of those who disagree, except in the most severe cases of principled objections where consensus is unattainable. Even the language that Jaggar cites approvingly from the *Women's Encampment Handbook* has an overtone of coercive agreement in characterizing a principled disagreement as a matter of "blocking consensus" and as requiring self-discipline to avoid.

There is an additional point here concerning the question of the domain and purpose of the discourse. Sometimes it seems from Jaggar's account that this mode of reasoning is intended to extend also to political communities and not simply to small participative groups or to discussions among friends or other face-to-face encounters. However, in such political contexts, particularly on a large scale, it seems to me that the relations of friendship, love, and care, which Jaggar claims inform this model, are usually too demanding, if not inappropriate. Further, in large populations, actual consensus is totally unrealistic. The question then remains how feminist values can be expressed in such large-scale political contexts.[2]

A second set of issues concerns Jaggar's assertion that feminist discourse (as against feminine discourse in general) involves a critical stance, namely, one aimed at ending the subordination of women and therefore one that consciously recognizes and exposes the various forms of this oppression. Jaggar is obviously correct in observing that such a feminist approach would be essentially socially critical in this way. However, her account of moral reasoning does not yet make clear how such a critical perspective emerges in the dialogue or what its sources are. It is not enough to say that in talking and listening and in voicing disagreements that the critical perspective will emerge. Nor is it likely to be derived simply from listening to women from different backgrounds and "from the working classes and other stigmatized groups, such as racial, ethnic, religious or sexual minorities." Jaggar writes that "Feminist Practical Dialogue assumes that it is precisely those women who may be best able to provide moral insight and even moral inspiration, especially in certain areas." But one problem with this is that in fact many of these women would tend to deny the reality of women's oppression and in addition many would defend unreasonable positions on such moral questions as abortion or welfare rights.

The notion that such women are "best able to provide moral insight and even moral inspiration" presumes that objective oppression produces a conscious critical response. But this is very often not the case, as Jaggar herself recognizes in citing Uma Narayan's account on this point. It is indeed important not to romanticize the situation of those less well off. Beyond this, we need to develop an explanation of error, that is, of why women often tend to deny their oppression or even to actively collude with it. There has been very little explicit discussion in feminist theory of this pervasive phenomenon.

A final comment concerns Jaggar's view that Feminist Practical Dialogue is distinctive and provides a new conception of moral reasoning. Jaggar usefully emphasizes such features of feminist discourse as the reliance on personal experience and first-person narratives as the basis of moral understanding and a source of moral reflection. She approvingly cites other accounts that stress the element of reciprocity in listening and the importance of attentiveness to the other and the ability to adopt the perspective of the other. These may indeed be distinctive elements of the new feminist moral reasoning that Jaggar seeks to describe here. However, if these are to be seen as new, then they must be further distinguished from analogous nonfeminist formulations of these very traits in the older philosophical tradition. I believe this can probably be done but Jaggar does not develop the comparisons with the earlier views here, though she notes in passing that her proposed new conception of feminist moral reasoning draws inspiration from some of them.

Such a study of earlier philosophical approaches might also give further dimension to the feminist account in various ways. Thus, for example, the reliance on personal experience has its older sources not only in traditional empiricism's emphasis on the experiences of the subject but also in the phenomenological and hermeneutic account of lived experience (*Erlebnis*) in both its social and individual dimensions. Similarly, the self-other relation has been developed in both epistemic and affective terms not only in the dialectical tradition generally in terms of intersubjectivity (in Kant, Hegel, and Marx, and later in Mead) but also in the nuanced form of relationship to the concrete other and being able to take the role of the other, e.g., in the I-Thou relation in Feuerbach and Buber, in Alfred Schütz's phenomenological sociology, in the Verstehen tradition, and in Personalism, among other approaches. It would be important to indicate the ways in which the conception of feminist moral reasoning goes beyond these earlier sources which, in agreement with Jaggar, I think it does.

In short, Jaggar's essay provides an important contribution to what is bound to become a central topic for philosophical feminist theory, namely, the articulation of a new approach to moral reasoning.

Notes

1. Virginia Held, *Feminist Morality: Transforming Culture, Society, and Politics* (Chicago: University of Chicago Press, 1993).
2. See Carol C. Gould, "Feminism and Democratic Community Revisited," in John W. Chapman and Ian Shapiro, eds., *Democratic Community: NOMOS XXXV* (New York: New York University Press, 1993), pp. 396–413.

Comments by Robert C. Solomon

I can imagine a disagreeable reader completing Professor Alison Jaggar's paper on "a feminist conception of moral reasoning" and asking, "what does this have to do with justice?—or, for that matter, with moral reasoning?" But such queries seem to me to betray not only the notable narrowness of so many recent discussions of justice but also the overly tedious and increasingly technical notions of "practical reason" that have come to define so much of the literature. The one ingredient that systematically gets excluded from those discussions, indeed, it is not even evident how it would fit in at all, is *listening*. Even if one learned nothing more from Jaggar's unusually detailed and even personal account of what she (unfortunately) calls "feminist practical discourse" (abbreviated with an acronym, one of the more annoying pretensions of the alternatives she is criticizing), the sharp reminder that listening is basic to any discussion of either justice or morals is a timely contribution to a discipline which has become all but entirely caught up in a cacaphony of competing theories and theorists, shouting to attract attention.

I found Jaggar's detailed account of the feminist movement, from "consciousness raising" to cross-subcultural and interracial dialogue and the egalitarian politics of conversation a welcome breath of fresh air in a field where consciousnesses tend not to be "raised" at all but rather reduced, to solipsistic deductive machines, to "rational capacities," where the primary reference to other cultures is to deny their otherness on a priori grounds, where conversation, even in the enlightened arguments of Jürgen Habermas, have much more to do with the conditions of unimpeded discourse than with the particular inhibitions and conversational structures of particular situations.

Jaggar rightly chastizes the dominant "adversarial" norm of philosophical and political discourse, and what she highlights is the need for cooperation and understanding—particularly in the face of what sometimes seems like insurmountable misunderstanding (e.g. between poor and exploited women of color and privileged university professors). I also applaud her emphasis on the need to pay attention to the emotions of participants, a notion that plays virtually no role in the many debates about "practical reasoning" in ethics, politics and political theory. But what is politics all about, if it is not "fear, confusion, indignation, powerlessness [and] rage," and why should these powerful motives be excluded from the "reasoning" process that aims to resolve, mollify or satisfy them? (p. 132) To so emphasize the emotions is not to encourage uninhibited primal screaming, banging one's shoe on the lectern or fisticuffs in the seminar room, the chaotic alternative often suggested by Robert's inhibiting Rules of Order. The emotions are not so opposed to reason or "reasoning," and Jaggar rightly emphasizes the *cultivation* of emotions, the *correction* of emotions and a welcome but usually unacknowledged link between emotions and *autonomy*. (Indeed, I think even Kant can be interpreted in this way, if one takes sufficiently seriously the extent to which respect, dignity, a sense of duty and other, more aesthetic "feelings" compromise his otherwise rigid dichotomy between inclination and reason, "nature" and "freedom.")

What bothers me about Jaggar's argument, indeed, I think, about the only thing that bothered me, was her own, albeit muted, adversarial stance, sometimes presented through quotations from other feminists, sometimes suggested in casual comments, indicating that the questions she raises are ultimately part of an unfolding feminist manifesto rather than important propositions about the very nature of ethics, politics and philosophical and political conversation. One need not deny that her accusations against traditional philosophical discourse are sound and solid, and statistically, quite obviously, most of the discussants in that tradition are men. But it hardly follows that these are peculiarly feminist issues, and thus polarizing the discussion— with or without acronyms—seems to me to be part of the problem.

4

Liberal Justice

William A. Galston

I

A liberal polity may be viewed as a cooperative endeavor to create
and sustain circumstances within which individuals may pursue—and
to the greatest possible extent achieve—their good. This view does
not deny the fact of social conflict. It implies, however, that this
conflict takes place within a framework of partial agreement and
potential mutual advantage.[1] The partial agreement is provided by the
liberal accounts of the good and of equality. The potential mutual
advantage consists in the obvious fact that in many circumstances
collaborative activities can be so arranged as to enable each individual to achieve more good than would be possible through uncoordi-
nated endeavors. The preambular references in the U.S. Constitution
to the "common defense" and the "general welfare" embody, it seems
to me, both the collaborative nature of the liberal polity and its di-
rectedness toward certain specific goods for individuals.

To say that individuals are joined in a collaborative endeavor is to
suggest that they may make special claims on one another. Within a
liberal framework, three kinds of claims are of particular importance:
those arising from the bare fact of membership in the community
(need); those arising from contribution to the community (desert); and
those arising from the voluntary individual disposition of resources in
areas left undetermined by the legitimate claims of others (choice). I
have discussed these claims at length in *Justice and the Human Good*[2]

(though I would no longer subscribe to every detail of my presentation there), and I offer only a brief summary here.

Need

As Michael Walzer has suggested, needs are the claims we can make on one another simply by virtue of fellow membership in a political community.[3] Within a liberal polity, these claims are defined relative to the basic elements of the liberal good. And because all individuals are equally members, need claims are imperative demands for equal access to the liberal good, or to the means to it.

So needs constitute a sphere of equality. But how extensive is that sphere? I think Walzer is right to stress the ineliminable element of local-historical particularity that enters into its specification. Even within a single community, there may be deep differences about the proper weights to be attached to the various elements of the (shared conception of the) good. Still, political processes of deliberation and negotiation tend to produce a certain consensus: within the United States, for example, that no one should starve for lack of food, or suffer for lack of primary medical attention, or go without the basic education needed to function as a competent citizen and contributory worker. Public policy does not always fully reflect these shared moral understandings, but when it does not, as in the case of U.S. medical care, other institutions and processes tend to take up much of the slack.

Because the principle of need is defined in relation to the good as a set of end states, it generates valid claims to widely varying levels of resources for different individuals. For example, resources required to preserve the lives of premature babies or to give handicapped people an equal chance to develop their capacities are typically significantly greater than for individuals born without such impediments. This differential ratio of resources to the good of diverse individuals means that conceptions of means (e.g., Ackerman's "manna") cannot possibly be an adequate benchmark for egalitarian (and more broadly, distributive) social policies.

To define the satisfaction of need claims as *access* to the good, or to the means to it, implies a social principle of respect for individual responsibility. In cases of normally responsible adults, societal obligation to meet needs is fulfilled by providing individuals access either to adequately remunerative occupations or directly to adequate levels of resources. The use individuals make of this access is not a matter of further collective concern: The refusal to accept a decent job, or the propensity to squander resources on drugs or drink, does not generate any additional need claims that society is obliged to honor.[4]

Desert

Desert, in the liberal understanding, is based not on personal virtue but, rather, on individual contribution to the cooperative endeavor to create opportunities for the good life. The concept of contribution to the community means that working versus shirking is a great moral divide in a liberal society. It implies, that is, a thoroughgoing critique of individuals who are physically and mentally able to make a contribution but nonetheless fail to do so.

The flip side is that the application of this principle is subject to the condition that opportunities to contribute are in fact available. It is clearly inappropriate to apply it to individuals who do not have equal opportunity to make a contribution. It is just as clearly inappropriate for a liberal society to deprive some of its members of that opportunity. This conception of contribution opportunity applies not only to the availability of jobs for adults but also to the availability of adequate opportunities for children and youth to develop their capacities to contribute .

The contribution-based desert principle implies that differences of natural endowments are not irrelevant and are not required to be nullified through social policy, as long as need claims are satisfied. To put it another way: Equal attention to needs reflects our understanding of the extent to which we are morally required to treat differences of natural endowments as a shared fate. As a matter of deep description of what "we" believe, John Rawls's total rejection of desert and its replacement with the idea of natural endowments as collective assets is simply mistaken. Nor for that matter does his position fare well under tests of wide justification.[5]

Contribution has both quantitative and qualitative dimensions. Key quantitative variables include sacrifice, effort, duration, and productivity. The key qualitative variable is the importance of different functions, as defined either by the community as a whole or (more typically) by some socioeconomic entity within the community.[6]

Two sorts of objections have been raised against the appropriateness, or possibility, of contribution-based desert claims. The first, by Rawls, is that the notion of an individual's contribution to society as a whole has no meaning, because "there is no set of agreed ends by reference to which the potential social contribution of an individual could be assessed. Associations and individuals have such ends, but

not a well-ordered society. . . . Contributions can only be locally defined as contributions to this or that association in this or that situation. Such contributions reflect an individual's worth (marginal usefulness) to some particular group. These contributions are not to be
mistaken for contributions to society itself, or for the worth to society
of its members as citizens."[7]

If my account of liberalism has even the most rough and approx-
imate validity, Rawls's thesis is mistaken. Because, as members of
the liberal community, we share a conception of the good (limited
and partial, but still significant), the liberal polity as a whole pursues
certain ends defined by that good, and individual contributions to those
ends can be assessed. Consider, for example, individuals who defend
the community against external aggression or against internal breach
of law. They contribute to the community's ends, and they serve the
legitimate interests of all members of the community. That, in part, is
why veterans are thought to have some special claims on the community after their term of military service, and why they receive special
access to housing, education, health care, and even employment ("veterans' preference"). Conversely, there are individuals whose lives
detract from the shared purposes of the community: mentally and
physically able individuals who could work but choose instead to be
burdens on society, or individuals whose repeated breach of law jeop-
ardizes the life and property of others and compels the polity to ex-
pend scarce resources on systems of law enforcement and incarcera-
tion.

Another criticism of contribution-based desert has been advanced
by David Mapel. There does not, he says, appear to be "any standard
measure for directly determining the relative value of all the diverse
sorts of tasks performed across the society as a whole. Instead, we
must rely on markets to indicate, through wages, the relative worth of
various economic activities."[8] This argument, it seems to me, proceeds
too briskly. As an empirical matter, a very high percentage of the U.S.
population works within large institutions, public and private, whose
internal wage structures are guided substantially by nonmarket criteria. This phenomenon is far broader than the movement for "comparable worth": Many public institutions and corporations have developed elaborate nonmarket formulas for determining the worth of
qualitatively different tasks, and there appears to be a significant
degree of convergence not only on the key variables but also on the
relative weights to be attached to them.[9] More generally, U.S. wages
tend to be a function of both market and nonmarket considerations,
and even wages that are in fact market-generated are subject to nonmarket moral critiques. (See Section II.)

Choice

Liberal societies are inclined to accept as legitimate the outcomes of the individual use of resources and opportunities legitimately held in accordance with need and desert claims. The liberal embrace of choice rests, as we have seen, on core aspects of the liberal conception of the good: on individual freedom, on the satisfaction of legitimate interests, and on the broader view that this conception is partial and limited, and allows for a very significant range of legitimate diversity.

Choice enters into the liberal conception of voluntary social groups, and it also helps define the extent to which liberals allow market determinations in the economic sphere. It means that the liberal conception of distributive justice is in part path-dependent: Certain inequalities are acceptable if they come about through the differential employment of legitimate holdings. So, for example, it is acceptable if different individual savings/consumption preferences at t_0 yield different holdings at t_1.

II

The identification of these three basic liberal claims—need, desert, choice—does not resolve, but instead sets the stage for, distributive debate. Indeed, many disputes revolve around their rank order, or relative weight. There is rough agreement that decency is offended by just ignoring basic needs of our fellow citizens, and that the urgency of these needs gives them a priority claim on the community's resources. (Although there is some disagreement about definitions of need and about the actual extent of deprivation, "welfare" programs are morally controversial only to the extent that they are seen as allowing capable adults to avoid providing for themselves and their families or as undermining their psychological ability to do so.)

The tension between desert and the market is one of the staples of contemporary social commentary. Many Americans are disturbed by the spectacle of (arguably) noncontributing paper entrepreneurs—hostile takeover artists, merger and acquisitions sharpies—reaping huge windfalls while ordinary wages and salaries stagnate. There is a vague but pervasive sense that the social contribution of the "helping professions" is not adequately compensated. Routine production workers are deeply ambivalent about salary differentials for managers and supervisors. Experimentation continues with comparable worth schemes that try to make nonmarket assessments of individual tasks within organizational structures. At the same time, the public tends not, in principle, to disapprove of huge market rewards garnered by rock musicians, movie stars, and professional athletes. (Audiences do feel entitled to value for dollar, however, and pop culture icons reap a rich harvest of moral disapproval if they shirk on the job or display contempt for their fans.)

Need, desert, and choice stand in complex tension not only in liberal conceptions but also in the institutions characteristic of contemporary liberal societies. The polity plays a significant role as the guarantor of basic needs; the market is the locus of choice; and conceptions of desert are embodied in the task and salary structures of large, complex, bureaucratic organizations, public as well as private. Debates among principles frequently take the form of struggles among institutions. To what extent, for example, should the polity enforce a public conception of need on employers through minimum wage laws? To what extent should notions of contribution be publicly enforced through comparable-worth standards and limits on compensation for corporate CEOs? To what extent, conversely, should the realm of market choice be expanded by privatizing public functions, weakening the geographical basis of public school selection, or providing alternatives to Social Security? I doubt that liberal philosophy can resolve these disputes, but it can certainly help us understand why they arise, and the significance of the concepts with which they are characteristically conducted.

Although the specifics of this discussion in this chapter have been drawn from the social and economic sphere, I believe that structurally parallel convictions apply in the political sphere as well. The principle of equality is satisfied by equal voting rights (as well as a range of other rights and protections); that of need, by fair opportunities to develop capacities for the exercise of citizenship; that of desert, by shared understandings of political excellence—distinctive capacities to contribute to the fulfillment of shared purposes (election campaigns serve in part to test the relative capacities of competing candidates); and that of choice, by the belief that when fair procedures govern a sphere in which public authority may legitimately act, the outcome is to be respected.

III

Liberal justice embodies a distinctive understanding of ways in which desert is to be developed, demonstrated, and rewarded. Specifically, many opportunities outside the sphere of need are to be allocated to individuals through a desert-based competition in which all have a fair chance to participate.

This principle entered American political thought under the rubric "equality of opportunity." Much of American social history can be interpreted as a struggle between those who wished to widen the scope of its application and those who sought to restrict it. Typically, its proponents have promoted *formal* equality of opportunity by attacking religious, racial, sexual, and other barriers to open competition among individuals. And they have promoted *substantive* equality of opportunity by broadening access to the institutions that develop socially valued talents.

In the remainder of this chapter, I sketch the grounds on which I believe equality of opportunity can be defended. In the course of doing so, I revise the generally accepted understanding of this principle in several respects. As I interpret it, equality of opportunity is less juridical and more teleological than is commonly supposed. It rests on an understanding of human equality more substantive than "equality of concern and respect."[10] It is broader than the traditional concept of meritocracy. And it is embedded in a larger vision of a good society.

My argument proceeds in four steps. First, I examine in summary fashion some propositions that provide the philosophical foundation for equality of opportunity. Next I explore the strengths and limits of four kinds of arguments commonly offered in defense of this principle. Third, I discuss some difficulties that attend the translation of the abstract principle into concrete social practices. Finally, I briefly respond to some recent critics of equality of opportunity.[11]

Full Development

Every human being is born with a wide range of potential talents. Some ought not to be encouraged—a capacity for ingenious and guiltless cruelty, for example. Among the capacities of an individual that are in some sense worth developing, a small subset are comprehensive enough to serve as organizing principles for an entire life. The fullest possible development of one or more of these capacities is an important element of the good life for that individual.

Equality

Corresponding to this developmental aspect of the human good is a principle of liberal equality: Despite profound differences among individuals, the full development of each individual—however great or limited his or her natural capacities—is equal in moral weight to that of every other. For any individuals A and B, a policy that leads to the full development of A and partial development of B is, ceteris paribus, equal in value to a policy that fully develops B while restricting A's development to the same degree. Thus a policy that neglects the educable retarded so that they do not learn how to care for themselves and must be institutionalized is, considered in itself, as bad as one that deprives extraordinary gifts of their chance to flower.

On one level, this proposal runs counter to our moral intuitions. It seems hard to deny that the full realization of high capacities is preferable to the full development of lower, more limited capacities. But this consideration is not decisive.

We would of course prefer a world in which everyone's innate capacities were more extensive than they are at present, and we would choose to be, say, mathematically talented rather than congenitally retarded. Accordingly, we would prefer *for ourselves* the full development of more extensive capacities to the full development of lesser ones. But it does not follow that whenever the developmental interests of different individuals come into conflict, the development of higher or more extensive capacities is to be given priority.

It may be argued, nonetheless, that there is something more horrible about the incomplete development of great capacities than about the waste of lesser gifts. Perhaps so. But one might say with equal justice that it is more horrible for someone who can be taught to speak to be condemned to a life of inarticulate quasi-animality than it is for someone who could have been a great mathematician to lead an ordinary life. Our intuitions about the relative desirability of the best cases are more or less counterbalanced by the relative unacceptability of the worst.[12]

The Good Society

This understanding of full, diverse, and equal development leads in turn to the idea of the good society. In such a society, the range of social possibilities comes as close as is feasible to equaling the range of human possibilities. Many worthy capacities, that is, find a place within it. Few are compelled to flee elsewhere in search of opportunities for development, the way ambitious young people had to flee farms and small towns in nineteenth-century societies. Further, worthy capacities are treated fairly in the allocation of resources available for individual development within that society.

These criteria, I suggest, are more fully satisfied in liberal societies than in any others. While liberalism tends to favor—and to screen out—certain ways of life, liberal societies historically have come closest to achieving the universality that excludes no talent or virtue. The development of great gifts encounters few material or political impediments. The development of ordinary gifts is spurred by education and training open to all. The fundamental argument for a diverse society is not, as some believe, that our reason is incompetent to judge among possible ways of life. It is, rather, that the human good is not one thing but many things. And it is equality of opportunity, understood substantively as well as formally, that mediates between the diversity of individual endowments and the relative openness of liberal societies.

Natural versus Social Endowments

Although the principle of equality of opportunity is embedded in this kind of society, the concept is nonetheless commonly thought to presuppose a sharp distinction between the natural endowments of individuals and their social environment. The life chances of individuals, it is argued, should not be determined by such factors as race, economic class, and family background. To the extent that these factors do tend to affect the development and exercise of individual talents, it is the task of social policy to alleviate their force. If malnutrition stunts mental and physical development, then poor children must be fed by the community. If social deprivation leaves some children irreparably behind before they start first grade, then compensatory preschool programs are essential.

The proposition that natural but not social differences should affect individual life chances raises a number of difficult problems. To begin with, natural differences are usually viewed as genetic endowments not subject to external intervention. But increasingly, natural endowments are viewed as malleable, and the time may not be far off when they can be more predictably altered than can social circumstances. This eventually will transform not only the distinction between the natural and the social but also its normative consequences. To the extent that, for example, modern techniques can overcome genetic defects or even determine genetic endowments, disputes will arise among families over access to these scarce and expensive techniques. Before the opportunity to develop one's capacities will come the opportunity to have certain capacities to develop. At this point— as Bernard Williams rightly suggests—equality of opportunity will merge into broader issues of absolute equality and the morality of genetic intervention.[13]

James Fishkin has reminded us of another crucial difficulty. In an argument that can be traced back to Plato's *Republic*, he shows that the family is a prime—perhaps *the* prime—source of inequalities that affect the development of natural talents and the ability to compete. Full equality of opportunity would therefore require, at a minimum, very substantial invasions of the family autonomy cherished as a basic freedom in a liberal society. Liberalism is a basket of ideals that inevitably come into conflict with one another if a serious effort is made to realize any one of them fully, let alone all of them simultaneously. It follows that our commitment to equality of opportunity—that is, to reducing to a minimum the impact of background social conditions on individual life chances—must be tempered by a sober assessment of the costs, at the margin, of such a reduction.[14]

Assuming that neither natural nor social differences are likely to be expunged, we can still ask why they are regarded so differently, that is, why differences of social background are thought to be impermissible determinants of social outcomes and, conversely, why natural differences are thought to be appropriate determinants. Why shouldn't the chief's eldest child be the next chief? This question is seldom asked because it seems absurd to us. We take it for granted that a competitive system ought to identify the candidate "best qualified" and that family membership is utterly irrelevant to this selection. But of course it need not be. If the tribe is held together by shared loyalty based in part on family sentiments, the chief's child may be uniquely qualified. Descent may be an important ingredient of social legitimacy and therefore an important claim to rule, especially when other sources of legitimacy have been weakened. India and Pakistan offer instructive examples of this sort of society.

Underlying the usual distinction between social and natural differences is the moral intuition that social outcomes should be determined by factors over which individuals have control. But the wealth and social standing of one's family are facts over which individuals cannot exercise control, and therefore, they should not matter.

The difficulty with this argument is that individuals do not control their natural endowments any more than they do their ancestry. The requirement that the basis on which we make claims must somehow be generated through our own efforts amounts to a nullification of the very procedure of claiming anything.[15]

The costs of this conclusion are high. Every conception of justice presupposes the distinction between valid and invalid claims, which in turn rests on some facts about individuals. There can be no theory of justice without some notion of individual desert, and no notion of individual desert that does not eventually come to rest on some "undeserved" characteristic of individuals.

It is perfectly true, as Rawls has urged, that from the "moral point of view" (as distinguished, say, from a theological point of view) the distribution of natural talents must be regarded as arbitrary. But this consideration is hardly decisive, for three reasons. From the moral point of view, the bare fact of our individual existence is just as arbitrary. So if undeserved talents cannot give rise to valid claims, undeserved existence cannot either.[16] In addition, our unearned characteristics are deeply woven into the fabric of our individual identity. Rawls's quasi-Kantian account of moral personality is just too parsimonious to do justice to the intuitive understanding of identity that we (properly) bring to social theory.[17] And finally, the proposition that natural talents are not to be regarded as "ours" for purposes of social justice violates what G. A. Cohen has called the principle of self-ownership, the intuitive force of which must (he argues) be acknowledged even by socialist critics of liberalism.[18]

For all these reasons, the contention that we must some how be responsible for the aspects of ourselves on the basis of which we make claims is less than compelling. The world's fastest sprinter doesn't "deserve" his natural endowment of speed, but surely he deserves to win the race established to measure and honor this excellence. There is nothing in principle wrong with a conception of individual desert that rests on the possession of natural gifts.

This does not mean that we are wholly unencumbered in the translation of natural gifts into social and material advantages. Desert claims are significantly constrained by claims based on need: Equal attention to needs reflects the liberal understanding of the extent to which we are morally required to treat differences of natural endowments as a shared fate.

The complex interplay of need and desert is more than an ad hoc compromise. It also reflects a deep duality in the human condition and in our response to it. As Anthony Kronman puts it, we must retain simultaneously a lively sense of moral arbitrariness and an understanding of the seamlessness of personal identity. The ambivalence we feel "reflects a general tension inherent in the moral point of view: although morality requires us to look at human affairs from the timeless standpoint of reason itself, its prescriptions must somehow be accommodated to the contingent and irrational features of the human condition."[19] I would suggest that the normative distinction between social facts and natural endowments is not so sharp as many interpretations of equality of opportunity presuppose.[20] This distinction provided the historical impetus for the development of the principle: The triumph of meritocratic over patriarchal and hereditary norms is an oft-told tale. But philosophically, the distinction between nature and society (or, for that matter, between what we have earned and what befalls us) must be reinterpreted as the distinction between relevant and irrelevant reasons for treating individuals in certain ways.

IV

To push this reinterpretation forward, I examine here four ways in which equality of opportunity can be defended.

First, and most obviously, equality of opportunity can be justified as a principle of *efficiency*. Whatever the goals of a community may be, they are most likely to be achieved when the individuals most capable of performing the tasks that promote those goals are allowed to do so. Such efficiency, it may be argued, requires a system that allows individuals to declare their candidacy for positions they prefer, and then selects the ablest. From this standpoint, equality of opportunity is a dictate of instrumental rationality, a measure of collective devotion to social goals.

But a complication arises immediately. Competition among individuals to fill social roles may not produce aggregate efficiency, even if the most talented is chosen to fill each individual role. To see why, consider a two-person society with two tasks. Suppose that person A can perform both tasks better than person B and is by an absolute measure better at the first task than at the second. If A is only slightly better than B at the first but much better at the second, it may be more productive for the society as a whole to allocate the first task to B, even though A will then not be doing what he or she does best.

In actual societies, the differential rewards attached to tasks can produce comparable distortions. If (say) lawyers are paid much more than teachers, the talent pool from which lawyers are selected is likely to be better stocked. Teachers will then tend to be mediocre, even if the best are selected from among the candidates who present themselves. This circumstance may well impose aggregate costs on society, at least in the long run.[21]

These difficulties arise for two reasons. First, applying equality of opportunity to a society characterized by division of labor produces a set of individual competitions whose aggregate results will fall short of the best that society could achieve through more centralized coordination among these contests. Second, equality of opportunity embodies an element of individual liberty. Individuals can choose neither the rules of various competitions nor their outcomes. But they can choose which game to play. The fact that society as a whole will benefit if I perform a certain task does not mean that I can be coerced to perform it. Within limits, I can choose which talents to develop and exercise, and I can refuse to enter specific competitions, even if I would surely emerge victorious. "From each according to his ability" is not the principle of a liberal society, for the simple reason that the individual is regarded (for most purposes, anyway) as the owner of his or her capacities. Equality of opportunity is a meritocratic principle, but it is applied to competitions among self-selected individuals.

I do not wish to suggest that this liberty is anywhere near absolute. Duties to other individuals, particularly family members who have made sacrifices on my behalf, may require me to develop and exercise certain abilities. Similarly, duties to my country may require me to become a first-rate general or a physicist, if I am capable of doing so. But after all such duties are taken into account, there will still be a range of choices into which a liberal society should not intrude. This will always be a barrier to the single-minded pursuit of efficiency, and to the use of coercive meritocracy to achieve it.

A second justification of equality of opportunity focuses on the notion of *desert*. For each social position, it is argued, a certain range of personal qualities may be considered relevant. Individuals who possess these qualities to an outstanding degree deserve those positions. A fair competition guided by equality of opportunity will allow exemplary individuals to be identified and rewarded.

Many critics have objected to this line of reasoning. It is a mistake, they argue, to regard social positions as prizes. In athletic competition, first prize goes to the one who has performed best. It would be inappropriate to take future performance into account or to regard present performance in the context of future possibilities. The award of the prize represents a recognition only of what has already happened. The prizewinner has established desert through completed performance. In the case of social positions, on the other hand, the past is of interest primarily as an index of future performance. The alleged criterion of desert is thus reducible to considerations of efficiency.

This critique contains elements of truth, but I believe that the sharp contrast it suggests is overdrawn. After all, societies do not just declare the existence of certain tasks to be performed. They also make known, at least in general terms, the kinds of abilities that will count as qualifications to perform these tasks. Relying on this shared public understanding, young people strive to acquire and display these abilities. If they succeed in doing so, they have earned the right to occupy the corresponding positions. They deserve them. It would therefore be wrong to breach these legitimate expectations, just as it would be wrong to tell the victorious runner, "Sorry. We know you crossed the finish line first, but we've decided to give the prize to the runner who stopped to help a fallen teammate."

To be sure, circumstances may prevent society from honoring legitimate desert claims. Individuals may spend years preparing themselves for certain occupations, only to find that economic or demographic changes have rendered their skills outmoded. Socially established expectations cannot be risk-free—a fact that security-seeking young people are not always quick to grasp. But this fact does not distinguish social competition from athletic competition. The Americans who worked so hard for the 1980 Olympic Games, only to be denied the right to compete, were deeply disappointed, but they could not maintain that they had been treated unjustly.

In short, no clear line can be drawn between tasks and prizes. Many tasks are prizes; opportunities to perform activities are intrinsically or socially valuable. These prizes are of a special character—forward looking rather than complete in themselves—which gives rise to legitimate disagreement about the criteria that should govern their distribution. There is no science that permits completely reliable inferences from past to future performance in any occupation.[22] But once criteria, however flawed, have been laid down, they create a context within which claims of desert can be established and must be honored if possible. Performance criteria may be altered, but only after existing claims have been discharged, and only in a manner that gives all individuals the fairest possible chance to redirect their efforts.

A third kind of justification of equality of opportunity focuses on *personal* development. When a society devotes resources to education and training, when it encourages individuals to believe that their life chances will be significantly related to their accomplishments, and when it provides an attractive array of choices, there is good reason to believe that individuals will be moved to develop some portion of their innate capacities. Thus, it may be argued, equality of opportunity is the principle of task allocation most conducive to a crucial element of the human good.

I accept this argument. But it has significant limitations. It ignores, for example, ways in which individuals may benefit from performing certain tasks even if they are less competent to do so than others. If apprentices are not permitted to perform the activities of their craft, they cannot increase their competence. In this process of apprentice-ship, the master craftsman must be willing to accept errors and inefficiencies. This is true even if the learner can never achieve the full competence of the best practitioner. Even individuals of mediocre talents can increase their knowledge, skill, and self confidence when they are allowed to discharge demanding responsibilities. Thus, developmental considerations may suggest rotating some tasks fairly widely rather than restricting them to the most able.

In addition, most individuals can achieve excellence in specific demanding tasks only when they concentrate on mastering that task to the exclusion of all others. Equality of opportunity is thus linked to the division of labor, to specialization, and to the principle of "one person, one job." An argument of considerable antiquity questions the human consequences of this principle. Perhaps it is better for individuals to be developed in many areas rather than allowing most of their capacities to lie fallow. Perhaps a system of task assignment that deemphasizes competence in favor of variety is preferable.

These considerations raise a broader issue. Human activities have both external and internal dimensions. On the one hand, they effect changes in the natural world and in the lives of others. On the other hand, they alter—develop, stunt, pervert—the character and talent of those who perform them. Neither dimension can be given pride of place; neither can be ignored.

Without a measure of physical security and material well-being, no society can afford to devote resources to individual development or to exempt individuals from material production for any portion of their lives. In societies living at the margin, child labor is a necessity, and scholarly leisure is an unaffordable luxury. But structuring a social and economic system to promote productive efficiency is justified only by physical needs and by the material preconditions of development itself. Thus a fundamental perversion occurs when the subordination of development to production continues beyond that point. A wealthy community that determines the worth of all activities by the extent to which they add to its wealth has forgotten what wealth is for. A system of training, education, and culture wholly subservient to the system of production denies the fuller humanity of its participants.[23]

For these reasons, I suggest, a prosperous society must carefully consider not only how it allocates its tasks but also how it defines and organizes the tasks it allocates. The very concern for individual development that makes equality of opportunity so attractive leads beyond that principle to basic questions of social structure.

Finally, equality of opportunity may be defended on the grounds that it is conducive to *personal satisfaction*. Within the limits of competence, individuals are permitted to choose their lives' central activity, and they are likely to spend much of their time in occupations they are competent to perform. No system can guarantee satisfaction, of course. But one that reduces to a minimum the compulsory elements of labor and allows individuals to feel competent in the course of their labor will come closer than any alternative.

Although this argument is probably correct, it is important to keep its limits in mind. To begin with, the satisfaction derived from an activity is not always proportional to our ability to perform it. We may want to do what we cannot do very well, and we may secure more pleasure from doing what we regard as a higher task in a mediocre manner than from doing a lower task very well. In addition, in a system fully governed by equality of opportunity, there would be no external causes of failure and no alternative to self-reproach for the inability to achieve personal ambitions.

An equal opportunity system stimulates many to strive for what they cannot attain. By broadening horizons, it may well increase frustration. Of course, this is not necessarily a bad thing. Such a system does induce many who can excel to develop themselves more fully. It is not clear that a system that increases both achievement and frustration is inferior to one that increases the subjective satisfaction of the less talented only by decreasing the motivation of the more talented to realize their abilities. And many people not capable of the highest accomplishments nevertheless develop and achieve more in a context that infuses them with a desire to excel. A permanent gap between what we are and what we want to be need not be debilitating. On the contrary, it can be a barrier to complacency, a source of modesty, an incentive for self-discipline, and a ground for a genuine respect for excellence.

V

I remarked at the outset that the principle of equality of opportunity gains both content and justification from the society in which it is embedded. There are, I believe, four major dimensions along which this abstract principle is rendered socially concrete; first, the range of possibilities available within a society; second, the manner in which these activities are defined and organized; third, the criteria governing the assignment of individuals to particular activities; and finally, the manner in which activities are connected to external goods such as money, power, and status.

I need not add much to the previous discussion of possibilities. A good society is maximally inclusive, allowing the greater possible scope for the development and exercise of worthy talents.

Opportunities for development are affected not just by the kinds of activities that take place within a society but also by their manner of organization. Consider the provision of health care. At present in the United States, doctors, nurses, orderlies, and administrators perform specific ranges of activities, linked to one another by rigid lines of authority. It is possible, and probably desirable, to redraw these boundaries of specialization. Nurses, for example, could well be given more responsibility for tasks now performed by doctors, particularly in some areas where judgment, experience, and sensitivity to the needs of specific individuals are critical. Similarly, it is possible to reorganize the process of production. At some plants, small groups of workers collectively produce entire automobiles, performing the required operations sequentially in the group's own area rather than along an assembly line. Proposals to expand managerial decision-making to include production workers have been tried out in a number of European countries. Behind all such suggestions lies the belief that the existing organization of social tasks rests more on habit and special privilege than on an impartial analysis of social or individual benefit. Occupational hierarchies in which all creativity and authority are confined to a few tasks while all the rest enforce routine drudgery are typically justified on the grounds of efficiency. Maintaining a certain quality and quantity of goods and services is said to demand this kind of hierarchy. In general, there is little evidence to support this proposition and much to question it. Besides, as we have seen, there are other things to consider—in particular, the effect of tasks on the development and satisfaction of the individuals who perform them. Equal opportunity requires an appropriate balance between the preconditions of productive efficiency and the internal consequences of tasks—a balance that may well depend on a far-reaching reorganization of social tasks.

Let me assume that a society has actually reached agreement on such a balance. The assignment of individuals to the tasks embodied in that agreement will remain controversial, because criteria of assignments are open to reasonable dispute. Some considerations are clearly irrelevant. Barring aberrant background circumstances, such factors as the color of one's hair or eyes should have no bearing on one's chances of becoming a doctor, because they have no bearing on one's capacity to practice the medical art. But beyond such obvious cases, there is disagreement—for example, about the nature of the good doctor. In the prevailing view, the good doctor is one who is capable of mastering a wide variety of techniques and employing them appropriately. But dissenters suggest that moral criteria should be given equal weight: The good doctor cares more about patients' welfare than about his or her own material advancement, gives great weight to need in distributing medical services, never loses sight of the humanity of his or her patients. Still others believe that the willingness to practice where medical needs are the greatest is crucial. They urge that great weight be given to the likelihood, or the promise, that a prospective doctor will provide health care to rural areas, small towns, urban ghettos, or other localities lacking adequate care. From this standpoint, otherwise dubious criteria such as geographical origin or even race might become very important.

This dispute cannot be resolved in the abstract. The relative weight accorded the technical, moral, and personal dimensions will vary with the needs and circumstances of particular societies. It will also vary among specialties within professions. In the selection of brain surgeons, technical mastery is probably paramount. For pediatricians, human understanding is far more important. Whatever the criteria, they must be made as explicit as possible, so that individuals can make informed commitments to courses of training and preparation. Those who control the selection are not free to vary publicly declared criteria once they have engendered legitimate expectations.

I turn now to the connection between activities and external goods. Here my point is simple. A fair competition may demonstrate my qualification for a particular occupation. But the talents that so qualify me do not entitle me to whatever external rewards happen to be attached to that occupation. I may nevertheless be entitled to them, but an independent line of argument is needed to establish that fact. So, for example, in accordance with public criteria, my technical competence may entitle me to a position as a brain surgeon. It does not follow that I am entitled to half a million dollars a year. Even if we grant what is patently counterfactual in the case of doctors—that compensation is determined by the market—the principle of task assignment in accordance with talents does not commit us to respect market outcomes. Indeed, the kind of competition inherent in a system of equal opportunity bears no clear relation to the competition characteristic of the market.

This distinction has an important consequence. Many thinkers oppose meritocratic systems on the ground that there is no reason why differences of talent should generate or legitimate vast differences in material rewards. They are quite right. But this is not an objection to meritocracy as such. It is an objection to the way rewards, not individuals, are assigned to tasks.

Indeed, one could argue that current salary inequalities should be reversed. Most highly paid jobs in our society are regarded as intrinsically desirable by the people who perform them. In moments of candor, most business executives, doctors, lawyers, generals, and college professors admit that they would want to continue in their professions even at considerably lower income levels. The incomes generally associated with such occupations cannot then be justified as socially necessary incentives.

There are, however, some rewards that are intrinsically related to tasks themselves. The most obvious is the gratification obtained from performing them. Another is status. Although I cannot prove it, it seems likely that there is a hierarchy of respect and prestige independent of income, correlated with what is regarded as the intrinsic worth of activities. Tasks involving extraordinary traits of mind and character or the ability to direct the activities of others are widely prized.

Finally, certain activities may entail legitimate claims to some measure of power and authority. As Aristotle pointed out, there are inherent hierarchical relations among specialized functions. The architect guides the work of the bricklayer and the plasterer. Moreover, if members of a community have agreed on a goal, knowledge that conduces to the achievement of that goal provides a rational basis for authority. If everyone wishes to cross the ocean and arrive at a common destination, then the skilled navigator has a rational claim to the right to give orders. But the navigator's proper authority is limited in both extent and time. It does not regulate the community's nonnavigational activities, and it vanishes when all reach their destination.

VI

To conclude this analysis of equal opportunity, I want to touch on four arguments that are frequently brought against it. The first objection is the *libertarian*, raised in its purest form by Robert Nozick. According to Nozick, equality of opportunity understates the individualistic character of human existence. Life is not a race with a starting line, a finish line, a clearly designated judge, and a complex of attributes to be measured. Rather there are only individuals, agreeing to give to and receive from each other.[24]

I believe that this contention overlooks important social facts. Within every community, certain kinds of abilities are generally prized. Being excluded from an equal chance to develop them means that one is unlikely to have much of value to exchange with others: Consider the problem of hard-core unemployment when the demand for unskilled labor is declining. To be sure, there is more than one social contest, but the number is limited. In a society in which more and more educational credentials are demanded for even routine tasks, exclusion from the competition for education and training—or inclusion on terms that amount to a handicap—makes it difficult to enter the system of exchange. Equality of opportunity acknowledges these prerequisites to full participation in social competition, and it therefore legitimates at least some of the social interventions needed to make full participation possible.

The second objection is the *communitarian*. According to this view, advanced by John Schaar among others, even the most perfect competition is insufficient, because competition is a defective mode of existence. It sets human beings apart from each other and pits them against one another, in an essentially destructive struggle.[25]

Certainly an equal opportunity system contains some competitive elements. But not all forms of competition are bad. Some competition brings human beings closer together, into communities of shared endeavor and mutual respect. (Consider the embrace of two exhausted boxers at the end of a match.) Moreover, competition can be mutually beneficial. Scientific competition may produce simultaneous discoveries, neither of which would have occurred without the presence of the competitor; gymnastic competition may inspire two perfect performances. And finally, the traditional antithesis between competition and community is too simple. Community rests on some agreement. A competitive system can be a form of community if most participants are willing to accept the principle of competition.

The third objection to equality of opportunity is the *democratic*. According to this objection, articulated by Michael Walzer among others, equality of opportunity is at best a limited principle because it cannot apply to the sphere of politics. Technical expertise may confer a limited authority. But because there is no rationally binding conception of the good, there is no technique for selecting the ends of political life. Political power does not look up to Platonic ideas, but rather around to prevailing opinions—that is, to the citizens' shared civic consciousness.[26]

I do not believe that any contemporary political thinker has adequately defended the crucial premise of this argument: that no rational theory of political ends is available. But let me set this question to one side and focus briefly on the qualities needed to direct a community in accordance with its own self-understanding.

I would argue that there are distinctive political excellences and virtues; they are necessary for the success of all political orders, including democracies; and they do constitute one valid claim to political authority, because they contribute to needed cooperation and to the achievement of shared purposes. Without them, a political community will lose its bearings and its self-confidence. It would be very fortunate if these virtues were widely distributed. But experience suggests that the percentage of individuals who possess them to any significant degree within a given community is small. This does not necessarily mean that democracy is based on a mistake. As Thomas Jefferson saw, the main problem of democracy is to achieve some convergence of participation, consent, and excellence. He believed that this problem is soluble, in part through social and political institutions that single out the natural *aristoi*, develop their special gifts, and reliably promote them to high office. From this standpoint, the purpose of elections is not just to register opinion but also to identify excellence. Indeed, the test of an electoral system is its propensity to confer the mantle of leadership on those most worthy to lead. Properly understood, the distribution of power in democracies is not wholly distinct from, but rather partly governed by, the merit-based principle of equal opportunity.[27]

The final, and surely the most ironic, objection to equality of opportunity is the *liberal*. (I say "most ironic" because equality of opportunity has fair claims to be regarded as the core principle of liberal society.) We have already encountered and addressed a version of the liberal critique, in James Fishkin's warnings against pressing equality of opportunity so far as to erode other liberal values. Another set of liberal objections is offered by Judith Shklar. There are, she argues, at least three problems with a social system based on equality of opportunity. It requires a powerful, and therefore dangerous, central authority to regulate its operation. It presupposes a measure of social agreement about goals, tasks, and qualifications that is most unlikely to be forthcoming. And to the extent that agreement does not exist, it invites public authority to behave paternalistically, "dispensing shares in accordance with his intuitions about the local meanings of the fair and the just.[28]

There can be no decisive response to these objections. But two considerations seem to me to diminish their force. To begin with, it is important not to overstate the role of central authority in administering a system of equal opportunity. Public authority will, up to a point, endeavor to establish fair background conditions within which individuals may strive to develop and exercise their talents. To the extent that some tasks are considered to be public offices, public authority will have to take responsibility for defining their qualifications. But beyond that, there will be a multiplicity of local and private competitions, each with its own definition of tasks and associated capabilities. Here, government will have a role only at the margin—to weed out patently discriminatory criteria and to ensure that private associations behave fairly (i.e., consistently with their own criteria) in the allocation of tasks and rewards.

Second, a system of equal opportunity does not presuppose any (fictitious) social agreement concerning goals and qualifications. It presupposes rather, as I have said, that there will be a multiplicity of competitive arenas reflecting differing conceptions of what is worthwhile. It also presupposes that in cases where some collectively binding determination must be made, standard liberal democratic decision-making procedures will come into play. A public school system, for example, may propose new criteria for hiring teachers; various individuals and groups will have their say; an elected, accountable school board will make the final determination—subject, of course, to correction at the next election.

I do not mean to suggest that there is no tension whatever between merit-based selections and liberal democracy. The point is, rather, that liberalism is guided not by one monistic or dominant goal but by a number of basic goals that can, when pressed to the hilt, come into conflict with one another. I quite agree that, taken too far, implementing equality of opportunity can pose threats to liberal freedom, diversity, and security. This is a perfectly good argument against losing our balance and mistaking the part for the whole. But it is no objection to equality of opportunity as such.

Notes

1. See William A. Galston, *Liberal Purposes: Goods, Virtues, and Diversity in the Liberal State* (Cambridge: Cambridge University Press, 1991), pp. 165–83.

2. William A. Galston, *Justice and the Human Good* (Chicago: University of Chicago Press, 1980).

3. For Michael Walzer's discussion, see his *Spheres of Justice* (New York: Basic Books, 1983), Chapter 3.

4. For useful full-length treatments of need, see Garrett Thomson, *Needs* (London: Routledge and Kegan Paul, 1988), and David Braybrooke, *Meeting Needs* (Princeton: Princeton University Press, 1987).

5. For the most detailed recent discussion, see George Sher, *Desert* (Princeton: Princeton University Press, 1987).

6. For an extended theoretical discussion of these points, see Galston, *Justice and the Human Good*, Chapter 6. For an empirical examination of the considerations bearing on the determination of "importance" within our society, see Karol Soltan, *The Causal Theory of Justice* (Berkeley: University of California Press, 1987).

7. John Rawls, "The Basic Structure as Subject," *American Philosophical Quarterly* 14, 2 (April 1977), pp. 162, 163.

8. David Mapel, *Social Justice Reconsidered: The Problem of Appropriate Precision in a Theory of Justice* (Urbana: University of Illinois Press, 1989), p. 27.

9. Soltan, *The Causal Theory of Justice*, Part II.

10. Ronald Dworkin, *Taking Rights Seriously* (Cambridge: Harvard University Press, 1978), pp. 272–73.

11. For another treatment of this topic, with which I am in general agreement, see S. J. D. Green, "Competitive Equality of Opportunity: A Defense," *Ethics* 100 (October 1989), pp. 5–32. See also James S. Fishkin, *Justice, Equal Opportunity and the Family* (New Haven: Yale University Press, 1983); and Ellen Frankel Paul, Fred D. Miller, Jeffrey Paul, and John Ahrens, eds., *Equal Opportunity* (Oxford: Basil Blackwell, 1987).

12. William A. Galston, *Justice and the Human Good*, pp. 159–62.

13. Bernard Williams, "The Idea of Equality," in *Philosophy, Politics, and Society*, 2nd series, Peter Laslett and W. G. Runciman, eds., (Oxford: Basil Blackwell, 1962), pp. 110–31.

14. Fishkin, *Justice, Equal Opportunity, and the Family*, Chapters 1–3. Green's focus on equalization of educational opportunity, though sound, leaves Fishkin's central point intact; see Green, "Competitive Equality of Opportunity," pp. 30–32. For a skeptical view of equal educational opportunity, and by extension equal opportunity as such, see Christopher Jencks, "Whom Must We Treat Equally for Educational Opportunities to Be Equal?" *Ethics* 98, 3 (April 1988), pp. 518–33.

15. Michael Zuckert, "Justice Deserted: A Critique of Rawls' *A Theory of Justice*," *Polity 13* (1981), p. 477; Robert Nozick, *Anarchy, State, and Utopia* (New York: Basic Books, 1974), pp. 224–27; Sher, *Desert*, Chapter 2.

16. Brian Barry extends this point pungently. In Rawls's hyperexpansive sense of moral arbitrariness, it must also be considered "radically contingent that the universe exists at all, that there is a planet capable of sustaining life, that human beings evolved on it, and so on. It seems to me that nothing of moral significance follows from this sort of radical contingency of every-

thing. The only possible reply, when the issue is pitched at that level, is that things might have been different but they were not." Barry, "Equal Opportunity and Moral Arbitrariness," in *Equal Opportunity*, Norman Bowie, ed. (Boulder, Colo.: Westview, 1988), p. 41.

17. On this point, see also Anthony T. Kronman, "Talent Pooling," in *Human Rights*, J. Roland Pennock and John Chapman, eds. (New York: New York University Press, 1981), pp. 71–77.

18. G. A. Cohen, "Self-Ownership, World-Ownership, and Equality," in *Justice and Equality: Here and Now*, Frank S. Lucash, ed. (Ithaca: Cornell University Press, 1986), pp. 110–12. For a broader discussion, see also G. A. Cohen, "On the Currency of Egalitarian Justice," *Ethics*, 99, 4 (July 1989), pp. 906–44.

19. Kronman, "Talent Pooling," pp. 76–77.

20. The same conclusion was reached by Green via a different route (see "Competitive Equality of Opportunity," p. 16); by Alexander Rosenberg, "The Political Philosophy of Biological Endowments: Some Considerations," in *Equal Opportunity*, Ellen Frankel Paul et al., eds., pp. 1–31; and by Brian Barry, "Equal Opportunity and Moral Arbitrariness," in *Equal Opportunity*, Bowie, ed., pp. 33–43. For a warning against carrying the acceptance of social facts such as cultural differences or group attitudes too far, see James S. Fishkin, "Do We Need a Systematic Theory of Equal Opportunity?" in *Equal Opportunity*, Bowie, ed., pp. 18–20.

21. Norman Daniels ably discusses the issues just raised in his "Meritocracy," in *Justice and Economic Distribution*, John Arthur and William H. Shaw, eds., (Englewood Cliffs, N.J.: Prentice-Hall, 1978), pp. 164–78. I am less sure than I once was, and than Daniels still is, that productivity represents the single best basis for understanding and justifying merit-based equality of opportunity. See the rest of Section IV.

22. For a discussion, see George Sher, "Predicting Performance," in Ellen Frankel Paul et al., *Equal Opportunity*, pp. 188–203.

23. Galston, *Justice and the Human Good*, pp. 261–62.

24. Nozick, *Anarchy, State, and Utopia*, pp. 235–38.

25. John Schaar, "Equality of Opportunity, and Beyond," in *Nomos 9: Equality*, J. Roland Pennock and John W. Chapman, eds. (New York: Atherton, 1967).

26. Michael Walzer, *Spheres of Justice: A Defense of Pluralism and Equality* (New York: Basic Books, 1983), p. 287.

27. For a more extended discussion of Walzer's view, see Galston, *Liberal Purposes*, Chapter 3. For a more extended discussion of Jefferson in the context of liberal-democratic political excellence, see Chapter 10.

28. Judith Shklar, "Injustice, Injury, and Inequality: An Introduction," in *Justice and Equality*, Lucash, ed., pp. 22–23. I do *not* mean to suggest that her stance toward equality of opportunity is wholly disapproving, or even on balance negative; see ibid., pp. 20–21.

Comments by Tibor R. Machan

The essay by Galston is a straightforward defense of a given kind of political system, roughly modern welfare state liberalism or, in European terms, social democracy. I will criticize it on two grounds, essentially. First, I criticize Galston's intuitionist approach to identifying the nature of justice, an approach I claim will only generate intractable disputation and not lead to fruitful public discourse. Second, I complain that this is not liberalism at all, and claiming it distorts the view to its unjustified benefit, by placing it on the side of human liberty when it is, in fact, supportive of widespread involuntary servitude.

To start with, it does not appear to matter much to Galston that the term "liberal" arises from the concept of negative liberty, so that liberalism in its original form deals with freeing people *from others*, mostly their rulers, and freeing them in the sense of respecting and protecting their sovereignty to strive for their success in life within the context of communities without resorting to ruling one another. Galston makes this clear early when he characterizes the liberal good in terms of need, desert, and choice, apparently in that order of importance. But, of course, need used to be (and remains today, especially in Western societies) the justification for subjecting people and treating them as lacking sovereignty of their own—they needed and need to be led, to be taken care of, to be provided for. The king and his gang were to take care of the realm where this care was needed and they ruled. Sir Robert Filmer, against whom the classical liberal John Locke argued so vigorously, asserted the merits of his illiberal political order largely on grounds of need. Desert, too, was one of the main reasons why illiberal systems gained support. The better, wiser, stronger, of more noble birth, et al. (based largely on how much better they could satisfy everyone's needs than could others), deserved to be rulers and to be privileged, while the rest, lacking in such fine qualities, did not. This was, in part, the doctrine of the divine rights of monarchs.

Choice, on the other hand, was not usually the basis for illiberal politics, although there have always been attempts to make it appear that some people's ruling of others will contribute to others' making their choices more effectively—nearly every measure of socialism and the welfare state gained some of its support from the view that true, informed, wise, and/or effective choice presuppose arranging the world so that the actions of agents are guided in these various ways, that they "choose the right way." So it seems that even choice, as understood by Galston and other modern liberals, supports not the genuine liberal order but some kind of system with considerable regimentation of human conduct (by monarchs, committees of good theoreticians, democratic assemblies, presidential health commissions, etc.), albeit for the sake of making other people's choices something better than they would be otherwise.[1] Now in order to criticize a political theory, one can do different things. First, one can show some contradictions, ambiguities, vagueness, impracticabilities, etc. Second, one can point to better argued or developed or otherwise more successful theories and note the theory's comparable inferiority vis-à-vis such theories. Or third, one can ignore the theory altogether and proceed as if it were not one of the contenders.

Galston employs the third alternative toward the sort of liberalism I regard as bona fide and very promising to boot—mentioning only one idea of Robert Nozick from that tradition[2] so as to indicate its strengths. Obviously I have not chosen the same approach. I will employ the first approach, having already employed the second in my own contribution to the constructive essays in this volume.

To start with, in his discussion of need, Galston invokes the idea of "societal obligation." This is nearly the most basic normative assumption in his essay, given that he uses the concept "we" with inordinate frequency and that his uses cannot be made much sense of without some notion of collectivity, both in the sense of there being some collective entity such as society and in the sense of that collective entity having some kinds of obligations or duties to fulfill. Yet it is just this idea that is left entirely undefined, unspecified, underdeveloped in Galston's discussion. Where do the societal obligations that place nearly everyone (other than perhaps some significantly impaired individuals) into a state of involuntary servitude "to meet needs" come from? Individuals have a difficult enough time to make a decent life for themselves and for those with whom they enter into voluntary company—family, friends, colleagues, partners, etc. Why is it not only wrong for them to address these tasks exclusively but to respect their liberty to decide whether to do this or to also take on the meeting of the needs Galston takes for granted we ought all be made to fulfill?

Here, I think, is a major problem with Galston's thesis. But its source is perhaps more interesting. As one reads Galston carefully, one will notice the significant metaethical role played by intuitions in his paper. This is not immediately evident since there is much talk about the good, or some conception of the good we share, or some such seemingly objective notion. If it is, after all, a conception of the good we share, we must somehow have developed it, based on some facts or experiences that are objective and that enable us to share the conception; otherwise it is mysterious that we would share them. If the good is, however, purely intuitive, then our sharing it would appear to be accidental, sporadic, unstable in the extreme. It is notorious what seemed intuitively good to people in the past—for example, public flogging of children, using women as chattel, regarding males as wholly expendable in holy wars, etc. If our current intuitions are to be treated as the last word in what our conception of the good is, and liberal justice is to be grounded on such a framework, it is hard to think how we have anything worthy of a political idea at hand here. Politics, after all, aims at establishing some kind of basic and ongoing framework for community life, not a set of loose, helter-skelter notions that will have moral force one day but lose it the next.

These are my most basic criticisms of Galston—his so-called liberal system is not really liberal except in the highly questionable sense that in America "liberal" has come to be distorted to mean "social democratic" or "welfare statist," losing nearly all connection with the intellectual tradition that prized the freedom of individuals from other individuals' intrusiveness and then left it to all individuals to make their way through life by means that did not abridge this freedom. The new liberalism lacks the confidence in human individuals to suggest that once they have their negative liberty secured by the respect of others and the protection of the government, they will be able to choose ways to reach their various aspirations, moving from a position they start from to a substantially improved one, although by no means supposing these positions to be uniform among members of the community. The most common ordinary rendition of this idea is that in a state of freedom we have the phenomenon of rags-to-riches and possibly back again. But the modern liberal or social democrat does not see individuals as possessing the capacity to exercise such initiative but requiring constant and repeated enablement, thus placing others into a state of involuntary servitude. Never mind that this is a self-defeating picture and invites the conclusion that in the last analysis all we have is a collection of human beings who are equally helpless and merely more or less lucky than their fellows. How we can conceive of social obligations which suggest some measure of individual moral responsibility and, therefore, personal initiative, is a mystery to me. It is here that the intuitionism of Galston, not unlike that of others (e.g., Rawls), builds up moral expectations without any foundation in a conception of human nature that is compatible with the very idea of moral responsibility. A bunch of people who are inert except for what others enable them to do are then expected to fulfill various moral and social obligations and to enforce these by means of politics. Just how is this possible? But when one begins politics from midair, as Rawls suggests that we do in his thesis of the independence of moral theorizing (taking, instead of a theory, one's intuitions as starting points for analysis), it is very troublesome to get different, more integrated results.

Let me now turn to some of the details in Galston's essay. My comments here presuppose the points raised above. Galston talks of how "There is rough agreement that decency is offended by just ignoring basic needs of our fellow citizens, and that the urgency of these needs gives them a priority claim on the community's resources." But he says nothing to make clear this sentiment. How rough is rough and how much does that matter—what if there is no such agreement? And what is the alleged agreement supposed to be (to actually do)? Should people and corporations make charitable contributions to those in need? Or should they force others, better situated, to make such contributions, directly or by means of somebody such as a protection racketeer organization or government? What would be the right thing to do if equally distressed citizens advance claims on resources that are inadequate—so that if equally distributed they simply do not help, but if unequally distributed this will be unfair? Galston brightly asserts that "welfare programs are morally controversial only to the extent that they are seen as allowing capable adults to avoid providing for themselves and their families or as undermining their psychological ability to do so."

But this is (a) dead wrong and (b) irrelevant—a political discussion of welfare cannot just take some kind of common belief as its ground, for that would then make all kinds of common beliefs, about the roles of members of certain races, sexes, nationalities, etc., morally decisive, leading to intolerably diverse moralities in different regions of the globe. Welfare problems are indeed morally controversial in part because they involve placing some people into involuntary servitude and thus making them subjects for the disposal of others. The rich, who may well be supposed to have their goals in life, some of them no doubt perfectly honorable, are usually the candidates for this but in fact, as economists have demonstrated, it is often the poor and middle-income citizens whose wealth goes to provide welfare for the rich, as in subsidies and trade restrictions and similar laws and regulations that mainly impose hardship on the general public so as to help the few.

Still, what is most important is that there is no justification given by Galston for the welfare system as such—taking from Peter to support the (let's admit for now) worse off Paul? This is not in itself to question the virtue of generosity or charity or the high mindedness of compassion or kindness—it is to question (a) distribution by force, and (b) the policy of just asserting its righteousness.

It is interesting, by the way, that even in his intuitionism Galston vacillates. At first liberalism is defended on the basis of some moral intuitions favoring charity and generosity. But later liberalism is characterized as something morally sound by reference to its minimal statism—"defend[ing] the community against external aggression, or against internal breaches of law." Galston is fudging the distinction between classical (capitalist, laissez-faire) and welfare statist (egalitarian, socialist) liberalisms. In his allusions to such features of the market place as that "the 'helping professions' is not adequately compensated," Galston invokes ideas that are confusing. To start with, contributions *are not* but contributors *are* capable of being compensated. Then, though at first Galston seems to reject the market's way of assessing value of anything (i.e., providing economically meaningful compensations for all varieties of contributions people make to and receive from others), later he seems to take money (or however else people can be compensated) as the measure of value, after all, since he complains that those who produce greater worth—in the way of the social cntribution of the helping professionals—do not get compensated enough.

But by what standard of "enough" is this to be evaluated? If I am a philosophy professor and make a third of what an IBM executive makes, but I get a great deal of satisfaction from my job, not to mention having the chance to allocate my working time more flexibly than the IBM exec, while he or she is strapped by a daily routine and frequent chores that are not to his or her liking at all, who is being more "adequately compensated"? If the moral rewards of the helping professions are as great as Galston's discussion implies, why should the social contribution of workers in these professions not be regarded as being "adequately compensated"? Why, in short, is cash and its equivalents (in-kind payments, perks, benefits) the measure of just reward, especially on the part of someone who evidently finds the system that generates more (monetary or economic) wealth than any alternative system not very elevating from the moral point of view?

Much of Galston's discussion suffers from a collectivism that does not only bear directly on his political ideas but on his method. Consider this sentence: "But it does not follow that whenever the developmental interests of different individuals come into conflict, the development of higher or more extensive capacities is to be given priority." By whom? How is one to make sense of the idea of giving priority to something without some notion of who is going to be involved and why those rather than others and on what grounds, and why those grounds and not others? Sure, such a process must come to an end somewhere, but Galston's discussion suffers from a repeated failure to take it far enough to some common ground that is genuinely evident to human beings as such, rather than to those who already share nearly all of his moral intuitions.

There is much else one could mention here, including the fairly lengthy discussion of equality of opportunity, the uses of such terms as "fleeing" farms as if this were comparable to fleeing a tyranny (thus begging the question as to the respective significance of negative and positive liberty for an understanding of justice). There is more. Let me, however, end with a point of strong agreement. Galston states, "The fundamental argument for a diverse society is not, as some believe, that our reason is incompetent to judge among possible ways of life. It is, rather, that the human good is not one thing but many things." Perhaps the most thorough investigation of liberalism based on this insight, by Douglas B. Rasmussen and Douglas J. Den Uyl,[3] discusses value pluralism within a naturalist metaethical framework and shows that it is just such value pluralism, understood from the viewpoint of morality, that supports the classical liberal system of *polity*, not some other in which the right to individual liberty is sacrificed.

Notes

1. A contemporary example will serve us here quite well. In her testimony before Congress on the health reform plan of the Clinton administration, Hillary Rodham Clinton noted that once this plan goes into operation, insurance companies will no longer be free to discriminate, regarding whom they will insure and at what cost, on the basis of who is and who is not at a higher or lower risk of becoming sick.

What this mandate from government does is legally coerce insurers to trade with those they do not wish to trade with—indeed with whom trade would be commercially disadvantageous—but, of course, that point wasn't stressed. Instead, the point that was stressed is that now everyone, however much a health risk faced by him or her, will be free to choose to be insured.

But this kind of choice existed when slavery reigned: masters were free to choose to obtain the services of slaves without having to reach terms of trade with them.

2. Robert Nozick, *Anarchy, State, and Utopia* (New York: Basic Books, 1974). Nozick, by the way, no longer identifies himself as an adherent of

such liberalism, and he among all the political philosophers who find such liberalism promising has done nothing since writing his book to advance the discussion about these issues. I am very tempted to consider the sort of attention Nozick has gotten, despite his refusal to answer criticisms or make any further contribution to the process of trying to find answers in this area, as little more than star gazing, which is not a very wise philosophical endeavor.

3. See Douglas B. Rasmussen and Douglas J. Den Uyl, *Liberty and Nature, An Aristotelian Defense of Liberal Order* (La Salle, Ill.: Open Court, 1991).

Comments by Milton Fisk

Galston's essay begins with a redefinition of liberalism and then discusses the principle of equal opportunity within liberalism as so conceived. I want to take note of what's new in his concept of liberalism. The new elements don't, I will suggest, make liberalism any more attractive a polity. He highlights the validity of needs claims, rewards for activity serving liberal goals, and market freedoms limited by basic needs. Emphasis on these features jibes with tendencies in current liberal democracies, without subjecting these tendencies to a critical test.

Needs. Classical liberalism always had a problem with welfare measures. Its emphasis on freedom as noninterference made welfare measures suspect. But as the welfare state developed, liberals became reconciled to its practices. Galston's redefinition of liberalism locates it somewhere between its classical and welfare state variants. He sees claims based on individual need as valid simply on the basis of community membership. This shift away from the classical emphasis on noninterference comes about through an appeal to community, which blurs the common contrast between liberalism and communitarianism. With the blurring of this distinction, one might expect a gentler type of liberalism. But though it may be gentler than classical Lockean liberalism, Galston's redefinition points in the direction of what today is called neo-liberalism.

Once having granted the validity of needs claims, Galston is quick to limit them on grounds of individual responsibility. This is where it becomes clear that what we're getting is far from a gentle liberalism. People have a responsibility to take care of themselves to the extent that they can. Those who can get adequately remunerative jobs are owed nothing more by society for their need satisfaction. The rest get subsidies for their needs.

But is there any problem with this? Social democratic defenders of welfare systems argue that some needs should be satisfied uniformly across the society. Otherwise, inequalities result that are harmful to the chances those either without income or with low income have of a rewarding life. We are talking here about needs that if not adequately satisfied jeopardize the chances of being a full member of the society. Even these fundamental needs of those depending on government subsidies and of those with low income will, under Galston's liberalism, tend to be satisfied to a lesser extent than the same needs of the better off. One gets then two-tiered education, two-tiered personal security, two-tiered justice, and two-tiered health care.

All this is hidden in the idea that the validity of needs claims calls for access to the "basic elements" people will need. How basic though are basic elements? In *San Antonio Independent School District v. Rodriguez* the Supreme Court saw education, not education that prepares students for political participation, as the basic element needed. Class-tiered education was sanctioned, and it was reaffirmed in a Texas referendum on school funding in 1993. Similarly, government subsidies intended to provide the basic elements of health care for low income people has already led to two-tiered health care in many countries. It will also lead to two-tiered health care in the United States. Experience elsewhere also shows that there will be progressive deterioration of the lower tier.

The answer is to recognize that the neoliberal emphasis on responsibility, even softened a bit with a commitment to respond to needs claims, reinforces unfortunate social consequences of inequality. Its net effect will be to undermine the community to which Galston appeals in order to ground the validity of caring for the needs of others. As inequality rends the society, the well off will resent provision for the less well off. The emphasis on responsibility, in regard to these fundamental needs, may satisfy the instinct of the disciplinarian, but it fragments the society. It should give way to an emphasis on treating the satisfaction of those needs as an entitlement.

Desert. In addition to claims of need, Galston also upholds claims of desert made by individuals who contribute to the community. The conflict on this point is with Rawls, who seemingly dismisses desert claims in treating contributions as social assets waiting to be distributed by principles of justice. Moreover, Galston sees equal opportunity as "the flip side" of the principle of contribution-based desert, for desert should be awarded only where all have the opportunity to make a contribution.

One way of reading Rawls on desert suggests a feasible alternative to Galston's treatment of it. Instead of reading Rawls as saying that desert is to be rejected altogether, one can read him as saying that desert claims do not stand on their own, but must pass a double test. It is only a metaphor to say that alleged deserts are a common asset pending passage of the double test.

First, desert claims must accord with publically stated criteria of desert. For example, it says in the Indiana University Bulletin that you deserve to graduate if you have passed 120 hours of course work. Or according to a Colorado statute you deserve the wealth produced from a lode your prospecting has uncovered. Nobody deserves to graduate unless there are criteria in an official book for doing so. *Pace* Locke, mixing labor with the ore in the lode does not create desert apart from common or positive law. So this requirement is incompat-

ible with the view of Nozick, for example, that there are natural
deserts, ones holding apart from laying down public criteria.

Second, desert claims must accord with criteria that satisfy norms
of justice. Equal opportunity is itself a norm of justice implicit in
most criteria for desert. But a criterion for desert that puts enormous
power or riches within the grasp of someone who wins the most votes
for the office of presidency might be judged unacceptable on grounds
of distributional justice. Again, deserts aren't natural, since they wait
upon justice.

If deserts aren't natural what's being said when Galston emphasizes that his liberalism gives importance to desert claims? He says this
importance is part of a "deep description of what 'we' believe" and
that, "There can be no theory of justice without some notion of individual desert." But the issue is just how desert enters a theory of justice. Does a theory of justice claim that it is just to treat those satisfying the existing criteria of desert as deserving? Or does it claim
only that this is just on condition that the criteria themselves have
satisfied the principles of justice?

Galston faces a dilemma here. In the former case the criteria suffice for justice. But only in this case does desert have the kind of
importance his liberalism wants to give it. For only then can we hold
desert up as largely independent of social democratic redistributive
schemes. In the later case the criteria for desert get legitimacy only
by being compatible with a general scheme of justice. Yet only in this
case does a criterion of desert avoid being merely an arbitrary agreement. How does he choose between liberalism and legitimacy?

Galston handles this dilemma by trying to straddle it with the double
requirement of need satisfaction for the indigent and equal opportunity for all. These are requirements of justice and by conforming to
them, criteria of desert aren't merely arbitrary. Still this is a pretty
thin slice from the panoply of all principles of justice that might be
thought relevant. Galston is, though, happy with its being only a thin
slice. If only these two requirements of justice are called in to assess
criteria for desert, then Galston can plausibly treat desert as at least
a quasi-independent factor in relation to a general scheme of justice.
It is not secondary to distributive matters going beyond a safety net,
but stands on its own in relation to them.

Galston can both satisfy neoliberals by treating desert as primary
in respect to other aspects of distributive justice and hope to satisfy
the Rawlsians by having desert conform to two minimal principles of
justice. Let's take a closer look though.

Consider the case of affirmative action, which Galston doesn't mention in this discussion of desert. Admission requirements are, we'll imagine, having the effect of excluding lower class students from entering law school, yet these students are not denied the opportunity for preparatory education. Should the requirements be modified to allow for an eventual allocation of the benefits of legal careers to more people with lower class backgrounds and to allow for a different mix of perspectives within the profession?

If this question is admitted, it is recognized that there may be considerations of justice, beyond bare equal opportunity and basic need satisfaction, relevant to deciding whether as things stand the dominantly non-lower class students who get to law school deserve to get there. Admitting the question, however it is finally decided, indicates that desert is not being treated as independent of considerations of justice going beyond equal opportunity and basic need satisfaction for the indigent. The denial of primacy to desert, in the manner of the above reading of Rawls, is sustained.

Choice. In Galston's liberalism the third fundamental type of claim a citizen can make on others, after need and desert claims, is that of the outcomes of free choice. If you choose certain associates and work to affiliate with them, you should not be denied association with them. If you choose to invest in the cable giant TCI, you reap the benefits (or losses) coming from doing so, once need and desert claims have been attended to. Galston observes that this legitimates "certain inequalities." Now the needs of the indigent are taken care of in a way that creates a two-tiered system. And deserts are limited only by basic needs and equal opportunity. So we can expect that the inequalities resulting from free choice will not be significantly reduced by the claims of needs and deserts. Should they be reduced farther?

We can begin by asking, what is the nub of the argument here for the legitimacy of possessing the gains made from a choice to use certain resources in a certain way? The nub is that the choice is free and that the holdings are legitimately one's own. This is just the classical libertarian argument, which has its own problems. What I'm interested in here is not these problems but Galston's qualification of the libertarian argument by the safety net and deserts. The beauty of the libertarian argument is that it seems to work only if there is no qualification: Free choice is the universal source of legitimacy, not depending on any other factor to work its magic. Satisfying the needs of the indigent had then to be charity, not an obligation. And what you deserved was what you made or were freely given. All beautifully simple.

But once he allows deductions from free enterprise to provide a safety net and to award civic prizes in recognition of desert, Galston weakens the moral force of libertarian liberty to legitimate the gains of choice. And then the question becomes: Why can't it be weakened even more? If we can weaken it to take care of the unemployed infirm why can't we weaken it further to end poverty rather than provide only a safety net for the poor. The stated intention of Lyndon Johnson's Great Society program was after all the elimination of poverty.

The answer is to be found in Galston's readiness to treat the market as a system of distributive justice, qualified in the two ways indicated. Again this fits with the neoliberal policy of tearing down barriers to free enterprise. What's missing in Galston's account is a reason why the decency to which he explicitly appeals doesn't demand a system of justice that is more than market rules and a safety net.

In sum, Galston's liberalism is a view that tries to avoid the egalitarian drift of certain forms of liberalism. It emphasizes individual responsibility for welfare, criteria for desert cut loose from a general view of justice, and the legitimacy of market inequalities. We can get a sense of what a society organized on this basis would be like. We need only look around us at the growing inequality and poverty, the frenzied competitiveness, and the decline in political participation and empowerment.

5

Social Justice and the Limitation of Democracy

Carol C. Gould

There are some hard problems in the theory of democracy that center around the question: When is it legitimate to constrain democratic decision-making in the interests of justice? If democracy is a central value in political and social life, what can justify limiting or overriding the decisions arrived at by the democratic process? Wouldn't any constraint undercut the very essence of democracy? On the other hand, justice is also a central value for politics, economy, and society. Can our commitment to democratic process allow for decisions or laws democratically arrived at that violate the requirements of justice? Where these two values conflict, what is the basis for judgment as to which will prevail? Even if we agree that in certain cases democracy ought to be constrained in the interest of social justice, who has the right or the authority to determine this?

Liberal theorists have discussed these issues in the context of political democracy. Here, the primary constraint on democratic decision-making has been seen as a constitutional framework that sets the boundaries of legitimacy for democratic decisions, by protecting the rights of individuals, and by specifying, limiting, and balancing the powers of government. Even in this political context, however, the issue of legitimate constraint on democratic decisions is not settled, and it becomes still more problematic if democracy is taken to extend to social and economic life. For in these contexts, there is only an informal framework of decision-making, not defined by the making of laws and usually not governed by a formal constitution. Moreover, norms of economic and social justice that could possibly serve to limit the scope of democratic decisions in these areas are not usually the subject of universal agreement in the way in which the norms of political and legal justice more often are. Therefore, what may be in contention is not whether the demands of social justice should override democratic process, but rather what exactly the demands of social justice are.

In contemporary political theory, we may observe that there have been two relatively separate conversations: one about justice and one about democracy. On the one hand, there has been an extended philosophical discussion about theories of justice that makes some passing reference to democracy and its place within such theories. On the other hand, there has been major renewed interest in democratic theory, but without much reflection on the relation of democracy to justice. There has of course been recognition of the relation between these two concepts in traditional theories of political democracy and in their contemporary versions. Thus, the protection of individual rights as a requirement of justice and the protection of minority rights against potential injustices by majority rule are seen to be essential constraints on democratic decision-making, which is taken to be embodied in a constitutional framework. Likewise, it is recognized that democratic processes may eventuate in unjust laws despite these constitutional protections, because of the limitations of human knowledge and judgments and conflicts of interest between majorities and minorities. Nonetheless, it is often argued that there is an obligation to obey even unjust laws if they are duly instituted, in the interest of preserving social stability and out of respect for the abiding institutions of democracy.

Although individual liberties and rights have been grounded in theories of justice in various ways, what has remained less than clear is whether the introduction of constitutional guarantees of these rights is legitimated by the democratic or the consensual procedures of their adoption, hence in some sense by the value of democracy, or whether their normative claim is independent of such procedures. That is, are such rights constituted as rights by their democratic or consensual recognition, or is the imperative to institute them based on their prior and autonomous status as rights? This question is further complicated by the fact that several recent theories of justice themselves ground rights in some consensual procedure, hence putting the principles of justice themselves in the context of some quasi-democratic decision-making procedure.

Another question that has not received sufficient attention is whether economic or social justice, where these lie beyond the traditional constitutionally protected civil liberties and political rights, should constrain democratic decisions. If the demands of economic or social justice were to constrain democratic decision-making as present constitutional rights do, would that impose too severe a limitation on the freedom of decision and pose the old problems about positive liberty that have been raised against the inclusion of such economic and social rights within the purview of government?

A wider question appears with the prospect of the extension of democratic decision-making beyond the sphere of politics to economic and social institutions. The difference here is that there is no established constitutional framework within these domains parallel to that in political life. Although of course the existing constitution and laws apply to these economic and social domains insofar as they fall under the law, the requirements of justice beyond these tend either not to be spelled out at all or to remain informal or ad hoc. Thus, for example, where a social institution like a university or a professional association, or an economic body like a trade union or the stockholders of a corporation operates in accordance with democratic procedures—specifically, by the election of officials or by the determination of policy by vote—the constraints of principles of justice or of rights are often left unarticulated or are vaguely formulated.

Another issue concerning the relation of justice and democracy that may be added to these has come sharply to the fore recently. This concerns the old question of rights of minorities against majorities but in a new form, namely, the question of what the demands of justice entail for the rights of ethnic minorities within a polity to cultural autonomy or, more radically, to political secession. In addition to the standard question of minority rights, this raises questions about the criteria of membership in a polity and what role nationality plays in generating political or cultural rights. In other words, does justice require rights of democratic self-determination for nationalities that would thereby limit processes of majority rule and universal suffrage as requirements of democracy?

The problems I have cited thus far introduce two sorts of cases. The first concerns the way in which democratic decision-making is explicitly constrained by constitutional considerations of justice and what the justification for this is. The second case concerns situations where the demands of justice lie beyond what is embodied in a constitutional framework. At a more theoretical level as well, namely, within political philosophy proper, we may observe that the relation between the norms of democracy and justice remains deeply problematic, where it is discussed at all. Some theorists (1) take the requirement of democratic decision-making to be entailed by a conception of justice itself, as realizing one of its requirements. Others, conversely, (2) see justice as required for democracy, namely, as rights instrumental to the protection and viability of democratic processes. Still others (3) see the value of democracy instrumentally as the best way to achieve just outcomes, where such just outcomes are understood either as (a) in conformity with standards of justice independently defined or as (b) whatever is produced by some ideal democratic or consensual procedure itself. In the latter case, democracy and justice are assimilated to each other.

In what follows, I will analyze these theoretical alternatives as a background for the articulation of my own argument concerning the relation of justice and democracy. This will permit a specification of the respects in which the demands of justice can legitimately delimit democratic decision-making. Within this framework, I will briefly consider the four issues with which I began: first, what legitimates the constitutional protection of rights and therefore the constraints on democratic processes; second, the status of the demands for economic and social justice as constraining democratic decisions; third, how to conceive of the requirements of justice that apply when democracy is extended beyond the political sphere to social and economic life; and finally, the issue of the rights of ethnic minorities to self-determination. The goal here is to make clear what is conceptually in question when the values of justice and democracy are seen to be in conflict with each other rather than a full account of each one of these issues separately, which is a subject for a larger project.

Alternative Conceptions of the
Relation of Justice and Democracy

The alternative theoretical formulations of the relation of justice and democracy may be divided into three main views. The first sees democracy as itself a requirement of justice. In such an account, justice is taken to be the prior value which entails democratic rights of participation in political processes or self-governance. Justice is understood here either as equal liberty or as equal consideration of interests. Equal liberty may be defined as freedom of choice protected against external interference (negative freedom) or again, as the equal freedom of self-development (equal positive freedom). On these views, equal liberty is seen to entail certain basic rights of self-determination or self-rule. Thus the legitimation of democracy is that it is required as the expression of the equal freedom of individuals which constitutes an essential part of the norm of justice. Rawls's discussion of his first principle of justice in *A Theory of Justice*, that is, the principle of equal liberty, suggests an account of this sort, insofar as it requires the right to vote and to stand for elective office (though he does not call this democracy).[1] Dahl also suggests a grounding of democracy in the prior value of equal personal autonomy and the equal consideration of interests.[2]

The second theoretical approach, by contrast, takes democracy to be the prior or basic value and sees the civil liberties and equal rights as required for the preservation and viability of democracy. On such a view, even the requirements of social and economic justice are seen as means for preserving or enhancing democracy. In this type of approach, the unalienable and primary right is that of democratic self-governance itself. Dahl sometimes seems to favor this sort of position. Thus he speaks of "fundamental political rights as comprising all the rights necessary to the democratic process."[3] Or again, "What interest, then, can be justifiably claimed to be inviolable by the democratic process, or, for that matter, any other process for making collective decisions? It seems to me highly reasonable to argue that *no* interest should be inviolable beyond those integral or essential to the democratic process."[4]

The third conception of the relation between justice and democracy sees democracy as the best means for arriving at just outcomes in decision-making or legislation. Thus democracy is legitimated instrumentally on this view. In contrast to the first case, where equal liberty requires equal opportunities to participate in decision-making independent of the outcome of the decisions, here it is the fact that democracy conduces to just legislation or to just outcomes of decision-making that recommends it. Rawls presents such a view in arguing that the institutions of a constitutional democracy satisfy the principles of justice and they do so because "Ideally, a just constitution would be a just procedure arranged to insure a just outcome."[5] Iris Young presents a different version of this view in suggesting that political democracy modified by procedures of group representation offers the best prospect for arriving at just outcomes, defined in terms of social and economic justice.[6]

Within this instrumentalist view, there are two different readings. On the first, the criterion for the justness of the outcomes of democratic decision-making is not merely the appropriateness of the procedure itself, since even with properly democratic procedures, unjust outcomes are possible. But this means that the standard of justice is independent of the procedure. Rawls's view of constitutional democracy is of this sort. Thus he writes, "Clearly any feasible political procedure may yield an unjust outcome. In fact, there is no scheme of procedural political rules which guarantees that unjust legislation will not be enacted. In the case of a constitutional regime, or indeed of any political form, the ideal of perfect procedural justice cannot be realized. The best attainable scheme is one of imperfect procedural justice."[7]

The second reading holds that an outcome is just if it is produced by some ideal democratic decision procedure. That is, there is no appeal to any independent criterion of justice beyond what the ideal democratic procedure would yield. Iris Young writes along these lines, "Without God or nature as the foundation of justice, the just decision must coincide with the decision that people in a democratic body freely agree to after listening to proposals, expressions of needs, arguments, etc."[8] Joshua Cohen in a similar vein introduces a conception of democracy as an ideal deliberative procedure which legitimates outcomes, but does not specify such outcomes in terms of their justness.[9] In this sense, though the reasoning is similar, Cohen does not here present an explicit conception of the relation of democracy to justice.

Jürgen Habermas presents an interesting perspective on this issue of the relation of justice and democracy. On the one hand, he speaks of democratic forms as merely a question of political organization, as a practical question of which "mechanisms are in each case better suited to bring about procedurally legitimate decisions and institutions."[10] This sounds like a purely formal and procedural characterization of democracy with no particular normative content. However, Habermas goes on to characterize "procedurally legitimate decisions and institutions" as those that "would meet with the unforced agreement of all those involved, if they could participate, as free and equal, in discursive will formation."[11] But the counterfactual condition of free and equal participation sounds very much like equal liberty as a traditional principle of justice. In these ways, Habermas's view seems to straddle the first and third conceptual alternatives. A further complication is that Habermas's account of the genesis of norms or of "discursive will formation" in an "ideal speech situation," which constitutes his notion of justice, tacitly makes appeal to a quasi-democratic notion of consensus. Thus what is essentially an ideal of democratic procedure, namely, a rational agreement among free and equal participants, itself defines the norm of justice. In this formulation, Habermas seems to be assimilating the concepts of justice and democracy, although he does not put it this way.

The Requirements of Justice and
the Limitation of Democracy

How then should we conceive the relation between justice and democracy in order to clarify the hard questions that arise when these two values conflict with each other? On first glance, it may seem odd to counterpose democracy and justice at all, since they seem to be not only closely related but interdependent values, which are grown from a common root. In the tradition of democratic thought and in an enlightened commonsense view as well, one of the main virtues of a democratic society is that it realizes the demands of justice. Therefore, if justice turns out to be needed as a constraint on the outcome of democratic processes, then it would seem as though something must have gone wrong somewhere. This is not to say that the outcome of democratic procedures like voting must somehow be guaranteed to come out "the right way." In fact, democratic decision procedures are in great part valid because they permit the freest choices by individuals which cannot be either predicted or preordained. Nonetheless, when such a procedure issues forth in an outcome that is unjust, we would tend to say that freedom of choice has somehow gone the wrong way.

The view that I propose concerning the relation of justice to democracy is developed within the framework of the democratic theory that I present in my book *Rethinking Democracy*.[12] There I take the common root or the common foundation that normatively grounds conceptions of justice and of democracy to be freedom. I argue that freedom is the criterial feature of human agency and conceive it as a process of self-development. Freedom is taken in a complex sense, not only as a capacity for choice but as a course of activity in which an agent realizes long-term projects and develops capacities. It is thus a process over time. This characteristic mode of agency or life activity is what I call self-development. Though it is necessarily the self-development of individuals, which I take to be the ontologically primary entities in social life, this self-developing activity both requires social interaction and is often expressed in common or joint activities oriented toward shared goals. Thus these individuals are to be understood ontologically as individuals-in-relations or as social individuals.

Self-developing activity requires not only the making of choices but also the availability of the means or access to the conditions necessary for making these choices effective. Thus the freedom to develop oneself as positive freedom requires access to the material and social conditions of such activity. Among the material conditions are means of subsistence and the means for carrying out the activities, and among the social conditions are freedom from domination and, correlatively, reciprocal recognition by the agents of each other's freedom. However, since free choice is a necessary precondition for self-developing activity, so-called negative freedom or the absence of constraint on the choices of individuals is also normatively required.

There is another step to the argument here which takes us to the conception of justice. Since freedom as agency or the capacity for choice characterizes all human beings as human and since the exercise of this agency in self-development is a normative imperative, and further, since this exercise requires conditions, I argue that there is an equal and valid claim—that is to say, a right—to the conditions of self-development on the part of each human being.[13] I call this equal positive freedom and take it to be the principle of justice. This is of course a telescoped version of an extended argument developed in my book, but it will serve to introduce the essential connection between justice and democracy.

I argue that the principle of justice thus conceived as a (prima facie[14]) equal right to the conditions of self-development requires democracy as the equal right to participate in decision-making concerning the common activities in which individuals are engaged. For engaging in such common activities is itself one of the main conditions for individuals' self-development and the opportunity for their self-development in these contexts requires that they be self-determining in this activity. If, instead, an individual's actions were determined by another, it would not be an exercise of the agency that is required for self-development. However, since such common or joint activity necessarily involves other individuals, the exercise of their agency in this context takes the form of co-determination of the activity, that is, rights to participate in decision-making about it.

In this construction, the principle of democracy is normatively derived from the principle of justice, understood as prima facie equal rights to the conditions of self-development, where it is taken in the context of common or joint activity. This principle of justice is ultimately based on the primacy of freedom as a value in human life, and specifically, on the equal freedom of each agent. Justice understood in this way therefore has normative priority over the requirement of democracy. In this sense, justice may legitimately constrain the democratic process when it leads to outcomes that violate the equal freedom of individuals. It is clear then, that this account falls under the first model of the relation of justice and democracy sketched above, namely, that which takes democracy to be a requirement of justice.

The particular theory of positive freedom and justice delineated here gives rise to a conception of certain rights that need to be recognized as human rights, that is, as rights that people possess simply by virtue of being human, and therefore, equally and universally. These are rights, which all individuals have, to the conditions necessary for freedom, understood as self-development. One may distinguish among these human rights between rights to the conditions that are minimally necessary for any human action whatever—these we may call *basic* rights—and rights to those conditions that are required for the free and self-developing activity beyond this minimum—these we may call *nonbasic* rights. Thus, for example, life and liberty are basic rights, whereas formal education and training are nonbasic. Human rights generally, as the expression of equal freedom, should not be violated by any democratic procedure, and serve to specify the constraints on democracy. We may say that they constitute rights against majorities in contrast to the majority rights inherent in democratic decision-making.

It might appear from this that the authority of democratic decision-making is so delimited by such constraints that it makes democracy a marginal thing indeed. For if the latitude of choice is so narrow because of the prescriptions set by the human rights, it would seem that democratic decision procedures properly exercised would be primarily a ratification of what is normatively predetermined. Or if democratic decisions are overturned by the courts to protect these rights when they are constitutionally guaranteed, then democratic process would again seem to be an exercise in freedom of choice only when it is correct. Yet, if democracy as the right to participate in decision-making is required by justice and in fact constitutes one of the human rights, then it cannot be so reduced as to become trivial.

This question over the marginalization of the freedom of democratic choice by constraints in the name of justice may be responded to in two ways, first with respect to formal freedom of democratic choice, and second with respect to what we may call substantive democracy. If we introduce a distinction between the form of democratic decision-making and the substance of democracy, we may argue in the first place that the form—namely, the actual procedures and the fact of participation—remains unaffected when a particular outcome of the decision procedure is overridden in the interests of justice. For example, when the Supreme Court declares a piece of legislation unconstitutional, it does not thereby delimit Congress's formal power to make laws. But it delimits those laws that are taken to be in violation of the Constitution. Formal democracy, then—for example, civil liberties and political rights—is not the subject of constraint.

The objection here may be that if many decisions were knocked down in this way, this formal freedom would tend to be a rather empty exercise. To this one may respond that the exercise of democracy deserves to remain empty when its outcome is such that it violates the very rights and liberties for the sake of which democracy itself has been instituted. For if democracy is a requirement of justice, its outcomes cannot be permitted to undercut its own foundation.

This makes appeal to what one may call a conception of substantive democracy. This refers to the practice of democracy as an activity of self-development on the part of the participants in which agents reciprocally recognize each other's freedom and equality in the process of making collective decisions. A democratic decision that violates these very conditions in effect is inconsistent with democracy itself in this sense and undermines it. For the function and justification of democracy, as we have seen, is that it serves freedom, understood as self-development. Democracy cannot therefore in principle undermine its own function with any normative justification. Therefore, the constraints that arise from the demands of justice do not delimit democracy in this substantive sense.

Four Hard Questions

In this last section, I want to consider in an initial way how this analysis of the relation of justice and democracy bears on a number of issues that I have characterized as hard questions. They are hard in the sense that they present conceptual difficulties not easily resolved, or difficulties in the implementation of principles. These concern what we name as (1) the constitutional circle; (2) the problem of positive freedom; (3) the institutionalization of rights in social and economic contexts; and (4) rights of ethnic minorities. I have a limited aim here: to formulate these problems in the framework of the previous discussion and to make some suggestions as to how they may be resolved. I will focus here mainly on the first issue and to some degree on the fourth. The second and third will be treated very briefly. A fuller discussion of them is given in my *Rethinking Democracy*.[15]

The Constitutional Circle

The constitutional circle refers to the justification of the decision to institute constitutional guarantees of rights that will delimit or constrain democratic decisions. The process by means of which these constitutional guarantees are to be instituted is some kind of constitutional convention or an equivalent decision procedure. Short of the authoritarian or dictatorial determination of these guarantees by fiat on the part of some ruler, the decision must involve some democratic or consensual procedure. But if these rights are instituted to delimit or to constrain any democratic decision that would violate these rights—that is, if these rights have normative priority over the democratic process itself—then the question arises whether there are rights that limit the very democratic or consensual process that determines the constitutional guarantees in the first place. To put this differently, would there have to be a prior determination of the rights that delimit the democratic decision in order to institute constitutional guarantees of rights? In short, is there an infinite regress here? In another formulation, isn't there a circularity involved in the establishment of constitutional guarantees of rights by means of a consensual or democratic procedure which in turn itself presupposes some of the very rights to be institutionalized? For the very idea of consensus implies the free and equal status of those who entered into the agreement and it is this freedom and equality that give the consensus its authority. For without this free and equal agreement to accept as binding what is agreed upon, the consensus has no force and is merely verbal.

This would be question begging only if it were supposed (1) that the rights established by the agreement were constituted as rights only in the agreement and had no prior status, and (2) that the force of the consensual agreement depended on the freedom and equality of the agents entering into it, where this freedom and equality are themselves the fundamental basis of the very rights usually constitutionally guaranteed, that is, freedom of speech, the right to vote, equality before the law, etc. The regress ends and the circularity is avoided if we take the democratic or consensual determination of constitutionally guaranteed rights as a recognition of those rights that are ingredient in human action, and more specifically here, as a recognition that it is these rights that are at the basis both of the authority of the consensual or democratic procedure that sets constitutional guarantees and of the democratic structures of self-governance that the constitution itself establishes. This then is an explicit recognition of the normative priority and of the ontological primacy of these rights vis-à-vis the democracy that exercises and protects them. In one sense, this is a bootstrap operation which institutionalizes rights ab initio. In another sense, however, these rights are recognized as rights prior to their institutionalization and it is this recognition that is brought to the consensual determination of these rights as constitutional.

There is a problem that remains, however, and that is the epistemological rather than the political problem of what guarantees that the appropriate rights have been recognized. It is always possible that a constitutional convention or its equivalent will fail to recognize either all the human rights or the scope of the rights it does recognize, and in fact such an epistemological shortfall is what characterizes the history of the development of constitutional freedoms and rights. If one takes an objective view of human rights as existing prior to and independently of their institutionalization or even their explicit recognition, then it is always conceivable that any consensual agreement about these rights will be in error. However, if the source of our knowledge of these rights is not some transcendental intuition but instead what is revealed in the very experience of human practices, then presumably a critical approach to any given constitution of these rights leaves open the possibility of correcting and deepening the recognition of them.

What reveals these rights, practically speaking, is the daily and recurrent recognition by individuals of others as being like themselves, namely, as agents with claims to the conditions for their self-developing activity. We may say that domination or exploitation of others is precisely the failure of this recognition, whether in personal or institutional forms, and that critical social and political theory and practice are just the attempt to achieve this recognition more fully.

What perhaps needs to be made clear here is that this conception of rights does not reduce to some atomistic distribution of rights to individuals considered as isolates—a charge sometimes brought against rights conceptions in general. Human rights are always rights of individuals, based on their valid claims to conditions for their activity, but individuals bear these rights only in relation to other individuals and to social institutions. "Right" is an intrinsically relational concept.

This discussion of the constitutional guarantees of rights which has so far been treated in terms of its conceptual difficulties suggests a consideration of the more applied question of how guarantees of rights against violations by democratic process can be implemented. Although these modes of implementation are familiar, it may be useful to list them in this context. We have considered thus far only the most obvious way, namely, the adoption of a constitution, by a democratically constituted founding convention, where the document itself sets out the principles and limits of the authority and legitimacy of democratic decision-making (as in legislation) or in the execution of the mandate of the constitution. Here, the constitution itself, as the higher law, supervenes upon lower laws and actions (as for example, where a constitutional Bill of Rights or an article or amendment of the constitution specifically names rights to be held immune from violation, or protections and privileges against which elected or democratically appointed bodies or offices may not act. In addition to such explicit proscriptions (e.g., "Congress shall make no law. . . ," etc.), the constitution may also set up instruments of review and interpretation, for example, judicial review of the compliance of laws with constitutionally guaranteed rights, or executive mandate to act to effect the priority of justice; or conversely, limitations of executive power where this may violate citizens' rights. Such a constitutional limitation of democracy is well established in the political sphere. A question arises as to how one would interpret such a self-limiting procedure in contexts of democratic decision-making in the economy or in social or cultural life where there are no constitutional structures analogous to those that obtain in the political sphere. I will take this up later.

The second way that democracy may effect its own limits is by legislative priority, where a legislature by its decision overrides the democratic decisions of a lower legislative body, in response to the demands of justice; or where it abrogates its own prior decision, on these same grounds.

Still another recourse is to popular opinion and the organization of mass support around demands for legislative, judicial, or executive action to change or abrogate unjust laws, or to institute conditions to satisfy the demands of justice. Here, education, consciousness-raising, political action, and demonstration are common means. The Civil Rights movement was a paradigm case.

Another method used to protest what are perceived as unjust outcomes of democratic decision-making, and to attempt to undo them in practice, is that of passive resistance movements, in refusal to obey unjust laws or to carry out the violations of justice mandated by such laws. One example is the case of civil disobedience, whether by an individual or a group.

In the fifth case, active abrogation or reversal of a democratically arrived at outcome by the administrative action of an individual or body in power may be undertaken on the grounds of the normative priority of justice. Here, the case is more complex, since such an action may be one taken simply by administrative fiat, pitting the authority of an office against that of a democratically constituted group. It therefore seems to be the exception, where democracy is contravened undemocratically, in the interests of justice. But the issue becomes sharpest, in terms of questions of legitimacy, when the social justice question is concerned with the representativeness of the democratic procedure that is being overridden, that is, where that procedure is not democratic enough because the group is exclusionary in its constitution, and especially where the impact of its actions is on just those individuals that it excludes from its ranks.

One may consider another case where administrative action on behalf of justice could possibly be justified, namely, that in which there is as yet no democratic constituency to make the decision that justice overrides. In such a case, for example, of a country or institution that has as yet no effective democratic structures of decision-making, one may argue that such democratic structures ought to be introduced but that in the interim, inherited and ongoing injustices need to be corrected even without popular support, or even perhaps against popular opposition. The danger of such an approach is that it may sanction authoritarianism in the name of justice. Such authoritarianism would violate the norms not only of democracy but of justice itself.

The Problem of Positive Freedom

We may now briefly turn to the second and third issues concerning the problem of positive freedom and the institutionalization of rights in social and economic contexts. Taking note of these issues here calls our attention to the fact that the relation of justice and democracy takes on a further dimension when it is considered in the context of social and economic values. The first of these issues concerns the constraints that the requirements of social and economic justice pose for the freedom of democratic decision-making. What makes this issue problematic is that it goes beyond the traditional civil liberties and political rights usually addressed in the context of constitutional democracy and it introduces the question of how far government can or should take part in matters concerning social welfare and economic justice. The argument has been that if these are to be made into rights on a par with civil and political rights, then the scope of democratic decision-making would be so severely constrained by the broader set of guarantees as to be rendered marginal. As will be remembered, I have partly dealt with this question earlier in the paper. Moreover, the issue of social and economic justice in relation to the role of government has been widely and intensively discussed. We may observe that Rawls's separation of the second principle of justice concerning economic justice from the first principle of equal basic liberties or political justice may have been motivated in part by a desire to avoid precisely this problem of constricting the role of democratic decision.

But there is the further objection raised against so-called positive liberty, classically by Isaiah Berlin,[16] that making the domain of social and economic welfare a matter of governmental responsibility quickly becomes transformed into the paternalistic or authoritarian prescription by government of what is good for people. Without entering into the labyrinth of issues that this poses, we may make one suggestion as to how to approach this question in a very different way. This involves rejecting the premise that the achievement of economic and social justice rests primarily on governmental decision-making. It may instead be more a matter of how economic institutions are set up such that they conduce to the achievement of economic justice, and how decisions concerning social and economic life are made. The proposal here is for the extension of democratic decision procedures not only to politics but to economic and social life as well. The substantial displacement of the requirements of social and economic justice from the arena of government or political democracy to these other spheres shifts the burden of decision-making. Nonetheless, it would remain a function of government to regulate or monitor the observance of basic social and economic rights within the spheres of social and economic life. This directly raises the third hard question concerning the institutionalization of rights in these contexts.

The Institutionalization of Rights in Social and Economic Contexts

This issue concerns social justice and the guarantee of rights in such institutions as the corporation, the university, the professional association, the trade union, the workplace, etc. Consider, for example, the widely discussed case of workplace democracy, where the workplace or the firm has itself been transformed into a democratic institution with participation by all those involved in its activity. In this case, all the workers may have rights to participate in decisions affecting production, wages, marketing, etc., though this may well involve the democratic election of managers rather than direct decision on and administration of all of these matters by the workers themselves. There are already numerous instances of worker participation short of self-management in the sense specified.

The normative issues concerning justice that would arise in the context of workplace democracy include the question of rights of participation in decision-making by members of the firm, that is, how long they have to be members in order to be full citizens, so to speak, and whether all members have such rights regardless of the status of their jobs or whether they are temporary contract workers. It also concerns how nonmembers may join a firm and under what conditions. Issues of justice also arise with respect to traditional questions of equal pay for equal work or of exploitation of some members by others or the creation of an underclass of workers or of a privileged elite. And finally, there is the question of when members of such a firm may be fired and by what procedures. Where the decisions arrived at by democratic procedures in the firm violate the rights of individuals in these contexts, there would seem to be the same justification as in the case of political democracy to constrain such democratically made decisions in the interest of justice. But here, the question of implementation arises, namely, how could one legitimately constrain such decisions in this context?

There usually is no appeal to any established constitutional framework within the firm itself. There is of course the constraint upon the firm as an institution, say in the United States, of falling under the general requirements of justice as specified in the U.S. Constitution and by legislation, both national and local, specifying equal rights and conditions of work, for example, having to do with wages, hours, discrimination, occupational health and safety, etc. Beyond this, however, the requirements of justice could be included in constitution-like articles of incorporation of a firm, and in the rules and regulations of its everyday procedures. In such a case, then, appeal could be made to such incorporated principles, which members would presumably accept when they join the firm, in order to forestall decisions in violation of justice or to justify overriding them should they occur.

But the question remains, by what means would such an override be effected or imposed on such a firm? Here, recourse to the courts as in other contexts is one important method, since members could sue the firm for violating the conditions of their contract. Further, those members of the firm who have suffered violations of their rights and those who agree with them could strike, paradoxical as this might sound in the context of workplace democracy.

Rights of Ethnic Minorities

The final issue concerning the potential conflict between the demands of justice and the freedom of democratic decision-making is a contemporary and presently vivid version of a classic problem. This is the question of the rights of ethnic minorities, as an update of the problem of the protection of minority rights against majority rule, a well-worn issue in political theory. Again, the aim here cannot be to do justice to this question in all its complexity but to see it as a case in point of the relation between social justice and democracy.

What is at issue are the rights of members of ethnic minorities to equal freedom to develop themselves, both individually and as a group in terms of cultural or linguistic autonomy, independent or separate institutions for the expression of their distinctive ways of life, and in terms of political representation. The problem arises when the equal freedom of minorities is put in jeopardy or denied by a dominant majority of a different ethnic identity. In the case of individuals who are discriminated against or suffer danger to life and limb as members of ethnic minorities, there are the straightforward requirements of justice to protect their human rights against those decisions of the majority that violate these rights, just as there would be for any other citizen regardless of ethnic identity. When the issue concerns the equal rights of self-development of the members of the group in terms of cultural autonomy or a distinctive ethnic way of life, the argument is more complex though basically similar. It is a matter of justice as equal freedom and requires the protection of the minority against the tyranny of the majority, where the majority denies the members of the minority any of the means for the expression of their cultural life. For example, this may consist in the majority's refusal to fund culturally or linguistically distinctive programs in social and cultural life, or in imposing a forced assimilation linguistically or culturally upon the ethnic minority.

A question here is whether the protection of the rights of ethnic minorities requires the introduction of a so-called group right. An alternative would be to understand this as a recognition of the rights of individuals to freely chosen paths of self-development, where these take the form of cultural identity or ethnicity.

Granting the demands of justice for ethnic minorities, and that there are rights to cultural autonomy (though what specific rights these are needs to be clarified), the question arises how justice could be implemented against the decisions of a majority that has denied the minority members their rights. One constraint on the majority may be to build in constitutional protection of minority rights. The difficulties here would include the question of whether this protection should be framed in terms of universal rights of individuals—for example, rights that affirm the freedom to choose their own language or culture—or instead, in terms of specific group rights.

Another means of implementing minority rights would be the promulgation of special laws for such protection. But this would require an enlightened majority binding itself not to trespass upon minority rights in the future. Implementing special laws or constitutional protections seems to run into paradox when the very majority that is violating minority rights is the same majority that would be needed to introduce these countervailing protections.

Two other means may be introduced for implementing minority rights. One way would be to provide structures for the special representation of the ethnic group's interest. For example, where there are many such ethnic groups constituting a population, there may be a council of such ethnic groups or of nationalities that functions as part of the legislative structure complementing the legislature as a body directly representative of equal individuals, that is, one-person one-vote. This would be an analogue for ethnic groups of the representation of states' rights in the bicameral structure of Congress with its Senate. But one may raise questions as to whether such a mode of representation is fully democratic. Yet another way in which ethnic minorities' rights may be expressed is in granting the right to secession of such minorities. But this is complicated by the requirement that these minorities be geographically discrete and separable and that the equal rights of those within its secessionist boundaries who are not members of the ethnic minority are preserved.

These are especially difficult issues in the present, where, on a world scale, ethnic identity and demands for cultural or political autonomy have burgeoned, and where secession and national independence of what were ethnic minorities in some federal or imperial states have become flashpoints of armed conflict. In the United States these questions have also come to the fore with the growth and increasing self-consciousness of ethnic minorities, and with the sometimes paradoxical and even conflicting demands for greater inclusion within the majority and for separation from it.

I have argued in this paper for the priority of justice in principle over the authority of democratic decisions. However, in conclusion, I would like to recall the argument for democracy, which is itself based on the requirements of justice as equal freedom. It follows therefore that the interventions on behalf of justice should be carefully delimited, and specifically to cases where fundamental rights have been violated.

Notes

1. John Rawls, *A Theory of Justice* (Cambridge: Harvard University Press), p. 60.

2. Robert Dahl, *Democracy and Its Critics* (New Haven: Yale University Press, 1989), pp. 97–105.

3. Robert Dahl, *A Preface to Economic Democracy* (Berkeley: University of California Press, 1985), p. 25.

4. Dahl, *Democracy and Its Critics*, p. 182.

5. Rawls, *A Theory of Justice*, p. 197.

6. Iris Marion Young, "Justice, Democracy and Group Difference," a paper presented at the meeting of the American Political Science Association, September 1990 (unpublished).

7. Rawls, *A Theory of Justice*, p. 198.

8. Young, "Justice, Democracy and Group Difference," p. 37.

9. Joshua Cohen, "Deliberation and Democratic Legitimacy," in *The Good Polity*, Alan Hamlin and Phillip Pettit, eds. (New York: Blackwell, 1989), pp. 18–27.

10. Jürgen Habermas, *Communication and the Evolution of Society* (Boston: Beacon Press, 1979), p. 186.

11. Ibid.

12. Carol C. Gould, *Rethinking Democracy: Freedom and Social Cooperation in Politics, Economy, and Society* (Cambridge: Cambridge University Press, 1988).

13. For fuller development of this argument, see ibid., pp. 60–71.

14. The equal rights are qualified as prima facie since there are other principles that potentially conflict with them. Cf. ibid., pp. 66, 153–56, 166–70, and 190–214.

15. Ibid., Chapters 7 and 9.

16. Isaiah Berlin, "Two Concepts of Liberty," in *Four Essays on Liberty* (Oxford: Oxford University Press, 1970). See also my discussion of this in *Rethinking Democracy*, Chapter 1.

Comments by Milton Fisk

In her contribution, "Social Justice and the Limitations of Democracy," Carol Gould moves from a discussion of the relation of justice to democracy to an attempt to show that freedom is prior to both justice and democracy. She uses freedom as a foundation for a political morality in which both principles of justice and the right to democratic participation are justified.

The kind of relationship her foundationalist view warrants between justice and democracy is one in which democratic rights are to be validated on the basis of fundamental principles of justice. Democratic rights will be limited by considerations of justice since, in her view, those rights are validated only if they can be derived from justice itself. My primary focus in discussing her interesting view of how freedom, justice, and democracy interrelate will be on her attempt to give democracy a foundation in freedom.

I am dubious about attempts to ground democracy in anything. We might, instead, say why at a practical level we should support even a nonideal democracy like that in the U.S. To support it we would take note of advantages flowing from it that we wouldn't find flowing from alternative forms of polity. This doesn't amount to giving it, or democracy generally, a foundation. By a foundation or a ground of democracy I mean something lying behind practical reasons and their sustaining social contexts which legitimates it whatever the social context.

But Gould wants something firmer than practical reasons for democracy. After all, reasons for supporting democracy will not be ones everyone accepts as good reasons. For her there would be a damaging incompleteness if we could not transcend the situation in which different groups have different reasons for supporting democracy and in which some groups even have reasons for supporting other forms of polity. This incompleteness might indeed leave us without hope of reaching unanimity. But that is damaging only if we can hope for unanimity.

To push back behind these reasons justifying the groups' practical support with the expectation of reaching a ground that transcends them may be a delusional process. What we come to might only appear to be independent of those practical reasons for supporting democracy. We may in fact only be interpreting certain of those reasons in such a way that they take on the appearance of transcending the context giving them their force.

I may be wrong about the limits of foundationalism as regards democracy. But at least in the case of the foundation Gould gives to democracy, I think there is reason to doubt that it is really a foundation. It is I shall argue no more than a practical reason for supporting democracy that has its force only in certain contexts. Thus to the extent that her argument for freedom as a foundation for democracy is persuasive, it depends on such a reason that has its force only in a given context. I shall reconstruct her argument as follows.

(1) Gould takes freedom to be essential for self-development. This means that free choices are required for self-development. She subscribes then to the principle of free self-development. This principle is about the structure of self-development itself.

(2) Not only is freedom at the core of self-development, but there is for Gould a normative imperative, call it the freedom imperative, to exercise free choice in a way that leads toward the realization of self-development. In short, we don't just have the capacity for freedom, but must exercise it, and indeed must exercise it toward the achievement of self-development.

(3) This imperative, according to Gould, calls in turn for a basic principle of justice—the principle of equal positive freedom. This mandates equal provision of material and social conditions for self-development. If we have to exercise freedom toward achieving self-development, we have to have the means to do so.

(4) We are not, Gould affirms, asocial individuals, so self-development necessitates common activity with others. The principle of equal positive freedom in (3) gives each of us, then, a right to the conditions needed for common activity. Otherwise we would have to exercise choice toward self-development without having a right to some of the essential conditions for such freedom, namely those needed for common activity.

(5) What are the conditions for common activity? One of the basic ones is self-determination. Gould claims—and this is a claim to be flagged for further consideration—that the opportunity for self-development through common activity calls for participation in decision-making in that common activity. If, instead, one were determined by others in common activity, then that activity wouldn't be in accord with the concept of self-development. Recall that by her principle of free development in (1) she makes freedom an essential aspect of self-development.

(6) Finally, Gould concludes—based on her principle of free self-development in (1), the freedom imperative in (2), and the principle of equal positive freedom in (3)—that there is a right to democracy, that is, an equal right to participate in decision. Let's return to the

claim flagged in step (5) above. This was the claim that if the self-development of social individuals calls for common activity then there must be freedom in that common activity and this freedom is possible only through participation in decision-making in carrying on that activity. The problem with this is the following: It seems we could use common activity as a condition of our self-development without it being necessary that this common activity is free, that is, involves equal participation.

Imagine you are in training to be a good feudal ruler, a king or a queen. Your self-development in this direction will involve common activities, such as learning from your tutor about customs and taking directives from the current king or queen. In all this your participation is not equal, since you simply learn what the tutor tells you and obey the king or queen. Yet without this common activity, which is nondemocratic, you don't develop your capacities for ruling your country and you won't realize your project of being a good king or queen. Since freedom is necessary for self-development, you exercise it in areas other than joint decision-making, as when you decide to spend more time than your tutor demands on Roman Law and equestrianism.

Now I think a fair response to this example would be that our prince or princess will fail to develop him or herself. What's missing is the development of those of his or her capacities that lead to respect for others and a taste for give and take. This is probably true, and it leads us to say that our prince or princess undergoes a one-sided development without equal participation in common activity.

It should then be stipulated that the self-development, for which common activity is a condition, not be one-sided and that as a consequence any such common activity itself be a field of equal participation. But in making this stipulation we have destroyed our foundationalist argument. We have built into the concept of self-development with which we started the requirement that, to avoid one-sidedness, self-development involve not just common activity but democratic common activity. Since we are not trying to define democracy but only to justify it, the appeal to democratic activity here introduces no objectionable circularity. So building democratic activity into the very concept of self-development may not itself seem fatal, rather than a quite legitimate way to get to the conclusion.

Why then has the argument been destroyed? Can't we simply say that this is just what a genuine concept of self-development entails? Well, the reason is that defending the genuineness of this concept is the hurdle we can't get over. There seem to be only two alternatives here: The concept of self-development with the requirement that self-development depends on equal participation is either genuine as an *a priori* concept or it is genuine as one that is abstracted from the context of a democratic culture where this type of self-development occurs. But on the one hand, we can't take this concept to be an *a priori* one, that is, one that is a condition for any possible view of a worthy life. After all princes and princesses got along for a long time without their lives depending on this democratic concept of self-development.

And on the other hand, we can't save the argument while treating this concept as a reflection of our democratic culture. In a democratic culture we would be willing to say, with J. S. Mill, that to avoid one-sided development people need to engage in democratic common activity. But then our justification of democracy depends on the kind of self-development associated with a specifically democratic society. This justification of democracy would not convince someone, like our prince or princess, struggling with self-development in a feudal culture.

To conclude, the foundational justification of democracy given by Gould fails in so far as it treats self-development as understood in a democratic culture as if it were an imperative for humanity in any context. A contextual norm has been transcendentalized.

Instead of this you might find your support for democracy to rest on a reason that is bound by your context. You might say merely that you give your support to democracy, even as it is in the U.S. today, because you see it as limiting tyranny. You object to tyranny since it could block the realization of your capacities for participation. There needn't be a suggestion that these capacities for participation must be universally realized.

You would be giving a practical reason for your support of realizing participation. Your reason would have greater weight, of course, if it made sense for everyone in a large group to which you belong. The foundationalist approach, as I mentioned earlier, seems to rest on taking such a practical reason and considering it still to be a reason when it is abstracted from the only contexts that make it a sensible reason.

Comments by James P. Sterba

In "Social Justice and the Limitation of Democracy" Carol Gould seeks to ground democratic political structures on an ideal of liberty understood as an equal right to self-development. In my judgment, her overall argument is quite successful. Those who endorse an ideal of liberty, understood in the way that Gould advocates, as an ideal of positive liberty rather than an ideal of negative liberty should endorse democratic political structures for just the reasons that Gould gives. I also endorse the view that Gould develops elsewhere which shows that her ideal of positive liberty leads to a feminist ideal of androgyny.[1] The only problem I have with Gould's account is that its normative foundation—an ideal of positive liberty—is not equally shared by adherents of other political perspectives. In fact, as Gould is well aware it is not even shared by libertarians who, like Gould, take an ideal of liberty to be their ultimate political ideal. This is because libertarians understand their ideal of liberty as a negative ideal of noninterference rather than, as Gould does, a positive ideal of self-development.

Now if Gould is aware of this problem, as I claim she is, why has she not done anything about it? Judging from her comments on my paper for this volume, I think the answer is clear. She does not think that anything can be done about it. Specifically, she does not think that there is a way to justify the conclusions she wants simply by appealing to an ideal of liberty understood as a negative ideal of noninterference. Of course, this is not to say that Gould would not be the first to endorse such an argument if it could be found, because it would obviously help to justify her normative conclusions if she could derive them from premises other than an ideal of positive liberty. She just thinks that this cannot be done.

In her response to my contribution to this volume, Gould also makes clear why she thinks that nothing like the conclusions both she and I defend can be justified by appealing to an ideal of negative liberty alone, as I try to do in my contribution to this volume and elsewhere. Gould's basic argument is this: So Gould thinks that I "succeed" in reconciling the libertarian and welfare liberal views only by "re-interpreting the concept of liberty," presumably giving it a positive interpretation, akin to her own, rather than the negative interpretation favored by libertarians. It is interesting to note here that this line of criticism of my work is being raised by Gould, who defends a socialist or radical welfare liberal view, rather than by Tibor Machan, who actually defends the libertarian view. Machan, in his comments on my contribution to this volume, and in his earlier published comments on my work, does not raise this sort of criticism of my work. He does not think that the problem with my reconciliationist argument is that I am employing a positive conception of liberty rather than the negative conception that is favored by libertarians. This is not to say that something like Gould's criticism of my argument did not occur to Machan earlier. As a matter of fact, in correspondence dating from around 1986, Machan actually advanced a similar criticism, and then, after considerable discussion back and forth, withdrew it.[2] Since that time, Machan has not claimed that my argument appeals to anything other than a libertarian concept of negative liberty.[3] Nor have any other libertarians who have published responses to my reconciliationist argument, such as John Hospers, Douglas Rasmussen and Eric Mack, made such a claim.[4]

Of course, it is possible that Gould has uncovered something in my argument that all these libertarians are missing, so let's examine her criticism in detail. Gould claims that "if liberty means freedom from external interference or harm by others . . . then the libertarian could argue that the rich person's retention of their wealth is not an external constraint of this sort upon the poor, whereas the liberty of the poor to take this wealth would involve an interference or harm, since it would presumably proceed by some kind of force or ingression, at least with respect to what the rich possess." Now I think that what Gould fails to see here, and what libertarians like Machan, Hospers, Rasmussen and Mack now acknowledge, is that there are two negative liberties in conflict here. First, there is the negative liberty of the rich not to be interfered with in using their surplus resources for luxury purposes. Second, there is the negative liberty of the poor not to be interfered with in taking from the rich what is necessary to meet their basic needs. Of course, one may want to object that the negative liberty of the poor is illegitimate, or not as important as the negative liberty of the rich, who, let us assume, created the surplus. But that is a second-stage attack on my argument. It assumes all that the first stage of my reconciliationist argument seeks to establish, namely, that there are two negative liberties here to be evaluated. Nor can Gould distinguish between these two negative liberties by claiming that the liberty of the poor not to be interfered with in taking from the surplus of the rich what is necessary to meet their basic needs *requires force to exercise* (presumably because the rich would resist its exercise) because the liberty of the rich not to be interfered with in using their surplus for luxury purposes also *requires force to exer-*

cise (because presumably at least some of the poor would resist its exercise as well, given that it interferes with satisfying their basic needs).

It may be, however, that what Gould really wants to object to in my reconciliationist argument is not its first stage where two conflicting negative liberties are recognized, but rather its second stage where I appeal to an interpretation of the "ought" implies "can" principle and its contrapositive, the conflict resolution principle, as a commonly accepted reasonable standard for deciding which of these two liberties should have moral priority. She writes,

> There is another aspect of Sterba's reconciliation argument that I would like to comment on here and that concerns his notion of reasonableness in moral contexts. . . . It is one thing for us to exercise of our moral intuitions and agree that it is not unreasonable to ask the rich to give something of their excess to the poor who are desperately in need of it; and it is equally acceptable to argue that the libertarian would want to have a moral resolution of a serious conflict between rich and poor, rather than a simple victory of the stronger. But to conclude from this that the libertarian would therefore agree that the rich be morally required to sacrifice and that policy of positive welfare rights would be rationally supported on prudential grounds seems beyond plausibility.

So what Gould is objecting to here is my use of the "ought" implies "can" principle and the conflict resolution principle as a reasonable standard for assessing the conflicting liberties between the rich and the poor. Again, it bears noting that this is not the type of criticism that libertarians themselves have used against my reconciliationist argument. Machan, in particular, endorses the use of the "ought" implies "can" principle in these contexts, and he does not contest my claim that in the conflict between the rich and the poor, *as I define it*, the liberty of the poor would have priority over the liberty of the rich.[5]

Could it be, however, that Gould has found reason to object here that has eluded Machan and other libertarians? Of course, everything is possible, but it is not likely in this case given that at least part of the reason why Gould thinks that libertarians can reasonably object to favoring the poor over the rich is her failure to see the conflict between the rich and the poor as a conflict of negative liberties. Hence, once it is granted that the conflict between the rich and the poor is a conflict of negative liberties, as the first part of my argument establishes, and once one takes into account the strong libertarian view that there is reasonable resolution of such conflicts that is acceptable to all sides of the conflict (i.e., the conflict resolution principle) as well as the comparative sacrifice to be imposed either on the rich or on the poor, one is driven inexorably to the conclusion that the liberty of the poor should have moral priority over the liberty of the rich in such conflict cases. This is the argument, which, I claim, grounds a negative welfare right of the poor.

It is possible that Gould was misled here into thinking that my argument against the rich is based on prudential grounds when it is not. I have not been arguing that it is in the prudential interest of the rich to favor the liberty of the poor over their own liberty in these conflict cases, but instead that favoring the liberty of the poor over the liberty of the rich is required by the "ought" implies "can" principle and the conflict resolution principle, which are clearly moral not prudential principles. Nevertheless, I do argue that once it is recognized that the poor have negative welfare rights, then it is possible to argue that it is *in the prudential interest* of the rich to bestow positive welfare rights on the poor, to prevent them, in the only way they legitimately can, from choosing when and how to exercise their negative welfare rights. So it is only at the last stage that any prudential considerations enter my argument at all. Now it may be that Gould was misled by my use of prudential considerations at this last stage of my argument into thinking the such considerations grounded the entire argument, which is clearly not the case. They only come into play after negative welfare rights are recognized as required by the "ought" implies "can" principle and the conflict resolution principle.

Hopefully, therefore, when all these clarification's of my argument are taken into account, Gould and I can then agree that the type of normative conclusions that we both favor can be supported not only by the ideal of positive liberty that Gould uses to support those conclusions but also by an ideal of negative liberty endorsed by libertarians. In that way, even more people will have grounds to endorse our shared conclusions.

Notes

1. Carol Gould, "Private Rights and Public Virtues: Women, the Family and Democracy," in Carol Gould, ed., *Beyond Domination: New Perspectives on Women and Philosophy* (Totowa: Rowman and Allanheld, 1984) and "Freedom and Women," *Journal of Social Philosophy* (1984), pp. 20–34.

2. See Machan's comment on my paper "The U.S. Constitution: A Fundamentally Flawed Document," and my response in *The U.S. Constitution*

and its American Philosophers, edited by Christopher Gray (Lewiston: Mellon, 1989).

3. Tibor Machan, *Individuals and Their Rights* (La Salle, Ill.: Open Court, 1989), pp. 100–11.

4. See John Hospers, "Some Unquestioned Assumptions," *Journal of Social Philosophy* (1991), pp. 42–51; Douglas Rasmussen, "Individuals and Human Flourishing," *Public Affairs Quarterly* (1989), pp. 89–103; Eric Mack, "Libertarianism Untamed," *Journal of Social Philosophy* (1991), pp. 64–72,

5. *Individuals and Their Rights.*

6

Justice and Universality

Milton Fisk

The position developed here is an elaboration of the idea that since justice functions to go beyond claims that have led to deadlock, it involves universality. The major task in this elaboration will be to specify the sense of universality involved. Difficulties will be pointed out with attempts to specify the relevant sense of universality through appeal to community consensus over norms. An alternative to such a "communitarian" basis for justice is provided by appealing to a theory of the interests of groups. In this way, the elusive character of community consensus can't vitiate the reliability and critical edge of notions of justice.

Social Homogeneity and Pure Universality

One way to locate the problem to be addressed here is by reference to a common assumption of currently contending schools. The assumption in question is that of both liberalism and communitarianism. Each takes the relevant social units for discussing justice to be homogeneous in a way that allows justice to have sufficient universality. In liberal thought, different social groups are not so different that it is impossible for them to have a common standard of justice. Thus different groups are "objects" of justice in that justice calls for toleration between them, but they are not "subjects" of justice in that each of them is not the basis for a different type of justice. Communitarian thought, in its turn, emphasizes that a community can't be so divided as to lack a common set of values on which a standard of justice could be based. This internal communal homogeneity could, though, exist alongside striking external differences between communities, leading perhaps to multiple standards of justice. After identifying the drawbacks of the common assumption of homogeneity, and of the accompanying notions of universality,[1] the problem becomes that of staking out a position beyond it, and hence beyond these contending schools.

Another way of identifying the problem to be discussed here refers explicitly to the contrasting categories of universality and particularity. Justice, most would agree, builds bridges between individuals, between groups, between nations. It reaches out beyond any particular interest to draw in some potentially conflicting interest. In drawing these particularities together, the just resolution acts like a universal. But paired with this universality is still a third particularity. For justice is done from a standpoint that does the drawing together. It is the standpoint taken up by some individual, some group, some nation. It doesn't escape into pure universality. The problem then arises as to how justice can be sufficiently universal so as to draw different tendencies together if it is never more than justice from a particular standpoint.

This is all forbiddingly abstract. To bring the discussion closer to earth, it is necessary to fill a gaping hole in the above views. To fill this hole we begin by asking what's going on in typical cases where calling for justice or doing justice becomes relevant. Universal and particular come on scene, not as themselves, but as part of conflict and compromise. Doing justice amounts to moving beyond the particularity of actual or potential confrontation toward the universality of a compromise that inevitably carries traces of some quite particular standpoint. The problem then does not emerge simply from the dialectic of schools or from the formal relations of concepts. There is no problem without the tensions of actual conflict that, in the luckiest of cases, work themselves out in the process of compromise. Our reliance on compromise will be seen as a regression by those who emphasize social homogeneity and pure universality. It is, however, only a regression to something more manageable and real.

Justice and Conflict

Doing justice is not tidy, mathematical business. It is the messy process of adjusting conflicting claims.[2] The conflicts here don't typically arise just from ignorance of overarching principles or even out of malicious disregard of them. To be sure, such principles could, through their prior acceptance, prevent a conflict from arising in the first place. But the difficulty is that it is usually not obvious why all parties to the conflict should be expected to agree to those principles. People are led to make conflicting claims from their different positions, rather than from ignorance or malice. Once they are made, the search for a just resolution begins, a resolution that will limit the potential damage of intensifying the conflict.

One side of the messiness of doing justice arises from the novelty of many of the conflicts that call for resolution. They are unanticipated by settled rules of justice and thus call for fresh reasoning. Such a fresh look will be open to an injection from current political forces. A related side of the messiness of doing justice arises from the fact that the conflicts involve people or groups fighting for their interests. Resolving such conflicts becomes, willy-nilly, a political intervention. For it will reflect or initiate a strand of politics in the arena of struggle. Thus justice is doubly political insofar as it calls for shaping new reasoning under political influence and for intervening directly into conflicts of interests.

Of course, this view is at odds with the idea that the messiness of doing justice is an accident stemming from human limitations. The substance behind the alleged accident is still represented by Justicia carrying scales that work according to settled rules, without her giving thought to why they work by those rules. And it is represented also by the blindfold that preserves her neutrality, keeping justice from being a political intervention. This icon, though, serves more to legitimate justice than limn it.

For the moment, put the political overtones of our agonistic view of justice aside so that we can concentrate simply on conflict and resolution themselves. Resolving the conflicts in the least destructive ways seems critical for getting on with social living. A resolution that deepens tensions might be inevitable when the conflict was a symptom that the social fabric was ripping apart anyway. A deepening of tensions can, though, be avoided in most cases. In general, deepening tensions result from the difficulty of finding a resolution that doesn't in a direct way favor one side while not promising at least indirect benefits to the other. The resolution fails to achieve the needed distance from one of the parties and seems too distant from the other. There is, in short, a failure to get beyond particularity to universality.

Universality here, as in other cases, implies something common that applies to both sides. But there is more to the universality of justice than that. First, the common thing is applied by an authority, which may be one of a variety of kinds. It could stem from an agreement by elders of both sides, a report from an extended process of dialogue between representatives of the sides, or a decision of a court of law. The authority vested with doing justice has a stake in seeing that the social bond is perpetuated rather than ruptured.[3] Given this goal, the authority seeks to resolve conflicts without getting too close or too far from either side. So, second, the common thing must be such that it protects the social bond by mediating the differences of the sides. The common thing is in fact the principle by which the limits on the sacrifices of the loser and the limits on the gains of the winner are set. Such a principle, whether explicit or implicit, sets limits in a way that brings the sides closer together rather than in a way that separates them still further.

Take the case of the Nazis marching in Skokie, Illinois, in the late 1970s. The Nazis claimed a right to march with swastikas and Skokie, with its large Jewish population, claimed a right not to be threatened by marchers bearing symbols that harked back to Auschwitz.[4] However, the claimed right to march with threatening symbols needs more to back it up than the mere interests the Nazis have in demonstrating, whatever those interests might be. At a bare minimum, this claimed right needs, if it is to become universal in the sense called for by justice, to be made applicable by some authority to both sides in the dispute. Jews as well as Nazis could, then, march with threatening symbols. Or, conversely, if the Jews' right not to be threatened is to be sustained, this right not to be faced with marchers bearing threatening symbols is to be extended to the Nazis as well. Without at least this minimal parity, the resolution would fail to distance itself sufficiently from one of the sides.

It might seem though that any time the claim of one party is upheld and that of the other is rejected, there is an objectionable one-sidedness. This calls for a distinction between two senses of one-sidedness. Doing justice is one-sided in the "weak sense" every time the claim of one party in a conflict is denied and that of the other is upheld. But this need not involve the kind of failure of universality that is called for by justice. Such a failure involves one-sidedness in a "strong sense," which focuses on the social effects of a resolution. Doing justice is one-sided in the strong sense whenever the social bond that has been severed by upholding one side and rejecting the other in a conflict is not re-established because it is not possible to affirm with any credibility that the claim upheld is also to be both a respected and a useful right for the side whose claim is rejected. The extension of the right to the loser would be purely formal when such a credible affirmation is not possible. In that case the right would not be an equal right, and its extension to the loser would be artificial. In such a case the effort at getting universality, and hence justice, would have failed because of strong one-sidedness.[5]

Assuming that the Nazis win the right to march with threatening symbols, would the same right be useful to the Jews of Skokie? What symbols would the Jews choose to threaten Nazis with? The asymmetry between the oppressed and their former oppressor together with their epigones like U.S. Nazi leader Frank Collin is crucial here. The asymmetry may be too great to allow one to say that the affirmation of the right to march with swastikas establishes sufficient distance from the Nazi side. In that case, upholding the right of the Nazis would be strongly one-sided. Although the Jews in Skokie didn't have to look at the swastikas, and were not then a captive audience, the threat to Jews intended by the Nazi demonstration remained, even if the Jews chose not to be present. If indeed the asymmetry between them were so great that it would be artificial to claim that an equal right had been upheld by the court in upholding the right of the Nazis to march, then one could expect the authority of the court to lose legitimacy with the oppressed. For the oppressed the decision would lack universality.

The Social Goal of Justice

The need to perpetuate the social bond creates the urgency to transcend conflicting claims and the willingness in general to accept the resolution of a conflict. There is a social bond where individuals willingly share burdens, treat others as having claims on them that limit their self-interest, and grant the bindingness of widely shared norms. An end to the social bond would turn interaction into a drab instrumental relation. The need to avoid such a change and to perpetuate the social bond is a teleological element that gives significance to doing justice and that is a standard for feasible resolutions of conflicts. This goal of perpetuating the social bond can be called "the social goal" of justice.

Without a social bond to start with, those making conflicting claims would be unwilling to accept the possibility that their claims would be rejected. Thus it is essential that we think of justice as having as an indispensable background, rather than as creating, the social bond. Since in El Salvador the social bond between the peasants and the

oligarchy had been attenuated, the oligarchy viewed even modest efforts at land reform in the early 1980s as assaults on their class rather
than as efforts to do justice.[6]

Where the social bond exists and can thus be the teleological element in justice, the question arises as to whether it imports a substantive conception of the good into the resolution of conflicts. Would the
conception of the good of ardent democrats, as distinct from that of
upholders of an aristocratic point of view, determine the outcome of
doing justice wherever the social bond happens to exist in a democratic society? The answer will depend on whether the social bond to
be reproduced is a neutral link rather than one that necessarily takes
on the character of the society it not only exists within but also is
indispensable for. A strong case can be made against the position of
neutrality. What the social bond implies will be different in different
kinds of society. The sharing of burdens, the respect for others, and
the binding norms—all needed for a social bond—will imply different behaviors in different societies. The commitment to perpetuating
the social bond would, then, be a commitment to these behaviors as
goods to be cherished. Thus perpetuating the social bond makes justice dependent on substantive goods.

This social goal is not recognized by strongly deontological views
of justice. These views see no incompatibility between doing justice
and destroying the community irreparably. They assert that justice must
be done whatever the consequences. John Sayles's remarkable movie,
Matewan, is a Kantian tragedy in which the justice of getting the mine
owner's gun thugs out of town is entwined with the realistic forebod-
ing that getting them out will destroy the town and with it the organizing drive by the miners' union. Strongly deontological views of
justice fail though to provide a motivation for doing justice beyond
pathological commitment to principle.

The transcendence achieved by doing justice is limited by the social goal. Resolutions of conflict that are one-sided in the strong sense
mentioned above not only uphold the right of one side over that of
the other but also fail to repair the damage this does to the social
bond. To avoid this strong one-sidedness calls for an affirmation that
the right upheld is also a right of the side whose claim is not upheld.
This affirmation must not express a mere formal equality, but must
also imply that in the circumstances the transcendent right will be
useful to the losing side. If this affirmation is to be true, it may be
necessary to initiate a process of social change so that the transcendent right will indeed be useful to those whose claim was not upheld.
Thus reestablishing the social bond, as called for by the social goal,

does not imply social stasis. The social goal will often require that social change be part of the process of doing justice.

Perhaps, though, the social bond shouldn't be reestablished in societies thought of as unjust. Wouldn't doing so only perpetuate their injustice? This situation presents no particular problem for the idea that a social goal is behind doing justice. For, if the society is indeed unjust, what will pass for doing justice in it will fail to avoid strong one-sidedness. The rights upheld by its so-called system of justice will not become equal rights, and hence the social bond, if there was one, won't be reestablished. The system of justice will, then, lack legitimacy. The conditions will be prepared for those denied equal rights to attempt to change the society in the direction of a genuine justice. Thus the social bond will be reestablished by justice only once the society has been changed to become a just one.

Perspectival Universality

More needs to be said about the standpoint from which justice is done. We have said only that doing justice is called for by conflicts of claims and that the reason it is called for is the social goal—the perpetuation of the social bond. A resolution is universal to the extent that it does transcend each side.

What needs to be added is that the social bond qualifies the universality of this transcendence. For doing justice is an effort to resolve conflict in order to perpetuate the social bond. The society that shapes the social bond will in turn give the transcendence in conflict resolution its special character. We can say the society provides the perspective from which justice is done. Doing justice in a particular case reflects the point of view of a society characterized by a social bond of a given kind.

What has been said so far shouldn't be taken to imply that doing justice is nothing more than the resolution of isolated conflicts. Rather, the resolution of one conflict bears on that of others, since the social bond will not be promoted when the resolutions of conflicts fail to cohere. Without coherent resolutions to conflicts, or at least some way of papering over incoherence by distinguishing cases, expectations become confused and individuals lose the trust needed for social intercourse.[7] With coherence, though, past resolutions begin to lay a basis for formulating principles of justice that achieve a higher level of universality than what would be involved if cases were taken in isolation. The great temptation is to confuse this higher degree of universality with an escape from any particular standpoint, to confuse universality with absoluteness.

Seeing justice in terms of perspectival universality is a feature of an old tradition that carries on today under the label "communitarianism." On the positive side, those in this tradition connect the motive for doing justice with acceptance of a certain social order. Justice is typically done from the motive of perpetuating the bond within a social order. There need be no appeal to ghostly motives, such as a pure respect for self-given law, the desire to implement arrangements worked out behind a veil of ignorance, solidarity with humans anywhere within the galaxy, or the urge to seek truth in a medium of uncoerced discourse. Instead of resting on such motives, which few humans feel even on occasion, the communitarian starts from where most of us are most of the time, that is, from our being bonded with others in a social order. Being thus bonded, we will accept—whether it be enthusiastically, merely implicitly, or only grudgingly—the social order into which such bonding fits. In the absence of an immediately available alternative to the social order we in fact accept, we have a motive to do justice in cases of those conflicts which if left to fester would erode that order. That motive is the perpetuation of the social bond of that order.

David Hume develops this positive communitarian theme when he argues for his claim that justice owes the approval humanity gives it solely to its tendency to preserve the order of society. He observes that "where the society is ready to perish from extreme necessity," such as a famine, the harm is already done that justice was intended to remedy by preventing the society from coming apart. Injustice cannot, at that point, increase this harm; so persons are left to themselves to survive, without justice regulating their interaction.

The notion of society here could be interpreted in either a broad way to include humanity or a narrow way to include only the agent's "own country." But Hume makes clear that attempts to do good for humanity come to naught "for want of a duly limited object." The perspective of justice is, then, society in the narrower sense. There will, though, be differences between societies in the narrower sense of subdivisions of humanity, differences important enough to affect justice.

Consider, for example, the contrast Hume draws between a society in which "birth is respected" and one in which "riches are the chief idol." The former favors military virtue and hence monarchy as its form of government; the later favors industry and hence a republican government. Hume concludes that each form of government will promote the usefulness of the characteristic custom of its society. The monarchical form, through the military, promotes respect for birth; the republican form, through industry, promotes the quest for riches. Hume does not go on to draw the conclusion, though it seems inevitable, that since the sole foundation of justice is the support of society, justice in these different societies will be different, otherwise one form of justice would be required to support conflicting goals.[8]

Freedom and Equality

On the negative side, those in the communitarian tradition reject the idea of an emergence of nonperspectival from perspectival universalism. Such an emergence might seem plausible if in the process of doing justice from a particular perspective a breakpoint is reached. At this breakpoint that perspective itself is tested. The significant thing is that the perspective has to be tested by adopting a moral stance with no tie to a particular social group. Such a nonperspectival moral stance would in some fashion be presupposed in the overall interactive process of doing justice from a particular perspective. It would then be argued that without presupposing a nonperspectival moral stance for testing any perspective the enterprise of doing justice is not a moral but only a political enterprise. It would be nothing more— as though everyone should see this as a fatal flaw—than choosing the best means for maintenance of the society.

Should there be, for example, reliance on the moral stance that those engaged in a just resolution of a conflict are free and equal as moral persons? If so, any perspective which rejects this stance would fail the test for being adequate for doing justice. This appeal to freedom and equality in the process of doing justice has deep roots in contract, as opposed to communitarian, views of justice.[9] Without presupposing freedom and equality, any resolution would be criticized by contractarians as instrumental.

As free, participants in doing justice would not be limited to preserving the social bond, since having to preserve it would be a restriction on moral reflection. The freedom of a moral person allows for questioning any tradition, any authority, any propriety. And as equal, the weight of their voice in the discussion would not be diminished even if they reject the social bond, since this would make acceptance of the social bond a condition on their qualifying as moral equals. Nations disqualify foreigners, ethnic minorities, and religious minorities from full participation in citizenship. But such discrimination is incompatible with the moral equality allegedly presupposed by doing justice. Freedom and equality would then certainly open up the discussion; there would be no binding rules of "political correctness."

The communitarian thinker will, though, want to know just why doing justice imports these nonperspectival requirements of freedom and equality into the discussion. They are, after all, quite rigorous standards, so rigorous that it is hard to imagine any being other than a detached and alienated spirit insisting on them.

But there is an easier way for the communitarian to attack the introduction of these nonperspectival requirements. In different social groups there are different standards of freedom and equality. Freedom and equality turn out themselves to be perspectival. In U.S. society the standard of freedom involved in the process of doing justice is compatible with important exclusions. For example, jury selection in criminal cases doesn't proceed on the basis that acceptable jurors can think that a classist and racist state has no right to punish. In appointments to U.S. judgeships, moreover, there has been a tendency to select those who do not see class as a suspect classification when it comes to determining whether there has been equal protection of the laws.[10] None of this need be taken to mean that in doing justice people lack freedom and equality. Instead, it reminds us that the standards of freedom and equality are fashioned by the society from whose perspective justice is being done. If there is an objection to such standards, then it is also an objection to the society in which they are standards. But such an objection would not lead away from all societies. It would point the direction to a different society, one with different standards of freedom and equality.

The urge still remains to say there is a noncontextual conception of freedom and equality that can serve as the test. This urge arises wherever communities cultivate the drive to have their own justice accepted by recalcitrant subgroups or distinct communities. Liberalism is often identified with an aversion to putting its concepts of freedom and equality in context. In fact, liberals with the greatest influence have always integrated a contextual element into their thought. Isaiah Berlin recognizes a "shifting, but always recognizable frontier" of freedom. Within these frontiers, people should be inviolable, and a "normal human being" would not overstep these frontiers without revulsion. The frontiers are "developed through history" and are "weighed against the claims of many other values."[11] With the recognition of the frontiers of liberty as shifting and value dependent, liberty can no longer lay the basis for a nonperspectival justice.

An even more concrete contextualization occurs when a specific social order is made the focus of discussion. It is democratic society of modern Western history that is picked out by John Rawls, in his work after *A Theory of Justice*, as the context for discussions of freedom and justice. Rawls would insist though that he stays clear of assuming any substantive goods when he picks out democratic society. He thinks this insistence makes sense because, in a democratic society, there will be respect and freedom for those striving for different substantive goods. Kantian autonomy or Millian individuality are not, then, assumed as goods. What Rawls assumes are only the mutual respect and freedom necessary if democratic procedures are to be workable. This freedom defines the frontier against intrusion, making it depend on the demands of democratic procedures. This freedom is not, then, the noncontextual autonomy Immanuel Kant makes central to his views. In addition, the mutual respect called for by democratic interaction is the appropriate sense of equality needed by Rawls in his pursuit of a "political" rather than a purely moral sense of justice.[12]

What has been said so far about the perspectival universality of justice is not something that liberals like Berlin and Rawls find abhorrent. Each contains a communitarian moment in his thought.

Homogeneity and Community

Building on communities is risky. They are made to carry a lot of weight in the argument for a social-based perspectivalism. In this argument, they provide the perspectives from which justice is done. The risk involved comes from the fact that there are all sorts of communities. Not all of them will provide a foundation for political morality in general or even justice in particular. Part of the problem comes from the widely lamented atomization of individuals that eventually destroys community. The problem also arises from the sharp divisions between reasonably well-defined groups that fracture what we are led to believe are communities. (The focus here will be on nation-sized communities, rather than on communities in the sense of traditions, which may involve only a small segment of a nation and may cross numerous national boundaries.[13]

We'll start with atomization. For John Dewey, the market and industrialization had ruptured the social bond as it had existed in small communities. As a result community had become a project, rather than a place ready for occupancy. Human relationships formed only a Great Society, an atomized aggregate resulting from the destruction of small-

er communities. Dewey could only anticipate a Great Community that
would replace the inchoate public of the Great Society.[14]

He took note of the tendency toward democracy present everywhere,
thinking that this tendency could be guided toward the realization of
a more ideal democracy, which would then be the Great Community.
But, he notes, this realization would not come about simply by more
democracy. There would have to be a qualitative improvement in the
kind of democracy presently existing, which suffered from the atomization of interests in a market society. So Dewey was pointing toward a community that didn't exist and furthermore wasn't the natural outcome of the democratic tendency that did exist. He looked
forward to it as a social thinker rather than as a member of a movement motivated by the Great Community as its shared ideal. It was a
project drawn to his own specifications. The Great Community could
not, then, claim to be an existing foundation, such as communitarianism requires, for a radical view of justice.

On to the problem created by social divisions. Contemporary communitarians are not as willing as Dewey to claim that there is only an
inchoate public. They would claim that there are social bonds strong
enough to make up communities rather than aggregates of individuals. Despite the atomization caused by markets, there is other-regarding behavior and many are willing to spend time for what they think
of as the good of the community. Such behavior might be attributed
to self-interest, to the need for recognition, or to an innate feeling of
solidarity. The communitarians would argue that the important thing
is not the origin of such behavior, but that it exists.

Where there is other-regarding behavior, there is what communitarians call civic virtue. This is a propensity for sociability, one that
builds social bonds and reinforces them institutionally. The state does
not make displays of civic virtue unnecessary but instead, at least in
the case of the democratic state, rests on civic virtue. Civic virtue is
necessary if the state is not to become totalitarian. A moral culture,
whether in a society with a democratic state or not, will have its roots,
at a level deeper than the state, in the sociability of the people. For
the communitarian, justice can in its turn be centered in this sociability, as a real rather than just an ideal foundation.

This type of view has many variants, running from the conservative to the neoconservative to the liberal and over to the social democratic.[15] Most variants share the belief that there are nationwide societies, each with a consensus in regard to a system of norms. With
such a consensus these societies can be considered communities. The
system of norms arms such a society with a moral culture that allows

for the orderly resolution of conflicts, which we are calling doing justice.

Can there be such a consensus and what might its nature be in a society with deep divisions along class, race, gender, or national lines? Jean-Jacques Rousseau raised just such a question concerning the compatibility of factions with the "general will."[16] The matter should be decided in precisely the way he did. He insisted that (a) a moral culture exists only when its adherents could freely adopt it in view of what is in their best interest, and (b) when there are social positions making for systematic conflict among them a people will not be able to freely adopt a common moral code. Given that in any society we can think of today there are social positions that generate such conflict, the kind of moral culture needed for justice on the communitarian view does not exist.[17]

John Rawls has adopted an ingenious way of avoiding this problem. If it is successful, the communitarian can still claim that, despite social heterogeneity, there is room for the moral homogeneity needed as a basis for justice. As already noted, Rawls appeals in recent writing to a democratic culture as a basis for justice. As Rawls was surely aware, there are important gaps in this culture in view of the reluctance of powerful groups to sacrifice their advantages by accepting the democratic process. Whites, for example, were for years willing to exclude African-Americans from the scope of democratic institutions. This involved the absence of political liberties, police repression with impunity, and the open denial of equal economic opportunity. Those who derived benefits from white supremacy in social, economic, and political terms saw these benefits as goods worth sacrificing a truly democratic culture for. Supremacy for whites and equality for African-Americans were conflicting goals that made it impossible for both groups to share a democratic culture.[18]

In this impasse, the way out suggested by Rawls is for both sides to experiment with democracy for enough time for them to recognize just how great its advantages are. At such a time they will be willing to modify their incompatible goals sufficiently so they can continue to enjoy the benefits of democracy.[19] Social heterogeneity would then allow for the moral homogeneity needed by the communitarian. His suggestion, though, is fraught with difficulties. Even if those in a privileged position were to enter into the experiment, there is no guarantee that they would find democracy better than their privileges. After all, when a sizable group is subordinated, the benefits in terms of everything from cheap labor to a political monopoly are enormous, at least for the most powerful in the subordinating group.

What makes their privileged position vulnerable is not mulling over the advantages of democracy but rather the possibility of a movement of the subordinated group for greater equality. The militancy of the African-American movement of the 1960s in the United States caught the attention of white liberals, thereby creating a coalition across racial lines that could not be ignored by white politicians. Playing the power card did, then, bring about an extension of democracy, based though on a truce rather than a fundamental change of goals.

The truce involved gains in civil rights for African-Americans but within the context of white-controlled institutions and of simmering white resentment at having to give up anything. There was an extension of democracy that did not eliminate, but only narrowed, the gap in democratic culture. For, so long as social inequality was still being promoted by attitudes and institutions, there could not be political equality and hence not a full democratic culture.[20] In the 1990s this 1960s truce is threatened as African-Americans of most strata recognize that their losses in the 1970s and 1980s were enormous. The heterogeneity in a society with unstable truces makes impossible the moral homogeneity the communitarian appeals to as a basis for doing justice.

Social Positions and Justice

Either there is no nation-sized community, but only Dewey's Great Society, or the nation-sized communities relevant today lack moral homogeneity, due to social fractures. In either case there appears to be no nation-sized moral culture on which justice could be based. Instead, the only place to look for a set of standards to base justice on seems to be in the individual groupings into which society is fractured. It is in these that there is a basis for normative unity on which justice can be based. There is no class-, race-, gender-, or religion-blind justice since the perspectives from which justice is done will be those of groupings defined in one of these ways. This shift from community to social position allows us to maintain perspectival universalism, but now the perspective is from a social position rather than from a community based on moral homogeneity.

The logic of this new view still sets out from the communitarian assumption that a social unit is a prerequisite for doing justice. This means only that they both share a perspectival universalism. But the new view differs from communitarianism in two respects, one of which has already been discussed whereas the other injects a new element.

The element already discussed has to do with the tendency of many communitarians to play up moral homogeneity where there are in fact deep social divisions. Nation-sized societies are fractured by criss-crossing divisions that make the unmanipulated common understandings needed for a common moral culture difficult to come by. The longing for community can underestimate the depth of the moral diversity in such societies. Dewey was closer to the mark when he said a nation-sized community is today no more than a project. Can we, though, find unitary moral cultures by pushing on to the subgroupings within nation-sized society, such as classes and races? I think not.

The new element is an insistence on social positions rather than moral cultures. The idea is that there can be opposed moral cultures within any grouping we settle on. This opposition will have complex causes but will in one way or another depend on the fact that it is an opposition within a single social position. Women in Operation Rescue have a pro-life, anti-gay, and pro-family moral culture that differentiates them from the women in the National Organization for Women with their pro-choice and pro-equality moral culture. It would, then, be a mistake to think of justice from the woman's perspective as rooted in a unitary women's moral culture. That is why there is a need to shift from moral culture, shared moral meanings, and normative consensus to speak about social positions.

Once this shift is made, it is no longer fruitful to think in communitarian terms. The appeal to community is an appeal to a bond established through a homogeneous culture, shared understandings, and cohering norms. Such an appeal is unfruitful in providing us with a basis for justice. The reason is simply that the moral cultures sought continue to break into multiple cultures as we push from nation-sized groups through various subgroupings. The appeal to social positions to which we now turn does not depend on there being a unitary moral culture within each grouping.

The shift in primacy from moral cultures to social positions puts a critical tool for assessing moral cultures within our reach. In this way it satisfies the classical liberal demand for reflection on moral cultures. Such a critical tool works in the following way. Through a social theory—an hypothesis about social positions and their links—one attempts to account for the fact that people in a given social position have the moral culture or cultures they do.

A sufficiently comprehensive social theory will also be able to account for the rejection of the explanation it itself offers of any moral culture by those adopting that culture. Thus the social hypothesis is not assumed to be beyond the conflicts in moral cultures it is dealing with. Its explanations will be contested and it will, if it is adequate, explain why they are contested.

In addition, a social theory can interpret moral cultures associated with a given social position as either coerced because of a need to cope with desperate circumstances or manipulated by agencies outside that position. Such an interpretation is of special interest here since it amounts to a critique of those moral cultures. It is a critique if it can be assumed that those in the given social position would not adopt any of those moral cultures on their own in the absence of desperate circumstances or manipulation.[21]

What does this general line of thinking imply for justice? As before, doing justice is a matter of transcending conflicting claims. And also as before, this transcendence is guided by a complex set of values. Such a set of values picks out ones that need to be realized to preserve the group. They are then part of a concept of a good society. With the communitarian it was possible to locate such a set of values where there was a moral culture or a shared moral understanding. But some moral cultures or shared moral understandings don't pass critical scrutiny in light of social theory. They show up as the coerced or manipulated cultures of a given social group. Thus the moral culture of Operation Rescue might fail to pass critical scrutiny as a morality for women on several grounds. Women who adopt that culture do so partly out of desperation. It helps them cope with the arbitrariness, the humiliation, and the threats they endure in the male dominated family as well as elsewhere. They also adopt it partly out of manipulation. Men promote such a moral culture as a way of protecting the privileges that equality for women would deny them. But where else, if not in moral culture, could a critically acceptable conception of the good society come from on the basis of which justice could be done?

The preliminary answer is that the values to be realized if a society is to be good will be based on the interests a social position will give its members. These interests will be ones that can pass the test of critique in the light of social theory. And if there are overlapping groups, it will be left to discussion in the light of social theory to undertake a conciliation of the interests of the various groups. According, then, to the general view taken here of the underlying values, justice will be done where conflicting claims are resolved in a way that advances the critically certified interests of a social position.[22]

An implication of this view is that justice itself will become a source of conflicting claims. Justice done from the perspective of one group will be countered by charges of injustice from the perspective of a conflicting group. Yet two such groups are often tightly linked, calling for a single justice between them. But by focusing on the interests arising from each group by itself, the way is barred toward such a single justice. For this reason a step beyond our preliminary answer is needed.

Before taking that step, in the next section, a word more about critical acceptability. There is no intention in appealing to social theory to ascend to a purely neutral level beyond the conflicts within and between groups. Thus the critical acceptability of a moral culture is not a mark of nonperspectival approval. As a caution, then, social theories should be indexed by the agendas they promote. This does not, though, destroy their critical impact. A well-documented account of the moral culture surrounding Operation Rescue based on a social hypothesis about the nature and interrelation of gender groups can be persuasive beyond those already committed to whatever agenda that hypothesis is associated with. Further, since finely articulated social theories aren't automatically available to serve every agenda, a developed social theory can get the edge simply for lack of a respectable competitor. The critical potential of a social theory does not, then, depend on its independence of the social context. Otherwise it would be hard to say how humans ever did critical thinking.

Governability and Universality

Though nation-sized communities are made impossible by social divisions, states manage to survive such divisions. Perhaps all along we should have been looking to states rather than to communities for justice. We could in that way have avoided the problem we just ran aground on while looking for the basis for justice at the level of social groups like classes and genders. It will turn out, though, that the false start with such groups pays off in getting clear about how justice can be located at the level of the state.

In doing justice, one needs to consider the big picture from somewhere within it. This is simply to reaffirm the view that justice involves universality with a tie to a perspective. But in this final attempt to understand justice, the big picture is to encompass the various subdivisions of society ruled by a state and the perspective becomes that of one of those subdivisions.[23] The perspective is not, then, that of the state itself. The motive for doing justice, where justice is still understood as the resolution of conflicts, shifts from being the cohesion of a community to the governability of a society. Conflicts between the elements of the society could, if allowed to intensify, make the society ungovernable and as a result undermine the society itself.

Governability, then, provides a motive for transcending the narrowness of group interest, making it impossible for any governing body to commit itself to advancing the interests of only one or a few of the groups in the society.[24] A balance must be struck between the interests of major conflicting groups that, on the one hand, limits their losses and, on the other hand, limits as well their gains. Exactly what formula for limiting losses and gains is adopted will depend considerably on the circumstances. The strength or weakness of the democratic impulse among a people, of the different conflicting groups, of the economy in the given period, and of the legitimacy of the ruling body will all be factors in determining how much gains and losses should be limited to ensure governability.

This picture isn't complete without emphasizing the role of group perspective. Losses and gains could be limited in a variety of ways. None of these ways corresponds precisely with the interests of any group in the society. For the point is to limit the interests of each group so that all groups can be governed together. However, each group will want to limit its interests as little as is absolutely required by governability. Here is where the group perspective of state justice shows up. All we need to do is ask what group or groups will be the positions defining the perspective of state justice. The perspective-defining groups will be the powerful social groups. They will have more resources with which to influence the doing of justice in the direction of their interests. In addition, a governing group standing above the society is more disposed to them since without their full support its ability to rule can be seriously undermined. It then makes sense for a governing group not to try to fashion the limits on losses and benefits as a neutral in the conflicts between social groups but in a manner that calls for the least sacrifices by powerful groups.

State justice is not, then, a carbon copy of the justice of powerful groups governed by the state. Still, by calling for the least sacrifices from the powerful groups, state justice is done from the perspective of those groups.[25] How is state justice related to the justice of the powerful groups? The governing group modifies the justice based on the interests of powerful social groups in such a way that governability is ensured. This will mean that the group justice of powerful social groups gets modified to take into account the interests of less powerful groups.

It was group justice that was elaborated in the previous section. It is being replaced here by state justice, which is neither more universal nor more absolute than group justice. It is not more universal since both can transcend conflicts occurring across the society. It is not more absolute since both involve a group perspective. They differ in that the governability of a divided society replaces the realization of group interests as the motive of justice.

The current escalation in the price of health care in the United States illustrates key features of this picture of state justice. Some limit needs to be put on the gains of the health providers and health related manufacturers. Otherwise, the government will be held accountable for allowing this sector to enrich itself far beyond the ability of the rest of the population to keep up. Similarly, some limit needs to be put on the losses sustained by those who have to pay the bill for health care. Inflation in the cost of health care is in part responsible for a high level of unemployment and for the large number of working people who have no health insurance. State legitimacy would be called into question without a state effort to alleviate this situation.

The health industry, though, wants to set these limits without sacrificing its chance to continue to increase its share of the gross domestic product, which in fifty years jumped from 4 percent to 14 percent. The majority of the population has, however, shown its preference in numerous polls for a system in which physician fees and hospital rates would be negotiated by health commissions and in which the health insurance industry would be replaced by a single payer.

In the U.S. context, this favored change will not take place now, since the justice that will be done will be done from the perspective of corporate power. This power is better organized, is closer to the governing group, and has greater resources than the inchoate majority favoring more radical change. At present this corporate perspective excludes a government takeover of any major industry and also excludes an effective mechanism of controls on fees and rates. On the issue of health care, this perspective of corporate power is eloquently expressed at regular intervals in *The New York Times* editorials.[26]

But the state's doing justice from the perspective of corporate power does not mean that it does exactly what that power wants. It is after all the state and not corporate power that is laying down the pattern of justice in health care from the corporate perspective. The perspective of corporate power is, then, no longer taken with the sole motive of realizing corporate self-interest but with the motive of preserving governability. Thus there will be an effort to extend coverage to many of the uninsured and there will be an effort, of dubious effectiveness, to have voluntary compliance on the part of the health care industry with price restraint. Despite the weakness of such a measure, it will become state justice in the health care field, barring an unanticipated groundswell of consumer protest which would strengthen it. Through it, conflict is temporarily defused and something more than narrow group interest is thereby achieved.

Objections

In closing, three objections call for comment. First, it will be objected that state justice is not the only kind. This must be admitted by introducing what can be called radical justice. But even this new species avoids the difficulties that have led us to state justice only by making reference to the state. Radical justice is different from state justice in two ways. On the one hand, its perspective is that of a group or groups that at the moment happen not to be those with the greatest power. It is the perspective of an underdog group. On the other hand, it is a perspective that, like state justice, takes into account the interests of what are currently the dominant groups. It takes them into account since it is a perspective that would promote the legitimacy of a state run not for the currently powerful but for the underdog groups.

Second, it will be objected that state justice is not merely a compromise worked out to preserve legitimacy. It is a matter of principle rather than compromise, and the principles involved can be found to be operative in the legal tradition of a democratic society like the United States.[27] The response to this made by Critical Legal Studies is adequate for our purposes as well. It is difficult to encase the history of legal conflict resolution in a consistent tradition of principle.[28] Legitimacy manages to be preserved over long periods through compromises that, if principles are present at all, involve changing and conflicting principles. These compromises are outcomes of debates that turn on the relative power of the groups participating and on the assumed goal of governability.

Third, it will be objected that as between the various justices—state justice and different forms of radical justice—there is a true justice, which will be that of dominated groups.[29] The reason is that only the interests behind the radical justice of dominated groups can be openly acknowledged without reducing the long-term chances of satisfying them. In other cases, the interests behind justice have to be obscured by ideology. State justice done from the perspective of the most powerful groups is, then, false since to admit openly its tilt toward the interests of those powerful groups would stiffen the resistance of relatively powerless groups. Thus if the interests of the powerful are to be promoted by state justice, its tilt to the powerful must be obscured with ideology about the common interest.

This is an initially attractive suggestion. But it comes to grief over the fact that in a divided society none of the sides—powerless or powerful—can reveal the true interests behind the kind of justice they wish to promote. There is a perfect symmetry here. The powerless, if they reveal their interest in overcoming their powerlessness, will only intensify the opposition to them of the powerful. The powerful will charge the powerless with declaring class war and will attack the powerless under the banner of the common good.

Can the radical justice of the powerless still be defended against a state justice based on the perspective of the powerful? Suppose the radical justice of the powerless calls for a society in which there is no power differentiation. Then in such an egalitarian society, the interests of those who promote the justice of this society can be proclaimed without threat to those interests. There is, though, no corresponding paradise for the powerful, since without the powerless to oppose them they are no longer the powerful. Here we seem to have reached asymmetry of the sort needed to justify the radical justice of the powerless.

Those who see power inequality as compatible with justice will, however, object in strongest terms. Any effort to do away with power inequalities for the sake of egalitarian radical justice will, from their perspective, involve an unacceptable use of coercion in order to divest the powerful of their power. Admittedly, after using coercion, a situation will exist in which people can express their interest in equal power without opposition. But what is at issue is precisely the present and not the future. Can a radical justice opposed to power inequalities be given validity within our present divided society simply by the fact that it points to a future society in which equal power can be affirmed publicly as a social good? The answer must be that its so pointing has no tendency to validate it. For, this radical justice can reach the goal it points to only by means objectionable to competing types of justice. Only if those competing types of justice were ruled invalid in advance could such a goal lend absolute validity to the radical justice in question.

Having dealt with these objections, we are in a position to claim that state justice, at least in state societies, must be central in treatments of justice. The impulse that leads to doing justice is one of finding a universal standpoint from which to reconcile particular forces in conflict. We have traced several steps in the attempt to find just what such a universal standpoint could be. We were led from communities to social groupings in a divided society and finally to states. Communities of at least the size of nations proved incapable of yielding norms generally acceptable within them due to the social divisions present in them. Social groupings within such nations might have been a structural basis for justice, but this left us with as many standards of justice as groupings. And yet due to the close interaction between such groups a single standard of justice is needed for dealing with conflicts between them. Rather than retreat to community to get such a single standard, we moved on to the state as the organizer of groups in conflict. Without presupposing social homogeneity, the state can claim to stand outside particular conflicts and adjudicate them on the basis ultimately of norms designed to promote governability. State justice is often at odds with radical justice, which shares with state justice a parallel structure but emerges from oppositional rather than dominant groups. While radical justice can offer a critical view of state justice, it cannot defend itself as ultimate.

Notes

1. On the connection between universality and community, see Alasdair MacIntyre, *Three Rival Versions of Moral Enquiry* (Notre Dame, Ind.: University of Notre Dame Press, 1990), pp. 59–60.

2. According to Ernest Baker, justice "balances, and thus reconciles (and thus, in the issue, 'joins'), the different claims." This is a fundamental theme of his *Principles of Social and Political Theory* (London: Oxford University Press, 1951), pp. 102, 150, 170.

3. Karl Marx and Frederick Engels, *The German Ideology*, editor C. J. Arthur (New York: International Publishers, 1970), p. 53. Here the conflict between the claims of individuals and the maintenance of the general interest is seen to exist even prior to classes and the state.

4. *Village of Skokie v. National Socialist Party of America*, 373 N.E. 2d 21 (Ill. 1978). The Supreme Court of Illinois upheld the right of the Nazis to march with swastikas, denying that swastikas are fighting words and claiming that, being forewarned of the demonstration, citizens could choose to be elsewhere, avoiding thereby being either offended or provoked to violence.

5. Consider the seeming justice of upholding the right to property, as claimed by the rich, by extending it to the poor. Suppose, though, there is no good-faith effort, by those doing justice, to protect the poor from common burglars, userers, environmental classism, and a regressive sales tax. The right to property for the poor is then artificial, and it doesn't become an equal right as between rich and poor. In these circumstances, denying the poor a right to take from the rich by upholding the right to property as claimed by the rich damages the social bond without an effort to repair it. The resolution is strongly one-sided, and thus the universality called for by justice fails.

6. Raymond Bonner, *Weakness and Deceit: U.S. Policy and El Salvador* (New York: Times Books, 1984), pp. 188–89, 313–19.

7. Ronald Dworkin, *Law's Empire* (Cambridge: Harvard University Press, 1986), pp. 219–24.

8. David Hume, *An Enquiry Concerning the Principles of Morals*, in *Enquiries*, editor L.A. Selby–Bigge (Oxford: Clarendon Press, 1972), pp. 186, 225 n1, 249.

9. Just as in John Locke's state of nature humans are free and equal, so too in Rawls's original position, humans are free and rational beings concerned with furthering their own interests in a situation of equality. "By acting from these principles [adopted in the original position] persons express their nature as free and equal rational beings . . ." John Rawls, *A Theory of Justice* (Cambridge: Harvard University Press, 1971), p. 252.

10. *San Antonio Independent School District v. Rodriguez*, 411 U.S. 1 (1973).

11. Isaiah Berlin, "Two Concepts of Liberty," in his *Four Essays on Liberty* (New York: Oxford University Press, 1969).

12. On the contrast between a comprehensive substantive moral view and a political conception of justice, see John Rawls, *Political Liberalism* (New York: Columbia University Press, 1993), p. 13.

13. Milton Fisk, "Community and Morality," *Review of Politics* 55, 3 (1993).

14. John Dewey, *The Public and Its Problems* (Athens, Ohio: Swallow Press, 1988), pp. 134–51.

15. For a survey of the different positions see Robert Booth Fowler, *The Dance with Community: The Contemporary Debate in American Political Thought* (Lawrence: Kansas University Press, 1991), chapters 5, 6.

16. Jean–Jacques Rousseau, *The Social Contract*, Book 2, Chapter 3.

17. For a perceptive survey of systematic conflict between class positions, see Ralph Miliband, *Divided Societies: Class Struggle in Contemporary Capitalism* (Oxford: Clarendon Press, 1989), chapters 3, 5, 6

18. However, the divisions between groups are not, for Rawls, so deep that they must ultimately refuse to agree to a conception of democratic fair play. They will, once having seen the advantages of such fair play in practice, go on to modify their comprehensive substantive goods so as to avoid run-ins. This does not mean that their comprehensive views will become identical, but only that they will become sufficiently homogeneous to provide a common moral basis for justice. Thus what he calls a "reasonable pluralism" is not just a limit on groups that will be tolerated. It is something most groups can become part of. For, they will see, in terms of their own values, the advantages of modifying certain among those values so that they can then adopt fair conditions of cooperation in respect to other groups. See Rawls, *Political Liberalism*, lecture 2, section 1; lecture 4, section 6.

19. This is the process emphasized by Rawls in "The Idea of an Overlapping Consensus" (*Political Liberalism*, lecture 4). In "The Priority of the

Right and Ideas of the Good" (*ibid.*, lecture 5, section 6), he stresses another tactic. Since civil society isn't fully formed apart from the state, he contends that conflictive divisions in civil society can be avoided by a just state.

20. This parallels the point about women made by Carole Pateman, "Feminism and Democracy," in *Democratic Theory and Practice*, edited by G. Duncan (Cambridge: Cambridge University Press, 1985), pp. 204–17.

21. Raymond Guess, *The Idea of a Critical Theory* (New York: Cambridge University Press, 1981), p. 79.

22. Milton Fisk, *Ethics and Society* (New York: New York University Press, 1980), pp. 218–20.

23. For an extension of this view to international justice, see Milton Fisk, *The State and Justice* (New York: Cambridge University Press, 1989), chapter 17.

24. Milton Fisk, *The State and Justice*, part 2.

25. A pattern of justice then becomes part of the set of ideas and practices that enables a dominant group or groups to become hegemonic in the sense intended by Antonio Gramsci, *Selections from the Prison Notebooks*, edited by Q. Hoare and G. Nowell Smith (New York: International Publishers, 1971), pp. 257–64.

26. See e.g. the editorials of the *New York Times*, 5/26/92, 6/22/92, 7/22/92, 9/26/92, 3/7/93, 8/18/93, 9/20/93, 10/28/93, 2/7/94, 2/22/94, 6/20/94, 8/9/94.

27. Ronald Dworkin, *Law's Empire* (Cambridge: Harvard University Press, 1986), chapter 6.

28. Andrew Altman, "Legal Realism, Critical Legal Studies, and Dworkin," *Philosophy and Public Affairs* 15, 3 (1986), pp. 205–36.

29. See the critique of the perspectival universality of justice in the discussion–review of Fisk's *The State and Justice* by Justin Schwartz, "Revolution and Justice," *Against the Current* 42 (1993), pp. 37–41. The criterion of publicity used in this critique can be traced to Kant's "To Perpetual Peace: A Philosophical Sketch," in Immanuel Kant, *Perpetual Peace and Other Essays*, translated by T. Humphery (Indianapolis: Hackett, 1983), appendix 2, p. 135. Here Kant lays out a transcendental formula of public right: "All actions that affect the rights of other men are wrong if their maxim is not consistent with publicity." This formula is subject to the difficulty pointed out below.

Comments by William A. Galston

In this essay Fisk makes an intriguing attempt to go beyond the liberal/communitarian debate over justice. Common to both liberals and communitarians, he argues, is an assumption of social homogeneity that provides a basis for the requisite universality of standards of justice. But this assumption is both contrary to fact and unnecessary. Rather, justice should be understood as conflict resolution spurred on by the need to "perpetuate the social bond."

The universal element of justice rests not on shared principles or understandings, but rather on membership in a polity the perpetuation of which is seen as desirable. To resolve conflict and preserve the polity, solutions put forward as just must reflect compromises struck among the interests of major competing groups that limit their losses as well as gains in a way that all will find at least minimally acceptable.

The particularity of justice reflects the fact that different societies will require correspondingly different strategies of preservation, and that even within the same society such strategies will vary over time with the shifting balance of power among its contending groups. As Fisk puts it, "Exactly what formula for limiting losses and gains is adopted will depend considerably on the circumstances. The strength or weakness of the democratic impulse among a people, of the different conflicting groups, of the economy in the given period, and of the legitimacy of the ruling body will all be factors in determining how much gains and losses should be limited to ensure governability."

It is not difficult to construct an objection to Fisk's argument from the standpoint of Rawlsian "political liberalism." Compromise in the interests of governability represents, not a moral position, but a (mere) modus vivendi in which powerful groups yield only as much ground as they must to one another, and little if any to the powerless. Fisk's response is straightforward. History confirms what social theory suggests, that conflict resolution is not and cannot be achieved within a "consistent tradition of principle." Not even common participation in what Rawls calls the public culture of a democratic society provides an adequate basis for an effective fund of shared universal principles. The resolution of this debate rests on the extent to which democratic public culture truly penetrates all groups within democratic societies—and on the extent to which broad democratic concepts such as freedom and equality can be specified through conceptions equally acceptable to all.

Without seeking to resolve this debate, which is as much empirical as philosophical, I want to raise a different question. Fisk says that the need to perpetuate the social bond is a "teleological element that gives significance to doing justice and that is a standard for feasible resolutions of conflicts. . . . Without a social bond to start with, those making conflicting claims would be unwilling to accept the possibility that their claims would be rejected."

The difficulty with this thesis is that in certain circumstances the maintenance of the social bond itself becomes a matter of political controversy. During the 1850s, for example, contending parties in the United States espoused a wide variety of positions on preserving the bond among the states. Radical abolitionists declared, "No Union with slaveholders." Fervent slaveholders rejected continued union within a federal government dominated by antislavery Republicans. And even those parties committed to the preservation of the Union relied on principles that turned out to be mutually incompatible—unionism and Abraham Lincoln's antislavery invocation of the Declaration of Independence.

This episode suggests a broader point. Perhaps Aristotle was not far wrong after all to suggest that some shared understanding of justice is what constitutes a political community. If so, the breakdown of that understanding can weaken the belief that the social bond is worth maintaining. Fisk argues that justice does not create, but presupposes, the social bond. There is something to this, of course: a sense of fellow-feeling, common history, shared fate may well make groups willing to endure compromises they would otherwise find unacceptable. But there is also merit to the opposing position that a shared conception of justice creates, or at least sustains, the social bond. This is not to deny the central fact of political conflict, which Fisk rightly stresses. But it is to suggest that the resolution of that conflict requires some basis beyond an ever-shifting modus vivendi.

Let me express this point in conceptual rather than historical terms. The goal of preserving the social bond, linked as it is to conflict resolution as a means, tacitly presupposes the preeminence of Hobbesian goals such as peace and civil order over the other moral and theological commitments (and conceptions of the good) that may divide groups within a polity. This presupposition may be justified. But it represents a more specific and substantive account of justice than Fisk suggests. On closer inspection, the apparent generic differences between (say) modus vivendi arguments and Rawlsian political liberalism may after all reflect competing political teleologies. For those of us who have long taken our bearings from Aristotle, this denouement hardly comes as a surprise.

Comments by James P. Sterba

In his essay Fisk argues that the search for justice is a search for "a universal standpoint from which to reconcile particular forces in conflict." He surveys various views concerning how this reconciliation should take place and opts for a conception which he calls "state justice" as being the most defensible view. According to Fisk, the goal of state justice is governability. Given this goal, state justice maintains that when faced with conflicts between social groups, it "makes sense for a governing group not to try to fashion the limits on losses and benefits as a neutral in the conflicts between social groups but in a manner that calls for the least sacrifices by powerful groups." Fisk considers the possibility that radical justice, whose "perspective is that of a group or groups that at the moment happen not to be those with the greatest power," might be considered to be preferable to state justice. Fisk rejects this possibility on the grounds that radical justice is simply the mirror image of the group justice favored by the most powerful and advantaged groups in a society (let's call this view "advantaged justice"). Both radical justice and advantaged justice are biased views unacceptable from the other perspective. Accordingly, Fisk claims that state justice with its goal of seeking only those compromises necessary for governability is preferable to both these forms of group justice.

It sometimes appears that Fisk would want to defend a conception of justice with more of a critical dimension than state justice, but he doesn't see how this is can be done. Nevertheless, I believe that the resources for a more critical conception of justice are available. Significantly, even Fisk's own conception of state justice contains a hint of such a conception. Fisk defines state justice as one that does not try "to fashion the limits on losses and benefits as a neutral in the conflicts between social groups but in a manner that calls for the least sacrifices by powerful groups." State justice then is defined by contrast with a view that is neutral in arbitrating the conflicts between social groups. This means that to fully understand what state justice is, we must have some understanding of what it is to be neutral in arbitrating the conflicts between social groups. Given that we have this understanding of neutral arbitration (let's call it "neutral justice"), why cannot neutral justice serve as a more defensible conception of justice than state justice with is constrained bias in favor of the more powerful groups? Moreover, the argument that Fisk gives for rejecting radical justice fail to apply to neutral justice. Radical justice simply favors the interests of "a group or groups that at the moment happen not to be those with the greatest power" and so is no better than advantaged justice, which simply favors the interests of the more powerful. But neutral justice is not tilted in favor of the interests of either the more powerful groups or the less powerful groups in society. Instead, it strives to be neutral between them. Why then is this conception of justice not preferable to the conception that Fisk favors?

Of course, one could accept the idea that neutral justice is preferable to state justice, but then contend that doesn't get us very far since many, if not all, contemporary conceptions of justice claim to be neutral in the sense that they strive to avoid bias, but then these conceptions of justice go on to endorse quite different practical requirements. So endorsing neutral justice, it may be argued, does not get us very far. We need to know which conception of neutrality we should endorse.

It is just here that the discussion of alternative conceptions of justice in my contribution to this volume and in my previous work is relevant. What I argue is that five contemporary conceptions of justice— libertarian justice with its ideal of liberty, welfare liberal justice with its ideal of fairness, socialist justice with its ideal of equality, feminist justice with its ideal of androgyny, and communitarian justice with its ideal of the common good—when correctly interpreted, can all be seen to support the same practical requirements, namely, a right to welfare and a right to equal opportunity. So if endorsing neutral justice is understood as endorsing any of these five contemporary conceptions of justice, we do know, or should know, where this leads. It leads to a right to welfare and a right to equal opportunity.

Now it may be that what is really bothering Fisk is that contemporary societies, like the United States, have not really secured basic human rights such as a right to welfare and a right to equal opportunity for all those who are entitled to them. At best, what contemporary societies have done is provide Fisk's state justice with its constrained bias in favor of the more powerful groups. Now I agree with Fisk that constrained bias in favor of the more powerful groups is normally what is practiced in most contemporary societies. And I think that Fisk would also agree with me that this should change. Where we disagree is whether a discussion of justice can be usefully employed to promote that change. I think it can, particularly if that discussion moves toward the practical reconciliation of alternative conceptions of justice that I think is possible. By contrast, Fisk would give to defenders of the status quo the "most defensible notion of justice." I think I have shown is that there are good reasons to resist this move. Justice is an important tool for changing society, and it would be a mistake to simply hand it over to defenders of the status quo. They simply don't deserve it.

7

Justice as Vengeance, Vengeance as Justice: A Partial Defense of Polymarchus

Robert C. Solomon

> If, then, anyone tells us that it is just to give everyone his due, and he means by this that from the just man harm is due to his enemies and benefit due to his friends—the man who says that is not wise, for it is not true.
>
> —Socrates to Polymarchus, *The Republic*, Book I.

"What is justice?" Socrates asked that question twenty five centuries ago, and ever since it has been one of the leading questions of Western philosophy. But from Plato to Rawls, philosophical discussions of justice have emphasized the supremacy of reason and rationality, and there has been too little appreciation of the role of feelings. Plato does insist on "harmony" between passions and reason, but he too often warns us against the unbridled emotions. (Socrates begins by dismissing any appeal to the sentiments in the *Crito*, for example.) Rawls devotes a late section or two to "the moral sentiments" and defends their ineliminability from human life,[1] but he too often tends to think of the sentiments as dispositions to act on rational principles and he seems to view them as inessential in the determination of justice.[2] Many other authors, of course, have simply dismissed the sentiments as mere "sentimentality" and insisted that the emotions only confuse and distort the rational deliberations of jus-

tice. Kant famously degrades the various "inclinations" as at best
secondary to morality, sarcastically dismisses "melting compassion"
or "tender sympathy" in an infamous passage on the injunction to "love
thy neighbor" and vigorously rejects any role for vengeance in his
retributive account of justice.[3] Harking back to a neglected tradition
in ethics, however, I want to argue that there can be no adequate
understanding of justice without an appreciation and understanding of
the role of the emotions. This includes not only those benign "moral
sentiments" such as sympathy, care and compassion and other "fel-
low-feelings" but also the nastier emotions of envy, jealousy, resentment and, especially, vengeance as well.[4]

Justice as Vengeance?
A Polemical Proposal

"As for Duhring's proposition that the home of justice is to be sought
in the sphere of the reactive feelings, one is obliged for truth's sake to
counter it with a blunt antithesis: the *last* sphere to be conquered by the
spirit of justice is the sphere of the reactive feelings!"

-Nietzsche, *On the Genealogy of Morals* (II, 11)

My thesis is, in part, that there is no a priori, non-reactive sense of
justice, such as so many philosophers from Plato to Rawls have tried
to delineate. Our sense of justice is always a more or less particular,
more or less personal, partially emotional response to a situation or
circumstances, even if at a distance or of global dimensions, often in
the face of disagreement, deprivation or disharmony. The contexts in
which justice is discussed and debated are various and sometimes
incommensurable. To begin with, the spheres of retributive and distributive justice are often separated, albeit with some embarrassment
and equivocation over terms, especially by anti-utilitarians. Within
the sphere of distributive justice, the perennial disagreements between
those who defend egalitarian, libertarian, need-based and various entitlement and merit-based conceptions of justice constitute a veritable
discipline unto itself, but it can and has been well-argued that these
different conceptions are in fact based on historical, contextual and
cultural as well as ideological differences.[5] Indeed, the delineation of
spheres of justice may well be much more fine-grained than that, and
these may indeed be incommensurable.[6] I do not intend to argue this

thesis here, although I am obviously sympathetic to it.[7] What I do want to argue, particularly with reference to retributive justice, is that justice essentially consists in part of a reaction to a more or less particular state of affairs, within a cultural tradition and with a substantial, concrete history.[8] In order to underscore that point in this paper, I want to suggest something moderately outrageous—that not only can vengeance be defended as a significant ingredient in (retributive) justice, but that there is a sense in which justice can be construed as a derivative of vengeance. Needless to say, I do not want to pursue this thesis too hard, nor should the reader take it entirely literally. But the idea is this: justice begins with a personal, impassioned reaction to a more or less particular, historical state of affairs, and if one then wants to generalize or theorize or raise the discussion to "a higher level of abstraction," it is nevertheless a mistake to jettison that personal, impassioned reaction as if it were nothing more than a coincidental inclination or a motive desperately seeking a justification.

Just as vengeance always consists of a personal, impassioned reaction to a more or less particular state of affairs, justice in general consists at least in part of a culturally scripted reaction to a historically set, more or less particular state of affairs—the punishment of a criminal, the rectification of wrongs suffered by a group after centuries of slavery or oppression, the establishment of a new nation still smarting from the abuses of a foreign king, the distribution of goods in circumstances of scarcity. Vengeance is certainly a misleading paradigm for justice insofar as it emphasizes only a particularly desert-minded conception of retributive justice and virtually ignores distributive and compensatory justice except insofar as these involve punishments and payback, but I want to suggest that the emphasis has been too lop-sided in precisely the other direction. Indeed, philosophers who write at great length about distributive justice often keep quite silent on matters of retribution (treating punishment as primarily a matter of either utility or an inadequately explained notion of fairness). Observing recent economic policy in the United States, both Western and Eastern Europe and the Pacific, however, one would be ideologically blind to deny that punitive concepts play no part in the suggested redistribution of the world's unequally distributed goods. Vengeance is also a misleading paradigm for justice in that it suggests that our sense of justice must always be actively provoked, but, again, I am exaggerating in order to make a point, that too often justice and our sense of justice is thought to descend from nowhere, or (what is the same) from pure practical reason, without reference to history or context or any provoking events. But, again, a cursory look at the actual context of even the most abstract philosophical debates about justice display a worldly relevance and reference, whether or not this is in any way explicit in the terms of the debate itself. Most current arguments about distributive justice in the United States and elsewhere, for example, whether liberal, radical or conservative, are provoked not only by the intolerable, increasing gap between rich and poor, whether this is taken to be a matter for shame, moral indignation or fear and defensiveness, but by sporadic, shocking acts of desperation, the Los Angeles riots of the Spring of 1992 being only the latest (as of this writing).

Vengeance is usually contrasted with justice, even opposed to it. ("I don't want vengeance; I want justice," is the obligatory retributive demand.[9]) Vengeance is said to be an Evil, a return of "Evil for Evil," and from Socrates in the *Crito* to contemporary debates about capital punishment, this formulation gets used to simply dismiss any further mention of vengeance from the discussion of justice.[10] Admittedly exaggerating the point, I want to suggest, as a counter to these traditional arguments, that vengeance should be seriously considered as a paradigm of justice. This perverse suggestion turns the usual considerations of justice on their head. For example, vengeance is personal, not impersonal.[11] Vengeance is passionate, not dispassionate. Vengeance is retributive, that is, it consists of an appropriate response to a particular situation. It is not an abstract theory which may or may not have any concrete application to the world we live in. And mainly, vengeance is (sometimes) justified. It requires measured reciprocity. It presupposes one's personal involvement, not the aloof and merely judgmental attitude of an observer, a judge, a jury, the Law or a philosophical game theorist imagining him- or herself in one or another version of the "original position." Vengeance may be more or less established and even respectable in a particular culture or society, but even so it is not as such a political institution. It is, almost wherever it is to be found, a social practice.[12] But it remains in the hands of the individual, the family or the local community, and it is not the product, the responsibility nor possibly even the concern of the law or of the larger society.[13] And yet, even in "a society of laws, not men[sic]," vengeance and its satisfaction, whether acknowledged or denied, continue to be an essential ingredient in the criminal law and provide a model for what we consider to be just and fair.

One might be willing to stretch this thesis into the realm of distributive justice as well. Vengeance generalized has a positive, nonpunitive aspect—having to do with rewards instead of punishments—although this always goes by other, more respectable names. I do not want to initiate here a discussion of the virtues and limits of a merit-based conception of distributive justice, except to note again the frequent failure of fit between merit-based theories of punishment, on the one hand, and merit-based theories of desert, on the other. But much of what goes under the name of "justice" is, one could argue, an elaboration of certain familiar feelings not dissimilar to vengeance (other, obviously, than a polar shift in "valence") rather than a grand scheme or blueprint for the rational organization of society. The fact that there are many such feelings and the fact that they do not in themselves determine any particular scheme or blueprint for society as a whole explains why there are and will continue to be very different, incommensurable, competing conceptions of justice.[14] Different cultures (and sub-cultures) cultivate different attitudes and outlooks, and different contexts even within a culture call for very different emotions.[15] The impetus behind general schemes of distributive justice, accordingly, is to be found in such situated and concrete emotions as sympathy, compassion, guilt, shame, embarrassment and pity, even when those emotions are evoked by the plight of people at a distance, large groups or even humanity as a whole. (It is worth noting, however, that we are most often "moved" not by horrendous statistics but rather, for example, by a photograph of a single, suffering child. The statistics then become horrific when we try, if we can, to multiply that singular compassion logarithmically.) So, too, our sense of distributive as well as retributive justice is moved by such straightforwardly "reactive" emotions as envy, resentment and revenge, even when directed against faceless institutions, political abstractions or, like Camus's Sisyphus, toward the universe or the gods themselves.[16]

I want to suggest that all of these emotions might be noted to resemble vengeance at least in their concrete, personal, responsive nature. They may involve one's own suffering or oppression, the suffering or oppression of others, the memory or vivid image of suffering or oppression, one's own suffering in response to the suffering or oppression of others or the desire that others suffer because of one's own suffering or oppression. Such emotions may result from the embarrassing or shameful recognition of one's own, unearned advantages. They may share in another's rightful sense of resentment or search for revenge, though they themselves have not been wronged. In general, it is the same shared sense of reciprocity in revenge that also dictates a general sense of desert and reward and of favors to be returned. It has often been suggested that no pattern of distribution is in itself unjust. It is only when it is compared to some ideal scheme or idealized personal expectations that it can be said to be so. (That is why, and not for lack of a "social compact," Hobbes was right in insisting that there is no justice in the state of nature.) It is only when one can claim (or have claimed on his or her behalf) *deprivation* that one or another conception of justice comes into play. And then it rarely becomes a matter of redistribution or even compensation alone, as some modern conceptions of entitlement and rectification make all too clear. They invoke the need to "get even" as well as any demand for equality. Wherever justice is at issue, the lingering shadow of vengeance is not far behind.

One of the emotions of justice which is most like vengeance, indeed, perhaps, its closest positive counterpart, is a sense of gratitude. Gratitude is a particularly undervalued sentiment both in philosophical discussions of justice and in our society as a whole. Social psychologist Shula Sommers, in a cross-cultural study, found that Americans in general ranked gratitude comparatively low on a scale of comfortable and uncomfortable emotions, and that American men, in particular, found gratitude to be a humiliating emotion.[17] One need not think or search very hard to find a plausible explanation for this, but its implications for some common attitudes concerning social justice are striking. Rather than being grateful for one's good fortune and painfully aware of the contingency of the less palatable alternatives, prompting sympathy and pity for those who are not so fortunate, we tend to pride ourselves on our own accomplishments and view good fortune as a reward for our own (inexplicable) merit. In place of, "there but for the grace of God go I," our culture and its philosophers tend to substitute game theoretical calculations of prudence and mutual advantage, abstract conceptions of equality and equal opportunity, minimally historical claims to entitlement, and, at its most vulgar, rationalizations for callousness: "Why can't he pull himself out of the gutter as I did (or could have)?" Instead of gratitude, we get abstract constructions of the original position and make-believe social contracts. Even at the most basic ontological level, it seems, it is far preferable to see ourselves as independent and self-determining rather than as dependent on luck and on others and, if we are lucky, appropriately grateful for our advantageous role in life.[18]

This view of justice as personal, passionate and situated can be found even in Plato and assuredly in Aristotle.[19] Before Plato, of course, "justice" (variations on *diké*) had this ineliminably personal and vindictive aspect, and in the *Iliad*, for example, it is typically introduced as a matter of personal (or tribal) honor.[20] In the complex weave of duties and morals in Homer's two immortal epics, justice appears again and again in the straightforward guise of personal retribution, coupled with appropriate rewards and demands for tribute. In Plato, the terms of justice change a great deal, not least in the central Socratic teaching that one should not under any circumstances do harm to others. But for Plato as for Aristotle, justice remains a personal virtue, whether or not it is also (in Plato, not in Aristotle) an abstract ideal. It does not eliminate the passions but employs them. And if vengeance as such is condemned (or, in Aristotle, subordinated to righteous anger), the particularist vision of justice as "giving each his due" nevertheless remains, however embellished and ontologically projected by Socrates.

In *The Republic*, however, the older, more Homeric conception of justice has its day, if only briefly. In Book I, Cephalus's son Polymarchus tries to defend the notion that justice is "giving each his due." Admittedly, he does not do a very good job of it, and Socrates undermines the argument at every turn and humiliates him. In one of its several versions the purported definition becomes, "be good to your friends and do harm to your enemies," which Socrates dispatches with his usual wit and dialectical skill. This invites the infamous but philosophically underrated bullying tactics of Thrasymachus, which Socrates also dispatches with humor and irony.[21] But it seems to me that the upshot of Socrates's arguments against both Polymarchus and Thrasymachus (and also the quick argument against Cephalus about returning weapons to a madman) is that judgments about justice are essentially contextual. They depend upon the situation and one's relationships vis-à-vis the other parties involved. If counter-examples show a proposed "definition" of justice to be inadequate, perhaps that is because there is no such general rule about justice that is not either incomplete or vacuous and will cover every case without regard to context.[22] Socrates also shows, with his usual flair, that the account as stated can be rendered self-contradictory, that it presupposes the (supposedly) intolerable claim that it is all right to harm some people sometimes, and that by "friends and enemies" Polymarchus can only mean those whom we *think* are our friends and enemies, rendering Polymarchus's definition intolerably subjective even within the overly personal interpretation. And yet, generously reinterpreted, I think that Polymarchus has a good case against Socrates. The emphasis on "friends and enemies" is an unfortunate way of underscoring the importance of particular attachments and relationships in justice as well as the feelings of reciprocity that motivate us. It is, more significantly, an insistence on the traditional emphasis on *personal context*, as opposed to Socrates' more idealized and abstract insistence on decontextualized virtue. Socrates attacks the very idea of punishment as a "return of evil for evil." Polymarchus wisely recognizes the necessity of doing or at least threatening harm to those who have done you wrong. Socrates argues against the appeal to emotion in ethics. Polymarchus rightly insists that personal feelings are not only important motives but also important grounds for ethical action. It would be stretching the intelligibility of the dialogue to suggest that Polymarchus represents what would later be called a "moral sentiment theory," but in spite of the brilliant dialectical maneuvering of Socrates, a case can be made for Polymarchus. Personal context is essential to ethics, although the "personal" here can be stretched to include such "impersonal" sentiments as compassion and sympathy and much more than personal theories of retributive punishment. The point is not to leave the laurels with Socrates alone, but to see, as in other dialogues, another side of the story.[23]

Socrates, it seems, had two very different lessons to teach us. The first, exemplified in his character as well as his discussions, is the importance of justice—admittedly in a broader sense than our use of the term—as a personal virtue, a way of responding to the world and other people. So conceived, justice is highly personal and always situated in a particular social context. Indeed, the political vision of *The Republic* can be viewed as an attempt to schematize just that social context which will most effectively manifest and cultivate that virtue in each and every citizen. The second lesson has to do with the more philosophical vision of a singular ideal Form of justice, which today translates into the search for an all-embracing philosophical theory. The two lessons are not all that obviously compatible, but in any case, they certainly urge us in two very different directions. There is no question in which direction Anglo-American philosophy has gone. Justice, we are reminded again and again and again, is a matter of abstract, dispassionate, impersonal, rational principles, now typically derived from some imaginative depersonalized account of the origins of society as such.[24] And if those principles or their consequences should turn out to be "callous"—as Nozick declares in his preface to *Anarchy, State and Utopia*—so much the worse for our feelings.[25]

It is this utter dismissal of the passions that I want to challenge here. I do not suggest that we in turn dismiss reason from the proceedings, but I would start by arguing that the distinction between reason and the passions is itself over-blown and the source of much mischief in the history of philosophy. Indeed, much of what is called "reason" in philosophy turns out to look too much like sophistry and insensitivity, and the impersonality and detachment with which we philosophers so often identify and on which we so pride ourselves

may be misplaced in social philosophy. What I am *not* suggesting—
let me be clumsily clear—is that favoritism and vindictiveness (say,
in a politician, a bureaucrat, or a dean of Liberal Arts) are in any way
justifiable or tolerable. Such well-defined positions make impersonality an essential virtue, and excessive expressions of compassion, affection or disdain a vice. And, to be sure, it is possible to be compassionate or vengeful and oblivious to justice as well as it is to be coldly
just and dispassionately fair. What I do want to argue is that our supposedly unphilosophical sense of caring, compassion and various other passions, too long swept under the carpet laid down by Kant and
other critics of "sentimentality," are essential to justice, to the framework within which even such well-defined dispassionate positons are
intelligible. Our emotions are not intrusions into an otherwise rational life. But I also want to argue that "negative" emotions such as indignation, outrage and vengeance are equally essential to justice. They
are not just incumberances or character flaws much less "human weaknesses." They are the stuff out of which our conceptions of justice are
constructed and in which they are anchored. Without emotion, without caring, a theory of justice is just another numbers game.

Emotions and Rationality:
An Untenable Dualism

Any doctrine that eliminates or even obscures the function of choice of
values and enlistment of desire and emotions in behalf of those chosen
weakens personal responsibility for judgment and for action.
               —John Dewey, in *Commentary*, July 1946

To insist on the central role of emotions in justice is an attempt to
put the supposed "impartiality" of justice in its place, to insist on the
priority of existing (and not merely hypothetical) attachments and
affections, to "ground" the abstract deliberations about justice in real
human concerns, not just the detached demands of reason. But to say
this is also to reject the opposition that is so often presupposed in
discussions of justice (and much else in philosophy), between the
emotions on the one hand and reason on the other. One of the most
enduring metaphors in philosophy is reason and emotion as master
and slave, the wisdom of reason firmly in control and the dangerous
impulses of emotion safely suppressed, channelled or, ideally, in harmony with reason. Hume's striking reversal of this ancient metaphor

fully presupposed its legitimacy. Reason and emotion remain opposed. Only the polarities have been altered. And nowhere has the unruly and threatening power of the emotions been more at odds with what has often been called "reason" than in the realm of justice, where compassion and gratitude and even love as well as vengeance have been condemned as disruptive, irrelevant, and, in the case of the last, at least, downright dangerous.

Arguments against emotion tend to focus on their alleged "capriciousness" and stupidity, although, alternatively, they are attacked with equal vehemence for their "intractibility" and their "bias." On the one hand, conservatives love nothing more than to lambast the "do-gooders" and "bleeding hearts," namely those who express their feelings rather than stick by some abstract and often ruthless but in any case "hard-headed" theory. On the other hand, there is the age-old insistence on "the rule of law," shared by both liberals and conservatives, which insists on "not returning evil for evil" and, accordingly, the foreswearing and condemnation of revenge. (That said, of course, liberals and conservatives then go on to have very different ideas about the aims and arguments for punishment.) But compassion and revenge are but two sides of the same coin, and that coinage is our sense of justice. Reason is not the master here, nor should it be. (Nor, of course, should it play the slave.) What must be and has been shown is that the emotions do not and should not play an inferior role in deliberations about justice, and that it is false that emotions are more primitive, less intelligent, more bestial, less dependable and more dangerous than reason.[26] Reason and emotion are not two conflicting and antagonistic aspects of the soul. *Together* they provide justice, which is neither dispassionate nor "merely emotional."

The conjunction of emotions, reason and justice would make little sense if emotions were only that which they have often been said to be, mere short-term, disruptive physiological disturbances or mere outpourings of personal prejudice. Plato seemed to sometimes so treat them, for example, when Socrates reprimands Crito for appealing to sentiments and the opinions of *hoi poloi*. James and Lange also treated them as such, when they defined an emotion as a "sensation" caused by a "visceral disturbance."[27] But recent work on emotion has shown that what was once called a "passion" is neither so unintelligent nor so opposed to reason as is so often supposed.[28] Emotions themselves are ways of coping, products of assessment and evaluation, modes of rational action. They are often enduring, even "intractable," lifelong programs rather than momentary distractions. This is nowhere more important than in the emotions of justice, where the sense of justice (and injustice) as well as more particular feelings such as caring and vengefulness are by their very nature not merely immediate but emotional commitments for the long haul. (That is why, perhaps, it is so much easier to recognize injustice than to identify, in general, what is just.) But one's sense of justice (and injustice) is not a passing sentiment or a merely "episodic" emotion. It is, for better or for worse, a way of life.

My own argument, briefly stated here, is that emotions already "contain" reason and practical reason is circumscribed and defined by emotion.[29] Nietzsche tells us, in his usual condensed style: "as if every passion didn't contain its quantum of reason!" Our emotions *situate* us in the world and so provide not so much the motive for rationality, much less its opposition, but rather its very framework. Every emotion involves what Robert Gordon has called a cognitive "structure" of judgments that can be well-wrought or foolish, warranted or unwarranted, correct or incorrect.[30] Anger involves judgments of blame, jealousy includes judgments about a potential threat or loss. Love involves evaluative judgments, typically overblown. So does hatred. Grief involves recognition of a loss, and vengeance—often maligned in philosophy—already involves a small-scale theory of justice, some crude version of "an eye for an eye" or what Kant less violently but more ambiguously called "equality."[31] In all of these examples, one can readily recognize what can go wrong in the emotion—and consequently what is required for it to go right. In anger one can be confused about the facts. He or she is still angry, but wrongfully so. And if one lept to conclusions or did not examine the readily available evidence, he or she is foolishly so. One can be right about the facts but wrong about the harm done or the blameworthiness of the person with whom one is angry. (The "intensity" of anger, I would suggest, has much more to do with the harshness of such evaluations than with the physiological accompaniments of the emotion.) One can be right about the facts and justified about the warrant for anger but yet go wrong in its expression, misdirecting it (a common problem with vengeance) or overdoing it. (The irrationality of emotions is often a fault in performance or timing rather than a mistaken emotion as such.)

Fault may also lie in the aim or purpose of an emotion, what Jean-Paul Sartre called an emotion's *finalité*.[32] It is an ingenious insight, that emotions not only serve purposes (in the sense of being functional or evolutionarily advantageous) but also involve strategies in their own right. Getting angry, falling in love, suffering grief are not just inflictions but tactics, ways of coping with a "coefficient of adversity."[33] But Sartre then goes on to accuse all of emotions of "escapism." They are all strategies for *avoiding* difficult circumstances. But without trying to reduce all emotional motivation to any single aim and strategy, one can provide a convincing argument that all of them either have some such aim and strategy or are responses to the breakdown of such aims and strategies. Such analyses are available for love and grief and every other emotion, even the seemingly simplest of them. Fear, for example, is not just a rush of adrenalin but the recognition of a danger, and one can be wrong about the danger, its imminence or its seriousness. Fear can be irrational, which means that it is subject to the judgments of rationality. It can therefore be rational as well. So, too, the sense of compassion, the desire for revenge, the sting of injustice and a generalized sense of justice. To say that these can go wrong and be irrational is just to say that, properly exercised, they can be rational as well. (Can a sense of justice be irrational? Indeed, I believe it can. Shakespeare's tragedies are full of examples.)

The claims so often made in the name of rationality in philosophical theories of justice are in part expressions of culturally sanctioned emotions. I do not know what it would be to defend the idea that people are created equal, the idea that people deserve what they earn, the idea that they are entitled to what they have or the idea that people have a right to what they need in the merely dispassionate terms that philosophers treat as matters of reason. Such ideas depend upon a set of social circumstances, a specific kind of culture and the perceptions and emotions that are taught and cultivated by that culture. Furthermore, I would want to argue that the concepts and judgments that are constitutive of our emotions are in turn constitutive of the criteria for rationality as well.[34] Thus my point is not just to defend the rationality of the emotions, a now well-established and much mulled over thesis, but to establish what one might call the emotional grounding of rationality. What I want to reject here is the now-prevalent idea that rational criteria are simply the presuppositions of emotion or the external standards by which emotions and their appropriateness may be judged. That would leave standing the idea of a rational framework *within which* the emotions may be appropriate or inappropriate, warranted or unwarranted, wise or foolish, and it would support the prevalent view that justice is essentially a rational or even formal construction within which such emotions as compassion, gratitude, envy and resentment can be judged to be (or not to be) rational or warranted. I want to suggest rather that emotions constitute the framework (or frameworks) of rationality itself, and justice is based on such emotions as compassion and the desire for vengeance as well as a standard for judging their appropriateness.[35] Of course, except in an exceptional case of singlemindedness or obsession a single emotion does not constitute such a framework, any more than a single correct calculation makes a student intelligent. A single emotion (or even an entire sequence of emotions) may be dictated by character, the circumstances and the overall cultural context, but altogether our emotions (appropriate to the general circumstances) dictate that context (as well as our character). Our sense of justice, as well as the grand theories that are constructed in expression of that sense of justice, is thus not a single emotion but rather a systematic totality of emotions appropriate to our culture and our character.

From this perspective, one might suggest that what best defines rationality is not any form of deliberation or calculative reasoning but rather *caring about the right things*, about one's friends and family, one's compatriots and neighbors, one's culture and environment, and, ultimately, the world. And caring in turn is the cornerstone of justice. But to care is already to perceive some sense of order, to recognize the pain of deprivation or loss in others, to acknowledge one's place in the interconnectedness of the world. True, some philosophers on both sides of the Adriatic tried to develop visions of a world without loss—the Stoics in ancient Greece and Rome, the Arab philosopher al-Kindi in the ninth century[36]—and many religions have tried to blunt the evident injustice of this world with promises of another one. But it is ultimately caring that counts, and it is not reason (as opposed to emotion) that allows us to extend our reach to the universal but rather the expansive scope of the emotions themselves. What one cares about is defined by one's conception of the world, but one's conception of the world is itself defined by the scope and objects of one's emotional cares and concern.[37] Our emotions thoroughly permeate our experience and they are not, as some honorable ancient views would have it, interruptions, intrusions or brief bouts of madness that violate the otherwise calm transparency of rational objectivity.

The Other Side of Vengeance:
Sympathy and the Moral Sentiments

How selfish soever man may be supposed, there are evidently some principles in his nature, which interest him in the fortune of others, and render their happiness necessary to him, though he derives nothing from it except the pleasure of seeing it. Of this kind is pity or compassion, the emotion which we feel for the misery of others. . . . The greatest

ruffian, the most hardened violator of the laws of society, is not altogether without it.

—Adam Smith

My aim in defending vengeance as a paradigm of justice is to re-
establish the role of the emotions in shaping and motivating our sense
of justice. But with that in mind it would be misleading, if not perverse, to focus only on the retributive side of justice and ignore the
benign sentiments that help shape and motivate our sense of distributive justice. All too often, distributive justice is debated in terms of
patterns of fair distrubution or, alternatively, as constrained by certain claims to entitlement. What is wrong with both of these philosophical positions is that they approach the subject of justice from
the "outside," so to speak, symptomatically imagining possible states
of affairs instead of confronting the very conflict-ridden world around
us. But our sense of justice is not prompted by the abstract sense of
"equality." It is rather prompted by the direct perception of inequality, the fact that others suffer while we do not or, alternatively, by the
fact that we suffer while others do not. In the latter case, we are moved
by envy and resentment (more on that later), but in the former case—
the usual fortune of most tenured philosophers—we are or should be
moved by compassion. Compassion is often contrasted with justice,
much as vengeance is contrasted with retributive justice. Compassion
is personal, justice is said to be impersonal. Compassion is directed
at isolated individuals (even if there are millions of them). Justice is
said to be concerned with the bigger picture, with the overall scheme
of distribution (or punishment). Compassion is merely an emotion, a
"sentiment," while justice is said to demand the judgments of reason.
But it is just these contrasts, between the personal and the impersonal, between the particular and the universal, between the emotions
and reason that I want to challenge. Compassion, I want to argue, is
an essential ingredient in our sense of justice.

As vengeance is a hostile reaction toward someone who is personally responsible for a wrong or an offense, compassion is a benign
reaction to the suffering of others, regardless of the existence of a
wrong or an offense. The recipient of compassion need not be a person of one's actual acquaintance, but compassion is felt personally
and directed at a person. Compassion is often taken to be a disposition, indeed, even the generalized disposition to feel whatever another person is feeling. What is right about this is that it underscores its
role as a reaction, but what is wrong with this dispositional view is
that it undermines compassion's special character. Compassion is first

of all caring, even if at a distance, even if intermingled with fear and loathing (the extreme version being pity). Compassion is implicitly comparative, not just "feeling with," a sharing of feelings. It is not compassion one feels for one's fellow sufferers, and one might well feel compassion for those who are in an otherwise enviable position, e.g,. when a billionaire pities those who cannot afford a Rolls. Compassion is an emotional reaction to those who are worse off than oneself (in some specific way), and it is compassion, more than any other emotion, that typically gets derided as "sentimentality." But it is also worth noting that compassion, as mercy, is also the sentiment that stands most directly opposed to vengeance, but as complements are opposed. The urge to get even is often (though not often enough) balanced by compassion for one's enemy, the realization that he or she has suffered enough or by way of the anticipation of the suffering to come. So considered, compassion is surely anything but "sentimentality," except, perhaps, to the irredeemably hard-hearted.

It has recently been suggested that what is missing from the standard analyses and theories of justice is an adequate sense of care and compassion.[38] This is, I believe, true and important. Even so pivotal a figure as John Rawls, whose liberal credentials and sense of compassion are not in question, finds it necessary to dress his sentiments in the formal costume of an impersonal deduction of rational principles, and most of the literature that has followed him has shown far more enthusiasm for his form than for his feelings. (Perhaps that is why so much of social philosophy today resembles a debate in game theory rather than an expression of concern for human suffering, even if "the needy" and "the least advantaged" often appear as players.) Justice is, first of all, a sense of compassion. Unfortunately, this important point has been politicized and polemicized as a difference between "male and female" and "masculine and feminine" approaches to ethics. Nell Noddings, for example, uses the division between "masculine" and "feminine" ethics as something of a Maginot Line, "the great chasm" in the war between the sexes.[39] ("Men of principle have been wrecking the world; caring women could save it.")[40] Instead of insisting that *any* adequate sense of justice presupposes care and compassion some recent authors have opposed the (supposedly male) concept of justice to (female) caring and compassion. But this seeming duality is no Kierkegaardian "either/or," impersonal justice *or* personal concern. Care (like *eros*) is neither exclusively a woman's nor a mother's emotion, and it is not an emotion that by itself can save the world. The kindly sentiments represented by care and compassion cannot by themselves explain the enormous range or the profound depth of the

passions that constitute our sense of justice, including our often vehe-
ment and not at all kindly sense of *in*justice. Sentiments alone cannot
account for the large policy issues that are (or should be) the ultimate
concern of those theories of justice, but any sense of justice whatever
begins with *caring*—about ourselves, our reputations and our belongings, about those whom we love and live with, feel akin to or responsible for, about the way the world is and the fate of the sentient creatures on it. Without that care and concern, there can be no sense of
justice. Why else would any of this *matter* to us—the distribution of
goods in the world, fair and equal treatment, just rewards and the felt
need to punish, even questions of life and death? Justice begins with
and presupposes our emotional engagement with the world, not with
philosophical detachment or with any merely hypothetical situation.

The Kantian turn in philosophy may be largely responsible for the
exile of the kindly sentiments and the "inclinations" in general from
moral philosophy.[41] But in the wake of this Kantian tradition, it is
always worth remembering how closely Kant (Rawls too) claims to
follow on the heels of his hero, Rousseau, one of the great defenders
of the natural inclinations.[42] Before Kant, and about the same time as
Rousseau, the "moral sentiment theorists" emerged in Scotland (and
elsewhere). The leading and best known proponents of moral sentiment theory were David Hume and Adam Smith. They defended the
centrality of the "natural" sentiment of *sympathy* in morals, distinguishing between sympathy and justice, which Hume, in particular,
declared not to be "natural" at all.[43] Moral sentiment theory began
with the view that the basis of morality and justice is to be found in
our natural disposition to have certain other-directed emotions. This
did not mean that morality is not, in part, a function of reason or,
above all, a matter of "doing the right thing." Both Hume and Smith
emerged as early champions of the importance of "utility" as well as
defenders of what is now called "virtue ethics." But it is clear that
the right things don't usually get done for the wrong reasons, and
justice is only rarely and ironically the result of malicious intentions.
And surely among the "right reasons" are the sympathetic emotions.
Contrary to much of the Kantian tradition, to be moral and to be just
does not mean first of all that one must act on principle. A good reason for helping another person in need is "I feel sorry for him." Indeed, one is hard put to think of any other reason that is so impervi-
ous to argument (which is not to say that it is indefeasible). And yet,
reading through the philosophy of the past two centuries, the ordinary
reader would be shocked that "I feel sorry for him" as a moral reason
is all but ignored, if not simply dismissed, as a basis for morality or

justice. Such sentiments are said to be capricious, naive, undependable, unpredictable and, in any case, beside the point. But I would
argue that without such feelings, some sense of deprivation and pity,
the calculations of just distribution are empty, soulless if not mindless exercises in equity.

Traditionally, moral sentiment theory was concerned with a family
of "natural" emotions, including benevolence, sympathy, compassion
and pity. Care and caring, instructively, were not part of the standard
list. In one sense, care and caring refer to that very general sense of
engagement and concern (the *Sorge* of Faust and Heidegger) that underlies and is presupposed by all emotional attachments. But there is
another sense, more specific than what the eighteenth-century philosophers called "beneficence," in which care and caring refer to a concrete psychological attitude which is often (but not necessarily) instantiated in *caring for* someone. Benevolence, beneficence, sympathy,
compassion and pity were often lumped together and not infrequently
treated as identical or as aspects of one and the same sentiment. In
the standard account of moral sentiment thinking, Francis Hutcheson's
"moral sense" theory is usually included as a moral sentiment theory,
despite the fact that Hutcheson explicitly denied any special moral
role to the sentiments. Jean-Jacques Rousseau is usually not included
as a moral sentiment theorist, though he was obviously a kindred spirit.
With his Scottish colleagues he attacked the "selfishness" theories of
Hobbes and Mandeville and argued for the naturalness of pity, an
emotion closely akin to compassion in particular. But as developed
by Hume and Smith, in particular, the exemplary moral sentiment was
sympathy. This sentiment, I suggest, is an awkward amalgam of several emotional states and dispositions, including compassion and what
we have come to call "care."

There is considerable confusion about the meaning of "sympathy,"
both in the writings of the moral sentiment theorists and in our own
conversations. In common parlance, sympathy means "feeling sorry
for" someone, while for many philosophers (notably Hume) it is con-
flated with benevolence. (Smith tries to keep these distinct.) "Feeling
sorry for" can be a sign of caring, but surely a minimal one, as we
can feel sorry for strangers and even our enemies. Benevolence has
much in common with the more activist concept of "caring for," but
benevolence has much greater scope than sympathy as such. We can
feel benevolence in the abstract without any particular objects) and
benevolence for those whose feelings are utterly malicious or indif-
ferent to us (e.g., in being merciful to a condemned and still hateful
wrongdoer, perhaps as an expression of our own largesse but out of

benevolence nevertheless.) We often use "sympathy" or the verb "sympathize" to register agreement or approval, although none of these qualify as an adequate philosophical conception or a correct dictionary definition of the term. Technically, sympathy (literally, "feeling with," like "compassion") is the sharing of feeling, or, as a disposition, the ability to share the feelings of others. Or, if one wants to insist that the emotions can be individuated only by virtue of the persons who have them and thus cannot be shared, one might say that sympathy is an "agreement of feelings," in the sense of "having the same [type of] emotion."[44] One need not "agree with" in the sense of "approve of" the feeling in question, of course, any more than one must always enjoy or approve of one's own emotions. The feelings may agree but we need not; sharing a feeling is one thing but accepting or approving of the feeling something quite different. (In grade B movies, we might well share the offended hero's rather fascist sense of revenge, as we might share the envy of someone who has been similarly deprived while berating ourselves for just that feeling.)

Adam Smith uses the term in this technical way, as "agreement of emotion," but he does not thereby imply the agreement of any particular emotion or kind of emotion. Thus there is a serious ambiguity between sympathy as a specific sentiment and sympathy as a disposition to share sentiments (*whatever* sentiments) with others. Sympathy so conceived is thus not actually a sentiment at all but rather a *vehicle* for understanding other people's sentiments, "fellow-feeling with any passion whatever."[45] One can sympathize with any number of feelings in another person, not only the kindly and social moral sentiments but such unsocial sentiments as envy and hatred as well. Sympathy is not an actual sharing of sentiments (in the sense of "having the same feeling") but rather an act of imagination by which one can appreciate the feelings of another person by "putting oneself in his place," "a principle which interests him in the fortunes of others."[46] This provides him with a way of accounting for how it can be that people are not essentially selfish or self-interested but are essentially social creatures who can act on behalf of others whose feelings they do not (and logically cannot) actually share. But this raises the question whether sympathy can be the sort of motivating factor in our behavior which moral sentiment theory seeks to defend, in opposition to the equally natural (and often more powerful) sentiment of self-interest and in contrast to the similarly selfless but also passionless dictates of reason. ("The approbation of moral qualities most certainly is not deriv'd from reason, or any comparison of ideas; but proceeds entirely from a moral taste, and from certain sentiments of plea-

sure and disgust, which arise upon the contemplation and view of
particular qualities or characters."[47]) But sympathy, according to
Smith's definition as "fellow-feeling" seems to be more concerned with
comprehension than feeling as such, and comprehension is too close
to the "comparison of ideas" to provide the "sentiments of pleasure
and disgust" to play the role that sympathy is called to play in morals.[48] ("As we have no immediate experience of what other men feel,
we can form no idea of the manner in which they are affected, but by
conceiving what we ourselves should feel in the like situation."[49])
Sympathy cannot mean merely "comprehension" but, on the other
hand, sympathy as shared feeling seems too strong for the role.[50] I
thus would argue that Smith is inconsistent. On the one hand, he wants
a mechanism for "fellow-feeling," on the other, a motive for morals.
It is not at all clear that he can have both, and it is arguable that
neither provides an adequate analysis of sympathy.

Hume's earlier theory of sympathy and justice, which greatly influenced Smith, is somewhat different than this, and to make matters
more difficult it is clear that he changed his mind between the writing of his early masterpiece, *A Treatise of Human Nature,* and his
later *Inquiry Concerning the Principles of Morals.* In the early work,
Hume treats sympathy rather casually, commenting that it is usually a
weak emotion compared with most of the motives of self-interest. In
the later work, Hume defends sympathy as a universal sentiment that
is sufficiently powerful to overcome self-interest in a great many cases.
In the *Inquiry,* in particular, Hume takes sympathy to be a form of
benevolence, a feeling for one's fellow citizens and a concern for their
well-being. But for Hume as for Smith, sympathy is too often countered and overwhelmed by selfishness and, for this reason, a sense of
justice is required. But whereas Smith takes the sense of justice to be
a somewhat natural revulsion at harming one's fellows, Hume takes
justice to be an "artificial" virtue which is constructed by reason for
our mutual well-being. It is an advantageous conventional "scheme"
rather than a natural sentiment as such. Thus for Hume sympathy is a
genuine moral sentiment and justice is not. Even so, Hume admitted
that justice was so beneficial that it became inseparably associated
with the moral sentiments, for what could be more basic to these sentiments than our sense of the general good for everyone, "a feeling
for the happiness of mankind and a resentment of their misery." He
writes,

> No virtue is more esteemed than justice, and no vice nore detested than
> injustice; nor are there any qualities, which go farther to the fixing of

character, either as amiable or odious. Now justice is a moral virtue, merely because it has that tendency to the good of mankind; and, indeed, is nothing but an artificial invention to that purpose.[51]

The whole scheme, however, of law and justice is advantageous to the society; and 'twas with a view to this advantage, that men, by their voluntary conventions, establish'd it. . . . Once established, it is *naturally* attended with a strong sentiment of morals.[52]

Hume does not go so far as to say that justice itself is a matter of sentiment, but he insists that the moral sentiments in general and in particular sympathy for others is so essential to morals that there can be no ethics without them. Both Hume and Smith are dead set against the Hobbesian view that people are motivated only by their own selfish interests and advocate the importance of distinctive, natural "social passions." Indeed, the core of their argument is, in Smith's terms, that "nature, when she formed man for society, endowed him with an original desire to please, and an original aversion to offend his brethren."[53] Moreover, "nature endowed him not only with a desire for being approved of, but with a desire of being what ought to be approved of, or of being what he himself approves of in other men."[54] It is not just sympathy but a whole complex of mutually perceiving and reciprocal passions that tie us together. Thus it does not take too much tinkering with Scottish moral sentiment theory to incorporate justice along with sympathy under its auspices and take the whole as a welcome alternative to both the "man is essentially selfish" thesis and the overly intellectual "morality is rationality" view of Kant and most current justice theorists.

Both Hume and Smith sometimes talk about sympathy as if it were no more than a generalized sense of altruism, a concern for others with no thought of benefit to oneself. But altruism like benevolence doesn't involve any sharing of feelings, as sympathy does, and Smith's phrase "fellow-feeling" too easily hides the distinction between "feeling for," "feeling with," and simple camaraderie, which is feeling oneself with but not necessarily feeling with the other. Altruism, on the other hand, might best be understood as the behavioral analog of benevolence, and sympathy is often used as a synonym for benevolence, a wishing well toward others, sympathy *for* others. This is the way that Hume often uses the term, and in the *Inquiry*, at least, he claims that this feeling "nature has made universal in the whole species." This is his way of denying the Hobbesian portrait of humanity as essentially selfish, and it is a mistake or at least unfair, I think, to attack Hume on the grounds that he is really an unreconstructed

Hobbesian individualist who brings in "sympathy" only as a desperate measure to explain the non-coercive validity of morals.[55] What both Hume and Smith are concerned to point out, against Hobbes, is that we genuinely and "naturally" do *care* about other people and we are capable of feeling *with* others as well as for ourselves. But it is obvious that there is considerable room for misunderstanding about what Hume and Adam Smith mean by "sympathy," and their various uses of the term seem inconsistent, or at best something of a grab bag of mixed kindly feelings and dispositions. Hume quite clearly changes his mind and his usage from the *Treatise* to the *Inquiry*, and Smith slips back and forth between the several vernacular uses of the term and the technical use (sympathy as a general disposition) that he sometimes insists upon. Hume equates sympathy and benevolence while Smith insists on separating them, but Smith does so in order to defend his "fellow-feeling" interpretation and Hume is too eager (at least in the *Treatise*) to downplay the actual motivational force of sympathy. By "sympathy" Smith seems to mean something very much like "compassion" while Hume wants it to mean something more like "care," but "compassion" and "care" here have rather emaciated meanings.

What is the relationship between sympathy and benevolence? Both emotional virtues suffer from an excess of scope and vagueness that makes their relative terrains difficult to map and identify. MacIntyre notes that "the new conception of the virtue of benevolence . . . in the eighteenth century is assigned very much the scope which the Christian scheme of the virtues assigned to charity. But, unlike charity, benevolence as a virtue became a licence for almost any kind of manipulative intervention in the affairs of others."[56] One might deny that benevolence too is an emotion; it is, perhaps, rather a motive or a broad category of desire. But what leads the moral sense theorists to so identify sympathy and benevolence is precisely the latter's motivational powers, whereas sympathy too readily remains nothing but a "feeling with" or "feeling for." Benevolence is indeed a much broader concept than sympathy, and though benevolence need not lead to action (it is a "wishing well" rather than a "making well"[beneficence]), it need have nothing to do with "feeling with" or even "for." (One can want to help others on principle, for example, or because one cannot abide their noisy suffering.) In such cases, one may well "care" but not care primarily for the well-being of the other.

But this is just the problem with sympathy. It always seems to suggest more than it actually provides. It is one thing to say that one is upset and has kindly feelings towards a fellow creature in pain, that one in some sense "shares" the suffering. But feeling sorry for someone is not the same as wanting to help them, and while benevolence typically leads to beneficence and helping behavior, "feeling sorry for" usually just stops at pity. One may be kindly or generous "out of pity," but though pity may motivate it readily remains a feeling unto itself—one of the reasons why Nietzsche launched such a relentless attack against it. "Feeling sorry for" isn't exactly sympathy either, even in the vernacular, for one can feel sorry for someone suffering without feeling anything at all, whereas we tend to think of sympathy, again in Smith's words, as something like a sharing of feeling. It is one thing to say that one shares feelings and something else— a much weaker claim—to say that one appreciates or "understands" the plight of another. Pity is even more problematic, for it includes within its structure an unmistakable sense of "looking down" at its object and, even on a more benign account than Nietzsche's, cannot be conceived of as an unalloyed kindly sentiment, which sympathy is so often said to be.

"Sympathy" (like "compassion") literally means and is often meant to mean "shared feeling," but, what is it to "share" a feeling—individuation problems aside (i.e., can one and the same feeling be shared by two people, or can each person have his and only his own feeling?). Insofar as sympathy involves actually *sharing* feelings, it is clear that the suffering one shares with the sufferer is, for the most part, pretty limp stuff and not nearly adequate to motivate ethical behavior. I may in fact feel slightly ill because you have just broken your leg in three places, but it would be absurd to compare my feelings to yours much less to say that I am "sharing" your suffering. Indeed, it seems absurd to talk at all about "sharing" feelings in most such cases. I may feel upset to hear that you have just lost your grandfather, been called for a general audit by the I.R.S. or have been fired from your job because of a general "downsizing." But the fact that I too have negative feelings (sadness, fear, indignation) *because* of you and even *for* you hardly adds up to a sufficiently equal measure of mutual emotion to call this "shared feelings." Of course, if indeed we share the situation, if it is *our* grandfather who died, *our* partnership that is to be audited or *we both* who are to be fired, it is perfectly plausible to say that we share the appropriate feelings. But this would not be a matter of "sympathy," for the idea behind moral sentiment theory is that I can and do feel for you on the basis of your suffering and not my own.

I may have a fairly mild sense of pathos caused by and in my concern about your rather awful suffering, and it makes little sense to compare the two much less to talk about them as "shared." It is for this reason that Smith, in particular, suggests that a sense of justice is needed to supplement sympathy, which by itself is not nearly powerful enough to counter the inevitably self-serving motives of most people. Justice, for Smith, is an internalized sense of fair play, and it is justice, not sympathy, which provides the main "pillar" that supports the whole society. Justice, unlike sympathy, is a passion with a determined content, albeit a negative one; justice is the sense that one should not cause harm to one's neighbor.[57] Sympathy and justice, together with a sense of benevolence, provide Smith with a portrait of human nature in his *Theory of the Moral Sentiments* that is very different from the usual Hobbesian interpretations of his later work, *The Wealth of Nations*, in which the wheels of capitalism are (wrongly) said to be moved by individual greed alone. Sympathy is "fellow-feeling," feeling not so much *for* as *with* one's fellow citizens, but especially when they are seriously suffering. Our sense of justice moves us to avoid harming one another, and between the two, the Hobbesian picture of human life as "a war of all against all" and as "nasty, brutish and short" gets replaced by the much more flattering portrait of a society of citizens who care about, feel for and naturally avoid harming one another.

Sympathy is often confused with "empathy," which is also defined as "identification with" another, "putting oneself in the other's shoes" and vicariously sharing his or her emotions, and certainly Smith, in particular, uses the one term to mean the other, and Joseph Cropsey's explicit identification of the two (in TMS) is not at all inappropriate as an interpretation of *some* of Smith's text. "[Smith argues that] every human being has the power to feel the passions of those other beings who come under his observation. The man who observes joy of another will himself experience joy."[58] But empathy, too, has been characterized not so much as an emotion as a technique or a strategy for sharing and understanding emotions, an ability to "put oneself in the other's place" as well as the actual sharing of feelings that results from such identification, and Smith elsewhere denies that we can ever actually share the feelings of another.[59] Moving from the eighteenth century to our own, however, we find that much the same debate and confusion continues, especially in the social sciences, where the validity of the "method" of empathy is much in dispute, e.g., in anthropology.[60] Recent studies of sympathy and empathy in psychology by Wispe and Natsoulos strongly suggest that the distinction has become largely a stipulative matter.[61] But we can take a strong hint from etymology and the observation that sympathy means "feeling with," (1) "agreement in feelings" and (2) "sharing feelings, esp. sorrow or trouble," while empathy means "feeling into" and "identification with or vicarious experiencing of the feelings or thoughts of another person."[62] Empathy, in other words, might better be thought of as shared feeling while sympathy is a more specific feeling, feeling sorry for, a kind of caring, but caring at a distance, as an observer rather than a "caretaker."

Alasdair MacIntyre has recently charged that sympathy is an emotion that was largely invented by Hume.[63] MacIntyre is primarily concerned with the tendency of the enlightenment philosophers—Hume in particular—to project their own narrow English property-owning ideology as a "universal" sense of morals, and he charges that Hume's presumed universal sentiment presupposed a very specific normative standard, "in fact a highly conservative normative standard."[64] MacIntyre denies explicitly that sympathy could "supply the defects of an argument from [long term self-] interest and utility," and suggests that the invention of an emotion called "sympathy" was Hume's attempt to "bridge the gap between any set of reasons for action which could support unconditional adherence to general and unconditional rules and any set of reasons for action or judgment which could derive from our particular, fluctuating, circumstance-governed desires, emotions and interests." MacIntyre adds, "later on Adam Smith was to invoke sympathy for precisely the same purpose. But the gap of course, is logically unbridgeable, and 'sympathy' as used by Hume and Smith is the name of a philosophical fiction."[65] I think that this analysis is unfair to both Hume and Smith, although it does betray a critical weakness in most prominent interpretations of these two great theorists, if not in their works themselves. The tendency to split the passions into a "selfish" set of sentiments and an "other-regarding" set such as sympathy and compassion raises deep problems about how such internal warfare can ever produce a coherent individual life much less a coherent and harmonious society. But I think that the soul-wrenching individualism that MacIntyre and many other commentators attribute to Hume and Smith is not the sole basis of their theories, and the sentiment of sympathy—however ambiguously defined—deserves recognition as a very real, indispensible and probably "natural" ingredient in our moral sensibilities. Both Smith and Hume were "classical liberals" (in other words, conservatives) and their individualism was always tempered by their sense of tradition and social unity. Thus I think that both Hume and Smith were struggling to formulate a more sociable sense of human nature, one in which mutual affection and approval are more important than self-interest as such, one in which shared emotions and feelings for others are more important than acquisitive desires. Their mistake, which they seemed to pick up from Shaftesbury and Hutcheson,[66] was to polarize the passions and characterize a few of these as "moral" or "social" and others "selfish" or "asocial," when in fact almost all passions and sentiments of any complexity at all pour across these artificial boundaries like clouds over state lines. Sympathy, in particular, is no simple sentiment and does indeed involve competitive and "self-interested" components as well as pure altruism and concern for the other. Accordingly, we should expect considerable strain in these theories, as Hume goes on to defend the British propertied classes and as Smith goes on to defend what has since been dubbed the "magic" of free-market capitalism. But the central and undeniable truth of moral sentiment theory, I believe, is that we are essentially and "naturally" social creatures with fellow-feeling, care and compassion for others, not only concerned with our own interests and ambitions in life and not then mysteriously moved by the impersonal promptings of practical reason.[67]

In Defense of Resentment:
A Plea for the 'Negative' Emotions

The slaves' revolt in morals begins with this, that ressentiment itself becomes creative and gives birth to values.
—Friedrich Nietzsche, *On the Genealogy of Morals*, I 10.

My argument is that a sense of justice is a passion or a set of passions to be *cultivated* and not an abstract set of principles to be formulated and imposed upon society. Justice begins not with Socratic insights but with the promptings of some basic emotions, foremost among them such 'negative' emotions as envy, jealousy and resentment, a keen sense of having been personally cheated or neglected and the desire to "get even."[68] This is not the usual list of "moral sentiments," to be sure. In Smith, in Hume, across the channel and a border or two in Rousseau, what we hear a great deal about are those supposedly basic feelings of fellow-feeling, compassion and sympathy. Of course these are essential, but the problem is that they are only a small piece—albeit an absolutely essential piece—of the picture. It may be worth noting, with some sense of irony, that sympathy and the other undeniably positive passions are often not just neglected but actually denied, for example, by those cynics who don't even think of denying the existence of the antipathetic passions—envy and resentment in particular. But could one have sympathy, much less empathy, with one's fellows if one did not know what it was to be envious, humiliated or embittered? Could one be resentful without at least the capacity to be sympathetic as well? What both conceptual analysis and empirical research will show, I anticipate, is that the emotions of justice essentially come in a "package." Just as one cannot feel love without the potential for grief and one cannot feel pride without the capacity for shame, one cannot have or develop a passion for suprapersonal justice without a primary sense of personal injustice.[69] The emotions of justice must be particular as well as general and when we speak of a "sense of justice" it cannot be just a universal sensibility, a Platonic love of the good, that we have in mind.[70] The sense of justice includes not just the noble or sympathetic emotions but the often nasty even hateful antipathetic emotions, sometimes generalized from personal maxims to universal political principles.

The usual set of altruistic or what Rescher calls "vicarious" passions is too limited to account for justice. The "negative" or *antipathetic* emotions are as essential as the sympathetic passions to our sense of justice. Envy and jealousy have as much to do with the origins and development of justice as pity and compassion. At the very beginning of our historical sense of justice (antedating our own rather ethnocentric notion of 'distributive justice' by several millenia) is the sense of justice as *outrage, resentment* and *revenge*. It is too easily assumed that a fully-developed sense of justice, because it is such a noble sense, must be derived only from equally noble (though perhaps more primitive) emotions. I think that this is wrong. Our sense of justice emerges as a generalization and a rationalization (not in the bad Freudian sense but rather in the good Hegelian sense) of a personal sense of *in*justice.

Our sense of injustice isn't a general sense of outrage—that comes later and already involves a number of grand generalizations. That sense of injustice begins with a personal slight, a perceived inequity. But perhaps the 'negative' emotions are not that negative after all. It has been argued, for instance, that envy is itself an important emotion, an engine of capitalism and the consumer society which encourages us to want more and be more competitive.[71] Nietzsche argued at length that resentment is the main ingredient in much of what we call morality, and Dostoesvsky (or one of his most famous characters) maintained that spite is the very essence of the free and autonomous self. The argument that I want to suggest if not pursue here is that our sense of justice cannot ignore and to some extent even develops out of these rather vile emotions. This is not to deny that justice requires and presupposes compassion, respect, and a sense of duty as well, but justice also involves the often despised and dismissed emotion of vengeance, which may, in fact, be (both historically and psychologically) the seed from which the entire plant of justice has grown.

Before we talk about vengeance as such, I would like to briefly discuss resentment, which has particularly close ties to our sense of justice and is also a kind of paradigm of a negative emotion, as Nietzsche argued at length.[72] Emotions ascribe responsibility, and this is utterly essential to our sense of injustice. To be sure, there are cultures in which ascriptions of responsibility are by no means so central a practice, and there are some aspects of distributive justice (e.g., the distribution of health care) in which considerations of responsibility are marginal.[73] But in general, injustice is not just getting the short end; it also requires that someone be to *blame*. Anger, indignation, outrage, vengeance are all emotions that ascribe responsibility (in the form of blame), but then so do gratitude, admiration and emotions of "debt," ascriptions of praise instead of blame and all evaluations of "desert" and "merit." Our sense of justice (but not every people's sense of justice) places a premium on personal responsibility. (This includes emotions of self-ascribed responsibility: shame, guilt, embarrassment, remorse, regret and humiliation; pride, self-love, sense of honor.)

How we feel about justice obviously depends, in part, on how we see ourselves and our roles in the world. John Rawls may appeal the liberal principles of justice to a selfless situation of rational deliberation, but I think that conservative critics are much closer to the mark when they argue (*ad hominem*) that liberalism is first of all a keen sense of personal guilt about one's own privileged place in the world. We first of all feel uncomfortable about our comparative wealth, health and opportunities; then we try to devise principles to give this discomfort some structure, to rationalize our privileges or at least allow us to live with them, to correct the inequities in some systematic way that is not wholly self-destructive at the same time. A big part of justice, in other words, is being able to blame (as well as praise) oneself, to admit one's responsibility for justice and not just delegate it to some "system" or social structure in which one is at most a contingent party or perhaps just an observer. The keenest sense of injustice, perhaps, is not our outrage at being slighted but rather our distress at finding that we ourselves are the beneficiaries of an injustice. It is there, perhaps, that our often childish sense of injustice turns into a sense of justice, not because we have learned to generalize our personal notions of "rights" and "desert" into an abstract theory but rather as we learn to see ourselves in others' places and realize that we are never mere observers in injustice but almost always at least passive participants.

At least in the Nietzschean context, we are so accustomed to thinking of resentment in its seething, vicious, most nasty embodiment that we fail to see that the same emotion invites a very different sort of interpretation.[74] Resentment is an extremely philosophical emotion. It is aware of the larger view. It has keen eyesight (the more Aristotelean analog of Nietzsche's sense of smell). It is quite conscious of not only how things are but of how they might be and, most important, how they ought to be. True, resentment always has a personal touch, one is always to some extent resentful *for oneself* but resentment has not only the capacity but the tendency to open itself up to more general considerations, namely, compassion and justice. It is a harsh and unfair analysis indeed that insists that the comraderie of the resentful is only of the misery-loves-company variety. *Schadenfreude* and other such emotions. It is commiserative, can be mutually supportive and conspiratorial. Resentment can provide inspiration. When I think of resentment, I think of Alexander Cockburn, pouring out invective in *The Nation* and *L.A. Weekly*—nasty, to be sure, but by no means impotent or ignoble. Would we rather have him write like John Kenneth Galbraith, or utter his theses in the platitudinous tone of an established mainstream politician? It is resentment that lies at the heart of democracy—Nietzsche was right about that—but it is not impotent resentment, not weakness, not slave or "herd" mentality. It is the "will to power" as a keen sense of *injustice*, which is, in turn, the foundation of our sense of justice.

What Nietzsche ignores—in part because of his own sense of biological determinism—is the legitimacy of the felt need to change the world. The sentiment of resentment may often be a legitimate sense of *oppression*. It is not the voice of mediocrity or incompetence but the passion of justice denied. None of this is to say that resentment isn't nasty. Of course it is. It is vindictive. It wants to change things. It looks vitriolically at those who are on top, who have the power. It wants to pull them down. But to insist that this is always mediocrity undermining excellence, the losers greasing the path of the winners, has little plausibility. Resentment provides the dialectic of the modern world, perhaps the basic dialectic of all human competitive relations, as Hegel suggested (hardly argued) in the "Master-slave" section of the *Phenomenology*. It may not be the ideal form of human community, but it will inevitably be at least an ingredient in all social relations so long as our sense of self-importance—as opposed to a selfless sense of community—is the basis of our thinking. And then it is the dialectic of communities rather than individuals.[75] One of the most common mistakes in discussions of emotion is the assumption that emotions (misconceived as "feelings") are to be ascribed only to individuals, not groups. But resentment, in particular, is an emotion that is often shared by whole communities or cultures, and even when it is contained within a single individual, resentment tends to be generalized to encompass the oppression of a larger community, however ill-defined.[76]

On the positive view, resentment is not just a selfish emotion, though it always has its self-interested element. Indeed, resentment often appeals to compassion, when it insists on projecting and objecting to its own sense of misfortune on the behalf of others. This is much more conceptually elevated than 'herd mentality,' which is unthinking, unreflective, imitative rather than compassionate. At the same time, I think that we should be cautious about concluding that this compassion amounts to anything like a sense of community.[77] But compassion lends itself to empathy, in that awareness of one's own suffering makes one prone to recognize suffering in others, and this in turn encourages (but does not guarantee) the recognition that other people are even worse off than ourselves. One may feel resentful just for oneself and for some slight offense or failure of recognition, and, indeed, we usually consider this to be petty, selfish and mean-spirited. But—and this is the crucial point—it is not the resentment that we so criticize, but its pettiness and limitation.

Vengeance as Justice:
The Rationality of Revenge

There is no denying the aesthetic satisfaction, the sense of poetic justice, that pleasures us when evil-doers get the comeuppance they deserve. The impulse to punish is primarily an impulse to even the score . . . That satisfaction is heightened when it becomes possible to mea-

sure out punishment in exact proportion to the size and shape of the
wrong that has been done . . . *mida k'neged mida*—measure for measure, *lex talionis.*

—Arthur Lelyveld

Finally, back to vengeance. Vengeance is the original passion for
justice. The word "justice" in the Old Testament virtually always refers to revenge. In Kant and Hegel, the word *"Gerechtigkeit"* certainly includes a strong concept of retribution, and throughout most of
history the concept of justice has been far more concerned with the
punishment of crimes and the balancing of wrongs than it has been
with the fair distribution of goods and services. "Getting even" is and
has always been one of the most basic metaphors of our moral vocab-
ulary, and the frightening emotion of righteous, wrathful anger has
been the emotional basis for justice just as much as benign compassion. "Don't get mad, get even"—whether or not it is prudent advice—
is conceptually confused. Getting even is just an effective way of being
mad, and getting mad already includes a generous portion of revenge.
The pleasure, the aesthetic satisfaction referred to by Arthur Lelyveld
in this section's headnote indicates the depth of that passion. The need
for "proportion" in vengeance already indicates the intelligence involved in this supposedly most irrational and uncontrollable emotion.
This is not to say, of course, that the motive of revenge is as such
legitimate or the action of revenge always justified. Sometimes vengeance is wholly called for, even obligatory, and revenge is both legitimate and justified. Sometimes it is not, notably when one is mistaken about the offender or the offense. But to seek vengeance for a
grievous wrong, to revenge oneself against evil—that seems to lie at
the very foundation of our sense of justice, indeed, of our very sense
of ourselves, our dignity, and our sense of right and wrong. Even sen-
timentalist Smith writes, in his *The Theory of the Moral Sentiments,*
"The violation of justice is injury . . . it is, therefore, the proper object
of resentment, and of punishment, which is the natural consequence
of resentment."[78] We are not mere observers of the moral life, and the
desire for vengeance seems to be an integral aspect of our recognition
of evil. But it also contains—or can be cultivated to contain—the
elements of its own control, a sense of its limits, a sense of balance.
Thus the Old Testament instructs us that revenge should be *limited to*
"an eye for an eye, a tooth for a tooth, hand for hand, foot for foot,
burning for burning, wound for wound, stripe for stripe" (the *"Lex
Talionis"*).[79] It was such "equality" that Kant took to be an absolute

rational principle in his *Philosophy of Law*, and, in more modern, jovial guise, there is Gilbert and Sullivan's musical *Mikado*: "an object all sublime/ make the punishment fit the crime." The New Testament demands even more restraint, the abstention from revenge oneself and the patience to entrust it to God. Both the Old and New Testaments (more the latter than the former) also encourage "forgiveness," but there can be no foregiveness if there is not first the desire (and the warrant) for revenge.[80]

Vengeance is often allied with such emotions of offense as anger and resentment, but it is something more than they in its core commitment to action. One can be angry or resentful and not feel the necessity to "get even"—indeed, there may be no sense at all to the idea of "getting even." (Aristotle, on the other hand, treats anger and the urge to revenge together, as one.[81]) Even when anger and resentment are tied to punishment, it is not necessary that one does, oneself, get to carry out the punishment. But this is essential to revenge. In that classic "spaghetti Western," *Once Upon a Time in the West*, the avenger (Charles Bronson) saves the life of the villain (wickedly played by Henry Fonda) just in order to be able to kill him personally at the climax of the movie. This is essential to vengeance (which is why, in Mickey Spillane's immortal words, "vengeance is mine," a phrase more often referred to the Bible). What is crucial to vengeance, in other words, is one's own essential part in the process of justice. This is just what makes it such anathema to the modern legal system, of course, for the system wants to retain justice, and in particular, punishment, for itself. It is also what makes it such an important if perverse paradigm for us here. Vengeance is personal, not impersonal, passionate and not dispassionate, engaged and not merely philosophical.

Not all passions, however, are explosive. Again, it is a serious mistake, in discussions of emotion, to assume that all passions are, by their very nature, episodic, momentary phenomena characterized by a rush of feeling and the usual physiological accompaniments. Many emotions are durable, on-going psychological attitudes, "simmering" perhaps but by no means episodic. Resentment is an obvious example. So, indeed, is love. But because love endures and may not manifest itself in a sensational bodily commotion for months or years, I have heard philosophers deny that love is even an emotion. (It is, perhaps, a "disposition" to have an emotion.) But this is absurd. Our sense of justice, to get back to the subject at hand, is also such an enduring passion, what Hume called a "calm" passion, though it may well explode in particular episodes, typically prompted by the per-

ception of injustice. Vengeance, too, is an enduring passion, so much
so that it may even seem to no longer be a passion at all. As the
Sicilians say, "revenge is a dish better served cold." The drama of
delay seems to be essential to revenge (but the delay is not, I hasten
to add, for the sake of drama). Retaliation is immediate, but vengeance
takes its time. Indeed vengeance can even become a raison d'etre, as
evidenced by so many movies and classic tales of revenge, from the
Count of Monte Cristo to *The Confessions of a She-Devil.*

Vengeance is not just punishment, no matter how harsh. It is a matter
of emotion, not public policy. Like punishment, it is always *for* some
offense. Questions of utility or rehabilitation ("teaching him a lesson") may enter into the demand for revenge, but they are certainly
not essential. Vengeance, accordingly, always has its reasons (though,
to be sure, these can be mistaken, irrelevant, out of proportion or
otherwise bad reasons). In some cultures, vengeance may be a matter
of obligation but it is first of all an urge, given shape and measure by
social practices, to be sure, but something more primitive than a social practice nonetheless. Perhaps vengeance cannot claim to be rational but neither is it obviously opposed to rationality. In cultures
where vengeance becomes a matter of obligation, it may thereby become a paradigm of rationality and a matter of family honor.[82]

Vengeance is the need to "get even," to put the world back in balance, and these simple phrases already embody a whole philosophy of
justice, even if (as yet) unarticulated and unjustified. Philosophers have
been much too quick to attribute this sense of "balance" or "retribution" to reason, but I would want to argue that it is also a function of
emotion. Kant, of course, immediately opts for the former, dismissing
the latter suggestion virtually altogether. Vengeance, he suggests, is
purely subjective, wholly irrational, undependable and unjustifiable.
It is wholly without measure or reason, devoid of any sense of balance or justice. In defense of retributivism, Robert Gerstein writes:
"Vengefulness is an emotional response to injuries done to us by others: we feel a desire to injure those who have injured us. Retributivism is not the idea that it is good to have and satisfy this emotion. It
is rather the view that there are good arguments for including the kernel
of rationality to be found in the passion for vengeance as a part of
any just system of laws."[83] But this kernel of rationality should be
taken very seriously, and I want to suggest that vengeance is just that
sense of measure or balance that Kant (and so many other philosophers) attributes to reason alone. But, of course, it is ultimately the
same old dichotomy that is most at fault here, the supposed antago-
nism between reason on the one side and passions on the other. Where

would our reasoning about punishment begin if not for our emotional sense of the need for retaliation and retribution?[84] To be sure, one might insist that what rationality and "measure" are to be found in vengeance are ingrained in various social practices rather than in the emotion itself, but this, I think, is a fruitless distinction. The social practice is, among other things, the cultivation of the emotion, and the emotion is, in part, the internalization of the social practice.[85]

Perhaps nowhere is the denial of what is most human about us (that is, our passions) more evident than in the various debates and concerns that surround the problems of punishment in criminal justice. The ongoing dispute between the "utilitarians" (who believe in a "deterrence" theory of punishment) and the "retributivists" (who believe that punishment is necessary in order to satisfy the demands of justice as such) not only neglects but explicitly dismisses any mention of that passion which alone would seem to give some fuel to the notion of punishment, namely the emotion of *vengeance*. This is not to say that punishment should serve *only* to revenge, but it is to say that punishment is in part the satisfaction of the need for vengeance and punishment makes no sense without this. Several years ago, Susan Jacoby argued that our denial of the desire for vengeance is analogous to the Victorian denial of sexual desire, and we are paying a similar psychological price for it.[86] But as with our hunger for sex, we do not succeed very well in suppressing our thirst for revenge.

How did our passion for retribution—our need for vengeance—come about? I think that evolutionary speculations can go a long way in answering this question. Earlier in this essay, I stressed the accounts of the moral sentiment theorists as an important insight into "human nature," but I hope that I was sufficiently careful not to give the impression that we are naturally "nice" in any ridiculous sense. Evolutionary theory has shown, conclusively I think, that there is demonstrable advantage for groups and species—if not always for individuals—in the evolution of cooperation. But cooperation has two sides, the willingness to cooperate, first of all, but then the resentment and punishment of those who do not cooperate as well. (This includes the expectation that one will be punished oneself if one does not cooperate.) One cannot imagine the evolution of cooperation without the evolution of punishment, and Robert Axelrod's now-classic "tit-for-tat" model of the former explains as well the latter.[87] In a repetitive "prisoner's dilemma" type situation, or in any on-going situation in which one person frequently has the ability to "cheat" the other(s), an optimum strategy for discouraging such cheating is to respond, dependably, with retribution. A creature endowed only with compassion, who would "understand" the motives of the criminal in every case, would be just as much of an evolutionary failure as a creature who did nothing but watch out for his or her own advantage and cheated every time. Swift and dependable retaliation is thus in the nature of social animals as well as the lesson of game theory. Vengeance is not the antagonist to rationality but its natural manifestation. To breed a social animal who has "the right to make promises" is to understand the evolution of a creature who has the natural urge to punish as well as natural sympathy and a sense of social solidarity.

Perhaps the point was overstated in the majority opinion in United States Supreme Court decision *Gregg vs Georgia* (1976):

> The instinct for retribution is part of the nature of man, and channeling that instinct in the administration of criminal justice serves an important purpose in promoting the stability of a society governed by law. When people begin to believe that organized society is unwilling or unable to impose upon criminal offenders the punishment they 'deserve', then there are sown the seeds of anarchy—of self-help, vigilante justice, and lynch law.

But at least the emotion of vengeance was taken seriously and not merely sacrificed to the dispassionate authority of the law. Retributive justice, however rationalized, is not as such a purely rational matter—but neither is it thereby "irrational" either. Most of the arguments that have been advanced against vengeance could, with only slight modifications, be applied to the standard notions of retributive justice as well—which is not surprising if vengeance and retributive justice are in the end identical. But in the end, it is perhaps not just a question of whether revenge is rational or not, but whether it is—at the bottom of our hearts as well as off the top of our heads—an undeniable aspect of the way we react to the world, not as an instinct but as such a basic part of our world-view and our moral sense of ourselves that it is, in that sense, unavoidable.

Retribution, accordingly, should be viewed as at least in part an emotion, a matter of personal involvement and intensity, not just an abstract obligation or a demand of detached rationality. Vengeance, as opposed to justice, is often said to be "blind," although it is worth reminding ourselves which of the two is depicted in established mythology as blind-folded. The truth is that vengeance, as a sense of justice, has or should have a reasonably clear picture of its ends and means.[88] Vengeance, it is said, knows no end. But, of course, every violation dictates (however vaguely) its "poetic" if not "natural" end,[89] and though one can get carried away with revenge (as with every emotion or motive), we are keenly aware of the point at which vengeance is excessive or fails to be satisfied.[90] Of course, there is danger in vengeance. It can be violent, disrupting the present order of things in an often impossible attempt to get back to a prior order which has itself been violently disrupted. Such impossibility breeds frustration, and the resulting violence often leads to more violence. An act of revenge results in a new offense to be righted. When the act is perpetrated not against the same person who did the offense but against another who is part of the same family, tribe or social group (the logic of "vendetta"), the possibilities for escalation are endless. Accordingly, the limitation of revenge through institutionalization is necessary. But it does not follow that vengeance itself is illegitimate or without measure or of no importance in considerations of punishment.

But to the dangers of vengeance unlimited it must be added that if punishment no longer satisfies vengeance, if it ignores not only the rights but the emotional needs of the victims of crime, then punishment no longer serves its primary purpose, *even if* it were to succeed in rehabilitating the criminal and deterring other crime (which it evidently, in general, does not). The restriction of vengeance by law is entirely understandable, but the wholesale denial of vengeance as a legitimate motive may be as much of a psychological disaster as its unlimited exercise is dangerous.

Just to be clear, I have not tried to defend vengeance as such, but my claim is that vengeance deserves its central place in any theory of justice and, whatever else we are to say about punishment, the desire for revenge must enter into our deliberations. The notion of "satisfaction" is particularly relevant here. Gerstein insists that "retributivism is not the idea that it is good to . . . satisfy this emotion," but it seems to me that it is precisely this good, when the emotion is justified, that justifies retribution. We speak of "satisfying one's thirst for vengeance" and, somewhat less metaphorically, we recognize that a given punishment does or does not satisfy the demand for retribution. The ten-month sentence handed down to a rapist does not satisfy the perfectly understandable demand for revenge on the part of the victim. The five-year sentence handed down to murderer does not satisfy the family of the victim. Anthropologist Steven Feld has described to me the practice of "buying off anger" in New Guinea and other cultures. A victim of an offense or his or her family demands compensation, and although it is clearly not a payment in kind it can provide "satisfaction" and avoid an escalation of violence.[91] Here, too, we are willing to hand over our grievances to the law for compensation and retribution, but only so long as we believe we will be satisfied. (It is not hard to see our current out-of-control system of liability law and tort action as our new version of this practice.) Any system of legal principles that does not take such emotions as the urge for vengeance into account, which does not motivate itself on their behalf, is not—whatever else it may be—a system of justice. Vengeance as such, I do not deny, is in any case dangerous. As the Chinese used to say (and no doubt still do) "if you seek vengeance, dig two graves." But I think that the dangers and destructiveness of vengeance is much overblown and its importance for a sense of one's own self-esteem and integrity ignored.

No discussion of vengeance, however brief, is complete without some final mention of mercy and foregiveness. It is worth noting that these are often *contrasted* with justice, e.g., in the Old Testament, where mercy undercuts the claims of justice as vengeance and retaliation, and we noted earlier that mercy, as a form of compassion, complements the desire for vengeance. Nietzsche, playing against the Biblical tradition, takes mercy to be the hallmark of true justice, and available only to god-like beings (e.g., his "*Ubermenschen*") and links up the desire for vengeance with resentment, the emotion of the weak. The New Testament, of course, makes much more of the virtue of forgiveness, but critics and commentators have often been perplexed about what sort of act or emotion this is supposed to be. Part of the problem, of course, is the typical pairing of "forgiving and forgetting." Why does one need both? I would suggest that forgiving means giving up one's plans or hopes for vengeance, but forgetting is something quite different and usually a matter of imprudence where it isn't simple distraction. Against the tradition that would distinguish mercy and justice (vengeance) and play them off against one another, however, I want to say that they are part of the same holistic package. They are contrasted because of an overly narrow conception of justice (e.g., as "getting even" or "giving him his due") instead of looking at the overall pattern of emotional and social relationships. One shows mercy because the crime does not really deserve the prescribed punishment, or one shows mercy because even though the punishment fits the crime it does not fit the criminal. He or she has virtues that speak louder than the crime. Of course, one might show mercy in order to show one's virtues, one's power, one's kindness, even one's whimsicality and unpredictability. But mercy is not opposed to justice (or vengeance). It is, in the larger picture, an attempt to see further that justice prevails, by way of a personal gesture instead of an abstract ruling or principle.

Conclusion

Back in the nineteenth century, the German philosopher Dühring elaborated a theory of justice along somewhat the same lines that we are attempting here, although Nietzsche, who was not at all unsympathetic to such motivational accounts, attacked this particular derivation of justice from the sentiments of resentment and revenge. ("As for Duhring's proposition. . . .[92]) Vengeance is, to be sure, not a proper paradigm of social justice, and to overemphasize the negative emotions at the expense of such emotions as sympathy and compassion would be to defend a truly perverse concept of justice. Accordingly, I have tried to suggest that an adequate account of justice would pay attention to both the "positive" and "negative" emotions, with the added complication that this simple-minded polarity too will disintegrate as we probe the social role and function of the various emotions. With that in mind I find myself attracted to the Nietzschean device of turning the usual priorities upside down and giving a primary place to vengeance. What I reject is the idea that some dispassionate mode of calculation, whether based on utility or quasi-legal entitlement or some less than empirical notion of "fairness," is the basis of our sense of justice. This is not to dismiss the relevance or the importance of such ideas, but when they lose touch with the feelings that provoke them or fail to recognize those feelings for what they are, the theory of justice suffers accordingly.

To put all of this in perspective, one might note that in a society where the sense of community and the all-importance of family relationships was taken for granted, an emphasis on impartiality and dispassionate judgment was absolutely essential to the corrective conception of justice. Thus the aristocracies of the eighteenth century were rightfully opposed by the new bureaucratic meritocracies, but this dialectic goes far further back than we usually imagine. Here, for example, are the "instructions" to the Vizier Rekhmire, the highest state official under the Pharoah Thutmose III, a thousand years before Socrates.

> Do not judge unfairly,
> God abhors partiality,
> Regard one you know like one you don't know,
> One near you like one far from you.[93]

In matters of state and social policy, such advice remains good today. But in a society where abstract individualism and an obsession

with contracts replaces what used to be taken for granted, impersonality and dispassion spread far beyond their proper "sphere of justice"
and threaten to become vices instead of virtues. A shift of perspective
is necessary. My argument, accordingly, is that justice depends not so
much on large scale schemes for redistribution or abstract arguments
about the necessity of punishment but on a more primary sense of
community and human relationships, including the violation of those
relationships. Plato was ultimately right, of course: The ideal of justice as a personal virtue depends on the structure and moral state of
society. So do our emotions. But justice is to be found neither in the
heavens nor in our various attempts to get beyond the State of Nature. The danger is that, like country singers looking for love, we are
looking for justice in all the wrong places.

Notes

This essay is based on my book, *A Passion for Justice*, (New York: Addison-
Wesley, 1990) and several related lectures and papers of the past several
years, including a Memorial Lecture at the University of Massachusetts,
Boston, for Shula Sommers in April 1989, a presentation at the I.S.R.E.
meeting in Paris in March 1988, a keynote address given at the conference
of N.A.S.S.P. at Oxford University in 1988 [published in book form in 1992,
W. C. Peden, ed.], an essay in *Social Justice Research* in 1991 and a
Festschrift for Nico Frijda in 1992. I would like to thank Nico and the various members of those audiences and editors of those journals and my editor
at Addison-Wesley, Jane Isay, for their advice, criticism, and encouragement.
Special thanks to Andrew Sharp (University of Auckland) for his good comments and criticisms of an earlier draft.

1. Rawls, p. 489. But cf. his more recent *Political Liberalism*.

2. Rawls, pp. 479, 481, 540. Of course, various emotions may enter into
the "reflective equilibrium" through which we evaluate our various theories
against pretheoretical intuitions (which Rawls variously describes as "intuitively appealing accounts," "various reasonable and natural presumptions"
and "initial convictions"). But Rawls rarely describes these as emotions and
seems to take their affective character simply for granted.

3. "*Schmelzender Theilnehmung*," Kant, *Grundlegung* (in *Werke*, Band
IV, p. 399) Kant, *Grounding of the Metaphysics of Morals*, trans. J. W. El-
lington (Indianapolis: Hackett, 1981), p. 12 (399 "melting compassion" is
Paton's translation, "tender sympathy" Lewis White Beck's and Elliston's);
Kant's account of retribution is in his *Philosophy of Law*, trans. W. Hastie
(Edinburgh: Clark, 1889).

4. Curiously, there seems to be no proper word in modern English for
the emotion(s) constitutive of vengeance. "Vengeance" itself is not the name

of an emotion but rather refers to the intended (or actual) outcome. So, too, one desires revenge, but revenge is the aim and not the desire itself. "Vengefulness" comes closer to describing the psychological state, but it tends to describe a trait of character rather than a specific emotion or psychological episode. "Wrath" is a good old Biblical word that actually does name the vindictive emotion in question but it is, perhaps tellingly, virtually out of use except in Biblical threats and phrases. In this essay, accordingly, I will treat "vengeance" and its cognates as the name of an emotion, with the understanding that this is not literally proper. I assume, however, that there is such an emotion (or functional set of emotions) and the problem here is nominal rather than substantial.

5. David Miller, *Social Justice* (Oxford University Press, 1976).

6. Michael Walzer, *Spheres of Justice* (New York: Basic Books, 1983).

7. I have done so in a limited way in my *Passion for Justice* (New York: Addison-Wesley, 1990).

8. By "substantial, concrete history" I mean to imply something more than the "thin" and conscientiously limited history suggested by Robert Nozick, in particular, in his argument against the "ahistorical" Rawlsian position.

9. A riveting discussion of this courtroom locution is Susan Jacoby's description of the post-Nuremberg Nazi trials, in which concentration camp victims and the families of victims were instructed to testify, almost robotlike, "We don't want vengeance; we want justice." What they wanted, of course, was revenge. Susan Jacoby, *Wild Justice* (New York: Harper & Row, 1983).

10. One of the best though admittedly not clearest discussions of the "Evil for Evil" formula as a deep misunderstanding of retribution can be found in Hegel's *Philosophy of Right* (Para 99). He, in turn, takes his cue from Kant, who defends punishment as "equality," but as a matter of purely practical reason, not vengeance.

11. This is ambiguous, of course. Vengeance is particularly personal in that it involves an offense or injury to oneself or someone very close to oneself. Not all emotions are personal in this sense. Some emotions are "impersonal" in that they have as their object *truth*, in the case of curiosity, for example, or moral principle (in indignation) or justice. I do not want to defend the (mistaken) position that all emotions are about the self or self-involved, but they are, nevertheless, personal in that one takes the matter in question personally. Thus curiosity reflects one's interest, and moral indignation reflects one's commitment to the violated principle in question. Robert Nozick (in *Philosophical Explanations*) suggests that we distinguish retribution from revenge insofar as the first is impersonal and, if according to certain standards, justified, while the latter is strictly personal, and therefore not justified at all. In the pages that follow, I want to undermine that distinction.

12. One way of putting the thesis I am beginning to formulate here is that vengeance is socially sanctioned and structured but the underlying motiva-

tion may not be socially created. Individuals in "the state of nature," like most "higher" animals, will retaliate in case of attack, typically in measured reactions. But vengeance as a social practice is cultivated according to certain cultural norms and concepts, including a notion of self (highly autonomous versus interdependent), a set of notions about what counts as an offense (although some of these, such as theft, rape and murder, may have a prima facie claim to universality), a set of standards of "fit," "balance" or "tit-for-tat" that distinguishes revenge from further wrongdoing.

13. In Marongiu and Newman's *Vengeance*, for example, the Sardinian code of "vendetta" is discussed in some detail as exemplary of a culture in which personal retaliation is considered not only acceptable but obligatory. But it is the aggrieved party, not the state, that has the responsibility for punishment. (*Vengeance*: [Lanham, Md.: Rowman & Littlefield, 1987]).

14. David Miller, in his *Social Justice*, distinguishes three very different social contexts and three competing conceptions of justice to explain, with a fair amount of anthropological data, why there is no single "correct" theory of justice. Context is the determinant of theories (or, more generally, conceptions) of justice. One might also consult, with some trepidation, Jean-François Lyotard's obscure but similar "anti-totalizing" thesis in his *The Postmodern Condition*.

15. Such subcultures include, for example, not only different generations and an occasional "counterculture" but also the business community, the homeless, the poor, the wealthy, blue-collar workers, small shopkeepers, the academic community, and those various shifting divisions and differences that are constitutive of ideologically like-minded groups. What separates liberals and conservatives, for example, are not the facts (which are simply rearranged or reinterpreted to fit or refute whatever recent theory is at hand) but two very different views of poverty, as shameful and as threatening, respectively. The neglected or repressed phenomenon of *class* thus determines much of our conception of justice. Paul Fussell, *Class*, and Benjamin De-Mott, *Class*.

16. It may be worth noting that Camus's Sisyphus has two very different and I would say opposed responses to the injustice and absurdity of the world. First and foremost, he throws himself into his task ("his rock is his thing") and survives by engaging himself in the moment. ("Each atom of that stone, each mineral flake of that night-filled mountain, in itself forms a world. The struggle itself towards the heights is enough to fill a man's heart. One must consider Sisyphus happy."). Such an attitude (what Nietzsche called "*amor fati*") seems to eclipse considerations of justice. But Camus's other reaction, which later informs much of his later work, is Sisyphus's "scorn and defiance" of the gods and his so-called "rebellion"—which might better be understood as sheer *ressentiment*. But resentment, as Nietzsche had pointed out a half-century earlier, can be a powerful impetus to stay alive and typically translates itself into the more impersonal, even "objective" demand for justice. Camus, *The Myth of Sisyphus*, trans. Justin O'Brien (New York: Vin-

tage, 1960). Nietzsche, *On the Genealogy of Morals*, trans. Walter Kaufmann, (New York: Random House, 1967).

17. Shula Sommers, "Adults Evaluating Their Emotions," in C. Izard and
C. Malatesta, eds., *Emotions in Adult Development* (New York: Sage, 1984).

18. It is with some irony that one observes some of the most brilliant and
best-paid moral philosophers of our time dismiss such obvious social advantages as intelligence and good up-bringing as utterly irrelevant to considerations of merit and, by the logical extension of the same argument, dismiss
merit itself as irrelevant to considerations of justice. Surely there is some
informal inconsistency here, though one hesitates to put a name to it.

19. I am willing to drop the "justice as vengeance" exaggeration, the point,
I hope, having been made. But if only I were a contemporary French philosopher, I could continue to defend the exaggeration, holding onto the germ of
truth and proclaiming the hyperbole as its rhetorical expression. But, alas,
I'm Midwestern to the core. No wonder contemporary "Continental" philosophy seems so exciting to some.

20. Agamemnon to Menelaus, concerning the fate of their prisoners: "Let
us not leave even one of them alive, down to the babies in the mother's
wombs," and Homer, commenting, tells us that "he turned his brother's heart,
and urged justice." *The Iliad*, 6.51–65, trans. R. Lattimore, 2nd ed. (Chicago: University of Chicago Press, 1975).

21. Translated into the admittedly obfuscating language of Michel Fou-
cault instead of the openly roughhouse vernacular of Thrasymachus, the thesis that "the just is nothing but the advantage of the stronger" becomes much
more plausible. I will not pursue this suggestion here.

22. I think that the best contemporary defense of this thesis is Michael
Walzer's *Spheres of Justice* (op. cit.), though I prefer the more Hegelian
notion of context to the rather Leibnizian image of a sphere just because
contexts so often and readily overlap and cause conflict whereas a sphere
(and many of Walzer's examples) seem overly self-contained. Socrates' argument with Polymarchus, in particular, cleverly shifts from context to closely
related context just enough to change the nature of the example. "Giving
one's due" and the differential treatment of one's friends and enemies are
not yet synonymous, but in any case the interpretation of "due" in terms of
friends and enemies moves the argument from a reasonable consideration of
context in general to overly personal preferences and affections. To be sure,
one may wish one's friends well and one's enemies ill, but this is hardly the
sort of personal passion that is constitutive of a sense of justice.

23. I have in mind *The Symposium*, for example, where it seems clear
that Plato is giving Socrates more than a run for his money and challenging
Socrates even within the confines of the dialogue. The very personal speech
of Alcibiades, for instance, provides a direct counterpoint to Socrates's overly philosophical account of *eros* according to Diotima's ethereal wisdom.
See, e.g., Martha Nussbaum, "The Speech of Alcibiades," in Solomon and
Higgins, ed., *The Philosophy of (Erotic) Love* (Lawrence: University Press
of Kansas, 1991), pp. 279–316.

24. In addition to the more traditional accounts of the so-called social contract and Rawls's original position, there are, for example, Bruce Ackerman's spaceship scenario, Nozick's somewhat different account of the growth of protective associations, and many hundreds of attacks on and tinkerings with these models. There is a great deal of literature about why these models aren't as "neutral" as they pretend to be, but I want to start at the other end and complain that they all begin with an excessive pretense of neutrality and ignore or rule out of order all of those preexisting personal relationships and affections without which justice would be just a hollow statistical calculation.

25. Robert Nozick, *Anarchy, State and Utopia* (New York: Basic Books, 1974).

26. Arguments to this effect go back at least to Aristotle, who in his *Rhetoric* as well as in his *Ethics* defended the importance and the rationality of emotions. One finds similar arguments in the Stoics (who, nevertheless, conclude that most emotions are irrational), in Spinoza and many modern philosophers. Today, of course, the thesis is widely endorsed and generally accepted. See, e.g., Ronald de Sousa, *The Rationality of Emotion* and Patricia Greenspan, *Reason and Emotion*. I have defended the thesis in my books, *The Passions* and *A Passion for Justice* and elsewhere.

27. William James, "What is an Emotion?" *Mind*, 1884. C. G. Lange, *The Emotions*. (Baltimore: Wilkins and Wilkins, 1922). But one can discern in James, at least, three different views of emotion, two of them in the aforementioned essay. First and best known, there is his "sensation" theory of emotion. But only a few pages later he offers us a behavioral account of emotion, summarized in his famous line, "a woman is sad because she weeps, she does not weep because she is sad," reversing the usual order of emotion and its expression. Finally, in his writing in the philosophy of religion, he offers us a very different view indeed, of certain emotions at any rate, whose significance is profound and whose nature is anything but merely sensational or behavioral.

28. A very brief list of recent authors would include the works cited by Ronald deSousa and Patricia Greenspan as well as others by Michael Stocker, Annette Baier and Amelie Rorty in philosophy and James Averill and Richard Lazarus, to name but two, in psychology.

29. Solomon, op. cit., 1976, 1990.

30. Robert Gordon, *Structure of Emotion* (Cambridge University Press, 1987).

31. Kant, *Philosophy of Law*, op. cit.

32. Sartre, *The Emotions: Sketch of a Theory,* trans. B. Frechtman (Philosophical Library, 1948).

33. Sartre, *ibid.*

34. I have argued this thesis in some detail in my "Existentialism, Emotions and Rationality," *Philosophy East and West* (Fall, 1992).

35. For a good discussion of the "appropriateness" of emotion, with ref-

erence to C.D. Broad, see Ronald de Sousa, "The Rationality of Emotions", Chapter 7 in his book, *The Rationality of Emotions* (Cambridge: M.I.T. Press, 1989) also reprinted in Amelie Rorty, *Explaining Emotions*, op. cit. (Berkeley: University of California Press, 1980).

36. See L. E. Goodman on "Medieval Jewish and Islamic Philosophers," in Biderman and Scharfstein (Eds.) *Rationality in Question: On Eastern and Western Views of Rationality*, pp. 95–99.

37. Against those overly rationalist conceptions of justice, I would argue that truly "dispassionate" judgment is more often pathological than rational and detachment more likely signals alienation than objectivity. (See for example, Michael Stocker's amiable piece, "The Schizophrenia of Modern Ethical Theories," *Journal of Philosophy* 73 (1979): 453–66. I find particularly valuable Martin Heidegger's punsical conception of *mood* (*Stimmung*) as our mode of "being tuned" (*Bestimmen*) to the world, because of its welcome shift in emphasis from detached knowing to holistic personal caring (*Sorge*). *Being and Time*, trans. Robinson and MacQuarrie, New York: Harper & Row, 1962). Unfortunately, Heidegger himself was most often in a bad mood, which is rather evident in his philosophy.

38. Cheshire Calhoun, "Justice, Care and Gender Bias," *Journal of Philosophy*, 1980. Nell Noddings, *Caring: A Feminine Approach to Ethics and Moral Education* (Berkeley: University of California Press, 1984).

39. "One is tempted to say that ethics has so far been guided by Logos, the masculine spirit, whereas the more natural and, perhaps, stronger approach would be through Eros, the feminine spirit." (Noddings, op. cit.)

40. "One of the saddest features of this picture of violence [in the world today] is that the deeds are so often done in the name of principle. . . . This approach through law and principle is not, I suggest, the approach of the mother. It is the approach of the detached one, of the other. The view to be expressed here is a feminine view. . . . It is feminine in the deep classical sense—rooted in receptivity, relatedness, and responsiveness." (Noddings, ibid., pp. 1–2, 5).

41. There are, however, larger social and cultural factors that seem to me to explain this move in philosophy, for example, the "sophisticated" reaction against growing women's literature in the eighteenth century and, more recently, a widespread bias against all emotion as "sentimentality." See, for example, Jane Tomkins, *Sensational Designs* (Oxford University Press, 1985) and my "In Defense of Sentimentality," *Philosophy and Literature*, 1991.

42. Jean-Jacques Rousseau is an interesting paradigm here. Although he is more often discussed in philosophy as one of the authors of social contract theory, he is also the philosopher who defended the benevolence of human emotion and influenced generations of romantics to follow. He is also the philosopher who is responsible for a particularly pathological if not paranoid notion of freedom which is, I would argue, a much more pervasive influence on contemporary conservative thought than most conservatives would ever allow. I would argue that he is also a more flattering model for

Rawl's theory of justice than Kant, who provided Rawls with much of his methodology. But in temperament, beneath the barbed wire language of his deontological system, Rawls's *Theory of Justice* seems to me more in the spirit of *Emile*. Rawls, pp. 140, 264, esp. 463 and 540. Of course, Rousseau was also the inspiration for Kant's moral philosophy, a fact that too often gets lost in a casual introductory paragraph and ignored in overly formal analyses of Kant.

43. For Hume, but not Smith, justice was an "artificial"—as opposed to a "natural"—sentiment, for it consisted of the calculated attempt to organize society on the basis of utility. But Hume was willing to recognize that, insofar as it had the ability to move us, justice was not just a set of utilitarian calculations but itself a cultivated sentiment that could be as spontaneous and heartfelt as his much celebrated sympathy. For Smith, justice was nothing more than our horror at seeing others harmed, and thus went hand in hand along with sympathy, which was the ability to perceive such harm in others.

44. Random House Dictionary, 1980.

45. *Theory of the Moral Sentiments*, I.i.5.

46. *Theory of the Moral Sentiments*, I.i.I.2.

47. *Ibid.*

48. Patricia Verhane, *Ethics and Economics: The Legacy of Adam Smith for Modern Capitalism* (Oxford University Press, 1990).

49. TMS, I.i.I 2.

50. I am particularly indebted to Charles Griswold for his excellent discussions of Smith's moral philosophy.

51. Hume, *Treatise*, p. 235.

52. Hume, *Treatise*, pp. 577, 579.

53. TMS, III.2.6.

54. TMS, III.2.7.

55. MacIntyre, *After Virtue*, p. 214–15. Milton Friedman, waxing eloquent on his own interpretation of Smith, gets it (characteristically) wrong: "Smith regarded sympathy as a human characteristic, but one that was itself rare and required to be economised," in "Adam Smith's Relevance for 1976" in *Selected Papers of the University of Chicago Graduate School of Business*, No. 50 (Chicago: University of Chicago Graduate School of Business, 1977), p. 16.

56. *After Virtue*, p. 47.

57. TMS, II.ii.2.1.

58. Joseph Cropsey, *Polity and Economy* (Westport, CT: Greenwood Press, 1957), p. 12.

59. TMS, I.i.I.2.

60. For instance, in the now classic dispute between Margaret Mead and Marvin Harris and in the more recent debate over Jean Briggs' book on Eskimo emotions, *Never in Anger* (Cambridge: Harvard University Press). See, for an extensive and varied account of this dispute, Levine and Schweder, eds., *Culture Theory* (Cambridge University Press, 1984).

61. L. Wispe, T. Natsoulos. See selected bibliography.

62. Random House Dictionary, 1980.

63. *After Virtue*, p. 47; *Whose Justice? Which Rationality?* 307ff. Chapter 17, pp. 244ff.

64. Ibid.

65. Ibid.

66. MacIntyre, *Whose Justice? Which Rationality?*, p. 268.

67. I am indebted to Annette Baier for letting me see some of her then unpublished work on Hume, and Patricia Werhane for letting me see some of her then unpublished work on Adam Smith. Their books have since been published as *A Progress of Sentiments* and *Ethics and Economics: The Legacy of Adam Smith for Modern Capitalism*, respectively.

68. The term "negative emotions" has been effectively employed by Lawrence Thomas, e.g., in an essay on "Grief and Guilt" in Myers, Irani, eds, *Emotion* (New York: Haven, 1983). He lists as his basic list of "negative" emotions not only grief and guilt (which I do not here discuss) but also envy, hatred, etc. The idea is that these are distinctively unpleasant and undesirable in themselves (unlike joy and love, for instance) but are to be valued rather for the "support" they give to such "positive" emotions. My argument here is somewhat different, but the overall point is much the same.

69. Laurence Thomas, *Living Morally* (Philadelphia: Temple University Press, 1983).

70. Martha Nussbaum has recently argued similarly with regard to "love and the moral point of view." She notes that Adam Smith, who defended the importance of all sorts of emotions, nevertheless denied love the status of a moral sentiment on the grounds that it was too exclusive and particular. See her *Love's Knowledge* (Oxford, 1990), esp. p. 338f. Nussbaum also makes the unfortunate claim that theorists of emotion have virtually ignored "the connection between emotions and beliefs about what is valuable and important" (p. 293 and n.15).

71. Schoeck, *Envy* (Harcourt Brace Jovanovich, 1970).

72. Nietzsche, *On the Genealogy of Morals*, II.

73. On the first claim, see Jean Briggs, *Never in Anger* (Harvard, 1975); on the second, see for example Daniel Callahan, *Living with Mortality* (New York: Simon & Schuster, 1993).

74. It is instructive that one of Nietzsche's best critics, Max Scheler, never took Nietzsche to task for being unfair to resentment; he only wanted to insist that Christianity and Christian morality were not necessarily based on this admittedly repulsive emotion. See his *Ressentiment* (New York: Free Press, 1961).

75. It is this aspect of the dialectic that is short-changed in Francis Fukuyama's recent take-off of Hegel, *The End of History and the Last Man*. Competition need not be confined to the economic sphere, of course, but rages much more destructively in the sphere of nationality and religion, two particularist aspects of human social life that have not been *aufgehoben*'d by

the end of the Cold War. But see Fukuyama's more recent acknowledgement of unyielding nationalism in Europe in *The Economist*, June 1992.

76. For a good discussion of group emotions, see Andrew Sharp, *Justice and the Maori* (Oxford University Press, 1990).

77. Jean-Paul Sartre comes dangerously close to this conclusion in his *Critique of Dialectical Reason*, in which it is a shared sense of oppression alone that forges a true sense of community or *"mitsein."*

78. Adam Smith, *The Theory of the Moral Sentiments*, p. 115.

79. *Exodus* 21:24–5.

80. Murphy and Hampton, *Mercy and Foregiveness*, (Cambridge).

81. *Rhetoric*, op. cit.

82. See, again, Andrew Sharp, *Justice and the Maori*, and G. Oddie and R. Perrett, eds., *Justice, Ethics and New Zealand Society*.

83. R. S. Gerstein, "Capital Punishment: A Retributivist Response," *Ethics*, Vol. 85 (1985), pp. 75–9.

84. We should stress here that retaliation and retribution should not be confused with reparation and mere compensation, which may in some cases "undo" the damage but in no case by themselves count as punishment.

85. A more general thesis hovers here, which often goes by the name "the social construction of emotions." I find much to applaud in this theory, although I object to its neglect of subjectivity and the phenomenology (the "experience") of emotion. But the thesis here is that an emotion is partially constituted by certain social norms and concepts. What more "natural" ingredients are also there is a delicate question which has been overly aggressively answered by sociobiologists and armchair anthropologists. For good statements of the social constructionist position, see Rom Harré, *The Social Construction of Emotions*, esp. the essay by James Averill (Oxford: Blackwell, 1986).

86. Susan Jacoby, *Wild Justice*, op. cit.

87. Robert Axelrod, *The Evolution of Cooperation* (New York: Basic Books, 1984).

88. The "should" here is worth dwelling on, for like every emotion, vengeance admits of excessive, crude, and genuinely stupid manifestations as well as refined, even exquisite expressions. Cultivated vengeance can be subtle and even sublime. Crude vengeance, the most common sort of example, is usually ugly and self-defeating.

89. I do not want to make it sound, as in the *lex talionis* ("Eye for eye, tooth for tooth") and in W. S. Gilbert's *Mikado* ("an object all sublime/ make the punishment fit the crime"), that this notion of "fit" is always all that obvious, even in the case in which it is most often taken as paradigm, the taking of a life for a life. As Albert Camus argued against the death penalty, "For there to be equivalence, the death penalty would have to punish a criminal who had warned his victim of the date at which he would inflict a horrible death on him and who, from that moment onward, had confined him at his mercy for months. Such a monster is not encountered in private life" (*Reflections on the Guillotine*).

90. Most movie plots assume the existence of such a point of satisfaction, and it is perhaps a sign of our bad taste that most revenge films involve only the most extreme kinds of wrongs calling for only the most extreme forms of vengeance. Most comedies, however, identify the point of satisfaction as something less than death and destruction, and the subtleties of humiliation constitute much of the plot as well as the satisfaction that follows. Perhaps the point is most evident when such satisfaction is withheld from the audience, for example in Woody Allen's acclaimed "black comedy," *Crimes and Misdeameanors* (1986). See William Miller, *Humiliation* (Ithaca, N.Y.: Cornell, 1993).

91. Steven Feld is professor of anthropology at the University of Texas and the author of *Sound and Sentiment*, a study of the Kaluli of Papua New Guinea. It is important to note that this concept of "satisfaction" is not necessarily equivalent to Kant's "equality." One can "buy off anger" precisely because one need not pay back in kind, and even in cases in which a return of like for like is appropriate, it may be judged offensive and simple-minded, as if we were to repay a friend who gives us a birthday present by returning a present that is exactly the same. It is also important to note that such exchange is first of all a way of fostering and tightening the community. It is not the fulfillment of any real or implicit contract. Indeed, the very idea of retribution is reestablishing and strengthening ties in the community, not pursuing individual grievances.

92. Nietzsche, *On the Genealogy of Morals*, II, 11.

93. From Miriam Lichtheim, *Ancient Egyptian Literature*, Volume II (Berkeley: University of California Press, 1976), reprinted in Daniel Bonevac et al., eds., *Beyond the Western Tradition* (Mayfield, 1992), p. 22.

Selected Bibliography

Aristotle. *Nichomachean Ethics*. T. Irwin, trans. Indianapolis: Hackett, 1985.

Augustine. *The City of God*. Philip Levine, trans. Cambridge: Harvard University Press, 1956.

Axelrod, Robert M. *The Evolution of Cooperation*. New York: Basic Books, 1984.

Blum, Lawrence. "Compassion." In *Explaining Emotions*, Amelie Rorty, ed. Berkeley: University of California Press, 1980.

Brentano, Franz. *The Origin of our Knowledge of Right and Wrong*. London: Routledge, 1889.

Calhoun, Cheshire H. *Feeling and Value*. Ph.D. Dissertation. University of Texas, 1981.

Calhoun, Cheshire H. "Justice, Care and Gender Bias." *Journal of Philosophy* 85 (Sept. 1988).

Camus, Albert. *The Myth of Sisyphus*. J. O'Brien, trans. New York: Vintage, 1955.

Descartes, Rene. *The Passions of the Soul*. S. Voss, trans. Indianapolis: Hackett, 1989.

Dostoevsky, Fyodor. *Notes from Underground*. R. Matlaw, trans. New York: Dutton, 1960.

Downie, R. S. Justifying Punishment. In *Issues in Moral Philosophy*, T. Donaldson, ed. New York: McGraw-Hill, 1986.

Frijda, Nico. *The Emotions*. Cambridge: Cambridge University Press, 1986.

Gerstein, R. S. "Capital Punishment: A Retributivist Response." *Ethics* 85 (1985): 75–79.

Gordon, Robert. *The Structure of Emotions*. Cambridge: Cambridge University Press, 1987.

Hegel, G. W. F. *The Phenomenology of Spirit*. A. V. Miller, trans. Oxford: Oxford University Press, 1977.

Heidegger, Martin. *Being and Time*. J. Robinson, trans. New York: Harper & Row, 1962.

Hume, David. *A Treatise of Human Nature*. Oxford: Oxford University Press, 1978

Hutcheson, Frances. *A System of Moral Philosophy*. Hildesheim: Olms, 1755.

Jacoby, Susan. *Wild Justice*. New York: Harper & Row, 1983.

James, William. "What is an Emotion?" *Mind*, 1884.

Kant, Immanuel. *The Metaphysical Elements of Justice*. J. Ladd, trans. Indianapolis: Bobbs-Merrill, 1965.

Kant, Immanuel. *The Grounding of the Metaphysics of Morals*. Ellington, trans. Indianapolis: Hackett, 1980.

Kant, Immanuel. *Philosophy of Law*. T. Hastie, trans. Edinburgh: Clark, 1889.

Lange, C. G. *The Emotions*. Baltimore: Wilkins and Wilkins, 1922.

Lelyveld, Arthur. *Punishment: For and Against*. New York: Hart, 1971.

Lerner, M. J. *Belief in a Just World*. New York: Plenum, 1980.

Marongiu, P., and G. Newman. *Vengeance.* Rowman & Littlefield, 1987.

Natsoulas, Thomas. "Sympathy, Empathy and the Stream of Consciousness." *Journal of the Theory of Social Behavior* 18 (June 1988):2.

Nietzsche, Friedrich. *The Genealogy of Morals*. W. Kaufmann, trans. New York: Random House, 1967.

Nozick, Robert. *Anarchy State and Utopia*. New York: Basic Books, 1974.

Plato. *Crito*. In *The Life and Death of Socrates*. Grube, trans. Indianapolis: Hackett, 1984.

Plato. *The Republic*. Grube, trans. Indianapolis: Hackett, 1985.

Rawls, John. *A Theory of Justice*. Cambridge: Harvard University Press, 1971.

Rescher, Nicholas. *Unselfishness*. Pittsburgh: University of Pittsburgh Press, 1974.

Rousseau, Jean-Jacques. *Discourse on the Origin of Inequality.* D. Cress, trans. Indianapolis: Hackett, 1983.

Sartre, Jean-Paul. *The Emotions: Sketch of a Theory*. New York: Philosophical Library, 1948.

Scheler, Max. *The Nature of Sympathy*. P. Heath, trans. London: Routledge, 1954.

Schoeck, Helmut. *Envy: A Theory of Social Behaviour.* Glenny and Ross, trans. New York: Harcourt Brace and World, 1970.

Schopenhauer, Arthur. *The Basis of Morality.* Payne, trans. Indianapolis: Bobbs-Merrill, 1965.

Smith, Adam. *The Theory of Moral Sentiments*. London: George Bell and Sons, 1880.

Smith, Adam. *An Inquiry into the Nature and Causes of the Wealth of Nations*. New York: Hafner, 1990.

Solomon, Robert C. *A Passion for Justice*. Reading, Mass.: Addison-Wesley, 1990.

Solomon, Robert C. *The Passions*. New York: Doubleday, 1976.

Sommers, Shula. "Adults Evaluating Their Emotions." In *Emotions in Adult Development*, C. Izard and C. Malatesta, eds. New York: Sage, 1984.

Thomas, Laurence. *Living Morally*. Philadelphia: Temple University Press, 1990.

Thomas, Laurence. "Morals, the Self and Our Natural Sentiments." In *Emotion*. Myers and Irani, eds. New York: Haven, 1983.

Walzer, Michael. *Spheres of Justice*. New York: Basic Books, 1983.

Wispe, L. "The Distinction between Sympathy and Empathy." *Journal of Personality and Social Psychology* 50 (1986).

Young, Iris. *Justice and the Politics of Difference*. Princeton, N.J.: Princeton University Press, 1991.

Comments by Alison M. Jaggar

Solomon's complex and rich discussion makes a number of interesting and important points about justice. I accept his view that justice necessarily includes a retributive element and I also agree that the sense of justice involves a package of cultivated emotions, of which some are negative as well as positive. Despite my sympathy with many key features of Professor Solomon's account, this discussion will focus on our major point of disagreement, namely Solomon's claim that vengeance is integral to justice. While I do not dispute his suggestion that vengeance may figure in stories about the psychological or social origins of justice, I disagree with Solomon's assertion that vengeance remains central in mature conceptions of justice so that, in order for justice to be done, victims' desire for vengeance must be satisfied. I am also unconvinced that the desire for vengeance lies "at the very foundation" not only of our sense of justice but also "of our very sense of ourselves, our dignity and our sense of right and wrong."

Solomon's claim that vengeance is central to our sense of ourselves as moral agents is startling in a moral climate where the desire for vengeance is regarded commonly as a moral failing to be overcome. His assertion that justice requires satisfaction of the demands of vengeance is even more provocative because justice is generally presented as an alternative to vengeance, a substitute for or means of transcending this morally reprehensible practice. Solomon mentions the first claim only in passing and, because it is not central in his present discussion of justice, I shall not address it here. Instead, I shall focus on Solomon's argument for his view that vengeance is an indispensable component of both Western institutions of justice and the Western sense of what justice requires.

Solomon presents vengeance as both a practice and an emotion. As a social practice, vengeance legitimates the infliction of harm by the victims of perceived wrongs on those perceived as having wronged them. Solomon asserts that the practice of vengeance requires: 1) that the punishment be inflicted through the direct agency of the victims of the original injury or their close associates; 2) that the punishment be slow in coming, unlike retaliation which follows immediately on the original injury; and, 3) that the punishment be in some measure of balance or proportionality to the original wrong. The emotion of vengeance, as Solomon describes it, is a desire on the part of individuals or groups who perceive themselves as wronged to inflict proportionate harm on those perceived as wronging them. While the practice and the emotion of vengeance can be distinguished conceptually, Solomon asserts that in fact they are bound up with each other. "The social practice is, among other things, the cultivation of the emotion and the emotion is, in part, the internalization of the social practice."

In what sense can the practice and emotion of vengeance be regarded as moral? The moral dimension of vengeance seems to be provided by three alleged features. First is the idea that the original injury is not just a harm but a wrong; second is the idea that the victim is entitled to seek revenge; and third is the idea that the revenge inflicted must be proportional to the original injury. Despite Solomon's assertion that vengeance necessarily involves "measured reciprocity," I disagree that revenge is necessarily proportionate to injury. Even if the punishments inflicted by those who perceived themselves as wronged were wildly disproportionate to the original injury, this would not disqualify them as acts of vengeance though it would disqualify them as acts of justice. Rejecting the third feature of vengeance undermines Solomon's assertion that "vengeance . . . already involves a small scale theory of justice," though it still leaves vengeance with an undeniable moral dimension.

As Solomon sees it, vengeance is distinguished from justice primarily in being personal whereas justice is impersonal. By this, Solomon seems to mean, first, that vengeance can be inflicted only by the victim or a close associate and, second, that individuals motivated by vengeance are interested only in avenging a wrong done to them or theirs. That vengeance is personal in this sense does not entail that it is unprincipled or nonuniversalizable; if victims perceive themselves as entitled to vengeance, they must presumably acknowledge that anyone else who had been similarly wronged would be similarly entitled to revenge. But vengeance provides no reason for people to care about anyone other than themselves or their close associates; it gives them no interest in the success of other victims' search for revenge.

The intrinsically personal nature of vengeance distinguishes it from retribution, which is an aspect of justice. As a practice, retribution differs from vengeance in requiring that those perceived to have wronged others be punished by agents who have no personal interest in harming the wrongdoers. As an emotion, the desire for retribution involves a sense that wrongdoers generally should be punished, regardless of whether or not we have any personal connection with the victims. Retribution is dispassionate rather than passionate. Unlike vengeance, it fulfils an interest that is public or impersonal rather than private or personal.

Solomon seeks to undermine the distinction between impersonal retribution and personal revenge by demonstrating that vengeance is a component and even a paradigm of justice, providing "a model for what we consider to be just and fair." He offers two arguments for these conclusions. The first argument is that "our" Western institution and sense of justice emerged historically from the social practice of vengeance—though not only from this practice. The second is that, on the level of individual moral development, the desire to harm those who injure us is one, though not the only, psychological prerequisite for developing a sense of justice. Solomon goes on to speculate that the "primitive urge" for vengeance is not only innate but an evolutionary imperative for a social species. Ontogeny recapitulates phylogeny.

Solomon's social and psychological claims seem to point in rather different directions. His assertion that "Our sense of justice (but not every people's sense of justice) places a premium on personal responsibility" suggests that vengeance is integral only to what he calls Jerusalem-based understandings of justice but his speculations regarding "the natural urge to punish" suggest that vengeance must be central to all conceptions of justice. Even if this unclarity can be resolved, however, his arguments fail, both separately and together, to establish that even Western conceptions of justice necessarily involve concern for the moral demands of vengeance.

I do not dispute Solomon's assertions that the practice of and desire for vengeance are prerequisites for the institution and sense of justice. Both of these empirical claims sound plausible to me, though, in the absence of a more detailed story, I do not know whether either of them in fact is true. But even assuming the truth of both, I cannot see how they establish that vengeance is a continuing component of either the full-fledged institution or the mature sense of justice. Even if vengeance must be part of any story purporting to relate the social or psychological origins of justice, to infer that vengeance remains untransformed in contemporary understandings of justice is to commit a genetic fallacy.

There is certainly an uncontroversial sense in which, if either the social or the psychological origins story were true, vengeance must indeed be a component of justice. It would be a component in the same sense as that in which flour and eggs are components of cakes. It would be "the stuff out of which our conceptions of justice are constructed." But the whole point of developing conceptions of justice is to transform stuff such as vengeance into something more morally acceptable, just as the whole point of making cakes is to transform their ingredients into something more palatable. To the extent that our conceptions of justice contain recognizable traces of vengeance, they remain half-baked, primitive and immature.

Conceptually, vengeance is quite distinct from retribution, though elements of both may be present on any given occasion. Solomon says that concentration camp victims and the families of victims at the post-Nuremberg Nazi trials really wanted vengeance rather than justice but, if this is true, they were wrong to pursue it through a judicial system. It is hard to imagine that any judicial system would permit those injured to take vengeance in the sense of inflicting personally whatever sentences were pronounced on the wrongdoers, precisely because such systems are typically concerned to present themselves as promoting (sometimes retributive) justice rather than vengeance. But even in the unlikely event that those who had been injured were permitted to impose the penalty personally, the symbolic meaning of imposing a legally mandated punishment would be quite different from the symbolic significance of exacting vengeance. Even if gaolers and executioners feel personal vindictiveness toward the wrongdoers they punish, indeed, even if they are punishing individuals who have wronged them personally, they are not simply exacting vengeance from those wrongdoers. The legal context and the officials' position as representatives of the state changes the social meaning of the penalty from vengeance to retribution. This is not to say that all situations of legal punishment involve only dispassionate retribution; wrongdoers may receive disproportionate punishment, in which case justice is not done; or those wronged may experience feelings of personal disappointment or triumph regarding the sentence, in which case an element of emotional vengeance is present. But the fact that some situations may contain elements of both does not undercut the conceptual distinctness of vengeance and retribution.

It may indeed be true that "justice can be construed as a derivative of vengeance" in the sense that vengeance is the stuff out of which justice is constructed. But this in no way entails that justice should respect the claims of vengeance, let alone that vengeance is "a paradigm of justice" or "a model for what we consider just and fair." Not only may vengeance be disproportionate, whereas it is logically impossible for justice to be so but, contrary to Solomon's claim that it is "a mistake to jettison the personal impassioned reaction," I have argued that this is precisely what must happen in order that vengeance may metamorphose into justice.

Comments by William A. Galston

Much of what Solomon says about justice is both true and important. While expressing a substantial measure of agreement, I want to draw some distinctions that are at best implicit in his argument and to urge some modest amendments.

Solomon suggests that underlying all our sophisticated propositions about justice is some primary—even primal—sense of connection to other people and to the world. Without some such connection, justice would be unmotivated and pointless. Solomon takes as his points of departure the sentiments of sympathy as the basis of distributive justice and (more controversially) vengeance as the basis of retributive justice.

He is, I think, right about this. A similar intuition underlies my longstanding unwillingness to accept the Rawlsian thesis that the right is prior to the good. In my view, an understanding of, and commitment to, a conception of the good undergirds and motivates our concern that the social world be well-ordered. The difficulty, of course, is that whether we express our sense of connection with the world in the language of goods or of emotions, we can experience connection in many different ways, some far less hospitable to the understanding of justice Solomon prefers. This emerges clearly in a humorous footnote in which Solomon first praises Martin Heidegger's conception of mood as attunement and then observes, rightly, that "Unfortunately, Heidegger himself was most often in a bad mood." Here, "bad" has a moral as well as psychological meaning: Heidegger's form of attunement was partial, peculiarly blind to crucial dimensions of human existence. Out of this blindness flowed a stance that was (to put it charitably) far too consistent with, and accepting of, the gravest forms of cruelty and injustice.

It seems, then, that our emotions are in need of standards that they themselves cannot fully supply. I don't think Solomon disagrees. He says, for example, that "what best defines rationality is not any form of deliberation or calculative reasoning but rather caring about the right things." Yes. But don't we argue about what we should care about, to what extent, in what order of priority? Isn't this a primary theme of Greek philosophy and tragedy, with family, polis, cosmopolis, and the god of the philosophers as sometimes competing claimants for our care? To say this is not to reinstate any simple dualism of reason and emotion. But it is to suggest that justice contains a moment (in Hegel's sense) of reflection that is distinguishable from, and irreducible to, the sentiments that may evoke it.

Another example—again, Solomon's. He says that fear is "not just a rush of adrenalin but the recognition of a danger, and one can be wrong about the danger, its imminence or its seriousness. Fear can be irrational, which means that it is subject to the judgments of rationality." This is virtually a paraphrase of Aristotle's *Ethics*, and it points once again to the moment of reflection. What is the right way to fear (say) the possibility of our own death in battle? One can hardly move toward an answer without a moral understanding (of courage, for a start) that will itself be embedded in larger vision of the world, of what is truly worthy of our care and concern.

Solomon goes on to say that his goal is "not just to defend the rationality of the emotions . . . but to establish what one might call the emotional grounding of rationality." Agreed. And this idea too can be traced back to the Greeks. For Plato, philosophy has little to do with Hobbesian calculative reasoning. It consists rather in a particular orientation toward wisdom, depicted vividly in the *Symposium*.

But here again the argument broadens in ways Solomon does not explicitly acknowledge. As Plato develops his understanding of eros, it comes to stand in tension with thumos—the psychological root of both aggression and anger at what is taken to be injustice directed toward oneself or others. Plato recognizes the facts of moral indignation and of the craving for vengeance, but he refuses to accept them as suitable points of departure for our understanding of justice. (This, I take it, is one of the great themes of the *Republic*.)

From the Platonic standpoint, then, Solomon is insufficiently critical of the emotions he takes as primary. For while reason is not motiveless calculation, it is not necessarily embedded in Solomon's emotional framework of revenge or, for that matter, of compassion.

Solomon's encounter with Kant is no less inconclusive. Solomon equates the Kantian tradition with acting on principle, which for present purposes he parses as "the calculations of just distribution." I don't think this is fair to either Kant or Rawls. In the Kantian tradition, acting on principle is a felt motive for action, not just an abstract proposition. Like many emotions, it is experienced as a formative force, and it is said to express our deepest sense of what it means to be human. The Kantian conception of practical reason is exposed to many powerful objections, but Solomon's charge of "empty, soulless if not mindless" calculation is not one of them.

About the Authors

James P. Sterba (Ph.D. University of Pittsburgh) is Professor of Philosophy at the University of Notre Dame, where he teaches moral problems and political philosophy. He has written more than 120 articles and published 14 books, including *How to Make People Just* (1988), *Contemporary Ethics* (1989), *Feminist Philosophies* (1992), *Morality in Practice,* Fourth Edition (1993), *Justice: Alternative Political Perspectives,* Second Edition (1993), *Earth Ethics* (1994), and *Contemporary Social and Political Philosophy* (1993). He is President of the North American Society for Social Philosophy and has lectured widely in the United States and Europe.

Tibor R. Machan (Ph.D. University of Santa Barbara) is Professor of Philosophy at Auburn University. His major publications include *The Libertarian Alternative* (1974), *The Pseudo-Science of B. F. Skinner* (1974), *Human Rights and Human Liberties* (1975), *The Libertarian Reader* (1982), *The Main Debate: Communism versus Capitalism* (1987), *Marxism: A Bourgeois Critique* (1988), *Commerce and Morality* (1988), *Individuals and Their Rights* (1989) *Liberty and Culture: Essays on the Idea of a Free Society* (1989), and *Capitalism and Individualism: Reframing the Argument for the Free Society* (1990).

Alison M. Jaggar is Professor of Philosophy and Women's Studies at the University of Colorado at Boulder. Her books included *Feminist Frameworks*, co-edited with Paula Rothenberg (third edition 1993); *Feminist Politics and Human Nature* (1983); *Gender/Body/Knowledge: Feminist Reconstructions of Being and Knowing*, co-edited with Susan Bordo (1989); and *Living With Contradictions: Controversies in Feminist Social Ethics* (1994). Jaggar was a founding member of the

307

Society for Women in Philosophy and is past Chair of the American Philosophical Association Committee on the Status of Women.

William A. Galston is Professor, School of Public Affairs, University of Maryland at College Park, and Senior Research Scholar, Institute for Philosophy and Public Policy. He is currently on leave serving as Deputy Assistant to the President for Domestic Policy. His most recent books are *Liberal Purposes* (Cambridge University Press, 1991) and *Virtue* (coedited with John W. Chapman, NYU Press, 1992).

Carol C. Gould (Ph.D. Yale University) is Professor of Philosophy at Stevens Institute of Technology and has taught previously at SUNY College at New Paltz, Lehman College of CUNY, Swarthmore College, and the University of Pittsburgh. She is the author of *Marx's Social Ontology* (1978) and *Rethinking Democracy* (1988), the editor of *Beyond Domination* (1984) and *The Information Web* (1989), and the coeditor of *Women and Philosophy* (1976) and *Artifacts, Representation, and Social Practice* (1994). She is currently working on a new book entitled *Hard Questions in Democratic Theory* and is completing the editing of an anthology on the topic of gender.

Milton Fisk (Ph.D. Yale University) is Professor of Philosophy at Indiana University. His major publications are *Nature and Necessity* (Indiana University Press, 1973), *Ethics and Society* (New York University Press, 1980) and *The State and Justice* (Cambridge University Press, 1989). He is Associate Editor of *Against the Current*.

Robert C. Solomon is Quincy Lee Centennial Professor at the University of Texas at Austin. He is the author of *The Passions* (Doubleday, 1976), *Love: Emotion, Myth and Metaphor* (Doubleday, 1981) and *About Love* (Simon and Schuster, 1988 and Littlefield Adams Quality Paperbacks, 1994), as well as numerous books on European philosophy and coeditor with Kathleen M. Higgins of *From Africa to Zen: An Invitation to World Philosophy* (Rowman & Littlefield, 1983).